Naomi Rolef
Framing the Sex Scene: A New Take on Israeli Film History

Cinepoetics

Edited by
Hermann Kappelhoff and Michael Wedel

Volume 8

Naomi Rolef

Framing the Sex Scene: A New Take on Israeli Film History

—

DE GRUYTER

Approved Dissertation Freie Universität Berlin 2018 – D 188

ISBN 978-3-11-110409-6
e-ISBN (PDF) 978-3-11-069474-1
e-ISBN (EPUB) 978-3-11-069479-6
ISSN 2569-4294

Library of Congress Control Number: 2020944935

Bibliographic information published by the Deutsche Nationalbibliothek
The Deutsche Nationalbibliothek lists this publication in the Deutsche Nationalbibliografie; detailed bibliographic data are available on the Internet at http://dnb.dnb.de.

© 2022 Walter de Gruyter GmbH, Berlin/Boston
This volume is text- and page-identical with the hardback published in 2021.
Cover image: Film still from GOING STEADY
Typesetting: Integra Software Services Pvt. Ltd.
Printing and binding: CPI books GmbH, Leck

www.degruyter.com

To Shlomo, Susan, and Rick

Acknowledgements

Any worthy academic study crystallises in an echo chamber of many voices. It has been a delight during my research to have encountered so much encouragement, support and inspiration, for which I respectfully extend my gratitude.

I am thankful to the Elsa-Neumann-Scholarship from the State of Berlin (Elsa-Neumann-Stipendium des Landes Berlin – Nafög) and to Cinepoetics – Center for Advanced Film Studies at Freie Universität Berlin, whose support and financial backing helped me launch my project and bring it to a close. I am also thankful to the German Academic Exchange Service (DAAD) that made my preliminary academic excursion to Israel possible.

Special thanks are extended to my supervisor at Freie Universität Berlin, Prof. Dr. Hermann Kappelhoff, and his wonderful team, particularly Dr. Christian Pischel, Prof. Bernhard Groß, Dr. Christina Schmitt, Dr. Eileen Rositzka, Prof. Sarah Greifenstein, Dr. Hauke Lehmann, Regina Brückner, Tatjana Schwegler, Eh-Jae Kim and Maximilian Grenz for accompanying me over portions in a long winding road, and generously providing much needed perspective and commentary. I likewise thank my second supervisor Prof. Dr. Tal Ilan for her support and encouragement.

My research benefited greatly from the medial and bibliographical sources that were made available to me. I would like to thank Karen Sitton the director of the Bloomfield Library at the Hebrew University in Jerusalem and Atara Kotliar, head of the media department, who generously granted me access to their valuable resources. I thank Meir Russo, Gad Astar, Nizar Natasha and Daniela Faingold from the Jerusalem Cinematheque archive for bearing with my requests and hosting me over many sessions with a kind and colloquial spirit. I thank Dr. Dror Yizhar and Tomer Kep from the Tel Aviv Cinematheque Library, who shared their gems with true friendliness and interest. An honorary mention is owed to the Jerusalem branch of The Third Ear. This video rental store catered in its former commercial capacity not only my work, but also the vibrant community of art-cinema enthusiasts of the city, as it continues to do in its present non-profit form.

I am indebted to many scholars from different countries, institutes and disciplines, who engaged with me in fruitful interactions over various aspects of my thesis, only a few of whom can be mentioned here. My gratitude is extended to Ralf Dittrich from Berlin, who shares my enthusiasm for Israeli "oldies", and gave me helpful guidance for my archival venture. I thank Dr. Christina Pareigis from ZfL Berlin, whose lectures about Jewish humour inspired the approach that I developed in this thesis. I thank Dr. Marc Siegel from the Goethe University in Frankfurt am Main, who generously assisted me in reaching new platforms, and Dr. Shmulik Duvdevani from Tel Aviv University, who never failed to offer his perspective and provide assistance. Special thanks to Dr. Jon Templeman for his excellent editing work. Last but not least, I thank Dr. Drehli Robnik from the University of Vienna for our regular invigorating discussions.

I had the privilege to discuss my thesis with many interested parties, Israeli, German and other outside the academic forum. I thank all those people for their contribution, and particularly Yoav and Deganit Arazi from Sha'ar Hagolan, who not only lent an ear and offered productive commentary, but also provided me with a copy of THE HERO'S WIFE that played such a major role in chapter 11. I would also like to thank Maayan Meir for helping me structure my work schedule.

My uttermost gratitude is extended to my family for their love and support. I am grateful to my mother, Dr. Susan Hattis Rolef, on whose devoted assistance I could rely every step of the way. I am indebted to her hospitality and generosity; her creative approach to uncovering information, which made the search itself exciting; and her inexorable aid as a proof reader. I humbly thank my father Shlomo Rolef and his wife Haya Vitelson Rolef for their unconditional material and spiritual support. I would like to commend the efforts they invested providing me with invaluable research material. My obliging gratitude is also extended to my aunt Rina Hattis, who read my thesis with "a fine-tooth comb" providing me with useful commentary. I thank my sister Dr. Tom Rolef Ben-Shahar for her long-standing support and interest in my project, as well as my brother Yoav Rolef, whose challenging questions and remarks helped me expand my own perspective.

Contents

Acknowledgements —— VII

Prologue —— XIII

Part I: **Setting the Stage: The Sex Scene and the Search for an Alternative Historiography**

1 *Qu'est-ce que la sexualité?* —— 3

2 The Sex Scene —— 8

3 Reflection on a Reflection: Earlier Discussions of Israeli Sex Scenes —— 14

4 Thesis and Antithesis —— 24

5 The Hypothesis of Repression —— 37

6 Contrariwise: The Applications and Implications of *Otherness and Alterity* —— 44
6.1 The Jewish Position: Sander Gilman —— 44
6.2 The Position of Resistance: Judith Butler —— 50

7 The Film Viewed —— 59
7.1 No Room of Their Own: The Disruption of Space —— 61
7.2 Figure This —— 68
 The Earnestness of Being Important: The Comic Figure —— 69
 How the Mighty are Fallen: The Victim —— 80
 "Whose Son is *This Youth*?": The Child —— 87
7.3 Where is My John Wayne? Where is My Muscle Jew? —— 92

8 Concluding Words —— 95

Part II: **The 1960s: Comedy, Victimhood and Paradise Lost**

9 The Introduction of Sex through the Prism of the Type Figure —— 99

10 "We Have a Little Sister and She Hath no Breasts": The Comic Figure and the Deterioration of Eroticism in MOTIVE TO MURDER —— 101

10.1 MOTIVE TO MURDER —— 101
    Through the Entrance Hall: The Disrupted Space —— 102
    The Podium: Comedy —— 103
    The Boudoir: Eros Disarmed and the Question of Female Promiscuity —— 106
    The Bedchamber: Sex Scenes —— 107
    On the Veranda: The Meaning of a Damaged Private Sphere —— 114

11 "We Are Both Crippled": Victimhood, Status, and Sex in Dramas and Melodramas —— 116

11.1 THE DYBBUK AND FORTUNA – Me Against Us: Victims of the Community —— 116
11.2 IS TEL AVIV BURNING? and EVERY BASTARD A KING – Us Against It: The Victim in the Community —— 119
11.3 ELDORADO —— 121
    No Place for Me: Space and Intrusion —— 121
    It's All About Me: Male Spectacle —— 122
    Poor Me: Victimhood Stardom —— 125
    Gain and Loss: The Sex Scenes —— 126
11.4 HE WALKED THROUGH THE FIELDS – Me Too: Following Sherman's Footsteps —— 131
11.5 THE HERO'S WIFE —— 134
    I am in Pieces: The Fragmented Individual —— 134
    Me, Not Us: Eroticism Rebels —— 138
    It's not You, It's Us: Yosef and The Unattractiveness of Community —— 139
    The Third Rival: Casualties of War —— 141
    War Time: The Synchronisation of the Communal Body —— 142
    Finally in the Frame: Sexual Climax —— 143
    Back to Life: The Return to Democratic Space —— 144
11.6 Shining Through: Conclusion and Commentary —— 146

12 Where is the Child? Where is the Adult? The Child Enters the Sex Scene in A NIGHT IN TIBERIAS, NOT MINE TO LOVE, and IRIS —— 148

12.1 A NIGHT IN TIBERIAS – Paradise Lost: The Clash between Childhood and Adulthood —— 149
12.2 NOT MINE TO LOVE —— 152

Jerusalem Personified: Internal and External Cityscapes —— 152
Thorny Routine: Eli's Perforated World —— 153
The Memory of the Mother, the Presence of the Son: Absence of Sovereignty —— 155
Mischief, Guilt, and Menace: Unsovereign Affairs —— 157
Once Upon a Time: The Recollection of Youth —— 159
Dysfunctionality: The Non-Sovereign Murderer and Unredeemed Rescuer —— 162
See Me, Feel Me: Male Anti-Spectacle —— 163
12.3 IRIS —— 165
Past Present: Untimeliness —— 165
The Winter of Our Content: The Abhorrence of the Present and the Celebration of the Past —— 167
"I Once Looked After Him ... A Little": Yoel's Misogyny, Lack of Mastery, and Sexual Surrender —— 169
Icon and Spectre: The Spectacle of Girlhood —— 170
Violence and Confusion: The Turbulent End —— 174
12.4 Children in Danger, Men in Crisis: Conclusion and Commentary —— 178

Part III: The 1970s: War, Protest and Youth

13 **Same Same, But Different: The Politics of Sex and Identity** —— 183

14 **Past/Present/Future: The Yom Kippur War in Melodramas** —— 188
14.1 THREE AND ONE and JUDGEMENT DAY —— 189
Cry, the Beloved Country: The Political Deployment of Melodrama —— 189
Common Ground: Family Crisis, Intergenerational Difference, and Men Behaving Badly —— 192
Differences: Circular vs. Linear Progression, Exterior vs. Interior Space, Desperation vs. Healing —— 195
Tenderness vs. Violence: Sexual Economies and the Dissipation of the Victim's Sensuality —— 200

15 **"They're Not Nice Guys": Oriental Jewish Identity Enters the Political Arena in the 1970s** —— 207
15.1 From History to Theory: Oriental Jewish Identity in Israeli Film Theory —— 208

15.2   Little Man and Highway Queen —— 211
         "He Who Fucks Alone, Dies Alone": Liberation from
         Comedy —— 211
         "It's Written All Over Your Face": Elevation and Degradation —— 217
         Social Oppression and the Struggle for Sovereignty —— 228

16 We Are Young, We're Not Free: The Face of a New Generation in Youth Films —— 229
16.1   Lemon Popsicle 2: Going Steady —— 233
         "C'mon Everybody": The Perpetual Impertinence of the
         Gang —— 233
         "I'm Singin' in the Rain": The Brazen Act of Self-Assertion
         and the Fragility of Togetherness —— 238
         "Let's Twist Again": The Teenage Clique as a Receptive
         Network —— 241
16.2   Dizengoff 99 —— 243
         "Tell Me You Love Me … Just for Fun": The Crystallisation of
         the Group and the Phantom of the Romantic Couple —— 243
         "Did You Get Many Responses to Your Ad in the Paper?": The
         Swinging Scene —— 247
         "The Most Natural Thing in the World": The Threesome —— 249
         "Don't You See You're Ruining Your Life?": Cinematic
         Self-Reflection —— 253
16.3   Tel Aviv, Sex, 1979: Conclusion and Commentary —— 255

Epilogue —— 257

Bibliography —— 259

Filmography —— 269

Name Index —— 273

Film Index —— 277

Subject Index —— 279

Prologue

This book constitutes the first broad historic study of the enactment of sex in Israeli film, providing a variety of analyses of sex scenes from their first appearance in the 1960s into the late 1970s. Its main goal is to present an alternative historiography of Israeli film to that which prevails in the research community today.

The focus on the enactment of sex, rather than sexual symbolism, puts an emphasis on the viewer's cinematic experience, rather than the critic's interpretation. Following the work of Michel Foucault and Linda Williams, the sex scene is defined here as a cinematic entity that constitutes an arena in which individual subjectivity and communal identity materialise. It provides a platform for us to reconsider popular perceptions of these attributes in Israeli film studies.

By reviewing existing research into Israeli film, we can identify the development of a paradigm which became dominant in the late 1970s, which is antithetic in structure. It describes two historic rifts in communal Israeli identity. The first of these is Zionism's departure from Diasporic Jewish identity at the end of the nineteenth century, and the second is a post-ideological turn within Israeli society in the last third of the twentieth century. In addition, this paradigm dictates that questions of identity and agency are primarily reflected through the prism of Otherness where the Zionist norm is defined as heroic masculinity.

I argue against this view of Israeli film history on two theoretical levels. Firstly, alongside Foucault and Anthony Wilden, I advocate a history of continuity, acknowledging that values and perceptions are never obliterated, but instead undergo transformation from one era to the next. Secondly, I examine the concept of Otherness developed by Sander L. Gilman and Judith Butler, demonstrating the limits of its binary divisions.

I present an alternative historiography, one based on four central motifs. The first of these is the enactment of intrusion, which resides in the sense of space. The remaining three embody a sense of being through cinematic prototypes: the comic figure, the victim, and the child. The enactment of intrusion by and upon the individual reflects an ambiguity within the Zionist movement regarding the ideal relations between individual and society, which may also be understood as the central predicament of modernity. This describes an imbalance between the public and private spheres. On the other hand, the three cinematic prototypes – the comic figure, the victim, and the child – all become comprehensible within the moral notion that the human subject must always be subordinate and secondary. The comic type figure, inherited from the Jewish Diaspora, is incongruous within its environment – revealing that it is both subjugated to that environment and fundamentally independent of it. The victim type figure embodies not just grief, but also an affirmation of the individual that is otherwise morally unacceptable. The child and adolescent type figures were prevalent as symbols in the early days of the Israeli society. Both are associated with innocence, fragility, instability, juvenility, and liminality. They enhance the sense of victimhood, insignificance, and volatility. With these motifs at hand I can now pursue a history of subjectivity as manifested in the viewer's physical sensations, which are affected by the incarnation of cinematic figures and the space that surrounds them. The 1960s and 1970s were a period of crucial change in Israeli society. Through my examination of sex scenes from these decades, I demonstrate how Israel renegotiated its identity in cinematic terms.

Sex scenes from the 1960s reflect the volatility of the boundaries between private and public spheres. They demonstrate the bond between subjectivity and eroticism, the way in which these are diminished in the comic figure and enhanced in the victim, and the destructive role sexuality plays in the presence of children. All of these motifs are presented within a wider cultural-historical framework. I take into account both the impact of historical events, like the Six-Day War, and cultural trends. Cinematic phenomena – the representation of promiscuity, the subjectification of the female and the objectification of the male in depictions of sex, the use of male bodies to bring about spectacle or lethargy, ambivalent representations of rape – are all placed in historical context.

My discussion of sex scenes from the 1970s is structured around three phenomena associated with that decade. Two melodramas correspond to the Yom Kippur War and the political crisis which followed it. The depiction of Oriental Jewish identity is associated with protest movements. Finally, the genre of youth films prominent towards the end of the decade reflects a new sense of reality following the Israel-Egypt peace agreement of 1979. I demonstrate that each of the analysed films operates within the patterns outlined above. The enactment of intrusion by and upon the individual persists and increases. So too does the use of incongruous comic figures and fragile, unstable, sometimes volatile adolescents. I contextualise the decline of the victim type figure and the ambivalent depiction of alternative sources of eroticism.

Through detailed analysis that associates the sensual with the political, this book provides a comprehensive exploration of the nature of sex scenes and their role in the Israeli cultural sphere during a defining period in the nation's history. The perspective offered by these scenes allows for a re-examination of Israel's cinematic history. As well as offering a new narrative of Israeli cinematic history, I offer insight into the ways in which this history is and has been narrated.

Part I: **Setting the Stage: The Sex Scene and the Search for an Alternative Historiography**

In part I, I outline the theoretical foundations of my work. Along with the role ascribed to sex and its cinematic representation, I also explore the value a discussion of the sex scene would offer for our general understanding of Israeli film. A thorough review of academic writing about Israeli fiction film reveals the dominant paradigm within which this film history is typically perceived. After presenting the theoretical basis for an alternative approach, I trace some major perceptions through which the individual, society, and subjectivity have and continue to be constructed in Israeli culture.

1 Qu'est-ce que la sexualité?

Foucault's writings, and particularly his trilogy, *The History of Sexuality*, have inspired a large number of studies on the representation of sexuality in film and other media. My own work is no exception. The existing body of work using Foucault's trilogy is considerable enough to include a variety of schools, with conflicting definitions of sexuality and its manifestations, and very different ideas of the "archaeological excavations" to be undertaken.[1] We must begin, then, by

---

[1] A fraction of this diversity can also be observed in the subjects and attitudes of scholars cited in this study. It is manifested in the plurality of eras and subjects that scholars focus on. On the one hand, Daniel Boyarin refers to Foucault when he explores sexuality in the Talmud in order to excavate a Jewish cultural and philosophical discourse distinct from the European, Greco-Christian one (Boyarin, 1993). On the other, Lynn Hunt applies a Foucauldian approach when she discusses explicit representations of sex in Europe before the emergence of pornography as a regulatory category in the nineteenth century in order to excavate its relations to libertinism, democratisation, privatisation, and political upheaval (Hunt, 1993). More central than the plurality of periods, subjects, and objectives that scholars refer to are the diversity of approaches they draw from Foucault's work. Most noticeable in this study is the disparity between two approaches to the meaning of sexuality which Foucault refers to, and the implications of his work.

Butler is a prominent representative of one such approach. She locates Foucault within a grand debate over the making of identity and the possibilities of subverting it. For Butler, Foucault's challenge to the Lacanian theory of repression, which places resistance in the inoperative realm of the subconscious, allows the development of an empowered concept of resistance. Power is not resisted but deflected, and its utilisation enables a radical making of subjectivity in and against historical hegemony, with the refusal of the type of individuality manufactured by the disciplinary apparatus. Sexual identity may be formed through and against its own prohibition. Butler identifies in Foucault a (revolutionary) call for remaking subjectivity beyond the shackles of law (Butler, 1997, pp. 97–101).

Williams, a prominent representative of the other approach, understands Foucault's historically and culturally constructed sexuality as a manifestation of sexual activities, rather than categories of identity. For her too, Foucault's most essential contribution is his challenge to Freud's "repressive hypothesis". However, the important thing is not the location of personal resistance, but the challenge to definitions of sex as an inherent force repressed by civilization. Williams observes that by defining sex, not as a force of libido, but as a discursive form of power, Foucault deflates the understanding of sexual revolution as liberation (Williams, 2008, pp. 12–13). From this perspective, Foucault does not offer a call for revolution, but a fundamental scepticism.

These two approaches, which will play a role in my theoretical discussion, are also present in debates about contemporary Israeli culture. Both Nitsa Ben-Ari and Raz Yosef refer to Foucault when they discuss sexuality in Israeli culture in two partially correlated timeframes. Whereas Yosef refers to sexuality as a category of identity, Ben-Ari sees it as practice. While he inscribes the queer perspective in Israeli film history, she tackles the development of sexual vocabulary. And while he describes and prescribes a challenge to hegemonic heterosexuality, she outlines a history of sexual conservatism (Yosef, 2004; Ben-Ari, 2006). Thus, although

https://doi.org/10.1515/9783110694741-002

delineating what in Foucault's work serves as the basis for my own. I rely primarily on the trilogy's first volume, *The Will to Knowledge* (*La volonté de savoir*), drawing both on his theoretical approach and some of his historical observations.

A central principle introduced in *The Will to Knowledge* is that the relation between sexuality and perception is not one of discovery, but of formation. In Foucault's (translated) words:

> Sexuality must not be thought of as a kind of natural given which power tries to hold in check, or as an obscure domain which knowledge tries gradually to uncover. It is the name that can be given to a historical construct: not a furtive reality that is difficult to grasp, but a great surface network in which the stimulation of bodies, the intensification of pleasures, the incitement to discourse, the formation of special knowledges, the strengthening of controls and resistances, are linked to one another, in accordance with a few major strategies of knowledge and power. (Foucault, 1990 (1976), pp. 105–106)

No less important is the acknowledgement that sexuality was primarily perceived as a "natural given", and remains so – something that allowed it to play a major role in the definition of truth and subjectivity.

According to Foucault, the scientific discourses which have constructed "new technologies of sex" since the eighteenth century inherited and modified pre-existing Christian discourses. The exigency of normality, inherited sin, and problems of life and illness inherited questions of the afterlife (ibid., p. 117). With such theological roots, sexuality came to possess considerable weight: "[S]ex was not only a matter of sensation and pleasure, of law and taboo, but also of truth and falsehood, that the truth of sex became something fundamental, useful or dangerous, precious or formidable" (ibid., p. 56).[2] Another significant development is the historical evolution of the discourse of sexuality. This prefigured the expansion of psychoanalysis, in which the repression and silencing of sexuality became a central feature. Sexuality carried truth, and its dangers were attributed to its repression (ibid., p. 128).

The discourse of sexuality which Foucault describes here has two combined objectives. The first is the attribution of subjectivity. The second, which derives from the first, is the definition and differentiation of social class. The sexualisation of the human subject "was a political ordering of life, not through the enslavement of others but through the affirmation of self" (ibid., p. 123), and Foucault emphasises that this was a constitutive act, rather than a repressive one. As such,

---

Yosef and Ben-Ari refer to the same culture and time, they seem to refer to two separate worlds.

2 Foucault writes this about late nineteenth-century Western society, but later dates its origin in the late eighteenth century (ibid., p. 128).

he argues, it served the middle class, which came to see its sexuality as "something important, a fragile treasure, a secret that had to be discovered at all costs" (ibid., p. 121). The sexual body became "the indefinite extension of strength, vigor, health and life" (ibid., p. 125). In that respect, "the intensification of the body" and "techniques for maximizing life" (ibid.) gave substance to the middle-class subject.

Nevertheless, sexuality did not remain the exclusive domain of the middle class: "[T]he nineteenth century witnessed a generalization of the deployment of sexuality, starting from the hegemonic centre. Eventually the entire social body was provided with a 'sexual body'" (ibid., p. 127). Nonetheless, it would be wrong to talk about the "universality of sexuality" (ibid.). Foucault reminds us that the middle class had repeatedly demarcated a difference between itself and other classes in order to maintain its own unique identity (ibid., pp. 127–128; see also p. 124). Different criteria were used in the deployment of sexuality toward different classes. The middle class used them as a tool for subjugating the lower classes (ibid., pp. 126–128). Still, Foucault emphasises that the act of "granting" sexuality to the lower classes marked their emergence, existence, and visibility in the public sphere (ibid., pp. 121, 126–127).

In conclusion, I adopt from Foucault the proposition that sexuality is not discovered but constructed, and that in Western culture it came to represent something fundamental, a natural given truth – the very essence of subjectivity. Furthermore, I accept his argument that repression became a central trope in the discourse of sexuality, that sexuality supplements social visibility, and that, as the mark of subjectivity, it can accentuate or undermine the humanity of the subjects it is ascribed to.

Crucial for us is Foucault's delineation of the link between subjectivity and identity. Because sex is, simultaneously, the essence of subjectivity and the bearer of social visibility and identity, the traces of "inner" subjective experience also provide evidence of "external" identity. Descartes' famous declaration, "I think, therefore I am", is transformed within this social discourse into: "I *feel*, therefore I am". Cinematically, this means that construction of sensual subjectivity sensed by the viewer correlates with the materialisation of identity.

It is clear that Foucault's historical observations relate to Western Christian civilisation. Can we apply them to a society that is neither predominately Christian nor, in my opinion, Western? Though not a part of the West, Israel and the societies that have evolved in it have never been completely isolated from the Western Christian world. Contemporary Israeli culture stands in a peripheral position to Western cultures, and inherited its discourse of sexuality and repression.

I make a number of departures from Foucault's approach. Foucault supported his claims using verbal and textual phenomena. In that respect, we already depart from his approach in applying his theory to other media.

Another difference involves the purpose and intentionality of the objects analysed here. Foucault describes the power in question as coming "from below" – it emerges from a multiplicity of relations (ibid., p. 94), is produced from moment to moment, and comes from everywhere (ibid., p. 93). However, he concentrates on the authoritative discourses of science and philosophy.[3] Although I refer to (authoritative) academic discourse in my work, the cinematic medium of fiction film is my main point of reference. As far as the modern history of sexuality is considered, in his efforts to portray the historical background of psychoanalysis and the "theory of repression", Foucault focuses on practices that relate to sex in pathological terms. Such practices are of little relevance to my work.

The implication of this last observation, seemingly mundane, are best understood by considering the proliferation of these pathological sexual concepts in some schools of film studies, under the influence of what Noël Carroll called the "psycho-semiotic approach" (Carroll, 1988, p. 9).[4] In the psycho-semiotic school, and its many offshoots, the cinematic experience is described as the manifestation of subjectivity. The nature of this subjectivity and the relations between viewer and screen are defined exclusively in terms of sexual pathology: voyeurism, sadism, masochism, and so on. In addition, cinematic imagery is "de-coded" into sexual objects, and the phallus is often "discovered" as part of the process of interpretation. Subjectivity is regarded as essential, and sexuality is the key to this essence. But this framework is not innate to film itself. Film is located in the matrix of relations which, according to Foucault, produces power, but is not necessarily subordinate to the authoritative terminology of psychoanalysis. The connection

---

3 Authoritative discourse is produced by agencies which have a claim to hegemony, but are not always in possession of control or authority. John Winkler refers to this phenomenon from a male-female perspective: "The more we learn [...] the more it seems that most of men's observations and moral judgments about women and sex and so forth have minimal descriptive validity and are best understood as coffeehouse talk [...]. To know when any such male lawgivers – medical, moral or material whether smart or stupid – are (to put it bluntly) bluffing or spinning fantasies or justifying their druthers is so hard that most historians of ideas – [including] Foucault [...] – never try" (Winkler, 1989, p. 6, quoted in Boyarin, 1993, p. 241). In that sense, Foucault stays true to his claim that he is not referring to general systems of domination exerted by one group over another (Foucault, 1990, p. 92).

4 In making use of this term (rather than referring to the "psychoanalytic" school), I signal both the semiotic elements this approach preserves, and the difference between it and the psychoanalytic school within psychology.

between subjectivity, sexuality, and the screen can be made using a different vocabulary and set of assumptions, as demonstrated by an alternative approach: neo-phenomenology. Here, too, subjectivity is central to relations, and sexuality (or rather, carnality and eroticism) is perceived as its medium.[5] Yet it is not confined as a signifier bound to pathological terms. Rather, it designates intensified sensuality. I follow the example of the neo-phenomenological approach, not by limiting myself to instances of intensified sensuality or its absence, but by diverging from psycho-semiotic discourse in my discussion of subjectivity and sexuality in film. I am not interested in uncovering phallic symbolism, or diagnosing any pathological conditions. In that respect, Foucault's observations regarding pathological sexual terminology are of little relevance to my work. I refer to this vocabulary directly in the relevant context, but I do not adopt it, or use it for the films I discuss.

I will return to *The History of Sexuality* in my discussion of the perception of history. First, however, I define which concrete manifestations of sexuality in film I will be discussing.

---

5 I refer here to the two dominant neo-phenomenological film scholars, Vivian Sobchack and Laura Marks. Sobchack does not grant sex a theoretical role, but it is nevertheless present in her work. It is implied in her sensual description of the bodies' register, her reference to the carnal sensuality of films, which film theorists are either too embarrassed or bemused to address (Sobchack, 2004, pp. 56–57), and to perception which "catch[es] the other in its own self-embrace" (ibid., p. 50). She demonstrates her perception on a sex scene from THE PIANO (1993, D: Jane Campion) (ibid., pp. 53–84).
Marks' use of sex is more explicit. She claims that the movement between the haptic and the optic is erotic, for eroticism is "the ability to have your senses, your self-control, taken away and restored [...] being able to become an object with and for the world, and to return to being a subject in the world" (Marks, 2002, p. xvi). The haptic in itself has erotic traits, for haptic visuality, which moves on the surface of the image is erotic (ibid., pp. 13 ff.), and "[h]aptic images pull the viewer close, too close to see properly, and this is itself erotic" (ibid., p. 16). Finally, the theoretical engagement with the haptic is also ascribed to eroticism, because, like a sexual encounter, it is based on trust which opens one to new experience (ibid., p. xvi).

2 The Sex Scene

I define the cinematic sex scene as a sequence in which sexual activity is played out. But this simple description does not allow us to classify what constitutes a sex scene. The matter is complicated by the fact that, in mainstream films, the sexual act itself is effectively absent. The depiction of sex has been a subject of moral/legal debate and censorship long before the invention of motion pictures.[1] Because of limitations on what may be shown, and the restriction of "graphic" imagery to pornography, implicit ways of depicting sex proliferated in motion pictures from their beginning. Consequently, the suggestive aspect of mimetic depiction is very present in any discussion of sex scenes. As Williams observes, "[m]ovies both reveal and conceal" (Williams, 2008, p. 2). More specifically,

> Sex is an act and more or less of "it" may be revealed but [...] it is not a stable truth that cameras and microphones either "catch" or don't catch. It is a constructed, mediated, performed act and every revelation is also a concealment that leaves something to the imagination. (ibid.)[2]

---

[1] In what generally came to be called the Meese Report, the U.S. Attorney General's Commission on Pornography notes that: "Descriptions of sex are as old as sex itself" (Attorney General's Commission on Pornography, 1986, p. 233), and that "sexually explicit descriptions and depictions have been around in one form or another almost since the beginning of recorded history" (ibid., p. 235). Although the regulation of sexually explicit materials is a comparatively recent phenomenon, "the very fact that many sexual references were veiled (however thinly) rather than explicit indicates that some sense of taboo and social stigma has always been in most societies attached to public discussion of sexuality. Yet although some degree of inhibition obviously attached to public descriptions and depictions of sexual acts, it is equally clear that the extent of these inhibitions has oscillated throughout history" (ibid., pp. 235–236). What constituted pornography, observes Hunt, was never a given, but defined over time by conflict (Hunt, 1993, p. 11). Censorship and the regulation of explicit depictions can be traced back to the sixteenth century in Europe (ibid., p. 10, and Attorney General's Commission on Pornography, 1986, pp. 237–240). After technological advances in the manufacturing and distribution of print, the mid-nineteenth century saw the development of the term "pornography", and legal action to persecute it in the name of morality around Europe and the United States (ibid., pp. 240–243; Hunt, 1993, pp. 12–13). When pornographic film material was produced and distributed, the premise that it could not circulate openly had long been established (Attorney General's Commission on Pornography, 1986, pp. 245–246). Equally established was the fact that the explicit depiction of sex in mainstream film was and remains restricted, even though these limits are tested and modified periodically.

[2] Williams' emphasis on cinematic sex being "constructed, mediated, performed" (Williams, 2008, p. 2) certainly echoes Foucault's terms for the manifestation of sex in culture.

What is revealed and what is concealed in the mainstream cinema may, to a certain extent, be described in concrete terms, since its parameters are predetermined, circumscribed by legal restrictions and corresponding industrial standards and ratings. Current rules dictate that, in mainstream cinema, some things may be presented, but not visually. The result is a split between imagery and narrative. A sex scene is defined as pornographic if its imagery is explicit and the sexual act is visible. A contemporary mainstream sex scene will not include such visual content. At most, it will present the viewer with implicit imagery. The narrative, on the other hand, leaves no room for the imagination. Viewers are left with no doubt that a sexual act is taking place, or at least being attempted – even if all they see onscreen are the pre- or post-coital moments.

Like other national cinemas, sexuality first appeared in the Israeli cinema in implicit form, both in imagery and narrative. The move from implicit to explicit narration of sexual acts in Israeli film can be traced to the early- to mid-1960s. In the few feature films produced in Israel in the 1950s, several female characters were marked within the diegesis, rightfully or wrongfully, with a heavy suspicion of doing "it".[3] Otherwise, the closest Israeli film came to "it" was a comic scene in A TALE OF A TAXI (1956, D: Larry Frisch), where a soldier meets a young woman in a barn for a roll in the hay, and her attempt to embrace him is frustrated by his jerky movements.[4] Things changed rapidly from the mid-1960s. Within a short time, sex had become part of dramatic compositions, not just sporadically but generally. The international trends that enabled the appearance of more "explicit" content in mainstream cinema (which meant explicit narrative and implicit imagery) arrived in Israel a strikingly short time after the local film industry finally succeeded in establishing itself and producing films on a regular basis.[5] Coincidentally or not, industrial maturity arrived

---

3 A female character could be "in the profession", like Na'ama/Naomi in LACKING A HOMELAND (1956, D: Nuri Habib); sexually unfaithful, like Miriam in CEASEFIRE (1950, D: Amram Amar); intimate with the wrong man, like Miriam in HILL 24 DOESN'T ANSWER (1955, D: Thorold Dickinson), who is publicly scrutinised in a café for getting involved with a member of the occupying British forces; or presented as the ultimate flirt, like Dina in BLAZING SAND (1960, D: Raphael Nussbaum). Public condemnation is used in these films to generate sympathy for the character, or disapproval, or, as in the last case, both.
4 The fact that these two figures literally role in the hay could already make this the very first sex scene on the Israeli screen. However, the sexual act here is not evident, and the question of whether it in fact takes place becomes negligible, since the comic (non-sexual) bodily function of the male figure remains the only real topic in the scene.
5 Until 1960, film productions in Mandatory Palestine/Israel were few and far between. In 1956, Yehuda Harell discussed the establishment of two independent film studios in the early 1950s, and legislation from 1954 that made screening Israeli films obligatory (Harell, 1956, pp. 230–236).

shortly before the sex scene became part of the picture(s).[6] Over the next five decades, sex scenes became a consistent element of Israeli film. As a flexible poetic component, such scenes were adjusted in terms of form, content, and affective impact, in order to comply with the genres they were being integrated into. In both respects, Israeli cinema is similar to other national cinemas in which such explicit content – which remains somewhat implicit – is not overtly restricted.

From a historical perspective, we must acknowledge that this process took place within a system of constraints, as Israeli films were subject to state-sanctioned restrictions. On the basis of censorship laws introduced by the British authorities in Palestine in 1927, Israel established a review board for film and theatre, with the authority to ban films or limit their viewers by age. The board's mandate was relatively expansive, and included "public morality". The representation of sex was one of aspect by which films would be judged, though by no means the only one (Shalit, 2006, pp. 105–107; Almog, 2004, pp. 1146–1147).

While distributors of imported films often removed "indecent" segments of films before submitting them to the board (Shalit, 2006, pp. 107–108), local filmmakers had to deal with the board throughout the production process (ibid., pp. 143–144). Local films were scrutinised more stringently and held to a higher standard by the board and other authorities, on the premise that they educated the public, and out of concern that they would represent Israel negatively abroad (ibid.). As a result, filmmakers complained that the amount of nudity and sex approved by censors for foreign films concurrently served to disqualify Israeli productions (ibid., p. 143).

In addition, Gertz cites a system of tax returns which was established in 1960, and which was highly beneficial for film production (Gertz, 1993, p. 21). The small-scale industry became strong enough to survive the financial crises that had hampered its earlier progress. In the 1950s, ten productions were released commercially, with the maximum of three films in 1956, and several years without any releases (1951, 1957, and 1958) (Schnitzer, 1994a, pp. 39–47). The 1960s saw some seventy commercial productions released, with a minimum of three productions per year (in 1960 and 1961), and a maximum of twelve (in 1968) (Schnitzer, 1994a, pp. 48–105; Jacob-Arzooni, 1983, pp. 347–352). It seems that 1960 marks the year in which feature films began to be marketed on a regular basis.

6 Historically, it is no coincidence that the early 1960s, a relative stable period for the Israeli state, saw progress within private initiative in the entertainment business, as well as commercial portrayals of intimate space. The intricate relations between those two phenomena, and the extent to which they are related, belongs to the field of film production history, and exceeds the scope of this book.

However, as we will see in parts II and III, censorship did not stop sex scenes becoming a convention in Israeli film during the 1960s, and growing in frequency and intensity during the 1970s. We can only speculate how the Israeli sex scene would have been affected if the review board had not existed in this form. It was not until the mid to late 1980s that the board lost its authority to ban films on the basis of public morality (Almog, 2004, p. 1155). By that time, sex scenes were well established in Israeli cinema, and this institutional change seems to have had no effect on their content, affective value, or frequency.

Of course, institutional censorship was not unique to Israel. Following earlier legal debates over obscenity internationally, some research into sex scenes has examined its historical development by mapping changes in practices of visual concealment and exposure, both of sexual activity and the human body. Discussing American cinema, for instance, Hermann Kappelhoff describes a historical shift in representations of sex and violence, as B-movies disclosed what classical Hollywood films cut out (Kappelhoff, 2009). Similarly, Williams has written about the effect of this development on sex scenes. Her book progresses from depictions of kisses to sexual penetration, and later to polymorphous sexuality (Williams, 2008). These approaches also share an emphasis on viewer's experience and sensual impact, something that has inspired my own work.

This history of exposure is an important feature in the development of the sex scene. In principle, such a history could also be written about Israeli film. The naked male torso had already served as a visual highlight in the 1930s. Female breasts were shown some thirty years later, in the 1960s.[7] Genitals – primarily male genitals – first appeared in the late 1970s and early 1980s, but only in the 1990s did they begin to appear in scenes involving sex.[8] When the sexual act was first shown, in the mid-1960s, it was often represented by pre- and post-coital scenes and symbolic sequences, but within a few years, by the end of the 1960s, a full enactment of intercourse became more common.[9] There are two

---

[7] The male torso is celebrated in the documentary AVODAH (1934, D: Helmar Lerski) and the feature film SABRA (1933, D: Aleksander Ford). The first glimpse of female breasts occurred in DALIA AND THE SAILORS (1964, D: Menahem Golan), in a more overtly sexual context.

[8] Examples of the former include PARATROOPERS (1977, D: Yehuda-Judd Ne'eman) and REPEAT DIVE (1982, D: Shimon Dotan). An example for the latter is LOVESICK ON NANA STREET (1995, D: Savi Gabizon).

[9] RACHEL (1960, D: Nuri Habib) was possibly the first Israeli sex scene (Lord, 1994, p. 66; Anderman, 2010). However, there are no surviving copies of the film, and hence no cinematic evidence of how sex was depicted in the film. The first pre- and post-coital scenes came in 1963 with ELDORADO (D: Menahem Golan). In the same year, THE HERO'S WIFE (D: Peter Frye) lingered on the sexual act, investing and obscuring it with visual metaphors. A playful use of visual implicitness can be found in TAKE OFF (1970, D: Uri Zohar) where sexual acts are

reasons – which are related, I believe – that I do not write about the history of Israeli sex scenes from such a perspective. On the one hand, it does not allow a satisfactory description of the intrinsic meaning embedded in those scenes. On the other, when I watch such practices, and the aesthetic conventions accompanying them, I notice that *we've seen it all before*: the very same elements have appeared beforehand in other national cinemas. To account for this is to recognise that the Israeli film industry – small in size, of limited international significance – did not influence global trends, or develop alternative practices. In acknowledging this, I do not wish to follow Nurith Gertz's claim that Israeli cinema is a late developer, a depleted replica of "real" arts like European cinema and Israeli literature.[10] Nor do I agree with Ella Shohat's claim that Israeli cinema wrongly followed Western trends, failing to orient itself around the more nourishing Third World cinema (Shohat, 1989, pp. 4–5). I do, however, recognise that it developed in a peripheral cultural environment and, as such, was subject to restrictions which made it a less likely source of aesthetic innovation.[11] Despite the fact that Israeli cinema has been a follower regarding the aesthetics of sex scenes, rather than a guiding light, such scenes still reveal something culturally specific, which can be sensed by the prospective viewer, and which is beyond the conventions by which body parts and sexual activities are exposed. As Foucault maintained, sexuality is historically perceived as "a fragile treasure", the essence of truth as well as subjectivity, and this perception of essence materialises in the sex scene. This is the added value we should consider in accounting for the frequency with which sex plays a role in cinema since its very beginnings, and the centrality of the sex scene in countless films. Both may not

---

depicted in accentual metaphorical representations without ever crossing the line to portraying the sexual act itself.

Zohar and other directors had already produced more explicit enactments of sex in films like Not Mine to Love (1967, D: Uri Zohar); He Walked through the Fields (1967, D: Yosef Millo); Iris (1968, D: David Greenberg); and Blaze On the Water (1969, D: Jacob Hameiri). More extensive enactments of sex appeared shortly afterwards, in films like Highway Queen (1971, D: Menahem Golan) and Boys Will Never Believe It (1971, D: Uri Zohar).

10 This major hypothesis is repeated in her historical account, and in her comparison between Israeli film and literature in *Motion Fiction: Israeli Fiction in Film* (1993).

11 These restrictions are the result of both material and spiritual constraints. Luiz Costa Lima describes the dynamics in arts and humanities which mark the difference between a central and a marginal culture – that is, between an economically and culturally stable environment and an unstable one. He demonstrates the logic which renders a peripheral culture more conservative, more true to canonical imports from the central culture, and less tolerant of deviation. In a stable environment, innovation will represent the *exploration of limits*, while in an unstable environment it will become a radical *explosion of limits*, which will at best gain recognition only from external circles (Lima, 2010).

only be guided by commercial requirements to satisfy the masses with erotic thrills. Images that "engage the eye *and* the body" (Williams, 1995, p. 37) evoke and communicate more than the sensational sensations of sexual activity.

The sex scene provides an instance in which perceptions of truth and subjectivity are manifested in concrete dramaturgical terms. It is an arena in which much is expressed about the human figures it contains. What we experience as viewers is both personal and interrelated. The scene contains the individual's characteristics, their (absence of) desire and behaviour. It also contains an interpersonal dynamic. Self-other and subject-object relations materialise in depictions of sexual activity, including self-gratification.

This dimension of the sex scene is instrumental in understanding those elements which are culturally unique to Israel. Foucault emphasises that the perception of sex as "a fragile treasure" is group-associated. He writes of a sense of subjectivity through sexuality which is not only exclusive to a social class, but is crucial to defining it. This organising principle has long been applied to cultures and nations.[12] I explore this cinematic sense of subjectivity within the context of Israeli history and culture, adding, in the latter case, a further dimension: a history of the physical sensation of Israeli subjectivity. In addition, I show that, in spite of the diversity within sex scenes at any given phase in Israeli film, what such scenes evoke can be historically charted.

---

12 This is reflected in the examples listed in footnote 1. Most conspicuously, the category of "class", dominant in Foucault's time, is almost completely replaced by that of "nationality".

3 Reflection on a Reflection: Earlier Discussions of Israeli Sex Scenes

In seeking the history of Israeli sex scenes, the question of how they have been thought about is almost as important as the question of what historical sex scenes reflect. How have sex scenes in Israeli film been perceived domestically over the years?

Newspaper and magazine articles wholly dedicated to the topic of nudity and sex in Israeli film only began to appear at the point in history where my study ends. Such articles appeared in entertainment and women's magazines, and in the weekend sections of non-religious newspapers, both popular and elitist, both socialist and liberal. These articles take a retrospective standpoint: while they offer an account of contemporary developments, they often also attempt to describe the historical dimension, revisiting the arsenal of sex scenes preserved in communal recollection and revitalising it with long forgotten scenes and films.

Most profoundly, media discourse about Israeli sex scenes changed very little between the late 1970s and the early 2010s. A breakthrough was occasionally declared. In 1978, for instance, Edna Fainaru hailed the bold, unprecedented cinematic representation of sensitive erotic settings in LEMON POPSICLE (1978, D: Boaz Davidson), something new to the Israeli screen (Fainaru, 1978, p. 18). In 1995, Dror Feuer announced that LOVESICK ON NANA STREET proved that Israeli cinema had revolutionised its approach towards nudity (Feuer, 1995, p. 40). In 2001, Yael Shuv proclaimed that LATE MARRIAGE (2001, D: Dover Kosashvili) was nothing less than a cinematic miracle, finally heralding Israeli cinema's sexual maturity (Shuv, 2001, p. 11). But these superlatives only highlight the exception – the new "avant-garde" that would hopefully catch on. They underline the general perception that the Israeli sex scene of the time – whether in the 1970s, 1980s, 1990s, or beyond – is a difficult topic.

Fainaru diagnoses a collective, deep-seated complex of shame, guilt, and provinciality in Israel as the root of the problem. A small, intrusive society and a conservative audience put pressure on the actors, preventing the directors from realising their vision (Fainaru, 1978). Indeed, most journalistic discussions of Israeli sex scenes in the following decades focus, in part or in whole, on their creation and public reception. Typically, the process by which these scenes are produced is described as a battlefield, and many reports are dedicated to stories from veterans: directors, producers, and most of all the actors. The latter sometime endorse unreserved sexual performances, or at least professional attitudes towards them. More often, however, they describe being mistreated during the shoot, or feeling exposed following the film's release (Fainaru, 1978; Shehori, 1982, p. 102; Feldmesser Yaron and Cohen, 1992; Hadas, 1993; Feuer, 1995; Roman, 1996; Shiram and Rom, 2003; Ginat and Arison, 2007; Ginat, 2007; Raveh, 2008; Bar-Haim, 2013, p. 34). Otherwise, the "problem" with Israeli sex scenes is traced back to conservatism (Fainaru, 1978), to ideology and macho-ism (Maiberg 1982; Schnitzer, 1994b; Shuv, 2001), and sometimes to a combination of all three (Israel, 1994; Bar-Haim, 2013).

At any rate, these authors agree that Israeli sex scenes are not erotic. Only the filmmaker Savi Gabizon refers to the absence of eroticism in positive terms (Feuer, 1995, p. 40). Otherwise, it is regarded as a shortcoming. Several critics argue that this failure derives from the simple fact that Israeli filmmakers do not know how to do "it". The term Fainaru uses in 1978 is "stuttering erotica" (Fainaru, 1978). Thirty-five years later, Gabi Bar-Haim used a variation of this term, adding that the local film industry still had tense relations with sex and sexuality. While films are produced in Europe which explore sexual boundaries, she argued, Israel was stuck in an earlier phase, still striving to achieve a basic cinematic depiction of intimate relations (Bar-Haim, 2013, p. 10). When a scene intended to be erotic finally appears onscreen, claims Yael Israel, viewers respond with indifference, laughter, or embarrassment (Israel, 1994, p. 11). Shuv claims that sex scenes in Israeli film are mostly embarrassing if not downright infuriating (Shuv, 2001, p. 11). If Israeli sex scenes cannot be sexy, they might as well be funny, argues Yishai Kiczales (Canetti, 2007, p. 56) – and indeed, asserts Meir Schnitzer, Hebrew orgies are ludicrous: good sex scenes appear once in every hundred Israeli films, and most don't actually include sex (Schnitzer, 1994b, pp. 64, 68). Many Israeli nude scenes are vulgar, exploitative, and sensationalist, Yair Raveh argues, but only a few intentionally so. In most cases, they only turned out that way because of the filmmakers' limitations (Raveh, 2008, p. 130). One should infer nothing from Israeli sex scenes about Israeli sexual activity, Amnon Lord suggests: the conventions for shooting sex in Israeli film simply have not yet been found (Lord, 1994, p. 66).

Rotem Danon diagnoses the problem slightly differently: Israeli cinema is abundant with sex, and always has been, but its representation remains shallow, primitive, and closely associated with stigma (Canetti, 2007, p. 56). As Ilan Shaul put it two decades earlier, every Israeli film contained at least one instance of sexual intercourse that bares all. In most cases, this insertion is utterly arbitrary. He blames this "disgrace" on Boaz Davidson, the representative of commercial cinema. Viewers are unmoved by Davidson's rushed sex scenes with their mass-produced intercourse (Shaul, 1983, p. 9). Gali Ginat depicts a more receptive audience, giving an ironic recipe for a successful Israeli film: take two hours, the average length of a feature film, add two to three shots of nice tits, firm, attractive male buttocks, and a short scene of a couple copulating wildly (Ginat, 2007, p. 54).

Ron Maiberg starts from the same premise, but reaches a different conclusion. There is sex in the Israeli cinema, and always has been. Most is blunt, violent, vulgar, and imposing, without love, eroticism, understanding, or tenderness. Sex in Israeli film is brutal and sweaty (Maiberg, 1982, p. 98). As the film scholar Shmulik Duvdevani remarks to Bar-Haim, Israeli cinema always had difficulties with emotions beyond the political sphere. There is something blunt, rude, and direct about the Israeli spirit. Suggestiveness is not our strong suit (Bar-Haim, 2013, p. 10).

The key to bedroom relations in Israeli film, Schnitzer argues, is that we are a military nation. Like good soldiers, we do it quickly, forcefully, and inelegantly – sexually speaking: violently, rapidly, and from behind (Schnitzer, 1994b, p. 68). Genuine erotic expression can only take place where the male and the female harmonise and balance each other, observes Israel. Eroticism in Israeli cinema has died in the womb from an acute lack of oestrogen (Israel, 1994, p. 11). Sex scenes in military settings are aggressive and lack tenderness, Shuv says, and the distance between them and rape is only a short one. Instead of passion, there is lust for conquest, which the camera shares with the man in the frame. Israeli filmmakers have long learned to condemn Israeli machoism, but most offer no alternative (Shuv, 2001, p. 11).

The Hebrew woman lacks sexual delight, declares Schnitzer, which is probably why female characters in the Israeli cinema find comfort in the arms of Palestinian men. Without the native Jewish ethos, the local man remains a sexually useless non-man. The Arab body is then annexed by women, and the Arab man loses his life as a result of female Jewish passion (Schnitzer, 1994b, p. 71). Perhaps it is no coincidence that two of the most beautiful, wild sex scenes in Israeli cinema occur between Israeli girls and young Arab men, writes Lord (Lord, 1994, p. 67).

Furthermore, he says, the prevalent identification of Israeli cinema with sweaty, markedly unsensuous horniness, is not justified (ibid., p. 66). Unlike other critics, Lord grants more than one Israeli sex scene a positive review, consistently praising the aura of the female performers. But even he sees a loss of sensuality and eroticism in the developments of the mid-1990s. Sex, he concludes, has returned to its natural place in Israeli cinema, lacking joy, immersed in a suffocating atmosphere, and even more subject to exasperating negotiations than the occupied territories – it has once again become, that is, an inseparable part of the hardship of living in the region (ibid., pp. 66–67).

Of course, media commentators are committed to capturing public attention, and yet are hindered by their level of subjective reserve. In dealing with something as potentially awkward as the sex scene, this may generally contribute to its histrionic representation. Nonetheless, the authors just discussed make valid points about the way in which Israeli sex scenes have been absorbed into public discourse: sex scenes are largely seen as formulations of communal identities, oriented and constructed by the terms in which the Israeli community can perceive itself, its means of expression, and the historical circumstances that shape it. The sex scenes are typically discussed in negative terms, and frequently perceived as an arena in which individuals and their struggles are mercilessly exposed. Judging from these authors, Israeli sex scenes have never led viewers to believe they present any form of utopia. And this is true of Israeli films in general.

Compared to journalistic discourse, academic discussions of Israeli sex scene are far more difficult to find. This is mainly because, within such research, sex scenes have never been at the centre of attention. Efforts to provide a systematic history of representations of sex in Israeli culture have been made for other media (as with Ben-Ari's work on literature) and other disciplines (as with Almog's sociological work).

The literary scholar Nitsa Ben-Ari has explored the representation of sex in Israeli literature. She offers a cultural background to these literary phenomena, adding an exhaustive etymological survey (Ben-Ari, 2006). The sociologist Oz Almog has provided an extended study of Israeli society, which also includes a section on sex, titled "Eroticism and Sexual Promiscuity". He approaches this through questions of norms, education, law, and media, commercial, and artistic representation (Almog, 2004, pp. 1043–1167). Ben-Ari and Almog take a similar perspective in their work, each focusing on questions of puritanism and promiscuity. They both describe Israeli society as fundamentally conservative, lagging behind more advanced societies and yet making progress in the adoption of liberal "Western" norms.

On Almog's account, this advance is straightforward. Jewish tradition dictated a puritan approach to sex, aiming to shroud and restrain the erotic. The Zionist movement was originally secular, and moved away from conservative religious conceptions to place new emphasis on the body. Nonetheless, Israeli society maintained sexual conservatism: along with the influences of a traditional upbringing and East European culture, new settlers were inspired by an ideological collectivism which had a prohibitive attitude toward private matters like love and sex. The sexual revolution only became possible in Israel in the second half of the twentieth century with the increase of individualism and Western influence (ibid., pp. 1043–1059).

Ben-Ari offers a more detailed explanation of the relationship between ideology and sexuality in Israeli society. According to her, Zionism, like other national movements, set puritan cultural standards. Full of Eros, but lacking sexuality, ideological passion was reserved for the common good. Sexuality was seen as inferior and marginal, a force that, at best, should be sublimated for pioneer activity (Ben-Ari, 2006, pp. 63–91). Ben-Ari's account of this development is more complex than Almog's triumph of humanistic Western values over conservatism. She agrees with Almog's claim that the Jewish Hebrew tradition lacked direct lexical references to sex, using suggestive language instead (Almog, 2004, p. 1044; Ben-Ari, 2006, pp. 258–259). While Almog diagnoses a full linguistic recovery, however (Almog, 2004, pp. 1055–1057, 1074–1085), Ben-Ari concludes that the hurdle has not been overcome. Sexual inhibitions are still present in contemporary Israeli culture, and the erotic linguistic repertoire has yet to shed its centuries of atrophy (Ben-Ari, 2006, pp. 358–361).

Ben-Ari and Almog's approaches were essential to my own venture into the world of sexual representation. They open the gate to a broad range of Israeli cultural references, something generally in short supply within Israeli film research. Both conclude that Israeli society suffered from failed development and is, in some way, lacking. That in itself marks the disadvantage of the work of both. Instead of offering a clinical diagnosis, they would have done better to ask what it is that motivates a society – or themselves, as members of this society – to perceive itself, or themselves, in terms of deficiency.

This is particularly clear in Almog's discussion of Israeli film, which maintains the hypercritical tone that characterises much journalistic discourse on the subject. He dedicates most of his discussion to the most popular film in Israeli history, LEMON POPSICLES, concluding that the sexual fantasy it depicts is in opposition to the ideological one featured in Israel's cultural past, and that the characters' sexual immaturity expresses the immaturity of past Israeli society (ibid., pp. 1156–1158). More generally, Almog claims that the sexual maturity typical of European cinema never occurred in Israeli cinema, and that the few scenes expressing sexuality are chauvinistic, offensive, and infantile. He argues that this is possibly an expression of male Israeli perception, or a result of some other "traumatic cinematic birth" that still affects Israeli sex scenes (ibid., p. 1155).

Using a single film, Almog recognises that its manifestation of sexual escapades and sexual inadequacy derives from a reflective rationale which pays tribute to, reproduces, and challenges existing cultural perceptions. In discussing Israeli cinema in general, however, this dimension is no longer taken into account, and film is considered a mechanical expression of deficiency, either of the society or industry that produces it. He invalidates the reflective discursive dimension in both the films and his own analytical position.

Naturally, it is not just sociologists like Almog who incorporate depictions of sexual activity into their work. A number of Israeli film scholars have also done so. None offer general observations about sex scenes in Israeli film, but they do discuss specific films or genres. Sex scenes are an integral part of Gertz's analysis of NOT MINE TO LOVE (1967, D: Uri Zohar), for instance (Gertz, 1993, pp. 125–127). Orly Lubin begins her article on the representation of women in Israeli film with a description of a sex scene in MOMENTS (1979, D: Michal Bat-Adam), which encapsulates everything she then explores in her article (Lubin, 2005, pp. 301–316). Igal Bursztyn takes a step further, incorporating the emergence of sex scenes and their function into his historical overview of Israeli cinema. According to Bursztyn, the sex scenes which appeared in the 1960s were a manifestation of the objectification, bourgeois materialism, and selfishness which replaced ideological commitment to the state (Bursztyn, 1990, pp. 89–120). He discusses the sex scenes in BOYS WILL NEVER BELIEVE IT extensively from this point of view (ibid., pp. 115–118). He goes on to argue that sex scenes from the 1980s, in NIGHT SOLDIER (1984, D: Dan Wolman) and ON A NARROW BRIDGE (1985, D: Nissim Dayan), reflect a failure to import international narrative formulas or to use local ones (ibid., pp. 126–132). Bursztyn's portrayal of sex in Israeli cinema is negative: in the early 1970s, it was a manifestation of bourgeois decadence, and a little over a decade later it became a foreign example which Israeli society failed to emulate. A recent study does the most so far to integrate sex into the history of film. Rachel S. Harris' book on women in Israeli film dedicates whole sections to sex, prostitution, and rape. She refers repeatedly to sexual activity in other sections of her book, acknowledging its proliferation in the films she discusses. Harris depicts the sex scene as a frontline in which women confront patriarchy (Harris, 2017).

In most cases, however, authors seemingly avoid discussing sex scenes, even when they are crucial to the topic under discussion. Amy Kronish, for instance, calls the director Uri Zohar's last five films "Sexual Comedies", but refrains from referring directly to any of the films' sex scenes (Kronish, 1996, pp. 38–40). Similarly, in her discussion of commercial youth film, Miri Talmon acknowledges the existence of sex scenes in DIZENGOFF 99 (1979, D: Avi Nesher) (Talmon, 2001, pp. 174–176) and LEMON POPSICLES (ibid., pp. 163–168), but they are left unanalysed.

Yosefa Loshitzky devotes two chapters in her book on Israeli film to the representation of Arab-Jewish love affairs in Israeli films of the 1980s (Loshitzky, 2001, pp. 112–168). More than half of the films she discusses include a sex scene, and in almost all of them it plays a central role in the plot. In Loshitzky's discussion, however, such scenes are only a minor element. Even the sex scene in ON A NARROW BRIDGE, which was constructed by the director and main actress with deliberate political intent, is dismissed as a subconscious gesture of "perversion" (ibid., p. 129). In her analysis of a sex scene in HAMSIN (1982, D: Daniel Wachsmann), Loshitzky focuses on the colours in the scene without any reference to the imagery of the sex act itself. This is particularly intriguing because, at the same time, she uses sex as a metaphor for the whole film, which she describes as "paced to the rhythm of a slow sexual intercourse progressing toward powerful orgasm" (ibid., pp. 124–125).

These elusive references to sex in film, where sexual metaphors are employed while the actual representation of sexual activity is evaded, are the most common approach to the subject in Israeli film research, and even more evident in texts that supposedly focus on sex. Yasmin (Max) Sasson, for instance, sets out to decode sexual relations in the film BIG SHOTS (1982, D: Jacob Goldwasser). Sexual relations play a major role in the film, but Sasson only alludes to them briefly (Sasson, 2008, pp. 174, 176). Instead, the sexual relations she dedicates her essay to are metaphorical ones, with the protagonists' attempt to crack open a safe read as a failed sexual penetration (ibid., pp. 171–178).

When Sandra Meiri and Yael Munk discuss GIFT FROM ABOVE (2003, D: Dover Kosashvili), they begin with the assertion that it "includes sex scenes unprecedented in Israeli cinema", and that it was "branded pornographic by both audience and critics" (Meiri and Munk, 2008, p. 66). But they do not analyse any of the sex scenes, or the dynamics by which sexual connotation permeates the film. Instead, they discuss the Freudian metaphor in two scenes in which sex does not take place (ibid., pp. 69–70), as well as hints and symbolism of gender transgressions (ibid., pp. 72–74), and, finally, "the notion of fetish" (ibid., p. 74).

In the article mentioned above, Lubin seems to takes a different approach. She begins with a description of a sex scene, and then discusses the female sexual body, arguing that Israeli films marginalise women and suppress sexuality (Lubin, 2005, pp. 304–305). Artists who use the penetrating gaze by placing the female sexual body at the centre of a film thereby subvert a hegemonic, patriarchal culture (ibid., p. 305). But the cinematic depiction of the body as sexual becomes conspicuously absent in the rest of Lubin's essay, and remains a mere thematic reference. For instance, when she discusses the burgeoning sexuality of Flora, the female protagonist in A THOUSAND AND ONE WIVES (1989, D: Michal Bat-Adam), she describes its construction in the original literary text (ibid., pp. 308–313), but omits any discussion of how this takes place in film. Sexual acts go unmentioned, except for a symbolic moment in which Flora cuts her finger (ibid., p. 311).

Once the spotlight is on questions about the depiction of sex in Israeli film, a frustrating game of academic hide-and-seek begins. On the one hand, sex and sexuality are dominant in academic vocabulary and theory. On the other, the phenomenology of cinematic depictions of sex is disregarded.[1] The sexuality in focus is simply metaphorically, and therefore mitigated, or else seems to have little to do with sex. The likely cause of this is the prevalence of two theoretical schools, which leave a trace in the examples just given: the psycho-semiotic school, and the politics of identity. There is no shortage of psychoanalytic terms and imagery in the texts above. Loshitzky's terminology, for instance, includes phrases like "voyeuristic primary scene" (Loshitzky, 2001, p. 125), "reversed Oedipal desire" (ibid., p. 139), and "double voyeurism" (ibid., p. 159). Meiri and Munk diagnose a fear of castration caused by the discovery of the woman's lack of a phallus and a resulting fetishism (Meiri and Munk, 2008, p. 70). Although Lubin distances herself from Freudian conceptions of womanhood (Lubin, 2005, pp. 302–303), she uses his imagery when describing self-inflicted injuries by women as an act of empowerment and desire, with the knife given the role of the phallus (ibid., pp. 310–311).

Beyond terminology, imagery, and perceptions, the true influence of the psycho-semiotic school lies in the type of reading it dictates. It takes the sexual arena as its prime locus. This is unconscious, and so is always veiled, appearing only in metaphor. Every cinematic composition ultimately possesses a clandestine sexual core. When everything onscreen is sexual, the unmasked representation of sex is of little significance. Furthermore, since meaning cannot be located on the surface, it must be found by a mitigated, indirect route, through metaphor. All interpretations are therefore conditioned by the reflex to search for hidden sexual metaphor, even where sexuality is materially present on the surface of the film.

In addition, all of the above texts deal with some form of identity politics, most through categories of ethnicity and sexuality. Sexuality as a practice is related to sexuality as a category of identity.[2] Lubin demonstrates that the two categories interact (Lubin, 2005). Loshitzky analyses how sexual practice poses a challenge to the ethnic category (Loshitzky, 2001). Meiri and Munk show how they are associated (Meiri and Munk, 2008, pp. 67–72). Nevertheless, in all the examples I mentioned above, sexuality as a practice is subordinated to the more dominant identity category. Lubin places it beneath gender and ethnicity (Lubin, 2005). Loshitzky, Meiri, and Munk discuss it alongside questions of homosexual identity (Meiri and Munk, 2008, pp. 67–68, 70; Loshitzky, 2001, pp. 161–165). It is

---

[1] Harris' study is set apart from others in its direct references to depictions of sex. However, Harris is generally concerned with plot, and refers very little to the cinematic dimension of what she describes.

[2] For an illustration on the elementary difference between approaches which demarcate sexuality as a category of identity, and those which demarcate it as practice, see my comparison of Butler and Williams in chapter 1, footnote 1.

far more common to find discussions of sexual identity in Israeli film research, covering both gender and sexual preference, than to find discussions of sexual practice. The word "sexuality" appears so often as a category of identity that it is treated as such for all purposes in academic discussion. Thus, for instance, when Raz Yosef dedicates two monographs to the topic of sexuality – *Beyond Flesh: Queer Masculinity and Nationalism in Israeli Cinema* (2004), and *To Know a Man: Sexuality, Masculinity and Ethnicity in Israeli Cinema* (2010) – he limits himself to categories of identity. Sex as practice, if it appears at all, is metaphorically mitigated, subordinated, and marginalised.

Psycho-semiotics and identity politics provide some explanation of the elusive approach researchers have taken towards depictions of sexual practices in Israeli film. The question still remains, however, of which metanarrative is embedded within them. Ben-Ari and Almog discuss the representation of sexual practice in Israeli culture within the context of a conservative-liberal divide. Bursztyn attributes it to materialism, individualism, and cultural inadequacy. Meiri, Munk, and Lubin, however, define it within an entirely different matrix.

Meiri and Munk explain the use of sexual practice in GIFT FROM ABOVE as a subversive act. According to them, Zionist ideology is constructed on the adoption and suppression of anti-Semitic perceptions of Diaspora Jews. In confronting Israeli audiences with two old anti-Semitic concepts – the exotic, hypersexual Jew and the effeminate, "castrated" Jew – the film presents an antithetic standpoint to Zionism's oppressive melting pot policy (ibid., pp. 66–67). This "return of the repressed" reveals that the new Jewish male sexuality is constructed on a fear of castration (ibid., p. 69). The fact that this depiction is attributed to the immigrant Georgian community broadens the sexual difference into a cultural one (ibid., p. 71). Lubin also uses Otherness as a key concept in explaining female difference. The normative world films construct is one in which woman is always perceived as inferior (Lubin, 2005, p. 302). Zionism serves as the norm that oppresses women and represses the sexual body (ibid., p. 305). Meiri and Munk describe repression as an expression of anxiety. In Lubin's framework, the sexual body is suppressed in order to privilege the body of the worker (ibid.). In both cases, the depiction of the sexual body is a subversive act. In the course of the subversive act, characteristics associated with the Other – women, Oriental Jews, Georgian immigrants – are manifested. According to Lubin, religious Oriental Judaism is set in contrast with European secularism (Lubin, 2005, p. 313). Along with rituals and customs, Meiri and Munk also mention vulgar or violent behaviour (Meiri and Munk, 2008, p. 72).

Generally speaking, in this context, sexual practice is attributed Otherness and placed in opposition to Zionist ideology. This, in turn, is labelled as masculine, and opposed to Jewish Diaspora existence. The fact that sexual practice is retained in this equation is arbitrary: almost anything could replace it. Indeed, within academic discourse on Israeli film, this Zionism-centred pattern is used in every possible way, and not just in discussions of sex. It is the most dominant paradigm applied to Israeli film. To explain my own theoretical approach, then, I must position myself in relation to this dominant hypothesis. The next chapter gives an overview of the evolution of this paradigm in Israeli film studies, and the two succeeding chapters (5 and 6) offer a critical discussion of its fundamental premises.

4 Thesis and Antithesis

This review of the history of Israeli film studies is based on the evolution of the paradigm described above, in which historical progress and identity construction are understood and organised in terms of opposition. I focus on academic texts about full-length feature films, to which I have dedicated my own research, rather than short or documentary films.

Like the film industry itself, academic research into Israeli cinema began slowly and developed only sluggishly. Its earliest moments were humble, and just as sporadic as early Israeli filmmaking itself. And, like the Israeli film industry, Israeli film research steadily grew and diversified once it had established itself.

Initially, the contributors belonged to the film industry. The first to write about Israeli film in a semi-scholarly manner was Yehuda Harell in 1956. The eighth and final chapter of his monograph on world cinema discusses Israeli film. Harell was an active participant in the film industry (Zimmerman, 2002, p. 920), and offers a compelling narrative of Israeli filmmaking since the 1920s as an ongoing uphill struggle (Harell, 1956, pp. 216–240). Similarly, in 1974, the producer Margot Klausner gave an autobiographical account of setting up her studios in Herzliya, a process riddled with dangers, difficulties, mistakes, and failure – all of which make her successes all the more miraculous (Klausner, 1974).

Initial discourse on Israeli cinema offered adventurous descriptions of film production, much in line with the widespread pioneer spirit, and discussions of the structure of the industry and the problems confronted by those attempting to participate in it. The focus was on early production narratives, and this spread from pioneering filmmakers to archivists, historians, and the occasional film scholar. It was continued in the published works by Natan and Yaakov Gross (Gross and Gross, 1991), Hillel Tryster (Tryster, 1995), Joseph Halachmi (Halachmi, 1995), Moshe Zimmerman (Zimmerman, 2001a; Zimmerman, 2001b, pp. 10–31), and Ariel Feldstein (Feldstein, 2009). David Shalit and Ulrike Heikaus' studies supplement these, discussing the early history of movie theatres and film-viewing culture in Palestine and Israel (Shalit, 2006; Heikaus, 2009). In their recent studies, the historian Ofer Ashkenazi and the film scholar Boaz Hagin have broken new ground in our understanding of the pioneers of Israeli film. Ashkenazi reflects upon the origins of director Helmar Lerski's aesthetic approach (Ashkenazi, 2016; Ashkenazi, 2017; Ashkenazi, 2018), while Hagin explores Klausner's cinema theory (Hagin, 2018).

Ora Gloria Jacob-Arzooni, who published the first wholly academic monograph on Israeli film in 1983, integrated this historical perspective into her work. Her book, based on her 1975 dissertation at the University of Michigan, takes a sociological view. She combines early production narratives with the history of Israeli theatre, as well as general historical and cultural insights. A further chapter offers a summary of sociological research on the film-going public. Her original research on audience numbers for Israeli films likely attracted more attention within the research community than her analysis of individual works (Jacob-Arzooni, 1983). As Zimmerman points out, Jacob-Arzooni's work remained isolated, and had no further influence on the research of Israeli film (Zimmerman, 2002, pp. 921–922). Shohat criticises Jacob-Arzooni's work as discourse "of the object", rather than "on the object": Jacob-Arzooni, she argues, refrains from taking a critical stance (Shohat, 1989, p. 12). Jacob-Arzooni does not refrain from criticism, but on the whole, like the filmmakers before her and unlike the scholars after her, her point of departure is integrative rather than critical. This conforms, perhaps, to Jacob-Arzooni's perception of Israeli history and society as part of an ongoing continuum: "Any review of the historic events in the life of the State of Israel and of the Israeli people must begin with the basic premise that Israel is a continuation of the Jewish people and not an entirely new entity" (Jacob-Arzooni, 1983, p. 326).

Before Shohat's own study appeared in 1989, a discourse had already developed in Israel through newspapers, magazines, and journals. *Omanut Hakolnoa* (1958–63) was the first Hebrew-language journal dedicated to film from an aesthetic and scholarly point of view (Shohat, 1989, p. 17; Gertz, 1993, p. 43; Zimmerman, 2002, pp. 919, 920–921). A corpus of academic and semi-academic writing about Israeli film accumulated during the 1970s and 1980s, in film journals like *Close-up* (1973–1978), *Kolnoa* (1974–1983), *Sratim* (1986–1990) and *Cinematheque* (1982–) (Shohat, 1989, pp. 12–13; Gertz, 1993, p. 43; Zimmerman, 2002, pp. 920–921), and in journals from other disciplines, such as the special edition of the literary journal *Keshet* dedicated to film, which appeared in 1968 (Klein, 2012).

Yehuda-Judd Ne'eman and Rennan Schorr's articles were the first to portray Israeli film history in antithetic terms. In his 1979 critique of contemporary commercial cinema, Ne'eman describes a dual opposition in Israeli film. Cinema was born during a time when Israeli society was moving away from the old pathos, and was ushered in by twin films: SALACH SHABATI (1964, D: Ephraim Kishon) was the prototypical commercial comedy, and HOLE IN THE MOON (1965, D: Uri Zohar) was the prototypical auteur film (Ne'eman, 1979, pp. 20–21).

In 1978, Schorr used the pioneer rhetoric of former writers to describe a new generation of filmmakers. His cinematic chronology describes an evolution. Until the early 1960s, feature films (excluding co-productions) were mostly a pale facsimile of contemporary reality, an apologetic perpetuation of an imaginary, heroic warrior and Sabra – or native-born Israeli – which the Diaspora wanted to see (Schorr, 1978, p. 32). In the early 1960s, melodramas and comedies widened the range of the cinema. But their subject matter was marginal and exotic, and the films anachronistic, rehashing successes and conventions from the theatre (ibid., pp. 32–33). The final step in Schorr's evolution, then, was the new wave of auteur filmmakers who made subversive cinema with non-linear narratives and a reflective view of cinema and history (ibid., p. 33). Filmmakers gained new freedom from structural convention, and began the process of demystifying the "Sabra" type figure (ibid., p. 34). Here, Schorr applies the standards of the European New Wave. More noteworthy, he organises the chronology of Israeli film into genres, corresponding to historical phases. He also gives an important role to the construction (by earlier films) and demolition (by later films) of the "Sabra" type figure. On his view, demolition is closer to the true sense of reality.

When Schorr reformulated his historical narrative in 1984, he maintained the division between two periods: Zionist propaganda films made until 1961,[1] and every film after that year, which are characterised by their focus on peripheral characters (Schorr, 1984, pp. 38, 42). He also uses Ne'eman's distinction, regarding the 1970s, between cheap commercial films and experimental films (ibid., pp. 42–43). But now he identifies a twofold failure. Ethnic cinema was repetitive, and debased the reputation of Israeli cinema (ibid., p. 45); meanwhile, the experimental wave failed to connect to the local culture, public, and industry (ibid., p. 43). Schorr claims that the schism between these two extremes weakened the national film industry. He ends with the re-emergence of mainstream film since 1977, and the beginning of a new era of normalisation (ibid.).

The use of this antithetic structure by Ne'eman and Schorr primarily reflects their own position in the Israeli film industry. Both belonged to a group of activist filmmakers who advocated for art films and who, in 1978, campaigned successfully for the establishment of a state fund for non-commercial films (Shohat, 1989, pp. 182–184). This historical narrative aided their efforts to assert themselves in film history. But the antithetic paradigm henceforth became common among scholars, who used it to present their own preferences.

Israeli film studies was consolidated with a number of books which appeared in the late 1980s and early 1990s. First and most famous was Shohat's 1989 *Israeli Cinema: East/West and the Politics of Representation*. Using a post-colonial approach, Shohat sets the stage for the antithetic paradigm with the claim that

---

1 Zionism generally understood as the national movement for the return of the Jewish people to establish a homeland and state in Israel (Zion).

Jewish national liberation took place upon the ruins of another national existence (Shohat, 1989, p. 6). Her narrative is constructed around three types of subjectivities – Ashkenazi/European Jewish, Sephardi/Oriental Jewish,[2] and Arab – and the main premise is that the first of these subjugated and suppressed the others. Her division remains much in line with that of Schorr and Ne'eman, relying on contrasts between early/late cinema and commercial/art films. She supplements these with an additional dimension which extends from European to Oriental identities. The historical development she describes moves from a European meta-narrative to the gradual emergence of the Orient.

Shohat divides Israeli film history into four periods: the first covers the years before the establishment of the State of Israel in 1948; the second extends from 1948 to the Six-Day War in 1967; the third goes from the late 1960s to the end of the 1970s; and the final period covers the 1980s. The first era is focused on the establishment of a Zionist form of self-representation. Shohat's analysis emphasises the centrality of the new Jewish protagonist and, as a consequence, the subjugation and misrepresentation of Arab figures within the cinematic matrix (ibid., pp. 1–56). The second era is a continuation of the first, depicting mythical Israeli heroes – Sabras, kibbutzniks, and soldiers – often in the context of the Israeli-Arab conflict (ibid., p. 57). In the third era, the "Zionist ethos" is deconstructed (ibid., pp. 185–197, 217–222, 227–236), and the Israeli-Arab conflict suppressed (ibid., p. 238). The "Palestinian Wave" films of the fourth era are a "return of the repressed", in which the way Arabs are represented differs fundamentally from the way they were shown in earlier stages (ibid., pp. 239–273).

In the second half of the book, Shohat equates the Sabras with their Ashkenazi descendants. European Jews are read as an oppressive force. Shohat argues that Sephardi Jews suffer discrimination in the Jewish state and are misrepresented in Israeli film. Traditionally, they appear either as faithful servants or as negative, violent threats (ibid., pp. 115–124). Most of Shohat's discussion of the third era focuses on how they are depicted. In her view, while ethnic comedy misrepresents the Sephardi population, it offers solace to working class Sephardis by delivering "carnivalesque" blows to characters who, for the Oriental collective consciousness, represents the oppressive centre (ibid., p. 131).

Ashkenazi and Sephardi filmmakers are then placed in opposition to each other. Commercial films by Sephardi filmmakers offer release, while those by Ashkenazi filmmakers reproduce repressive misconception (ibid., p. 135). Similarly, Sephardi art films offer warmth, and truths about Sephardi existence

---

[2] Shohat uses the term "Sephardi" to refer to Jews from the Orient. Successive scholars prefer the term "Mizrahim" for the same group. I follow the term used by each scholar.

(ibid., pp. 166–178) while those by Ashkenazi filmmakers express the crisis of Zionist ideology (ibid., pp. 205–209), narcissism, individualism (ibid., pp. 209–210), rootlessness, and alienation (ibid., pp. 215–216). The values Shohat attaches to single films are no longer dependent on era and genre but on inherent identities. Twenty-three years later, Rami Kimchi developed this idea further by distinguishing between commercial comedies produced by "Ashkenazi" filmmakers, and the ones produced by "Mizrahi" (Oriental) ones (Kimchi, 2012, pp. 59–143).

Following Shohat came Bursztyn's *Face as Battlefield*, in 1990, and Gertz's *Motion Fiction*, in 1993.[3] At first glance, these monographs are very different. Bursztyn, a filmmaker, focuses on an aesthetic element, the portrayal of faces, and asks how Israeli films might improve in the future. By contrast, Gertz, a literary scholar, offers an academic comparison of Israeli literature and film from the 1960s to the 1980s. Nonetheless, the Israeli film cosmos described by Bursztyn and Gertz is very similar. Like Shohat, both recognise a division between earlier and later periods, and between commercial and art cinema. Both refer to the history of Israeli cinema as one of failed development, and the progression they both describe is from national collectivism toward bourgeois materialism and individualism.

According to Bursztyn, the first two eras of Israeli film are dominated by ideology which is antithetical to human truth and dynamic narrative (Bursztyn, 1990, pp. 30–88). Counter-reactions by later eras include dynamic materialism (ibid., pp. 89–99), deconstruction and self-reflection (ibid., pp. 100–108), and individual truth and self-indulgence (ibid., pp. 109–120). Like Schorr, Bursztyn sees commercial cinema and art cinema as opposites in terms of what they possess and what they lack. Art films lack the dynamism of commercial films. On the other hand, art films possess internal truths which low culture (in his term "folklore") excludes from commercial films (ibid., pp. 126–203). The cultural war is carried over materialistic objectification, which commercial films promote and art films wish to escape (ibid., pp. 206–207).

While Burstyn discusses these developments on an aesthetic level, Gertz writes in terms of a systemic power struggle. She argues that, after collectivist national norms were replaced by individualist ones in the 1960s (Gertz, 1993, pp. 13–14), national cinema adopted bourgeois norms from the cinemas that would later replace it (ibid., pp. 16–27). Popular and elitist forms of cinema both fought against the pathos imposed by national cinema (ibid., p. 27). Popular

---

[3] Gertz's work serves as a basis for her 2015 publication with Munk, *Revising Israeli Cinema: 1948–1990*.

cinema had little institutional support, but enjoyed broad popularity. The opposite was true for elitist cinema. Both forms of cinema suffered from a weak position within the culture, which is why they offered alternatives to national norms but did not confront them (ibid., pp. 27–49). This confrontation took place a decade later, in the "cinema of the outsider and anomalous" of the 1980s (ibid., pp. 176, 183). According to Gertz, mainstream cinema is continuous with popular cinema, while the cinema of the outsider and the anomalous is continuous with elitist cinema. The rise of the political right has made it highly political (ibid., pp. 176–182). Its main target, however, is the earlier national cinema, whose prototypes, clichés, dynamic sense of time, and optimism it opposes (ibid., pp. 176, 195, 203–204, 226). Throughout her discussion, Gertz not only qualifies the cinemas she discusses using antithetic logics, but contrasts them constantly to literature. Literature sets the norm by which the cinema's shortcomings, weaknesses, and slow development are measured (ibid., pp. 37–40, 182–185).

Shohat, Bursztyn and Gertz, each offered a unique perspective on Israeli film. However, they did so on the basis of shared hypotheses about the periodisation of Israeli film and genre, and about the antithetic structure of meaning. These hypotheses became dominant in Israeli film studies. The timeline and rationale behind them are adopted in work like Ariel Schweitzer's research on Israeli art films of the 1960s and 1970s (*The New Sensibility*), Eldad Kedem's dissertation on the representation of the kibbutz, Lev Hakak's book on film adaptations of modern Hebrew literature, and Kronish's chronology of Israeli film history. Schweitzer dedicates a chapter to national and commercial cinemas as paradigms against which art cinema asserted itself as an alternative (Schweitzer, 2003, pp. 25–59). Hakak and Kedem each adopt and repeat the periodisation and chronology established by previous writers (Hakak, 2001, pp. 17–31; Kedem, 2007, pp. 39–40, 61–63, 72–76). Kronish, too, follows the historical landmarks established in earlier writing: the pre-state cinema, the "heroic" cinema which followed the establishment of the state and the Six-Day War, commercial comedies, and art films. The films of the 1980s and 1990s are organised by topic, and departures from the norm in the early cinema are noted for each decade (Kronish, 1996). This is repeated in Kronish and Safirman's reference guide to films (Kronish and Safirman, 2003). By now, it should be quite clear that early cinema is viewed as the ultimate thesis against which every antithesis is structured.

Talmon fleshes out the historical shift from collectivism to individualism, portraying the evolution of Israeli cinema and society through the depiction of the group. In early Israeli cinema, Talmon views groups as expressions of optimistic, activist male codes promoting individual effort within collective solidarity (Talmon, 2001, p. 42). In turn, this is enacted through an initiation process (ibid., p. 62), exclusion, and othering (ibid., p. 51), and through dynamic, educational, positive plots (ibid., p. 62). At the next stage, the cinema of the 1960s and 1970s still maintains conformity and integration even while deconstructing and parodying the group (ibid., pp. 63–64), which becomes an object of nostalgia (ibid., pp. 66–67), while "Others" become visible in their struggle for legitimacy (ibid., pp. 52–53). During the third stage, from the late 1970s, the purpose and aim of the cinematic group is undermined (ibid., p. 42). Conformity ceases to be attached to a cause, and becomes a goal in itself (ibid., pp. 65–66). In the final stage, in the 1990s, manhood opens up to "female" properties like passivity, emotionality, and underachievement (ibid., p. 68). The group structure then gives way to the romantic couple (ibid., p. 276).

Although the changes Talmon describes go from one social structure to another, she is describing, in effect, a process of deconstruction. The earlier perspective is viewed as perfectly affirmative. Changes are largely described as subtractions. In articles dealing with the myth of the binding of Isaac in Israeli film, Anat Zanger, too, describes change as subtraction where central cultural myths are first affirmed and then rejected and protested (Zanger, 1999, pp. 270–273; Zanger 2003). She views art cinema's persistent relationship with traditional myth as a failure to unburden itself of traditional symbolism (ibid., p. 96).

There is an apparent consensus among writers that the early phase of Israeli film and the society it reflects is optimistic and active in nature. In an article from 1999, Ne'eman provides a rare case in which this phase is associated with negativity. As he explains, the Zionist ethos of martyrdom sanctified death. Modernist art films proposed a reversal, a negation of negation, involving both attraction to and rejection of the death wish propagated by Zionist culture (Ne'eman, 1999, pp. 119–122).

In Loshitzky's study, hegemony and Otherness are dominant categories. She dedicates her book to questions about the identity of Holocaust survivors and their children, Mizrahim (particularly the second-generation), and Palestinians. All of these groups, she argues, are connected by the way in which the Zionist state victimises them. The dominant narrative oscillates between an ethos of self-sacrifice and one of involuntary victimhood (Loshitzky, 2001, pp. xiii–xiv). Loshitzky exemplifies the antithetic approach when she argues that an inseparable part of her research of "Other" identities is an analysis of "the" identity, the "New Jew" (Loshitzky, 2001, pp. 1–14). Identities possess a dual structure and are engaged in a duel with their counterparts. They are defined in terms of centrality and, more often, marginality.

It is not just those identities specific to Israel which count as marginal. The universal category of women is a central trope. Régine-Mihal Friedman describes woman as the suppressed Other. According to her, woman is absent from Israeli film. She is not even an object of the male gaze. The film relinquishes her. The male protagonist and male group take her place, and male fraternity – for instance, the military squad – substitutes for male-female love attachments. The female body, a source of abjection, disappears completely (Friedman, 1998, p. 42). Two academic generations later, Rachel Harris describes women and Mizrahi as inherently oppressed by the superior male and the Ashkenazi (Harris, 2017). Lubin, on the other hand, uses these categories interchangeably. As illustrated in chapter 3, Lubin describes woman in Israeli film as a peripheral being who commits an act of subversion by reappropriating the marginal sexual body (Lubin, 2005). Lubin employs a similar concept in another article, describing the Oriental Jewish immigrant as peripheral. His act of subversion takes place in Israeli films of the 1980s, within the marginal space of the transit camps established for newcomers in the state's early years (Lubin, 1991).

Distinguishing a group as Other becomes a key part of its definition. It is inseparable part of Ursula Raberger's venture to classify and index queer films within Israeli cinema (Raberger, 2015, pp. 104–231, 246–306), and of Nir Cohen's analysis of "proclaimed cinematic representation of gayness" (Cohen, 2012, p. 3). Yosef takes a further theoretical step when he describes the homosexual and Oriental as the ultimate counterpart to male hegemony. Zionist phallic masculinity is constituted through the exclusion of the queer, the (homo-)eroticised Mizrahi, and the Palestinian male "others". The sexualised "Other" is first identified with and then disavowed (Yosef, 2004, p. 1). In Zionism, masculinity and the queer "Other" are internally connected. Queer subjectivity can only be understood as counter to Zionist masculinity, and Zionist masculinity only as a disavowal of queer subjectivity.

Which antithetic Other is chosen depends on scholars' preferences. As Gilad Padva argues, in Zionist cinema there were no effeminate men with bleached hair, platform shoes, soft voices, camp gestures, colourful shirts, and tight pants (Padva, 2008, p. 8). Otherness does not exhaust itself in women, Arabs, Oriental Jews, or homosexuals. Other "Others" are occasionally cited as new subjectivities that appear in film or are yet to appear, including residents of the geographical periphery, members of religious and ultra-orthodox communities, immigrants from the former Soviet Union and Ethiopia, and foreign workers (Kedem, 2007, p. 107; Loshitzky, 2001, p. xv).

A notable shift took place in the common Israeli film chronology regarding the point in time at which the "old" values gave way to the "new" ones. Schorr locates the beginning of the new era in 1961, and Ne'eman in 1964–5, conspicuously close to the generational changeover in literature (Zimmerman, 2003, p. 139). Just over a decade later, Shohat and Gertz allowed for an historical overlap in the 1960s, in which the "national" cinema existed alongside those cinemas that undermined it. The Six-Day War was regarded as a thematic stimulus which endorsed a moribund narrative (Shohat, 1989, pp. 103-114; Gertz, 1993, pp. 22–23). The fact that the watershed moment is stretched out facilitates the delineation of additional events that mark further breaks from the early narrative. Gertz, for instance, points to the electoral victory of the political right in 1977 (Gertz, 1993, pp. 177–185), while Zimmerman focuses on the eruption of the Six-Day War and the Yom Kippur War (Zimmerman, 2003, pp. 142–143).

I believe that this indicates another gradual paradigmatic change in the way historical progress is recorded. In the early 1990s, Gertz payed tribute to the generational gap in her chronology. Since films from the 1980s played against a Zionist ethos some twenty years after this ethos reportedly lost its dominance, she attempts to explain why a rebellion took place against the founding fathers – against the "grandparents", rather than the "parents" (Gertz, 1993, pp. 182–184). Later scholars have been less inclined to provide such historical motivation. The longer the antithetic paradigm is used, the more Zionist hegemony becomes an ahistorical phenomenon which Israeli cinema is permanently determined in contrast with. Both Munk and Kedem, for instance, argue that Israeli cinema of the 1990s is constructed in opposition to Zionist hegemony (Munk, 2004, p. 7; Kedem, 2007, p. 104).[4]

The Zionist narrative and its protagonist, the "New Jew" or "Sabra", have become the central configuration against which everything else is contrasted. How are they described? In their early writings, Ne'eman and Schorr associate the early mode of depiction with pathos and grandeur (Schorr, 1978, p. 32; Ne'eman, 1979, pp. 20–21). Shohat described it as a combination of Eastern-Bloc socialist realism and Western colonialist ideals (Shohat, 1989, pp. 24–25, 42). In 1992, Ne'eman called it a combination of Zionist accomplishments, collectivist ideals, disasters in Europe, struggles with the wilderness, and clashes with the local population (Ne'eman, 2006 (1992), p. 134). Nitzan Ben-Shaul observes that, in the pre-state phase, the Sabra's labour as an agricultural pioneer was emphasised; after independence, the focus shifted to his fighting prowess (Ben-Shaul, 1997, p. 13).

"Utopia" and "ideal" are the key words here. Zimmerman describes early Israeli cinema as imperialist, youthful, and eternal (Zimmerman, 2003, p. 134), idealising the figures it depicts (ibid., p. 136) and creates a complete correlation between the mythical and the concrete (ibid., p. 115). In her 2004 book, Gertz describes a cinematic Hebrew man who dominates the space around him

---

[4] Munk's dissertation, cited here, served as a basis for *Exiled in Their Borders: Israeli Cinema at the Turn of the Century* (Munk, 2012).

through action and gaze and who in fact imitates an imaginary ideal (Gertz, 2004, p. 13). While those who focus solely on early cinema recognise ideological mobilisation as a dominant component (Cohen, 1991), epic attributes are ascribed to early cinema only by those who play it up against the cinemas that follow.[5]

Another prominent component in general perceptions of the Zionist protagonist is that this constellation itself is seen as the product of opposition. The Sabra is not identified as the thesis, but rather an antithesis in itself. Whereas, in 1978, Schorr described early cinema as an apologetic attempt to please the Jewish Diaspora (Schorr, 1978, p. 32), by 1989, Shohat could regard it as a counter-image to anti-Semitic associations with the European Diaspora – unhealthy, self-tormenting, cowering in small spaces, with no attachment to a land (Shohat, 1989, pp. 29, 35). Other scholars followed with similar arguments. The Sabra image provided a counter to the rootlessness, spirituality (Talmon, 2001 p. 118; Gertz, 1993, p. 17), and passivity attributed to Diaspora Jews (Talmon, 2001, pp. 51, 62). The Sabra is seen as a reversal of European Jewish masculinity (Cohen, 2012, p. 18). As Ne'eman argued in 1992, the European Jew, the ultimate Other of Western society, suddenly wore the uniform of the utopian man (Ne'eman, 2006, p. 134). Gertz postulates that Zionism needed the identity of the Diaspora Jew in order to define itself as its antithesis (Gertz, 2004, p. 13). Talmon suggests that the process was gradual. The descendants of the pioneers were the first to adopt the heroic image for themselves, projecting victimhood onto the Diaspora Jew (Talmon, 2001, p. 119).

If the Zionist narrative and its protagonist are constructed in opposition to each other, representing a swing of the pendulum away from the Diaspora, then the opposition to this opposition, a negation of this negation, is mostly seen as a swing in the other direction, back to the allegedly negated identity. Everything that was alien and other in films of the 1940s and 1950s takes centre stage in the 1960s and 1970s, Gertz argues. The margins became the centre (Gertz, 2004, p. 42). Zionist secularism pushed Judaism to the margins, adds Schweitzer, and the post-Zionist era is exemplified by the rehabilitation of disfranchised traditions (Schweitzer, 2003, p. 200). Third- and fourth-generation immigrants refused to ignore Jewish heritage as their parents had, explains Yuval Rivlin, and the two stages involved – alienation and the return to traditional Jewish identity – are critical for understanding modern Jewish identity (Rivlin, 2009, pp. 10–11). As we

---

5 In his 2016 article on Lerski's work, Ashkenazi apparently offers an exception to the rule. Like his predecessors, he attributes a mythical disposition to early Zionist films, and Lerski's in particular (Ashkenazi, 2016, pp. 98–101). But he immediately undermines this by providing an alternative reading of Lerski's film (ibid., pp. 101–114).

have seen in chapter 3, Meiri and Munk argue that anti-Semitic concepts of Jewish identity crept up from the Zionist subconscious as late as 2003, as true representatives of difference (Meiri and Munk, 2008).

This antithetic paradigm has remained dominant in Israeli film studies from its emergence to the present day. Have any alternative perspectives been offered in Israeli film studies over the years? If so, how different were the narratives they offered? Schnitzer's 1994 book is widely seen as an attempt to offer an alternative to Shohat's account (Ben David, 2008, p. 20). It provides the first systematic index of commercial Israeli productions – a potential source for an alternative film history. But Schnitzer keeps to the antithetic paradigm in his historical summary. He draws a sharp distinction between the early, mobilised, affirmative norms and the critical ones that follow (Schnitzer, 1994a, pp. 15–22). He also emphasises the presence of Others: the religious, Holocaust victims, Palestinians, and women (ibid., pp. 22–25).

Ilan Avisar proposes an alternative historical perspective, pointing out that early Israeli cinema did not generate epic films about superheroic pioneers and warriors. Such films were made in Hollywood, and the local film industry had neither the means nor the inclination to produce them (Avisar, 2005, p. 131). In his chronology, however, Avisar still refers to early Israeli films using the term "heroism" (ibid., pp. 132–133). Rather than questioning the antithetic structure of film history, Avisar argues that, in the new millennium, the pendulum swung back to the affirmative mode of early film (ibid., pp. 142–143).

Liat Steir-Livny applies similar scrutiny to a specific film in revising the image of Uri, the protagonist of HE WALKED THROUGH THE FIELDS. Her analysis shows that Uri is the opposite of a mythological hero (Steir-Livny, 2007, pp. 292–303). She claims that the film departs from the concept of a mythological "New Jew" (ibid., pp. 291–292). Since she does not question the term's validity, however, she remains in the same premise, in which all is motivated by the Zionist myth that can either be affirmed or shattered.

Different paradigms do sporadically appear in Israeli film studies, but without significant consequences. Zimmerman, for instance, alternates between two discourses. He applies an enthusiastic pioneer narrative in his writings on early Israeli film, crediting it with the establishment of later genres, as well as difficulties that would later repeat themselves (Zimmerman, 2001a, pp. 89–112). However, he does not continue this into his discussion of productions from the 1960s onwards, where he exclusively uses antithetic historiography (Zimmerman, 2003).

A new film history could emerge if we changed the premises by which it is discussed. Zanger's 2012 monograph which promises just that, releases itself from a traditional, time-oriented, narrative-based approach in favour of a space-oriented one, which supposedly enables a non-hierarchical perspective (Zanger,

2012, p. xvii). Her spatial motifs – maps, borders, the military zone, water, the desert, gardens, Jerusalem – are instrumental in introducing concepts and myths which have never been applied in Israeli film studies. And yet, in spite of her new approach and her extended corpus, Zanger does not break away from the old paradigm. The history she addresses is still one founded on Zionism and breaking away from it (ibid., pp. 14–18). The female protagonist still serves as an ultimate Other (ibid., pp. 57–97), and spaces are defined by the Otherness they contain (ibid., pp. 99–150).

In their article, Hetsroni and Duvdevani declare that their main objective is to challenge the traditional, overly selective Israeli film historiography (Hetsroni and Duvdevani, 2000, p. 99). The dichotomy between art films and ethnic comedies has left most commercial films unaccounted for (ibid., pp. 101–102), they claim and propose that these belong to a third, disregarded lineage of hedonistic, nihilistic films which were both high-quality and popular. This lineage begins in the late 1970s, and dominated the screen in the 1990s (ibid., pp. 111–112). Pablo Utin offers new terms to define films from the mid-1990s, drawing a distinction between understated films (which he calls "tip of the Iceberg") and political films (which he calls the "reversed iceberg") (Utin, 2008, pp. 9–27). Whereas Hetsroni and Duvdevani undermine the antithetic paradigm by introducing a third, integrative lineage, Utin introduces a new vocabulary while maintaining the antithetic structure. He contrasts the trends he discusses to the political films of the 1980s (ibid., p. 14), and establishes an antithetic dichotomy between political and non-political (ibid., pp. 17–18). In any case, Hetsroni and Duvdevani and Utin all focus on specific contemporary trends, rather than revising Israeli film history more profoundly.

The only scholar of Israeli films to offer a systematic history of cinematic continuity, rather than antithesis, is Ben-Shaul. He does so by emphasising historically repeated patterns. According to his article from 1989, the motif of the siege unifies Israeli film. Ben-Shaul argues that political films depart from earlier cinema in their advocacy of political change, but still share its sense of enclosure (Ben-Shaul, 1989). In his book from 1997, he expands this into a historiography, which follows the sense of siege as it contracts and relaxes following the political atmosphere. It acts as a seismograph for the changes the Israeli society undergoes, and does not stand in opposition to any other element (Ben-Shaul, 1997). Accordingly, Ben-Shaul does not interpret the depiction of war in pro-Zionist productions of the 1950s as an antithesis, but rather as representation that encompasses contradiction. The war is both the expression of a long history of Jewish persecution and a sign that such history is changing (Ben-Shaul, 1997, p. 14). Note, however, that Ben-Shaul limits his observation to a narrow corpus of films, and never attempts to apply it on a larger scale.

Israeli film studies has grown and diversified throughout its many years of existence. It has never presented a unified front, or spoken with one voice. And yet its consolidation was accompanied by the emergence of the antithetic paradigm. Its dominance has persisted, and alternatives have never solidified which could provide a rival metanarrative. This is reflected in two anthologies on Israeli film: *Fictive Looks*, edited by Gertz, Lubin and Ne'eman, which was published 1998 in Hebrew; and the 2011 English-language anthology *Israeli Cinema: Identities in Motion*, edited by Talmon and Yaron Peleg. While not all of the essays they contain use the antithetic paradigm, the majority do. Moreover, the essays are organised into periods and topics that reproduce the way the antithetic paradigm has taught us to visualise Israeli film history.

The existing corpus of Israeli film research has allowed me to recognise the periodic nature of film genres in Israel, and to understand that changes in the Israeli *Zeitgeist* were impressed upon and, simultaneously, constructed by film. But the dialectical historical narrative and the binary, antithetic framework used by the vast majority of film scholars has restricted possible ways of understanding Israeli cinema. Early cinema had come to be seen as negation, manifesting what it is *not*, and later cinema as a negation of this negation. Regardless of what was shown in individual films, they have primarily come to be viewed as a cinema of everlasting difference. This is the central concept I wish to question.

To do so, I undertake an excursion outside the cinema and into theory, which will provide the framework and context for my discussions of films. I begin by offering a critical perspective on the dialectic readings of history described above, and then turn to the difficulties caused by the term "Otherness" and by binary identities.

5 The Hypothesis of Repression

I have chosen to explore the evolution of the sex scene in Israeli film from its emergence in the first half of the 1960s through to the end of the 1970s – a period of a decade and a half. Not coincidentally, as I showed in chapter 4, Israeli film scholars have located a breaking point in this period, a moment at which the pendulum altered its direction and collective Israeli identity changed. I do not wish to deny that a dramatic change took place in Israel at that time, as society began to shift away from the mobilised, ideological disposition that had characterised it from the very outset. Within that time, Israel participated in three wars, entered a historic peace agreement, experienced an economic surge and depression, witnessed a rise in protest movements, and underwent its first democratic change of leadership. Those events brought changes to society and communal identity that manifested themselves in every form, including cinema. But the framework in which these changes and their consequences were integrated into Israeli film studies are, I believe, in need of revision.

To carry out this revision, I turn once again to Foucault. In this context, it is his methodology which is essential, rather than his historical observations. I embark on what Foucault terms an archaeological excavation on a discursive level, to be conducted "in order to discover far less 'immediate' relations than expression, but far more direct relations than those of the causality communicated through the consciousness of the speaking subjects" (Foucault, 1972 (1969), p. 163). In other words, my revision is aimed first and foremost at the context in which history is read, which resides on a theoretical rather than an empirical level. Foucault's objective is to test historiographical categories, to overcome their familiarity, and to replace them if they do not withstand scrutiny (ibid., p. 26). My task, then, is one of re-contextualisation.

The historiography shared generally by Israeli film scholars, which I described in chapter 4, is apparently based on a Hegelian dialectics of negation. Zionism is perceived as an ideology which generates progress through the negation of the past. As I argued, if the Diaspora is the thesis, then Zionism is the antithesis, and the "Post-Zionist" phase functions as a kind of synthesis, a negation of the negation – clearly interpreted by most as the negation of the antithesis. As I said in chapter 4, this movement resembles that of a pendulum, swinging between opposite poles. To investigate the idea that this pattern is the organising principle underlying historical cultural change, I now examine its origins: the dialectic model introduced by Georg Wilhelm Friedrich Hegel – or, rather, Wilden's reconstruction of it.

As Wilden observes, negation is an important concept for Hegel, "a divine power" which is the source of progress (Wilden, 1987, p. 245). He describes the Hegelian dialectic of negation:

> For Hegel the real is rational, and the rational is real. The "negativity of the dialectic" is the supposedly self-generating and self-renewing source of motion, growth and change in nature, society and history.
>
> An idea or concept is posited or put forward (forming a thesis, literally "set down, placed"); it is said to be negated by its opposite (its antithesis); the fusion of thesis and antithesis is then said to be negated by the "negation of the negation" producing the synthesis – which becomes the thesis to be negated at the next stage of the supposedly inevitable dialectical process [...].
>
> The synthesis *"suppresses and conserves"* both thesis and antithesis but at a new level and in new context, the context created by the dialectical process itself. The synthesis thus bears with it the insignia of its origin – its memory, in fact. (ibid., pp. 246–247 emphasis mine)

For Hegel, negation is not simply the formation of oppositions, but progress through change, by which the former constellation is both rejected and upheld. In the idea of dialectic preservation lies the difference between the Hegelian concept and a dialectic model described in chapter 4, which is exclusively based on oppositions. Wilden demonstrates this difference through a comparison with Karl Marx and Friedrich Engels' interpretation of the term "dialectic". He observes that, while Hegel's dialectic occurs on the level of in-formation (the organisation of knowledge), Marx and Engels place it in the material sphere, viewing it as a mechanical or electromagnetic metaphor (ibid., p. 247). The conceptual shift in the Marxist model enables accounts like the following:

> [W]hen the object moves beyond the limits of what it is, the object ceases to be what it is and it becomes in what is not. Is [sic] "negated" and in this sense a movement is generated (in the Aristotelian sense of the term, not in the Newtonian sense) both in nature and in human thought. (Hernández, 2013)

This contention – that a changed object becomes the antithesis of what it once was – depends on the idea that everything outside the object is antithetic to it, and that change causes negation. According to Wilden, this mechanical model does not hold for nature and human history, as no entity is truly the opposite of another:

> "I" cannot be the opposite or the "other side" (of the coin) of "not-I", for "I" is a particular, whereas "not-I" is a general relation englobing the rest of the universe. "Not-I" is the environment of the system "I", and open system and environment are not of the same level of logic, communication, or reality. (Wilden, 1987, pp. 251–252)

The confusion is not only between system and environment, which are erroneously equated, but also between the rational and the real. Wilden argues that reality, as a rule, is not within the grasp of negation, because it does not obey its basic function: "'Not' can only signify absence, zero, opposition, or exclusion in a system with only two options, as in the binary code (1,0) of the digital computer, where 'not-1' has no alternative but to mean '0'" (ibid., p. 251).

Having uncovered a preservative element in Hegel's dialectic, Wilden goes beyond this concept to define a dialectic process in which negation has no central role:

> In the dialectic of invention and science and history unexpected novelty emerges from the insoluble or tangled contradictions [...] of the old system, often quite suddenly but also over centuries, and a new technique, a new machine, a new understanding, a new mode of production, a new social order becomes dominant over the old, which survives in a subordinate role marking the distinction in the continuity between the past and the future created by the system's radical change in structure. (ibid., p. 248)

Not only is the old order preserved (even) in the process of radical change, but the creation of opposition is not the motivating force behind it. This is because development causes dialectic progress, and not vice versa. Moreover, the realisation of dialectic change occurs primarily in hindsight:

> The structural changes are continuous but in retrospect we detect a discontinuity: the process displays emergent qualities. In every instance of change – in analytic logic change is impossible to explain – the paradox of the discontinuous in the continuous comes in and out of being like the Cheshire Cat. (ibid.)

The discontinuous can only advance within the continuous, and therefore appears only elusively. Such progress applies not just to material change, but also to ideas within a learning process. As Wilden points out, Freud calls the dialectic of learning the "theory of deferred action", or "learning after the event" (*Nachträglichkeit*). Information that endures through memory acquires new meanings, in new contexts, through passage in time and space (ibid., p. 249).

For Wilden, negation plays no part in this dialectic process:

> The dialectic leap that results in the discrete Event of Events, the change in levels, the framing of new contexts, the repatterning and restructuring of the old order, has nothing to do with "not", "negation", or (Hegel's) so-called "third law of dialectics": "the negation of the negation". Negation is a linguistic operation, not found in nature or history or communication between organisms. (ibid., p. 250)

By associating dialectic process with restructuring, rather than negation, Wilden is calling for a transition from an antithetic chronology to a continuous one – a chronology that focuses, not on what has been negated, but on what has been sustained.

Foucault, too, believes that history is continuous. Unlike Wilden, he does not reflect on the logic of the forces that effect change, but rather on his own position as a historian (or "archaeologist"). He considers his ontology as an observer, drawing a distinction between "*extrinsic* contradictions that reflect the opposition between distinct discursive formations" and "*intrinsic* contradictions [...] deployed in the discursive formation itself", which are the sole objective of archaeological description (Foucault, 1972, p. 153–154, emphasis in the original). Archaeology explores the depths of a single discursive lineage, rather than bringing wholly separate discourses together. It is the principle of continuity which eliminates the notion of an abrupt break in history:

> One can see the emergence [...] of a number of disconnexions and articulations. One can no longer say that a discovery, the formulation of a general principle, or the definition of a project, inaugurates, in a massive way, a new phase in the history of discourse. (ibid. p. 146)

> The idea of a single break suddenly, at a given moment, dividing all discursive formations, interrupting them in a single moment and reconstituting them in accordance with the same rules – such an idea cannot be sustained. (ibid. p. 175)

Because change in not abrupt and absolute, even a radical change occurs within continuity:

> To say that a discursive formation is substituted for another is not to say that a whole world of absolutely new objects, enunciations, concepts, and theoretical choices emerges fully armed and fully organized in a text that will place that world once and for all; it is to say that a general transformation of relations has occurred, but that it does not necessarily alter all the elements; it is to say that statements are governed by new rules of formation, it is not to say that all objects or concepts, all enunciations or all theoretical choices disappear. (ibid. p. 173)

More compelling than Foucault's theoretical remarks is his application of them in his historical analysis. In the first part of *The History of Sexuality: An Introduction*, Foucault examines the "discourse on modern sexual repression", which is based on distinct oppositions. The historiography Foucault proposes to revoke has a similar structure to the cultural history of Israel described in chapter 4. In this history, the Victorian age, like Zionism, is the antithesis which sets things in motion. The pendulum moves from a time in which "sexual practices had little need of secrecy" (Foucault, 1990, p. 3), to the "monotonous nights of the Victorian bourgeoisie" in which "sexuality was carefully confined" (ibid.), and back to contemporary times in which one liberated oneself from "those two long centuries [...] of an increasing oppression" – something that required "nothing less than a transgression of laws, a lifting of prohibition, an irruption of speech, a reinstating of pleasure within reality" (ibid., p. 5) in order to reinstate freedom.

Like Wilden, Foucault sees such chronologies as a gross misinterpretation of the structure and dynamics of the forces at play. He gives three "doubts" about its existence in practice: on the historical level, he asks if the repressive force really existed (ibid., p. 10); on the historico-theoretical level, he asks if power only manifests in a society through prohibition, censorship, and denial (ibid.); and, on a historico-political level, he challenges the idea of a rupture between critical discourse and the historical network it denounces, and inquires about their affiliation (ibid.). In the second and third of these, Foucault argues for a historiography of continuity. On the theoretical level, he questions the idea that negation takes the form of repression. On the political level, he doubts that there is a genuine rupture between the critical era and the one preceding it.

But how can we trace continuity when the historical rupture seems obvious? Foucault provides an example through an "analytics of power", which defines a domain formed by relations of power (ibid., p. 82). Foucault demonstrates how continuity is sustained in discourse when moral codes or principles endure through extreme changes in the political system. To begin, he claims, institutions gained acceptance by presenting themselves as agencies of regulation (ibid., p. 86). For instance, since the Middle Ages or earlier, monarchic power has engaged in judicial discourse. Law was not simply a tool for the monarchs: rather, they manifested themselves and generated their own acceptability through law (ibid., p. 87). European monarchies were constructed as a system of law, and expressed themselves through theories of law (ibid.). In later years, those who wished to criticise and subvert these monarchic powers did not challenge judicial codes of power, but instead adopted them, using them to condemn the monarchy (ibid., p. 88). The fact that the judicial code endured beyond the system that contained it, being adopted by its successors and opponents, left a mark on the consequential historiography. Instead of being recognised as the source of the judicial code, monarchic power was viewed as an authority which violated it: "A tradition dating back to the eighteenth or nineteenth century has accustomed us to place absolute monarchic power on the side of the unlawful: arbitrariness, abuse, caprice, wilfulness, privileges and exceptions" (ibid., p. 87). An obsolete power can be harshly judged by the very moral scale it once maintained and propagated.

As we can see, Foucault's revisionism involves substituting an antithetic model of development for an integrative one which manifests continuity. His own revolutionary aspirations do not compel him to organise history in the form of oppositions.

To explain how Wilden and Foucault's approaches apply to my own revision of Israeli film history, I refer to a further observation from Foucault regarding the temporal dimension of the theory of oppression. He argues that, while supporters of this theory claim to be currently aware of past oppression, this is not enough to release them from it. The process by which this oppression is overcome is ongoing and everlasting (ibid., p. 5). The promise of a new age resides in the future (ibid., p. 7). The present is determined by the importance of the battle against old patterns (ibid., p. 6).

This resonates with the historiographical discourse on Israeli culture and film. As I showed in chapter 4, almost all film scholars agree upon two major historically detectable changes, two major swings of the historical pendulum: one towards the Zionist concept, and the other away from it. Avisar and Utin argue that other changes followed (Avisar, 2005, pp. 142–143; Utin, 2008, pp. 9–27). For many scholars, though, Zionist hegemony evolved into an ahistorical phenomenon against which Israeli cinema is permanently determined.

For the last fifty years, then, the heroic ethos and the heroic protagonist have been continuously undermined. Every reference and context is overshadowed by an allegedly sinful self-perception that must be circumvented and denounced, and by a father figure that must be destroyed. The time which had passed since the alleged era of heroism ended does not affect this intensity. As Benny Ben David puts it, the increase in studies linking Israeli cinema with the Zionist metanarrative renewed the myth of the fortitude of Zionism. Reflected in critical literature, the Zionist myth is revitalised after years of disintegration, and attributed power and dominance it never had (Ben David, 2008, pp. 21–22). As a result, perceptions of historical progress stagnate. The decades differ in the genres they generate and sustain. Their main frame of reference is not immediate history, but a concept which is no longer present. They are little more than variations of the same theme: counter-reaction to the Zionist model, distinguished from each other only by the attitude and angle they use. This historiography loses its contextual rationale after the 1980s.[1]

---

[1] That this historical model provides a plausible narrative for Israeli cultural and film history until the end of 1980s, and no further, is demonstrated on a film-poetic level in the documentary A HISTORY OF ISRAELI CINEMA (2009, D: Raphaël Nadjari). The film follows this dominant historical paradigm in the narration of Israeli film history. The first half of the film, which portrays Israeli cinema until the 1990s, develops in a coherent dynamic form illustrating dialectic progression. The second half, on Israeli cinema from the 1990s, offers no historical perspective and develops through a series of isolated topics – manifestations of Otherness. Its fragmented structure is striking when compared with the first half of the film.

An alternative to this approach is offered by the TV documentary series HAGIGA: THE STORY OF ISRAELI CINEMA (2015, D: Noit Geva). Its makers adopted a chronological approach to Israeli cinema

Although my study concludes long before the 1990s, it is nonetheless motivated by the need to offer an alternative to a history that ultimately "loses its swing". My thesis is guided by three tenets: continuity over disruption; repatterning over negation; and the revision of concepts established on the premises of disruption and negation. Since my alternative historiography is one of discursive continuity, I do not dispute that, over the decades, there has been much repetition in the premises of Israeli communal self-perception – premises by which the individual, society, history, and their relations have been defined and articulated. I argue that this evolving discourse did not begin in the 1960s, but can be traced back through the different phases of the preceding ideological age, and that some aspects of it can already be found in discourses that existed in the Jewish community before Zionism emerged. I also claim that this continuity, manifested in repetition, is not the result of a process of negation or some sort of periodic trauma. The cultural process Israeli society went through – which I trace out here through its embodiment in film – is dialectic, in Wilden's sense of the term: it is a repatterning, reordering, and restructuring of an older order. It is a gradual metamorphosis by which Israeli society changed the terms in which it perceived itself and, at the same time, preserved them.

And what of the *heroic* type figure, a spectre hovering over communal Israeli identity all the way to the present? Although it will not play such a central role in my analysis, I do not wish to dismiss it completely, but to place it in a different context. The heroic figure plays the roles of both Icarus and the Golden Calf. It is the insignia of a moral code, an omen inherited from Jewish tradition, maintained in Zionist thinking, and (as in Foucault's example of judicial authority) deployed against the ideological system which bore it. I do not dispute that early Israeli cinema was infused with the Zionist cause, and with the corresponding imperatives. Rather than accept the claim, described in chapter 4, that early Israeli cinema was utopian, ideal, mythic, and *heroic*, I examine the motivations which led scholars to project these notions onto it. To reflect on the reasoning which helped keep the heroic spectre alive, I refer to another concept which found a stronghold in Israeli film historiography: the concept of *Otherness*.

---

from the 1960s to the present day, concentrating on the filmmakers' perspectives in order to avoid the fragmentation that results from the prevailing academic methodology (Raveh, 2015).

6 Contrariwise: The Applications and Implications of *Otherness* and *Alterity*

As Wilden points out, no entity is truly the opposite of another (Wilden, 1987, pp. 251–252). But the binary perception of identities, in which individuals and groups are seen as contraries, is rooted in human history. In the twentieth century, as part of the attempt to explore and challenge this phenomenon, a cluster of academic theories of *Otherness* and *Alterity* emerged, focusing on the experience and identity of the object of binary perception, the person(s) viewed as "Other(s)".

As I showed in chapter 4, this theoretical approach was widely adopted in Israeli film studies. Using theoretical work of two central scholars in the field, Sander L. Gilman and Butler, I take a closer look at the mechanism of this approach and some of the obstructions it poses. Neither Gilman nor Butler apply their theories to Israeli film, although both incorporate questions of Jewish identity in their work. They nonetheless articulate key concepts for understanding *Otherness* in contemporary Israeli film studies. Elaborating on their concepts will help us to define the logic of its theoretical application in this field.

6.1 The Jewish Position: Sander Gilman

Jean-Paul Sartre's *Réflexions sur la question juive* (*Anti-Semite and Jew*) was published in 1946, a year after the end of Second World War and the Holocaust. Sartre sought to redefine three protagonists in French culture: the anti-Semite, the democrat, and the Jew, who serves as an archetype of Otherness. The focal point of his analysis are the protagonists' interrelations, in which the anti-Semite and democrat effect the Jew: "[M]an is defined first of all as a being 'in a situation'. [...] He cannot be distinguished from his situation, for it forms him and decides his possibilities; but inversely, it is he who gives it meaning by making his choices within it and by it" (Sartre, 1965 (1946), pp. 59–60). Sartre consequently maintains that anti-Semitism is not just a trend faced by Jews, but a dominant attitude that defines them and determines their position:

> It is neither their past, their religion, nor their soil that unite the sons of Israel. If they have a common bond, if all of them deserve the name of Jew, it is because they have in common the situation of a Jew, that is, they live in a community which takes them for Jews. (ibid., p. 67)

The Jew is defined as Other, not because society cannot assimilate him, but because it does not wish to (ibid.). Christian society has created the Jew by hindering his assimilation and providing him, in spite of himself, with a function (ibid., p. 68). Sartre goes on to describe the inferior position projected on the Jew, and the position of inferiority from which the Jew develops different strategies of negotiation (ibid., pp. 55–141).

Gilman, a cultural and literary historian, adopts this concept of Otherness, extending the existential social framework with a psychological dimension. He locates it in the process by which, in the earliest stages of development, all human beings become individuals. This process is set off by the discovery that the world is not the extension of the Self (Gilman, 1985, p. 17):

> [T]he child begins to combat anxieties associated with the failure to control the world by adjusting his mental picture of people and objects so they can appear "good" even when their behavior is perceived as "bad". [...] The child's sense of self itself splits into a "good" self, which, as the self mirroring [of] the earlier stage of the complete control of the world, is free from anxiety, and the "bad" self, which is unable to control the environment and is thus exposed to anxieties. [...] With the split of both the self and the world into "good" and "bad" objects, the "bad" self is distanced and identified with the mental representation of the "bad" object. Stereotypes [...] perpetuate a needed sense of difference between the "self" and the "object" which becomes the "Other". (ibid., pp. 17–18)
>
> Anxiety arises as much through any alteration of the sense of order (real or imagined) between the self and the Other (real or imagined), as through the strains of regulating repressed drives. [...] We project [...] anxiety onto the Other, externalizing our loss of control. [...] The "bad" Other becomes the negative stereotype; the "good" Other becomes the positive stereotype. The former is that which we fear to become; the latter, that which we fear we cannot achieve. (ibid., pp. 19–20)

Anxiety is the source in which Otherness is conceived and within which it re-emerges. Otherness is a social category. Every social group has set a vocabulary of images for an externalised Other, and these manifest its history and culture (ibid., p. 20). The categories in which Otherness is perceived are bipolar, framing the Other as the antithesis of the self. They are mutable and constantly shifting (ibid., p. 23). The coding of Otherness is determined by the group's needs at any given moment – it is protean, and its qualities are interchangeable (Gilman, 1986, p. 5).

Both Sartre and Gilman focus less on the reference group which defines the Other, and more on the object of their projection – in this case, the Jews. One of the strategies, Sartre argues, that Jews may use to negotiate anti-Semitism is to attempt to "blend in", getting rid of their Jewish attributes and becoming invisible as Jews (Sartre, 1965, pp. 95–103). Gilman agrees with Sartre's final observation that the desire to become invisible makes invisibility all the more prominent as a sign of the Jew's difference (Gilman, 1991, p. 192). Sartre describes a related strategy:

adopting anti-Semitic positions towards fellow Jews (Sartre, 1965, pp. 102–109). Gilman dedicates much of his work to this phenomenon, which he calls "self-hatred". He argues that it occurs when outsiders accept a false image of themselves generated by the group they wish to integrate into. It contains an inherent contradiction: on the one hand, there is a liberal fantasy that anyone can share the power of the reference group *if* they abide by their rules; and, on the other, these rules exclude the Other from sharing this power. The outsiders imagine that there is a message: Become like us, abandon your difference, and you can be one with us. At the same time, they hear the conservative curse: The more you resemble me, the more I know the true value of my power, and the more I am aware that you are only a shoddy counterfeit, an outsider. The privileged group desires to integrate the outsiders, and so to remove the image of its own potential loss of power. At the same time, it wants to put them at a distance, and validate its own power through the presence of the powerless. As one approaches the norms of the reference group, the group's approval recedes: even as one becomes identical with the definition of acceptability, one is still not accepted, because the ideal and unattainable state is never to have been Other in the first place (Gilman, 1986, pp. 2–3).

The cycle is complete when the "integrated outsiders" reproduce this projection. They subconsciously integrate their own rejection into their self-definition, projecting their sense of an unresolvable dichotomy onto an extension of themselves. They select some fragment of the category they have been included in, and see in it the essence of Otherness, embodying all the qualities projected onto them by the power group. This second level of projection is never complete. Even as one distances oneself from this "essence", the message from the internalised power group remains: under the skin, you're still just like them (ibid., p. 3). Caught in an impasse, "Others" attempt to escape negative perceptions of themselves by adopting the reference group's position, projecting that negative perception onward – only to be haunted by it further.

How far is the "Other" limited to becoming either the object or the subject of negative projection? Gilman describes two possible ways out. One is to make the terms involved positive:

> "Race" as a concept, can be a positive quality – it can provide for a group cohesion or group identity. One need not have only "an over-intense admiration or indeed worship", to evoke Isaiah Berlin's phrase, for the majority culture in which one lives. One can understand oneself as a Jew, or as an African-American, as different. (Gilman, 1991, p. 241)

Because of the weight of history, however, Gilman sees this path as inadequate:

> The success of the idea of alterity which seems now, at the beginning of the 1990s, to provide a positive sense of "racial" identity for individuals in American society, also contains an historical legacy, one which is negative and disturbingly self-renewing. The

concept of "race" is so poisoned in Western society that it is difficult to imagine how it can be resurrected. (ibid., pp. 241–242)

Another path lies in acknowledging that, against Sartre, "Otherness" is not the only factor that determines a minority group's identity. Gilman resolves this critique by retracting Sartre's claim of exclusivity:

> Sartre's definition, departing as it does from the question of the nature of anti-Semitism, does not reflect any internal continuity of Jewish identity, only the reaction of the Jew (or the outsider) to the world in which he or she is found. This does not deny an internal group identity; it only places this identity, whether strong or weak, in a greater social context. (Gilman, 1986, p. 12)

But Gilman does not set out to integrate this internal group identity, whether strong or weak, into his account of history, which is dedicated to the apparatus of Otherness and self-hatred as a major motivating force. It is a history of Jewish identity, determined by those who label Jews as Other (ibid.). Gilman's discussion offers valuable insight into the position and conduct of Jewish individuals and communities at different times. But he does not include any factors beyond the realities of Otherness, and so his scope remains limited – and, at times, problematic. Reducing Jewishness to two options – either being the object or subject of negative projection – means that the only source of identity is the anti-Semite. In Gilman's narrative, no matter whether Jews suffer from or replicate anti-Semitic prejudice, they internalise anti-Semitism. The main result is that Gilman fails to account for the rejuvenating influence of positive coping strategies. We see this in his discussion of Jewish/minority humour. Gilman locates the birth of Jewish comedy in the eighteenth century. He argues that the type figure of the Jewish schlemiel, the prototypical awkward bungler, was a product of the Enlightenment's corrective efforts – conceived as the counter-image of the enlightened Jew, a double of the negative image of the Jew in Germany (ibid., pp. 107–114). He notes that Jewish jokes, which began to appear in collections in the early nineteenth century, were seen as a response to "centuries of persecution", a weapon for Jews to defend themselves against attacks from the Christian communities. Joking is a verbal strategy used by those who lack strength and must therefore use their wit (ibid., p. 257; Gilman 1985, pp. 180–181). At the turn of the twentieth century, these jokes allowed German Jews to react to the threat they felt East European Jews posed to their own integration, by consigning them to a distant world of comedy and fiction (Gilman, 1986, p. 255; Gilman 1985, p. 178). Inversely, self-deprecating humour was also used by Jews and other minorities to discharge the hostility against them, to adapt to the majority environment, and to seek acceptance (Gilman, 2012). Over the centuries, as a means of defusing anxiety, the jokes presented in softened and refined tones those same things that the mobs in the streets were shouting about the Jews (Gilman, 1986, p. 259; Gilman, 1985, p. 182).

In short, Gilman finds in Jewish humour various strategies used by Jews, both inwardly and outwardly, to respond to their predicament as outsiders. He limits the utility of Jewish humour to such strategies, and denies that humour conceived in such circumstances might have any redeeming qualities. Gilman continues an academic tradition associating Jewish humour with psychopathology, and overlooks that tradition which focuses on the emancipating power of Jewish humour. Both of these traditions will be discussed in my analysis of the comic type figure in section 7.2. Intriguingly, Gilman connects his own remarks to the opus magnum which inspired both traditions, Freud's *Jokes and their Relation to the Unconscious*. Gilman does not focus on Freud's work itself, but on the way in which it may have evolved from his status as Other. Freud, Gilman asserts, identifies himself with the East European Jew because of his father's Galician background. In Vienna, the language of the East European Jew like Freud's father was seen as both comic and sexualised (Gilman, 1985, pp. 185–186). The death of his father was the catalyst for Freud's self-analysis, and so for the development of psychoanalysis. In turn, this is manifested in the approach Freud develops to neurosis, and to humour – where sexualised and comic language plays a major role (Gilman, 1986, pp. 264, 266; Gilman, 1985, pp. 186–187).

Freud's achievements are completely attributed to his struggle with Otherness, and his theory is seen as an act of suppression. He suppresses the role Jewish identity and language play for a patient, Anna O. (Gilman, 1986, pp. 259–261; Gilman, 1985, pp. 182–184). Similarly, he suppresses the role of Jewish jargon in the jokes he analyses (Gilman, 1986, p. 265; Gilman, 1985, pp. 186–187). Gilman concludes that Freud's theoretical analysis repeats the gesture illustrated by his model of the sexually aggressive joke, in which the object of the story vanishes through the identification of the storyteller with the listener: "The Jew in the 'Jewish' joke [...] vanishes in the presence of the idealised German self as both raconteur and listener, turning the teller's desire for identification with his reference group into hostility at the outsider, himself, who does not permit this" (Gilman, 1986, p. 267; Gilman, 1985, pp. 187–188). Freud's scientific language, according to Gilman, draws a distinction between him and the language attributed to the Jews. He publicly identifies with the non-Jew, rather than the non-Jew's caricature of the Jew. As a consequence, his scientific language is tainted with anti-Semitism (Gilman, 1986, pp. 267–268; Gilman, 1985, p. 189). As a theorist, Freud is placed in the position of the oppressive subject of negative projection. And this position is, apparently, assigned to any theorist who attempts to introduce a new theoretical approach. For instance, in his discussion of Max Nordau, the co-founder of the

World Zionist Organisation, Gilman remarks that his advocacy of regular physical exercise as a Zionist ideal draws from the anti-Semitic rhetoric of "Turnvater" Jahn. Nordau's call for the creation of the "new muscle Jew" is based on the premise that Jews are degenerate. Furthermore, according to Gilman, Nordau's claim that the muscle Jew will have a healthy body and a healthy mind condemns his Jewish critics as weak both in body and mind (Gilman, 1985, pp. 157–158; Gilman, 1986, p. 291). As a consequence, Nordau's plea for liberation has anti-Semitic roots and is, in reality, an act of oppression against his opponents.

In essence, any advocacy for reform incorporates a rejection of some variation of the present and/or past. But Gilman even finds anti-Semitic roots and negative consequences in the writings of philosopher Martin Buber, who advocates a sense of continuity in Zionism with present and past existence. Buber's affirmative account of a unique Jewish identity, distinct from acculturation on a "foreign" soil, is based on racial ancestry, and so only duplicates standard anti-Semitic racial paradigms in positive terms (Gilman, 1986, pp. 273–274). Also, Buber's positive view of East European Jews is paired with a negative evaluation of West European Jewish identity (ibid., p. 273). Gilman argues that Buber's favourable approach to East European Jews originates in a West European Jewish dilemma, and is invested with West European values and with a misconception of East European Jewish language and traditions (ibid., pp. 275–277). In Gilman's view, then, Buber, like Nordau, is inspired primarily by anti-Semitic views. Moreover, he fosters an oppressive attitude both toward the West European position he condemns and the East European position he endorses. As the last two references show, Gilman sees the foundations of Zionism as anti-Semitic. Zionism is not singled out as a set of beliefs, but integrated into an unbroken chronicle of self-hatred.

Gilman's definition of the Jewish position, like Sartre's, rests on the Jews' minority status. His theoretical approach does not account for a Jewish majority – something that came into existence with the establishment of the Jewish state in Israel. Gilman does not mention this in his work. Still, given the consistency of his theoretical structure, we can easily infer how it would view a community in which Jews are the majority. On the one hand, this would be identified as a rupture in Jewish history and identity: the peripheral position which defines Jewishness no longer applies. On the other, continuity comes through the application of anti-Semitic perceptions, which, in Gilman's model, are the only source of identity. From a central position in the social structure, the Israeli Jewish community establishes its identity on the axis between Us and Them, between "good" and "bad", and establishes a vocabulary of images for an externalised Other. In that, it emulates the nations which once repressed it, taking on elements of their collective image, including negated mirror images of the Otherness once projected upon them. This Otherness continues to exist, projected upon those marked as the new outsiders.

The scenario outlined here is not only a plausible continuation of Gilman's theory, but an assumption which has in fact been made about Israeli society. Ofra Nevo, for instance, shares Gilman's view of Jewish humour as derivative of oppressive conditions – either destructively, through the internalisation of negative stereotypes and identification with the aggressor (Nevo, 1984, p. 195), or constructively, as a means to cope with harsh conditions and rebuff external aggression (Nevo and Levine, 1994, pp. 126–127). She concludes that Jews in Israel, no longer oppressed as before, exchanged Jewish humour for a "humour of the strong". The Arab minority became the butt of the joke, rather than themselves, and they grew less reliant on Jewish tradition (Nevo, 1984, pp. 195–196; Nevo and Levine, 1994, p. 127).

Ultimately, Gilman's theory is most valuable for understanding how theorists view the formative years of Israeli Jewish culture during the mobilised phase. Most scholars of Israeli film are guided by the assumption that there was a dramatic rupture with earlier modes of existence, by the negation of former Diasporic Jewish identity, and by an identification with a heroic "New Jew" – in this context, a replica of the nationalistic European collective image from which Jews were mostly excluded.

6.2 The Position of Resistance: Judith Butler

In an article from 1982, Foucault suggested that, to understand what power relations are all about, we should investigate forms of resistance and attempts to break apart these relations. He makes a number of remarks about the reasoning behind modern "oppositions", or contemporary theoretical stances of resistance. He describes an original, specific characteristic of these:

> They are struggles which question the status of the individual: on the one hand, they assert the right to be different and they underline everything which makes individuals truly individual. On the other hand, they attack everything which separates the individual, breaks his links with others, splits up community life, forces the individual back on himself and ties him to his own identity in a constraining way. These struggles are not exactly for or against the "individual", but rather they are struggles against the "government of individualization". (Foucault, 1982, pp. 211–212)

This is well reflected in the following words of Judith Butler, a philosopher, gender theorist, and literary scholar, whose work gained international acclaim only a few years after Foucault's essay: "I am in favor of self-determination as long [as] we understand that no 'self', including no national subject, exists apart from an international socius" (Butler, 2004, p. 99).

Much of Butler's work focuses on questions of collective and individual identities, and the relations of both to their respective environment. Alterity and Otherness play a major role in her analysis. While Gilman offers a historical perspective, tracing the conditions in which certain kinds of subjectivities and rationalities developed, Butler's thought is anchored in the present. She does not attempt to decipher history, but to establish a theoretical framework from which an ethical position toward contemporary events can be best sustained. Her position is critical, emphasising the revolutionary potential of the theories she analyses and formulates. She quotes Foucault's call, in the article just mentioned, to "promote new forms of subjectivity through the refusal of this kind of individuality which has been imposed on us for several centuries" (Butler, 1997, p. 101, quoting Foucault, 1982, p. 216). By maintaining the paradoxical relations to individuality Foucault describes, however, Butler refrains from "following the call" and forming a perception of subjectivity which would offer a truly independent alternative. Furthermore, the difficulties of Butler's philosophy, perhaps less noticeable in her earlier writings on gender, become clear in her later work as she turns to issues of nationality and political ethics.

To begin, Butler perceives all contact between subjectivities as disharmonious: ethical relations to alterity are based on the fact that the latter *interrupts* identity (Butler, 2012, p. 5, emphasis in the original). Furthermore, the "I" is always dispossessed to some extent by the social conditions of its emergence (Butler, 2005, p. 8). As the formation of individual subjectivity occurs through relations, and in the presence of others, it too constitutes an ambivalent site. The subject is subordinated from birth through passionate attachment and primary dependency. She maintains that, because of this initial attachment, subordination is central to the subject's becoming. Furthermore, a subject is not only formed in subordination, but also provides its continuing conditions of possibility. This subordination is repressed and repeated in the subject's pursuit of its own dissolution (Butler, 1997, pp. 6–9). As a result, it ultimately represents a destructive force. This also means that the subject – which, according to Butler, is the position individuals occupy and the linguistic condition of their intelligibility, existence, and agency – is an effect of subjection (ibid., pp. 10–11).

Indeed, Butler offers a grim vision of socialisation, subject formation, and the individual's relationship with their environment. She therefore seeks the ways in which this system of suppression is subverted through resistance – moments in which the subject opposes her subordination and reiterates her subjection using the very power which subjects her (ibid., pp. 11–13). She locates the moment of reversal in the transition from the power that acts on the subject to the power she enacts. Agency then may operate in relations of contingency and reversal towards the power that makes it possible (ibid., p. 15). For Butler, this does not only take place on an individual level, but among groups and nations in the international arena. A hegemonic regime may claim to be "universal". It may assimilate particular discourses, and elevate its particularism to universality, concealing its hegemonic power. In turn, it is contested by the true forces of universalization:

> The point is not to convert the inassimilable into the assimilable, but to challenge those regimes that require assimilation to their own norm. Only when those norms break apart does universalization have a chance to renew itself within a radically democratic project. (Butler, 2012, p. 23)

Butler takes four things from her reading of Foucault: his radical construction of subjectivity, which is formed in and against historical hegemony; a refusal of individuality, which is identified with the disciplinary apparatus; a subject shaped by the prohibitions imposed upon her; and the transformation of harmful interpellation into a site of radical reoccupation and resignification (ibid., pp. 100–103). She finds the performative gesture that facilitates a radical constitutive act in the writings of Hannah Arendt, who makes a strong case for performative speech (Butler and Spivak, 2007, p. 27): when she *redeclares* the right of man, this declaration is an important rhetorical movement, both a call to freedom and the exercise of that freedom (ibid., pp. 47–48, emphasis in the original). According to Butler, there can be no radical politics of change without performative contradiction. Such contradictions must be relied upon, exposed, and worked on in order to move toward something new. This involves a deformation of the dominant language and a reworking of power. Alteration takes place in language and its public space (ibid., pp. 66–67).

Butler discusses the example of the widespread demonstrations that took place in California in 2006, most dramatically in Los Angeles, when illegal residents took to the street (ibid., p. 58). Singing the American anthem in Spanish, they defied the claim of the president, George W. Bush, that the anthem could only be sung in English (ibid., pp. 58–59). By performing in the street, they enacted the freedom of assembly in defiance of its prohibition by law. In their performative politics they defied the law which recognition they demanded (ibid., pp. 63–64). They spoke freely in order to demand the right to speak freely, and exercised the right that precedes legal right – the right to have rights, which is one of the social conditions of equality (ibid., pp. 64–65).

Butler is particularly concerned with constitutive acts, performances which generate and assert the positions of individuals and groups. But she only endorses these constitutive acts as long as they resist and defy hegemonic structure. In her disharmonic account of the subject formation and encounters with alterity, she leaves out any positive potential of socialisation, and so the possibility that the individual, the becoming subject, may be empowered rather than oppressed by the forces imprinted upon her. There is never a claim that the model of being she describes is exclusive, and yet she never considers other forms of existence besides that of oppressed individual and groups. To use her own principal term, all other forms of existence are foreclosed and, in effect, delegitimised. For instance, the act of singing the American national anthem in Spanish is commendable only because it is done in defiance – because there is a hegemonic American president who will oppose such an action and, in the act of opposition, acknowledge it (ibid., p. 69). Not coincidentally, she emphasises how much she enjoys the sound of protestors singing by saying that she would not want to hear Arendt or Nietzsche sing (ibid., p. 66). In her preference for the deprived, she contrasts them with figures of (philosophical) authority. Butler asks: "[I]s it still an anthem to the nation and can it actually help undo nationalism?" (ibid., p. 69), and reminds the reader that the ritual constitutive act may just as well reaffirm a non-suppressed social entity as strive against it. The anthem may be sung by members of an existing state or nation, and she categorically rejects this act of affirmation. Butler will only acknowledge a collective ethos that has become anachronistic and imposes itself on the present through violence (Butler, 2005, p. 5). She will not consider those occasions in which the collective ethos may serve as a source of vitality. Resistance, then, is meant to be permanent, and reconciliation is not an option. Since normalisation involves preserving and perpetuating the destruction of subject formation (Butler, 1997, p. 92), renormalising "abnormalities" like homosexuality will only reduce them to their "abnormal" category (ibid., pp. 93–94).

This unyielding position is followed accordingly in Butler's reference to measurable results and outcomes. Because resistance, as a rudimentary position, is at the heart of the constitutive act, the goal of that act should at best be unattainable. When discussing the protests in California, she raises the question of its possible futility, but does not resolve it; indeed, she dismisses the question of the potential outcome in favour of the protest's symbolic value (Butler and Spivak, 2007, p. 64). Butler expresses her disinterest in practical outcomes more directly when she acknowledges that her favoured solution for the Israeli-Palestinian conflict – the establishment of a bi-national unified state – is commonly seen as impractical even by its supporters. Its inapplicability allows her to elevate the concept to an inaccessible ideal (Butler, 2012, p. 28), preserving and protecting her initial disposition towards resistance.

The reasons for the centrality of resistance in Butler's philosophy, and the logic which shapes the line she draws between the constitutive acts of resistance she welcomes and the constitutive acts of sovereignty she condemns, become clear when she discusses Arendt. She expresses ambivalence and revulsion towards Arendt's thought, even while adopting some of her ideas, as demonstrated above (Butler and Spivak, 2007, p. 14 and pp. 25–26).

Butler points out on more than one instance that Arendt, in her emancipated attitude toward individual action, fails to account for the involuntary conditions that facilitate it. These include economics (Butler and Spivak, 2007, p. 26), the social condition under which the constitution of personhood and the exercise of judgment become possible (Butler, 2012, p. 170), and the unfreedom which sets conditions on cohabitation and freedom, and on which politics is founded (ibid., p. 176). Butler not only emphasises the environmental consequences of existence, outside the control of the individual who comes to be, but also draws a distinction between "haves" and "have nots", and establishes the different perspectives from which they are to be judged. She also criticises Arendt for separating the public and private spheres (Butler, 2012, p. 74). In *The Human Condition,* Arendt emphasises the need to draw a line between the public, in which politics takes place, and the private (Arendt, 1998 (1958), pp. 60–61, 63–64, and my discussion in section 7.1). Butler is critical of this segregation of the private and the political (Butler and Spivak, 2007, pp. 14–15), and accuses Arendt of depoliticising life (ibid., p. 38). Although Arendt states that an exclusively private life is deprived (Arendt, 1998, p. 58), she claims that Arendt ignores the disenfranchised trapped within the private sphere (Butler and Spivak, 2007 p. 19). She takes Arendt's conception of the public sphere, partitioned from the private one, as evidence of an anti-democratic ethos (ibid., p. 22).

It is no coincidence that Butler refuses to accept the notion of a private sphere, separate and in need of sheltering from the public sphere. In her view, communality exceeds individuality. She adopts Arendt's concept of freedom as a voluntary exercise that takes place in concert, rather than solitude (Butler and Spivak, 2007, p. 26). She emphasises the need for joint action in Arendt's concept of revolution, where the transformation of "I" into "we" is a precondition (ibid., p. 56), and quotes her: "[...] man can act in and change and build a common world, together with his equals and only with his equals" (Arendt, 1951, p. 297, quoted in Butler and Spivak, 2007, p. 56). It follows from this, Butler claims, that individual action must seek first and foremost to establish equality so that action can become plural action (ibid., p. 57). While she endorses actions to bring about equality, she does not endorse Arendt's vision of the democratic arena which would follow such equality, as a competitive field in which participants distinguish themselves through individual action (Arendt, 1998, p. 41).

Butler lingers on an occasion in which, she believes, Arendt's performative gesture and constitutive act rhetorically place her in the position of the sovereign: when she formulates her own death sentence for Adolf Eichmann (Butler, 2012, p. 160).[1] In condemning Eichmann to death, Arendt takes the type of action which Butler would otherwise label a radical constitutive act:

> She not only makes the case for the priority of moral philosophy to legal institutions, but invests moral philosophy with fictive, performative, spontaneous, and aspirational character [... She] obeys no law [but bases her judgment] on an independent judgment of what law should be. (ibid., p. 169)

Why does Butler see Arendt's action here as a sovereign one, rather than a radically constitutive act of resistance, beyond her essential objection to the death sentence? We must first clarify Butler's conception of sovereignty. Discussing sovereignty in another context, she calls it as an anachronistic force. It once provided legitimacy for the rule of law, offering a guarantor for representational claims of state power, and was supposedly replaced by governmentality,[2] which regulates the population by policies and law. The re-emergence of sovereignty replaces governmentality, suspends and limits jurisdiction, and poses a threat to the democratic rule of law (Butler, 2004, pp. 51–56).

Like the act of resistance described above, sovereignty is made tangible when it diverts from the dominant laws and norms. It becomes material by undermining them. If both sovereignty and radical resistance operate in the same fashion, there is little difference between them, except that sovereignty, unlike resistance, is considered primary and invested with authority. Butler's case against Arendt is that she reserves the sovereignty she denies the nation and the state for her own judgement (Butler, 2012, pp. 153–154): "[S]he has certainly taken a distance from the notion of equality and the process of pluralization and universalization that characterize both her social ontology and the benefits of her theory for democratic politics" (ibid., p. 175).

Butler's confrontation with Arendt reveals the similarities between her own concepts of resistance and sovereignty. She shows that these labels are a matter of perspective: one either sides with laws and norms or opposes them. She also

---

1 The idea that Hannah Arendt takes on the position of the sovereign and "sends" a man to his death poses such a challenge to Butler that she takes pains to moderate its harsh implications. She suggests that Arendt's voice is entangled with that of the judges; that it is spilt into an agonistic struggle with itself; that Arendt is highly emotional; that she is airing out what she would have said, and utters the a penultimate (death) sentence, without really meaning it; and that, on the other hand, she adopts the voice of the plurality and fades in the background as an individual (Butler, 2012, pp. 164–168).
2 "Governmentality" (*gouvernementalité*) is a term coined by Foucault in the late 1970s to refer to the art of government. Foucault's work on the subject has inspired a burgeoning corpus of political, social, and cultural research (Inda, 2005, pp. 2–11).

emphasises her fundamental objection to individuality and the isolated private sphere. The deprived may undertake constitutive acts in order to achieve equality, but equals may not do so to achieve distinction. Although constitutive acts are central in her philosophy, they can only take place under the guise of resistance – otherwise, they ultimately clash with her conception of pluralisation, universalisation, and democratic politics. An entity that is not perceived as oppressed and resisting has, according to Butler, no legitimacy to perform self-constitutive acts, as those acts – within and in the name of this entity – run the risk of suppressing others. In this respect, like Gilman, she associates positive action and constitutive acts with oppression. Because Arendt envisions a public realm constituted by unoppressed equals in a space separated from the private, Butler deems it inherently oppressive, unacceptable to a radical democratic political vision (Butler and Spivak, 2007, p. 22).

Butler provides a clearer example with regards to public ritual. In her discussion of the oppression and repression of homosexuality, she argues that grief is an important constitutive example. When grief is foreclosed, the inability to relate to the lost homosexual object descends into melancholia (Butler, 1997, pp. 132–143). She also recognises the communal function of grief in the Jewish tradition: "[P]ractices of mourning (sitting Shiva and saying Kaddish) within the Jewish tradition insist on the importance of the communal and public acknowledgement of losses as a way of continuing to affirm life" (Butler, 2012, p. 21).

Nonetheless, Israeli communal grief over casualties of conflict is unacceptable. Such cases are an act of oppression and repression against the Palestinians:

> If Jews only mourn the loss of the Jews in the conflicts of the Middle East, then they affirm that only those who belong to one's own religion or nation are worthy of grief. This way of differentiating between valuable and nonvaluable populations emerges not simply in the aftermath of violent conflicts, but provides the epistemological condition of the conflict itself. (ibid.)

Butler's critique is aimed specifically against the political instrumentalisation of public grief, but she goes beyond such condemnation, and categorically rejects the very practice of communal grief among Israelis, denying them this constitutive act.[3] She not only denies the ritual self-constitution of the non-oppressed-and-therefore-oppressive entity, but also ontological self-definition. She refers to Emmanuel Levinas' argument that the essence of Israel lies in its

---

3 In comparing traditional Jewish and Israeli mourning rituals, Butler leaves out two factors. One is that the Jewish ceremonies she mentions are only practiced within Jewish communities to commemorate Jews. One does not say Kaddish and sit shiva for a non-Jew. On the other hand, communal grief over casualties in Israel includes (military and civilian) non-Jews.

predisposition to involuntary sacrifice and its exposure to persecution. From those, Levinas argued for Judaism's sustained concern for universal responsibility towards the Other. As Levinas uses it, "Israel" could mean the People, the Community, or the Jewish State. Butler takes it to mean the latter, and formulates her objections on that basis. In equating the fate of Israel and that of the Jews, Levinas dismisses Diasporic and non-Zionist traditions. In acknowledging Israel's suffering, Levinas ignores its violence. She abides by the logic of either-or, claiming that Jews who are defined as persecuted cannot be considered persecutors, and therefore that Levinas' definition of Israel justifies violence because it makes it possible to treat it as "self-defence". He encourages irresponsibility, not responsibility (Butler, 2005, pp. 93–96). Butler negates a constitutive definition which, according to Levinas, plays an affirmative role by connecting Israel (either the people or the state) with Jewish history and providing a basis for its moral position. She dismisses it as doubly offensive: it obliterates *other* Jewish identities, and justifies violence toward *others*.

For Butler, evidently, Israel is oppressive to its core, and any constitutive act on its part is ultimately an act of oppression and aggression, and cannot be legitimate. The twofold offence just mentioned is central to her account. She does not just repeat the claim that Israel existence is infused with the subjugation, expulsion, and dispossession of the Palestinians (ibid., p. 1), but also argues that Zionism "colonializes" Jewish identity and exercises hegemonic control over it (ibid., pp. 3–4). The latter claim cannot be substantiated by the Zionist tradition, since no strand of Zionist thought ever claimed possession of Judaism or Jewishness in its totality. Its roots can only be traced to Butler's own position. To make her argument for the dissolution of the Jewish State (ibid., pp. 32–35), she must, like the subjectivities she describes, relate to it within the binary framework of oppressor and oppressed. In her view, Israel not only constitutes a hegemonic force, but also threatens to occupy her own identity.

My intention here is not to discuss Israel's right or lack of right to exist. Nor do I claim that Butler's political agenda for the region is necessarily shared by the film theorists I discuss. Rather, using Butler's theory, I want to demonstrate the philosophical stance which dominates within Israeli film studies. This standpoint fails to reconcile the public and private sphere. It places the constitutive act at its centre, both valuing and condemning it. Because of this double bind, the constitutive act necessarily takes the form of a struggle. Rather than being perceived and accepted as an independent act, it is necessarily located within a framework of hegemonic relations of oppression and resistance. It may amount to a negative act of sovereignty, or to a positive act of resistance. Because film figures are generally identified as constitutive elements, they may only embody the hegemonic sovereign or, far more often, the resistant Other.

The suppressive dimension is generated in every single character, which must be seen as a pair – for each hegemonic sovereign contains an oppressed Other, and more importantly, every Other contains a sovereign it must resist.

In analysing the theories of Gilman and Butler, we recognise that, while each uses very different sources and parameters, their perspectives are determined by a common standpoint. Both see various types of constitutive act as suspect, leading them to discuss these acts in a moral context. In that process both generate a duality, as the constitution and growth of one entity is counterbalanced by the subjugation and oppression of another. The constitutive act always presents a danger. Any alternative to this shared paradigm requires a more lenient perspective. If we acknowledge that, in every constitution of individual or collective identity, there is an act of affirmation as well as one of suppression, the question of what is affirmed in the establishment of this identity becomes just as important as the question of what is suppressed. By moving away from the dual model of suppression, we can explore Israeli identities which are not just suppressive or subversive. We can regard the affirmative aspects of identity as something other than acts of aggression.

Another liberty we gain by moving away from the dual, duelling structure of oppression is that it enables more flexibility in our discussion of the various identities embodied in cinematic figures. They must no longer be seen in a dual perspective, to be matched with concrete or abstract partners for the enactment of oppression. It also lets us identify cases in which figures that supposedly represent opposites (proletarian vs. bourgeois, Oriental vs. European, male vs. female) in fact share common premises in their identity. Figures of different social significance may share a communal narrative – and not just as opposite sides of a conflict or hierarchy. I will describe, then, some of the common denominators inherited and shared over generations by different parts of Israeli society, and these will serve as the foundations of my discussion of film.

7 The Film Viewed

So far, I have explained my decision to focus on sex scenes in Israeli film as a way of understanding the cultural perception of communal and individual identity, and have critically examined the prevailing discourse on Israeli film. In the final sections of part I, I pursue both of these tasks by presenting the central motifs I use in analysing sex scenes, placing the emphasis on the individual's relations with their environment, and offering an alternative to the existing terms in which Israeli film is predominantly analysed. To do so, I turn to the more practical aspect of Foucault's search for "far less 'immediate' relations than expression, but far more direct relations than those of the causality communicated through the consciousness of the speaking subjects" (Foucault, 1972, p. 163, quoted in chapter 5). The practical aspect resides in the question of how the "clandestine" historical relations Foucault refers to come to be "revealed", and where exactly they materialise. To answer this question with regards to film, I use the concept of *film utopia* as described by Kappelhoff, who associates it with theorists like Alexander Kluge and Jacques Rancière.[1]

Film utopia is the concretisation of conditions and circumstances into sensual experience. Kluge promotes it as a concept of politics in which the individual's scope of experience is central (Kappelhoff, 2008, p. 11). Rancière views film as an art which combines feeling, perceiving, and thinking. In his film utopia, the image utopia makes the world comprehensible for the viewer while simultaneously allowing a physical-sensory experience of being-in-the-world. It delivers the forces and construction of the social world as personal sensory evidence. Through it, the possibility of perceiving reality and community is continuously reshaped and re-thought (ibid., pp. 14–15).

My argument is that the terms by which members of the Israeli community perceive themselves and their environment are captured in the sense of being-in-the-world imparted by the films they produce. The central arena of this work, the sex scene, is delivered within a sensory system that correlates with a cultural context. This context, this shared gesture, is omnipresent inasmuch as it is familiar and taken for granted. It is like an axiom which can support different, even contradictory implications, but which primarily bears a very basic sense of common reality. In this shared, sensual space, the demarcation of subjective sensual experience also describes the contours of individual identity within the community.

---

[1] In adopting this term here, I do not wish to associate it with utopian aspects of the Zionist project.

The sex scene is an arena in which the individual and their relation to the environment is characterised and explored, something that can only be generated and made palpable within the viewer's experience of the audio-visual space constructed by film. It takes place on the surface of the film, not in its hidden crevices, and in the course of it existing cultural pattern materialise and are re-enacted and re-negotiated on the corporeal level. Their repetition serves as the basis for historical continuity.

The common denominators I discuss are part of the viewer's sensual experience, and reflect patterns in the relations of the individual and their environment, they bear a specific sense of subjectivity which re-emerges when they appear. These elements exist on the sensory level in two forms: in the world and in being – in other words, in a particular sense of space, which I discuss further in section 7.1, and in the particular presence of type figures, which I discuss in section 7.2.

In my discussion of the first two elements – disrupted space and the comic type figure – I will describe more extensively the moral and philosophical matrix that affects the sense of being-in-the-world in all four configurations. Having provided this background, my discussion of the last two elements – the type figures of the victim and the child – focuses on their cultural presence and subtexts. My choice of the four elements is based on a survey of hundreds of Israeli films produced from the very early days of Israeli cinema, in the 1930s, up to the present, by which I established that they recurred frequently and continuously. My contention is that all four elements are part of a continuous history, which means that they were present on the Israeli screen before sex scenes were introduced. A comprehensive review of their use before 1960 goes beyond the limits of this study. Nonetheless, I pay tribute to earlier history by exploring the presence of these elements in Israel's first full length feature film, ODED THE WANDERER (1932, D: Chaim Halachmi). This pioneering silent film tells the story of Oded, a boy from a Jewish settlement in Palestine. On a school trip to the desert in the company of a foreign tourist, Oded wanders away from the group in search of peace and quiet, and loses his way. He is rescued, not by the search team organised by the settlement's adults, but by his classmates, Micha and Yigal. During the search, the tourist is captured and accused of theft by a Bedouin tribe. After he escapes, they return to the settlement together, to the joy of its inhabitants.

The presence of all four elements in ODED THE WANDERER is the earliest cinematic testimony to their immanence in Israeli culture. Each element is captured on film before and outside the sex scene. In each section, then, I include an analysis of how the element in question occurs in this first full-length Israeli feature film. Just as the discussion of our four elements as they occur in the film enriches my account of them, my analysis will reveal the complexity of the poetic gesture in ODED THE WANDERER. I close my discussion by reviewing the elements of the film that conform to the widespread thesis I challenge in chapter 5. I explore the film's utopian potential by analysing the depiction of the Hebrew protagonists as dominant, male, and active. In doing so, I provide a further perspective on the relations between the prevailing academic view of Israeli film and my own.

7.1 No Room of Their Own: The Disruption of Space

> [...] and my life that collapsed without reaching you, was surrendered to the streets and the drums.[2] (Nathan Alterman, "I Shall Come to Your Threshold")

The fabrication of space within film is related to the way in which space is organised and places are marked in human culture. As the anthropologist Marc Augé has said:

> Collectivities [...] need to think simultaneously about identity and relations; and to this end, they need to symbolize the components of shared identity [...], particular identities [...] and singular identities [...] The handling of space is one of the means to this end. (Augé, 1995 (1992), p. 51)

Other than being occupied by its inhabitants, "anthropological place" as Augé describes it (ibid., p. 42) is space invested with meaning (ibid., pp. 51–52). It is ceaselessly re-constituted, and the notion that it is founded is only half fantasy, because it is substantiated, cultivated, and protected. Nonetheless, it is never sheltered from the realities of other groups or sets of meanings (ibid., pp. 46–47). The place, in Michel de Certeau's words, is an instantaneous configuration of positions, and the elements within it, however distinct and singular, are seen as interrelated (ibid., p. 54).

Ben-Shaul (discussed in chapter 4) gives one cinematic materialisation of such a configuration in Israeli film: the sense of siege, which involves representations of confined space, and strained relations between the characters (Ben-Shaul, 1989 and 1997).

Intrusiveness is constituted by the configuration of positions I focus on here. It converges at some points with the phenomena that Ben-Shaul refers to, but possesses a life and biography of its own. As a configuration, intrusiveness established itself very early on in Israeli film, and is present in all the films

---

[2] Alterman, 1972 (1938), p. 56, my translation.

discussed in parts II and III. Generally speaking, throughout the history of Israeli film, the individual is depicted as intruding and intruded upon. Not only is there a persistent movement between the private and public spheres, but the borders between the two are constantly visited, reflected upon, and disturbed. Like Ben-Shaul's sense of siege, this pattern is disharmonious by nature.

Intrusion and precarious relations between the individual and their peers are evident from the very beginning of ODED THE WANDERER. The exposition opens with a series of tranquil shots of the Oded's settlement. Entering the school, we see a notice announcing a school trip the next day, which disappears as children gather in front of the board. The children's society is first presented as a crowd, setting a vibrant contrast to the settlement's serenity. Oded and a foreign tourist – the two central characters, who will eventually lose their way in the wilderness – are initially shown interacting with the crowd. The tourist is first seen at the beginning of the film, in front of the school, arranging with the teacher to join the school trip. A growing stream of children leaves the school, increasingly resembling a force of nature. It is a very mild version of the powerful mobs in the Keystone Cops' silent films. Grabbing hold of one of the children, the tourist is swept into the yard. He is shown in close-up, from a low angle, with a smile to show that the attention from the children empowers him. After the stream of children had rushed by, carrying the tourist, Oded appears at the school entrance. He walks slowly toward the teacher, reading a book, and the teacher acknowledges him. From that moment onward, Oded becomes the film's protagonist of the film. Because he first appears in isolation, Talmon concludes that he represents a form of Otherness (Talmon, 2001, p. 82). However, when he enters a conflict, it is Oded who gangs up with his peers against a smaller boy, Micha. After the children set up camp, Oded writes in the diary his parents packed for him. Micha stands close to him and peeps behind his shoulder, violating his private space. Oded stands up and confronts him. In the ensuing fight, his companion, Yigal, bends over behind Micha, causing him to fall over when Oded shoves him. Oded, Yigal, and two other boys burst into laughter, and Micha, whose sullen expression appears in close-up, vows revenge.

A stream of children rushes to greet the tourist, who arrives late at the camp. Shortly afterwards he becomes the vehicle of Micha's revenge. Out on a field trip the group takes a break. Oded returns to his diary, and the tourist attempts to take a picture of him. As Oded turns his back, the tourist moves in front of him. Micha appears, winks, and summons a group of children with his hand. They storm the tourist, bent over his camera, and start a game of leapfrog over his back. The bouncing bodies and laughing children are shown in close-up. The camera jerks when a group runs toward it. Oded, now surrounded by children, gets up and walks offscreen, and Micha immediately takes his place. Oded finds a new spot to continue writing, but Micha quickly joins him and stands directly over him. Before Oded can get away, he and Micha are encircled by a ring of girls. Oded must now wrestle his way through the crowd. In the next shot, Oded is finally absorbed in writing undisturbed in a third location. When the teacher gathers the children to continue the trip, Oded, who is not among them, is left behind.

The events of the film are set off by the overpowering force of the crowd and violations of the private sphere. This is how it all begins. When the question of boundaries arises again toward the end of the film, it revolves around the tourist, who the locals see as an intruder. He takes a pause during the search for Oded, and a Bedouin woman sees him patting one of her goats and its kid. She accuses him of theft, and he is taken captive by her tribe. The characters' trials do not end when Oded is found. The last challenge for the tourist and his rescuers involves interacting with the Bedouins. The film's final crisis is occasioned not by uncultivated nature, but by social order. The source of the intrusive configuration is not merely the awareness of the presence of other realities, sets of meanings, and narratives in the space inhabited by the community, as the confrontation between the Bedouin tribe and the tourist might indicate. It enacts a discord between the individual and the social environment, revealing a discrepancy in the communal structure – something demonstrated by the main conflict between Oded and Micha.

Film scholars have recognised at least some of these discrepancies, manifested in films shot decades after ODED THE WANDERER. They were by and large perceived, justifiably, as indications of a struggle between collectivism (recruiting the individual for the urgent good of the community) and individualism (championing the unheeded independence of this individual). As I showed in chapter 4, several scholars have made use of this assumption, interpreting it as the symptom of a change in Israeli society as it moved away from mobilisation. Collectivism is generally seen as a product of Zionist indoctrination, and individualism as an antithetic force marking the decline of the ideological impetus. (See my references in chapter 4 to essays from the 1990s by Bursztyn, Gertz, Talmon, Loshitzky, and Ne'eman.) Kimchi is exceptional in his reference to an earlier source for intrusiveness, which he identifies as a convention in Yiddish *belles lettres* of the mid-nineteenth century and early twentieth century (Kimchi, 2012, pp. 95–99, 174–183). He does not draw the connection, however, to questions of individualism vs. collectivism.

As I demonstrated through ODED THE WANDERER, the incongruities in question predate the era in which Israeli society underwent demobilisation. The struggle they articulate between "collectivism" and "individualism" can be traced back to the early days of Zionism – the same era that was the golden age of Yiddish literature Kimchi refers to. Intrusiveness sprang up from deep roots in Israeli identity, from a paradox that has not yet been resolved, and emerges persistently in Israeli film.

We find a major indication of the way in which relations between individual and environment are perceived in attempts to engineer them. The term "New Jew" was coined during one such attempt. As I have shown in chapter 4, film scholars who apply the paradigm of oppositions use this term to refer to the protagonist of the "Zionist ethos", who embodies the utopian subjectivity in the early phases of Israeli film. As the historian Anita Shapira has shown, the term "New Jew" first appeared in Zionist discourse of the late nineteenth century, and was in fact utopic. Inspired by the revolutionary discourse of the "New Man" in Europe, the Zionist movement saw one of its goals as the education and formation of a new type of human being, the subject of a new society in the Land of Israel (Shapira, 1997, p. 155).

The "New Jew" represented a multiplicity of ideas and aspirations, some of which were contradictory – partly a result of disparities in the Zionist movement, and partly a result of ambiguity on the part of those who theorised it. Shapira overcomes the pandemonium within this discourse by identifying four prototypes for the "New Jew":

1. A secular, educated being whose knowledge is rooted in the Jewish tradition, and who is immersed in liberal Jewish culture – a culture shielded from the non-Jewish world, and not modified to suit it. Shapira associates this type with the tradition of the Jewish Enlightenment movement, and particularly with Ahad Ha'am, a Hebrew essayist and the founder of cultural Zionism (ibid., p. 159).
2. An antithesis to everything that was recognised and despised as Jewish, whether in manners, occupation, or physical appearance. Shapira associates this prototype with German and Russian culture, an acute awareness of how non-Jews perceived Jews, and with the influence of Theodor Herzl, the founder of the Zionist Organization and of political Zionism (ibid., pp. 160–161).
3. A mythical, mystical "New Jew" who can evade the burden of culture, tradition, and reason and return to nature, beauty, and primitive instincts. This vitalist Nietzschean prototype, a "Jew made of flesh and blood", frees himself from the grip of history to shape his own fate (ibid., pp. 162–164).
4. A socialist prototype who overcomes the innate human tendency towards egotism and rivalry, exercising altruism and sacrificing personal advantage for the good of the community (ibid., p. 167).

Film scholars employed the second, third and fourth prototypes in their portrayal of the "New Jew". However, unlike Shapira, they do not address the inherent inconsistencies between them. Shapira notes that the prototypes of the "New Jew" share several attributes, but her emphasis is on the differences and contradictions, which she organised thematically (ibid., p. 171). Since all of the prototypes are reflected in formal and non-formal Israeli education systems, young people in Israel absorbed a mixed set of contradictory values: universalism and national particularism, love of humanity and antagonism toward gentiles; tolerance and militant fanaticism; devotion to the Jewish nation and disdain towards Diaspora Jews; yearning for peace and reconciliation and callous aspirations towards power (ibid., p. 173). Shapira refers to the contradictory mixture of "Nietzscheanism" and socialism. While the former glorifies creative egotism of the individual and releases him from social and moral constraints, the latter advocates the subjugation of individual interests to those of the community and the superiority of the collective over the individual. It presupposes that individuals can only fulfil themselves within community, and that the collective must defend the weak. In short, Nietzschean vitalism rebels against the Judeo-Christian morality in which socialism is rooted (ibid., pp. 169–170).[3] For Shapira, these incongruities were resolved during the process of simplification and vulgarisation that all ideological schemes undergo when translated into practice – which, in this case, sharpened the similarities between the ceremonial performances of the two perceptions (ibid., p. 170). Nevertheless, two prototypes representing mutually exclusive frameworks for structuring communities and characterising individuals were joined together under a single heading. The contradiction was never resolved and, rather than causing a rupture, was sustained.

This paradox endured long after the revolutionary forces had lost their predominance and the term "New Jew" had become irrelevant. The following generations were alienated from the term, but did not resolve the paradox. The external self-image was shed and the old terminology was replaced by a new one, but the contradictory notions of communal and individual identities, and the unease that the discrepancy between them produced, were upheld. The configuration of intrusiveness is not an expression of a conceptual breach and

---

[3] This contradiction between the influence of Nietzschean individualism among early Zionists thinkers and a widespread disposition toward collectivism, which ultimately determined the institutional structure of Israeli settlements, is also addressed by the historian Jacob Golomb. According to him, this apparent paradox poses a challenge to all scholars of Nietzsche's impact on Zionism (Golomb, 1999, pp. 97–98).

a generational gap, but a manifestation of an heirloom passed down across generations.

Having accounted for the source, I explore another aspect of the supposed clash between individual and community using the perspective offered by Arendt in *The Human Condition*. While recognising the impact of the Judeo-Christian morality Shapira discusses, Arendt examines the concepts of collectivism and individualism, rather than subscribing to them. Instead of writing on the individual and the collective, Arendt draws attention to the differentiation between the public and private realm. Her use of spatial concepts can be usefully applied to the cinematic concretisation of social structure in lived experience.

In Arendt's view, the distinction between the private and public realms is fundamental, and indicates the proper location of human activities, inasmuch as some need to be concealed and others to be publicly displayed (Arendt, 1998, p. 73). Both realms are essential to human existence:

> Since our feeling for reality depends utterly upon appearance and therefore upon the existence of a public realm into which things can appear out of the darkness of sheltered existence, even the twilight which illuminates our private and intimate lives is ultimately derived from the much harsher light of the public realm. Yet there are a great many things which cannot withstand the implacable, bright light of the constant presence of others on the public scene. (ibid., p. 51)

No human life is completely fulfilled in the absence of either realm. A life led exclusively in the private realm is impoverished (ibid., p. 58), and one spent in the public realm without the possibility of retreat lacks quality (ibid., p. 71). Just as vital as the existence of the two realms is the boundary between them. Arendt argues that there are signs of this even in early human history:

> The law originally was identified with this boundary line, which in ancient times was still actually a space, a kind of no man's land between the private and the public, sheltering and protecting both realms while, at the same time, separating them from each other [...] The law of the city state was neither the content of political action [...] nor was it a catalogue of prohibitions [...] It was quite literally a wall. (ibid., pp. 63–64)

Accordingly, it is in the nature of the relationship between the public and the private sphere that the disappearance of the public realm would be accompanied by the threatened liquidation of the private one (ibid., pp. 60–61).

Arendt's history of Western civilisation traces the shifts in the location of the borderline between public and private (ibid., pp. 28–78). Rather than portray the modern age as progressive, she argues that it is characterised by the obscuring of the difference between the two realms, and the blurring of the gulf between them (ibid., pp. 28–29, 33, 38–41). Arendt consequently associates modernity with the potential danger of losing both the public and the private realms (ibid., pp. 57–58, 70).

Among the phenomena and dangers she describes, two correlate directly with the experience of intrusion. One phenomenon is that the performative act can no longer legitimately take place in the public sphere, as it should. As I mentioned in section 6.2, Butler commends Arendt's use of the performative act as both a call to freedom and an exercise of that freedom (Butler and Spivak, 2007, pp. 47–48). For Arendt, the performative act taking place in the presence of peers is a competitive endeavour, aimed at distinguishing oneself and proving one's own excellence through unique deeds and achievements. In antiquity, the public realm was reserved for individuality through the performance that took place in it (Arendt, 1998, p. 41). In modern times, however, the situation has changed: "While we have become excellent in the laboring we perform in public, our capacity for action and speech has lost much of its former quality since the rise of the social realm banished these into the sphere of the intimate and the private" (ibid., p. 49). The performative act depends upon its place in the public sphere, but cannot take place there.

Another of Arendt's concerns is the revelation of the private realm: "[T]he four walls of one's property offer the only reliable hiding place from the common public world, not only from everything that goes on in it but also from its very publicity, from being seen and being heard" (ibid., p. 71). Consequently, "[t]he greatest threat [...] is not the abolition of private ownership of wealth but the abolition of private property in the sense of tangible, worldly place of one's own" (ibid., p. 70). Arendt equates this need for a privacy with elementary bodily needs (ibid., pp. 70–71). It is indispensable, and any threat to it is correspondingly serious.

Delegitimised public performance and threatened privacy are two faces of intrusiveness. An act with no legitimacy in the presence of others is perceived as intrusive. So too is the penetration, destabilisation, and destruction of private space. From Arendt's perspective, while an injury of private space presents a clear case of harmful dispossession, the fact that a public act loses legitimacy does not mean that it lacks reason and merit.

Whether one sides with the intruder or the one intruded upon, in both cases intrusiveness marks the disruption of balance between the public and the private realms. In a community like Israel which has never settled the boundaries between the two realms, the cinematic enactment of intrusiveness becomes an accessible expression of the unease and apprehension which reality entails. This means that the configuration of intrusiveness – dominant in my analysis in part II and part III – is, at its very core, a concretisation of a social condition.

7.2 Figure This

Having presented the spatial component, I now turn to the other three elements that will be central to my analysis: the comic figure, the victim, and the child, all of which are prototypes of cinematic figures.[4] I call them type figures, following a concept presented by the philosopher Stanley Cavell.

For Cavell, the cinematic figure embodies aspects specific to the medium, and set film apart from other art forms. The constellation he describes reconciles two fundamentally disparate qualities: distinctiveness and seriality. On the one hand, the viewer experiences a kind of intimacy with a cinematic figure which occurs in no other medium:

> It is an incontestable fact that in a motion picture no live human being is up there. But a human *something* is, and something unlike anything else we know. We can stick to our plain description of that human something as "in our presence while we are not in his". (Cavell, 1979, pp. 26–27, emphasis in the original)

The performer is essentially not an actor but the subject of somebody else's study of him. He is the figure in the flesh (ibid., p. 28). Taking another perspective on this intimacy, Kappelhoff locates the figure's origin in the viewer. The figure is not created in front of the camera, or in the plot, but in the darkness of the movie theatre, as a specific way of hearing and seeing when the simulated perceptive world of the figure fuses with the viewer's aesthetic perception (Kappelhoff, 2004, pp. 45–46).

On the other hand, paraphrasing Erwin Panofsky, Cavell says that cinematic figures appear within a "fixed iconography", and their conduct is "predetermined accordingly" (Cavell, 1979, pp. 32–33). Conventions may alter, but the principle remains. Iconographies which are specifically associated with figure types will inevitably change with the times. Nonetheless, as a general rule, iconographies remain specific and associated with particular types (ibid., p. 33). This does not mean that movies create types instead of individuals: "What it means is that this is the movies' way of creating individuals: they create *individualities*. For what makes someone a type is not his similarity with other members of that type but his striking separateness from other people" (ibid., emphasis in the original). That such types cannot project but are projected permits their

---

4 In my terminology, I make a distinction between three related terms: I refer to *type figures* as the general figure-patterns I describe in this section; *character* refers to specific fictional persons that appear in the film; finally, *figure* also refers to the visual materialisation of the *character* and the viewer's experience of them in the cinematic space.

sublime comprehensibility. That photos do not ontologically favour humans over other objects means that the object world in the film provides more than just props for the type figure. It has an equal share in this sublime comprehensibility (ibid., pp. 36–37).

The type figures I discuss are cinematic materialisations of patterns that exist in cinema, as well as in other mediums of Israeli and Jewish culture. I show that their existence can be understood as part of an ethical discourse and communal self-image within Israeli society. As I demonstrate in part II and part III, they form a cinematic presence that is unique in each of its incarnations, and nevertheless recognisable as they recur.

Cavell claims that movie cycles are genres, and that genre is the cinematic medium (ibid., p. 36). In his discussion of types, however, he avoids direct use of the word "genre", giving a multitude of examples instead. This might be because not all "fixed iconographies" are genre-bound; even if they are, they could still function outside the limits of any specific genre, as long as their presence as types were distinguishable by the viewer. For that reason, I do not associate the type figures I discuss within specific genres, though each of them could hypothetically be assigned to one (comedy, melodrama, coming-of-age drama). In part II and part III, I show how pervasively the type figures I discuss exceed the confines of any particular genre.

The Earnestness of Being Important: The Comic Figure

Comic figures are dominant throughout the history of Israeli film, and their function resides in the topography I described in my discussion of intrusion: in the relations between individual and society, and the construction of "I and thou". My understanding of these type figures is based on Freud's theory of jokes and the academic research into Jewish humour that it inspired. I examine Freud's theoretical model within a larger context, in view of other major theorists in the field, focusing on the social role each theorist attributes to jokes and humour.

In *Leviathan,* published in 1651, Thomas Hobbes condemned laughter as a destructive force in human relations:

> *Sudden Glory*, is the passion which maketh those *Grimaces* called LAUGHTER; and is caused either by some sudden act of their own, that pleaseth them; or by apprehension of some deformed thing in another, by comparison whereof they suddenly applaud themselves. (Hobbes, 1914 (1651), p. 27, emphasis in the original)

The moral predicament described by this situation, in his view, places comic figures in an inferior position, and one is compelled to look down on them. Laughter serves as self-indulgence for the weak. It counteracts any form of didactic conduct which aims to improve oneself and others: "For great minds, one of the proper works is, to help and free others from scorn; and compare themselves only with the most able" (ibid.). From Hobbes' perspective, laughter involves a sense of superiority which inhibits empathy and any acknowledgement of one's own inferiority – an acknowledgement, he thinks, that encourages ambitions for growth. It is an antisocial act, a challenge to society's morality.

Writing in defence of laughter a century later, Francis Hutcheson, a member of the Scottish Enlightenment, did not dispute society's role in dictating individual conduct. But he did challenge the disruptive function Hobbes attributes to laughter (Hutcheson, 1750, pp. 13–15). Hutcheson describes laughter predominantly as a balancing force. It alleviates unpleasant emotions (ibid., pp. 26–27, 32–33), encourages social bonding (ibid., pp. 27, 32), and can be used as a corrective (ibid., pp. 31, 35–38). It may occur in good company and bad (ibid., p. 35). In that respect, ridicule may be used with or without empathy, depending on its context and intensity (ibid., pp. 31, 34–35).

The twentieth-century spiritualist philosopher Henri Bergson adopted Hutcheson's view that laughter serves the social order. The expression of individual or collective imperfection sets in motion a corrective reaction: "This corrective is laughter, a social gesture that singles out and represses a special kind of absentmindedness in men and in events" (Bergson, 1980 (1900), p. 117). Bergson allows a wider range of possibilities for the object of laughter, and allows for some ambiguity:

> [W]e find it very difficult in the majority of [...] cases, to say whom we are laughing at [...] A word is said to be comic when it makes us laugh at the person who utters it, and witty when it makes us laugh either at a third party or at ourselves. But in most cases we can hardly make up our minds whether the word is comic or witty. All that we can say is that it is laughable. (ibid., p. 128)

While Hobbes assumes that the subject of laughter is alienated from its object, and Hutcheson permits empathic relations, Bergson not only presumes identification, but also an unconscious obscuring of boundaries and differences. The object of laughter could simultaneously be the speaker, the listener, and a third party.

Hutcheson, like Hobbes, emphasises good social measures and values, which require boundaries. Comedy ends where tragedy begins: one could not laugh at a serious crime, or a calamity (Hutcheson, 1750, p. 30). Likewise, "any great being, character or sentiment" should be protected to avoid abuse (ibid., p. 35). Greatness is off limits. At the beginning of the twentieth century, the focus is no longer on social propriety, but individuality, and so Bergson connects seriousness, not with values, but with individual sovereignty:

> All that is serious in life comes from our freedom. The feelings we have matured, the passions we have brooded over, the actions we have weighed, decided upon and carried through, in short, all that comes from us and is our very own, these are the things that give life its ofttimes dramatic and general grave aspect. (Bergson, 1980, pp. 111–112)

According to him, it is the disavowal of this sovereignty that produces comedy (ibid., p. 112). "The comic is that side of a person which reveals his likeness to a thing, that aspect of human events which, through its peculiar inelasticity, conveys the impression of pure mechanism, of automatism, of movement without life" (ibid., p. 117). Because the emphasis shifts from common values to individual coherence, while Hutcheson is concerned with setting boundaries, Bergson sees their transgression as the basis for laughter. Disavowing the foundational coherence of individual identity is a cathartic moment and is central to Bergson's theory.

When the literature scholar Mikhail Bakhtin introduces his concept of the grotesque, however, he does not contrast individual coherence with social order, but aligns them, showing how both are dispelled through base humour. In his view, social order and individualism are both the unfortunate fruits of pre-socialist order. According to Bakhtin, in the framework of feudal and class politics, the medieval carnival and marketplace festivals were established as a second life for common folk, a utopian realm of community, freedom, equality, and abundance (Bakhtin, 1968, p. 9). The carnival laughter that forms a crucial part of this utopia is not individual. It is the laughter of all the people, directed at everyone (ibid., p. 11). Likewise, the bodily element

> is presented not in a private, egotistic form, severed from the other sphere of life, but as something universal, representing all the people [...]. The material body principle is contained not in the biological individual, not in the bourgeois ego, but in the people, a people who are continually growing and renewed. (ibid., p. 19)

Bakhtin replicates Bergson's undoing of the individual. While Bergson associates it with mechanisation, however, Bakhtin associates it with primordial Mother Nature (ibid., p. 21). Nevertheless, although he dislikes individuality, Bakhtin differentiates external from internal truth, indicating the autonomy of the individual from "the people":

> Laughter is essentially not an external but an interior form of truth [...]. Laughter liberates not only from external censorship but first of all from the great interior censor; it liberates from the fear that developed in man during thousands of years: fear of the sacred, of prohibition, of the past, of power. It unveils the material bodily principle in its true meaning. (ibid., p. 94)

Bakhtin is referring to material, bodily, true meaning – but what he seems to be describing is laughter as an outlet for the subconscious, a concept that stems unmistakably from Freud. Bakhtin's "Freudian slip" is paradoxical: in the theory of humour, Freud lies on the opposite pole to Bergson and Bakhtin, as a champion of individuality. For Freud, laughter, like other personal human activities, is not generated in order to repress individual autonomy, but to support it.

In *Jokes and their Relation to the Unconscious*, published in 1905, Freud focuses predominantly on the joke – a social event involving interaction and cooperation. He locates its source in a libidinal impulse that becomes positively hostile if confronted by an obstacle (Freud, 1960 (1905) p. 99). Like Hobbes and Hutchison, Freud sees curbing aggression as the main function of social order: "Since our individual childhood, and, similarly, since the childhood of human civilization, hostile impulse against our fellow men have been subjected to the same restrictions, the same progressive repression, as our sexual urges" (ibid., p. 102).

Diverging from the propriety that characterised the Enlightenment, Freud does not regard the expression of this aggression as violation, but as relief. Jokes represent rebellion against authority and liberation from its pressure (ibid., p. 105). As subversive agents, they veil both their message and the fact that the message is prohibited (ibid., p. 106). They give quiet support for forbidden wishes and desires, and offer fresh insight into morality's ruthless demands (ibid., p. 110). What Freud calls "tendentious" (purposeful) jokes are obvious examples of this rebellion against social order, as they are obscene, hostile, cynical, and sceptical (ibid., p. 115). He expands the range even further when he claims that non-tendentious jokes, too, reduce inhibitions and offer relief against the restrictions of rationality and the burden of intellectual thought (ibid., pp. 127–128).

Bakhtin's utopianism suggests that social order is exclusively oppressive. Freud, on the other hand, may regard social order and any human system as repressive by nature, but like Hobbes and Hutcheson he deems them indispensable. Jokes and humour provide an unresolvable duality. They constitute a necessary, justified individual rebellion against a system which is nonetheless also necessary and justified. In comparison with Bergson and Bakhtin, Freud offers an important twist. While the former see laughter as a challenge to individual sovereignty, Freud detects the presence of this challenge in the very conditions of laughter. For Freud, laughter is where the individual counteracts, reflecting both the threat to her sovereignty and her resistance to it.

The implication of Freud's thesis – that both the producer and audience of jokes rebel against the system – is that they are both subjected to the system, and relate to it as underdogs. This became clearer when Freud discussed the source of comic attitude further in his article "Humour", published in 1927. The comic attitude reflects a person's refusal to suffer. In adopting it, they emphasise that the real world cannot harm their ego, victoriously maintaining the pleasure principle (Freud, 1960 (1927), p. 163). Humour is the triumph of narcissism (ibid., p. 162). In contrast to other methods, however, it does not overstep the bounds of mental health (ibid., p. 163). It is orchestrated by the superego, which inherits parental agency (ibid., p. 164). Departing from its usual stern approach, the superego offers words of comfort to the intimidated ego (ibid., p. 166), making trouble seem small and trivial (ibid., p. 163). While jokes are attributed to the impulsive id, humour is attributed to the nurturing superego. And, while jokes help overcome the repressions of mandatory social decorum, humour overcomes a reality which is not justified but which cannot be changed.

More than any other major theorist, Freud describes laughter as serving the individual. And, like no other theorist, he upholds a number of paradoxical dualities. Jokes are described as an act of aggression, and at the same time an elevating protective measure; humour is a narcissist departure from reality, which nonetheless takes place within the boundaries of sanity; social structure is vital, and so is rebellion against it. Consequently, Freud is the most useful, and most popular, among theorists of Jewish humour, to whose field of study he also made a minor contribution.

In *Jokes and their Relation to the Unconscious*, Freud is positive about Jewish jokes. He attributes their power to their intimate origins, and to the identification of the subject with the object of the joke: "A particularly favourable occasion for tendentious jokes is presented when the intended rebellious criticism is directed against the subject himself, or to put it more cautiously, against someone in whom the subject has a share" (Freud, 1960, p. 111). The paradox of rebellion against the self is consistent with his other dualities. Freud associates self-criticism with quality, and this is a reason Jewish jokes form a major source for his own discussion. He praises their frequency in the Jewish community as a rare phenomenon (ibid., pp. 111–112). Jewish jokes are superior to foreigners' jokes about Jews because "they know their real faults as well as the connection between them and their good qualities, and the share which the subject has in the person found fault with create the subjective determinant [...] of the joke-work" (ibid.).

Jewish jokes reflect oppressive social order and religious dogma, the conflict between old and new value systems, and the many hopeless miseries the Jews are subjected to (ibid., pp. 112–114). The folklorist Dan Ben-Amos notes that the jokes Freud discussed are particular to his era and social milieu (Ben-Amos, 1991, p. 40). But we can extract from Freud's example a more general observation: that Jewish jokes express both internal and external conflicts.

As is often the case with phenomena at the focus of academic attention, Ben-Amos argues that the actual definition of Jewish humour – a term which first appears in the modern era – is ambiguous: "Jewish humor is only a reified collective term that does not actually exist. If it is conceived as an abstract construction, actual examples will contradict its basic tenets" (ibid., p. 36). "Jewish humour" is not synonymous with every form of humour used by Jewish communities across time (ibid., pp. 36–37).[5] The date of birth of the protagonist of Jewish humour, usually referred to as *schlemiel*, is unclear, as the literary historian Ezra Greenspan explains:

> The schlemiel, of course, did not spring up suddenly, full-blown, from the soil of nineteenth-century Eastern Europe [... He] can be seen taking gradual shape over the long centuries of Exile: in the traditional Jewish aversion from Talmudic times onward, to western notions of heroism, in the self-deprecating humor of Ibn Ezra and Heine, and in the early Hasidic tales told by and about Rabbis Nachman and Levi-Yitzchok. (Greenspan, 1983, p. 4)

The discussion of Jewish humour and comic protagonists does not focus on historical demarcation, but, predominantly, on poetic and aesthetic characterisations. Here too, descriptions vary, although self-deprecation – referred to by Freud – remains a permanent feature. (See, for instance ibid., p. 3; Juni and Katz, 1998, pp. 290–291; Nevo and Levine, 1984, p. 127.) The Yiddish literature scholar Ruth Wisse describes numerous individual types in the Yiddish repertoire, including fools, the luckless, and the inept (Wisse, 1971, pp. 13–14): "[The] schlemiel was at first only one of a vast number of almost synonymous types, each of which, nevertheless, represented a somewhat different shade of folly or loss" (ibid., p. 14).

The schlemiel is the dominant and most memorable character, and is paired with the *schlimazel*. While the schlimazel is the passive victim of bad luck, the schlemiel disseminates it (ibid.). The two appear together in a series of comic anecdotes. As well as the most famous, in which the schlemiel spills soup into the lap of the schlimazel, the literary scholar Sanford Pinsker describes one which offers a sharper distinction between their respective comic principles: "[W]hen a *schlimmazzel's* bread-and-butter accidentally falls on the floor, it always lands butter-side down; with the *schlemiel* it is much the same – except that *he* butters his bread on both sides!" (Pinsker, 1971, p. 5, emphasis in original) In a sense, lack of luck and lack of logic are two sides of the same

---

[5] As part of his argument, Ben-Amos dismisses the possible affiliation between Europe-based "Jewish humour" and the Oriental humour personified by Djuha, the fool-trickster character from Islamic Mediterranean and Near East, which was adopted by Jewish communities there and successfully introduced to Israel when they immigrated (ibid., p. 36). But it is doubtful that such a categorical segregation between European and Oriental comic type figures could exist in Israel to such an extent that no similarities or mutual influences ever surfaced.

coin. Both express a conflict between individual and environment, much like the scenarios Freud associates with Jewish jokes.

Freud's duality encouraged two approaches to the self-deprecating aspect of Jewish humour. On the one hand, there is the "negative" approach, which sees it and all other forms of humour as aggressive.[6] Psychoanalytic authors like Theodor Reik and Martin Grotjahn see it as an outlet of "self-hatred", "self-aggression", "masochism", "paranoia", and "identity instability" (Ben-Amos, 1991, p. 37). This is the approach taken by Gilman, who we discussed in section 6.1. On the other hand, the "positive" approach sees Jewish humour as a survival mechanism. As Pinsker puts it, "perhaps, Jewish humor was never really humor in the ordinary sense of the word; rather, it was a weapon in the uphill battle for survival" (Pinsker, 1971, p. 14).

According to Wisse, the oppressive narrative is adopted and rearranged on the external social front:

> In fashioning the schlemiel, the Jew admits how weak and foolish he appears to those who dominate him, and up to a point, he shares their view [...]. Yet beyond that point, he does not submit to self-hatred, and stands proudly on his record [...]. The schlemiel is the Jew as he is defined by the anti-Semite, but reinterpreted by God's appointee. (Wisse, 1971, pp. 5–6)

According to the psychologists Samuel Juni and Bernard Katz, in internal psychological terms, a similar process takes place when Jewish humour operates as an adaptive mechanism. Its deeper meta-messages about the Jews are positive. The negative message serves only as a vehicle. Rather than being masochistic, Jewish humour is used for ego mastery. It is a tool for maintaining a sense of control and superiority over oppression. It features a triumphant turnaround which converts insults into victory, and which opens the way to victory through defeat (Juni and Katz, 1998, pp. 291–292).

But Jewish humour represents a balancing act, not a complete reversal. According to Wisse, schlemiel literature avoids sentimental effect through a humour that cuts simultaneously into the character and those belittling him (Wisse, 1971, p. 24). "At its best, the finished irony holds both the contempt of the strong for the weak and the contempt of the weak for the strong, with the latter winning the upper hand" (ibid., p. 6). The potential butt of the joke is both the individual and the environment she clashes with. No one is ever "off the hook". Jewish humour epitomises Freud's principle by supporting both the governing viewpoint and those who rebel against it. Wisse explains this within a specific cultural context: "Since Jewry's attitudes toward its own frailty were

---

[6] See the folklorist Elliot Oring's discussion of this tradition (Oring, 1981, pp. 43–45).

complex and contradictory, the schlemiel was sometimes berated for his foolish weakness, and elsewhere exalted for his hard inner strength" (ibid., p. 5).

Like the overwhelming majority of scholars, Wisse connects Jewish humour and comedy with Diaspora existence. While Wisse, Pinsker, and Greenspan associate it directly with historical persecution (ibid., pp. 25–29; Pinsker, 1971, pp. 14, 19; Greenspan, 1983, p. 6), Juni and Katz see it as a result of inherent marginality, as does the philosopher Vladimir Jankélévitch (Juni and Katz, 1998, pp. 294–296; Jankélévitch and Berlowitz, 2008, pp. 148–149). For Arendt, the schlemiel is just another name for the pariah, the eternal outsider. Alienation is at the centre of her discussion, and it is irrelevant whether the figure she labels as "schlemiel" appears in comic or Jewish settings (Arendt, 2000).

As we saw in section 6.1, Ofra Nevo argues that, since Jews in Israel are no longer oppressed, they substituted Jewish humour with a "humour of the strong" (Nevo, 1984, pp. 195–196; Nevo and Levine, 1994, p. 127). Ben-Amos is more sceptical, both toward the notion that Jewish humour is a direct response to a history of suffering, social marginality, and tensions between tradition and modernity, and toward the idea that Jewish humour has vanished in Israel (Ben-Amos, 1991, pp. 38–39). I agree with Ben-Amos' objections. The categorical split between Jewish and Israeli humour has not been substantiated. Even if the harsh conditions of the Diaspora were influential in the formation of what came to be known as Jewish humour, they were not necessary for its continued existence.

ODED THE WANDERER serves as a test for the matter. We can see it as a link between the Diaspora and the new land, with immigrant filmmakers bringing their traditional comic trappings to local realities. There are two kinds of comedy employed in the film: the children's comic performance, and the comic situations that befall the tourist.

I mentioned in the section 7.1 that the children's first appearance, three minutes into the film, constitutes a milder version of a Keystone Cops-style mob. Thus, their first movement as a group generates a comic effect. This is repeated when they greet the tourist at the camp and are depicted at play a while later, where they are seen defying gravity in various forms of balancing acts. The clashes between Oded and Micha, described in section 7.1, are orchestrated in a comic manner. Along the repeated use of herds of playful children, close-ups during the fight highlight the exaggerated gestures and grimaces of individual children. Yigal and Micha maintain a comically quaint appearance through their similar physical and facial expressions, even much later, when the conflict is over and they set out to search for Oded. The comic effect is also maintained by the repeated appearance of a girl first seen bidding farewell to her father in a state of excitement. She reappears among the group of children setting off on an excursion the following day, and again when the settlers, rejoicing at Oded's return, run toward the camera at the end of the film. Her mischievous expression is a recurring motif.

On the other hand, the tourist's appearance is not comic. Rather, the comic effect comes from the situations in which he finds himself. He proclaims at the start of the film that he is punctual, but he arrives late. The donkey he rides in search of the group stands in a field of reeds, refusing to move, and two minutes later runs away from him. As I described in section 7.1, the children use his bent back for their game. On an expedition to find Oded, the tourist loses his hat to an angry hedgehog, and is later mistaken for a thief by a Bedouin tribe. The children appear comic, whereas the tourist generates a comic effect through his clashes with every possible native inhabitant. It is clear that the tourist, who is constantly out of step with his environment, lends himself to interpretation through the prism of traditional Jewish humour by personifying a schlemiel. As long as they operate as a human stream, the children's comic effect is reminiscent of Bergson. Once we move to individual close-ups, however, their quaint appearance becomes more important, and they evoke what Freud defined as the purpose of jokes and humour: rebellion against the social order and the laws of nature.

What purpose the comic effect of these characters fulfils is best clarified by considering the ethical dimension of Jewish humour, which also provides an explanation of the survival of Jewish humour beyond oppression and Diaspora. The main premise is that the protagonists of Jewish humour, whether schlemiels or otherwise, do not only lack power and logic – they are also typically innocent, and so blameless (Wisse, 1971, p. 9; Pinsker, 1971, p. 18). They do not identify with the world's injustice (Pinsker, 1971, p. 18), or the pessimism that it should cause (Wisse, 1971, p. 22). They function on entirely opposite terms to Hobbes. As small and imperfect beings, they attract the audience's admiration and identification, rather than its scorn. In Judaism, the children of Israel are accustomed to the judgemental gaze of a divine presence that deems them imperfect, as Wisse explains:

> The generation of Jews who lived as God's people, sanctifying every act of private and communal life in accordance with their understanding of His Commandments, considered all afflictions as rebukes in His ongoing efforts to forge a righteous nation. The Jews of secular modern times, who saw themselves not only through God's judgement, but through the eyes of their neighbors, found their infirmity more difficult to interpret. (ibid., p. 5)

Humour can be seen as a kind of surrogate to religion, as Pinsker suggests: "[W]hen religion began to lose its capacity, even among the devout, to impose dignity and trust on daily life, the Jew was driven back on his sense of humour"

(Pinsker, 1971, p. 18). It is central within the rules of the Judeo-Christian morality that man is not of primary significance, but is subjected to God. Like other ethical values drawn from religion, this extended further: subjugation continued to be imperative even when God's ethereal presence seemed to fade. The reality of subjugation overpowered ancient Jewish tradition. From the humble position of the wretched, the alleged Biblical emphasis on success and the activities of its strong-willed heroes seem not just taunting, but utterly inconsistent with Jewish identity (Wisse, 1971, pp. 9–10). There is an inherent moral preference for the position of the weak. Jankélévitch supports Odysseus as long as he is in beggar's clothing, and ceases to do so when he kills his wife's suitors and regains control over his household (Jankélévitch and Berlowitz, 2008, pp. 140–141).

This powerful position is an ambivalent, morally dangerous one (ibid., pp. 144–145). Humour offers a solution by never aspiring to the throne. Jewish humour ridicules the oppressor without any pretence to an alternative truth. Self-deprecation ensures that the shattered idol is not replaced by another (ibid., pp. 149–150). The schlemiel is a little man, sympathetically conceived as small by sociological rather than moral standards (Wisse, 1971, p. 23). Juni and Katz translate this into psychoanalytic terms. The superego features prominently in the religious/ethnic heritage of the Jews through the use of guilt and blame. Humour is used to defend the ego (Juni and Katz, 1998, p. 290). Whereas the principle of Greek tragedy is that guilt is atoned for by destruction, Jewish guilt offers the lesser evil – suffering as redemption (ibid., p. 291). The schlemiel is a victim who comes to grips with a total lack of power. His strength is in his will to live without mock heroics or undue soul-searching (ibid., p. 293).

In ODED THE WANDERER, we find an example of the disarming effect of the schlemiel in an altercation between the tourist and another comic figure, the Bedouin woman. Like the children, the Bedouin woman enacts performative comedy through exaggerated gestures and facial expressions. She is accused of losing a milking goat. Two minutes later, seeing the tourist tending to the goat and its kid, she announces the "theft" to the men in her tribe, and as a result the tourist is held captive. Comic interludes give the film a light atmosphere, but its political implications are evident in this clash. A conflict between Jewish settlers and a Bedouin tribe is depicted as a misunderstanding between one comic figure, prone to mishaps, and another, prone to exaggerations. The film, in effect, reduces human conflicts to palatable comic affairs.

As the literary scholar Paul Lewis observes disapprovingly, the only liberation the joke offers is psychological release from the burden of being serious (Lewis, 1987, p. 66). This complies with Aristotle's idea that comedy is a representation of inferior people, and that the laughable is a form of error and ugliness which is not painful and destructive (Aristoteles, 1987, p. 6). The true value of this lies in the fact that this unimportant protagonist is not simply a manifestation of human lack of sovereignty, as Bergson would have it, but rather, as Freud suggests, a fleeting display of disobedience. From its marginal standpoint, Jewish humour is rebellious (Juni and Katz, 1998, p. 296). Its protagonists are not only small and unimportant, but also *autonomous*. As I showed above, both Wisse and Pinsker point to the historical parallel in the nineteenth century between the rise of secularism and the rise of Jewish humour (Wisse, 1971, p. 5; Pinsker, 1971, p. 18). The comic type figure's autonomy may explain the face, mentioned by Greenspan, that it materialised earlier (Greenspan, 1983, p. 4). It produces a form of subjectivity that, on the one hand, does not defy subordination and, on the other, is not completely dominated by the system.

During Zionism's mobilised period, personal subordination to God was replaced by subordination to the cause. I argue that the perseverance of the ethical principle of subservience facilitated the adoption of practices of Jewish comedy and humour. Ben-Amos makes an empirical argument that similarities exist between Israeli humour and its Diaspora predecessor, manifested in local versions of international Jewish jokes and in stories about jesters, tricksters, and fools whose names may differ from those in the earlier Jewish repertoire, but who play similar roles (Ben-Amos, 1991, p. 38).

Comedy has always been a dominant genre in Israeli cinema, one that appeared frequently from its very beginning. Even before ODED THE WANDERER, the three known short fiction films produced in Palestine were comic sketches: YERACHMIEL THE SCHLEMIEL, a ninety-second sketch directed by Nathan Axelrod, filmed sometime between 1928 and 1930; THE ADVENTURES OF GADI BEN SUSSI (1931, D: Baruch and Yizhak Agadati), an eight-minute animated film; and ONCE UPON A TIME (1932, D: Chaim Halachmi), a seventeen-minute feature. ODED THE WANDERER is not a comedy like its predecessors, but as I have demonstrated above, it still makes extensive use of comic elements, as did many Israeli films in the following years. The Jewish stage, film and literary traditions were not simply transferred to the Israeli screen. Various forms of comedy and humour – not all of them "Jewish" – were employed by a wide range of filmmakers over the years. Over the decades, however, comedy continued to produce and reproduce manifestations of small subjectivities that maintained traditional clashes and conflicts, both internal and external.

Given its broad presence in Israeli cinema, academics have paid relatively little attention to comedy. As we saw in chapter 4, Shohat distinguishes an "Ethnic" genre of comedy in the 1970s, defining it as carnivalesque, in Bakhtin's sense of the word (Shohat, 1989, p. 131). But what she describes is more of a rebellious antagonistic aversion to authority, rather than the general disintegration of individuality into a utopia of "the People" which would be truer to Bakhtin's theory. Kimchi describes the same comedies as an adaptation of Yiddish humorous literature, where Oriental characters take over the traditional role of the European Jewish literary characters (Kimchi, 2012, pp. 30–31). The function of these characters, according to him, is "negative" – a manifestation of anti-Semitic perceptions (ibid., p. 56). The comedies themselves serve as masquerades that manifest fissures in Israeli society, with Jews of European and Oriental descent taking pleasure in seeing members of the other community impersonate them (ibid., pp. 233–235). He employs Hobbes' theory of superiority, disregarding the ritualistic viewing practices which evolved in Israel around films he discusses – practices which indicate substantial identification and admiration.

In chapter 3, we saw how Munk and Meiri view a comedy from 2003 as a manifestation of anti-Semitic imagery erupting from the Zionist subconscious (Meiri and Munk, 2008). Loshitzky refers to the comic figure in DAY AFTER DAY (1998, D: Amos Gitai), and to the cinematic persona of the actor Moshe Ivgi from films made during the 1990s (Loshitzky, 2001, pp. 150, 209n63). Her description is more "positively" oriented than that of Munk and Meiri. She describes the character as a "kvetcher" and a "nebbish" (prototypes from the Jewish comic arsenal), as an Israeli version of the Diasporic "schlemiel" and the Good Soldier Švejk. Like Meiri and Munk, however, Loshitzky also concludes that the "new antihero" is only an answer to the mythological Sabra and national heroic genre (ibid., p. 150).

As I show in chapter 10 and part III, understanding comic types in Israeli cinema as subjectivities forged in Jewish tradition, manifesting both subjugation and rebellious independence, provides a much-needed insight into the mechanisms of Israeli film.

How the Mighty are Fallen: The Victim

Israel has a highly developed culture of mourning and commemoration, one that some scholars describe as a national obsession (Weiss, 2002, p. 84). This culture is particularly potent in relation to casualties of war. As the anthropologist Meira Weiss remarked in 2002: "Today the fallen soldier is perhaps nowhere more publicly honored than in Israel" (ibid., p. 67).

From the beginning of Jewish settlement in Israel, the Hebrew fighter's death was viewed as voluntary and altruistic, and accordingly associated with the ancient tradition of Jewish martyrdom (Almog, 2000, p. 40). This developed as part of a commemoration culture for early settlers, who died not just in conflict but through the hardships of life on the frontier. As Yael Zerubavel points out, a heroic death for the fatherland was regarded as a more active form of martyrdom than was achieved by those who sanctified God's name in exile (Zerubavel, 1995, p. 19). Nevertheless, the heritage of martyrdom which continuously evolved in the Diaspora provided the customs, symbols, and myths on which the Zionist culture of commemoration was based. Among the various traditional narratives that accommodate this practice, the most widely used is the Biblical tale of the binding of Isaac, in which Abraham follows God's command to sacrifice his son Isaac, but is stopped at the last instant by an angel (Genesis 22:1–19). Almog maintains that the association of the fallen soldier with the binding of Isaac emerged in Europe in the nineteenth century, and was later adopted by the settlers in Israel. It appeared in the first memorial anthology *Yizkor*, from 1911, and was used frequently in commemorative literature and Hebrew poetry and prose (Almog, 2000, pp. 39–40; see also Weiss, 2002, pp. 71–72). It was explored extensively, both from a canonical national standpoint and a critical, satirical perspective which undermined it (Weiss, 2002, pp. 73–74; Zanger, 2003, pp. 96–102).

Almog observes that the traditional myth underwent several changes as it was translated to a Zionist context. Originally an act of total submission to divine will, it became an act of heroism, a battle to the last bullet. While the purpose of the sacrifice in the Biblical story was not disclosed to Abraham, in the Zionist context it became the realisation of an ideal. The story's centre of gravity shifted from Abraham's relationship with God to his relationship with his son (Almog, 2000, pp. 40–41).

With all this in mind, it is nonetheless crucial that the story which came to be associated with death in combat is not one of the numerous Biblical tales of armed battles, but one in which the potential victim is an unsuspecting, innocent, passive child. Moreover, the change of focus from divine will to the sacrificial victim's family relations made it an outlet for personal agony. Poems written in the aftermath of the War of Independence did not express a sense of victory, validation, or even reconciliation with sacrifice, but the painful premonition and realisation of bereavement. These include lines by T. Carmi and by Ayin Hillel[7]:

Tonight I dreamt that my son did not return. (T. Carmi)

But your son, your only son whom you love, There was no ram to replace him. (Ayin Hillel)

---

[7] Both cited in Weiss, 2002, p. 72.

Unlike the poems mentioned above, THIS IS THE LAND (1935, D: Baruch Agadati), a partial documentary celebrating fifty years of settlement, clearly endorses martyrdom. Following a public speech by an elderly pioneer, twelve minutes into the film, of the hardships he and his fellow pioneers endured, including thirst and malaria, we see a corresponding scene. A pioneer ploughing a field collapses. A fellow pioneer rushes over and, instead of tending to him, continues the ploughing. A close-up of the pioneer applauding his comrade with his failing breath is superimposed on this image. On his death bed, the pioneer delivers an oration calling for the continuation of the settlement for which he sacrificed his life (Bursztyn, 1990, p. 44). Nevertheless, the film uses substantial pathos to dramatise the loss of the individual. The sight of his body lying on the ground is superimposed on the shot of the earth turned over by the plough and trodden on by his comrade, as though the body itself were being worked into the ground. This image disappears as the scene repeats, with another plough followed by another pair of feet. At his deathbed, the settler is attended to by a weeping female companion. Bursztyn interprets this as another expression of collective values (ibid.). However, it is her presence that underlines his loss, for he disappears from the bed as she sits there weeping. She tenderly strokes the empty pillow, and a close-up on her tearful expression hovers for ten seconds, before a pan shot of the tombstones in the pioneer graveyard appears. Despite its endorsement of sacrifice, the scene emphasises what the jubilee speech and the tombstones cannot: the savagery of the individual's death, and the pain and sorrow it inflicts. Although several means are used to portray this death as a conscious act of self-sacrifice, the sense of painful personal loss is enhanced rather than obliterated.

In the case of ODED THE WANDERER, the voluntary sacrificial aspect is absent. Oded's disappearance and the prospect of his loss is not harnessed to any cause. It is an adversity triggered by an innocuous peer rivalry. The focus is on the misery suffered by the boy, his family, and the community. From the moment Oded and the others discover that he is separated from the group, the film's chief emotional gestures are fear, alarm, and anguish, all manifesting their personal disaster. Because of this, we can categorise ODED THE WANDERER as a melodrama. The potential loss of Oded by his parents and community dominates the film.

When Oded first begins to search for his peers, the vast plains of the wilderness are used to emphasise his smallness, as he runs frantically in all directions before stopping to cry at the top of his lungs, to no avail. The vast plains are also captured in a pan shot as the desperate teacher stands up on a hill and looks out for Oded in vain, the wide horizon emphasising the difficulty of tracing the boy. Between these two scenes, the teacher sits lethargically smoking a cigarette on the side of the road, and then stands up to meet the tourist and the children who return, empty handed, from the search for Oded. They move more slowly as they approach him, dramatising the gravity of the matter. This gesture is repeated more elaborately by the teacher when he returns to the settlement and faces the mother, who ends the scene in tears. The motif is extended when a search party of men on horseback led by the father returns slowly to the settlement, having failed in their mission. They are met by reaction shots of grim children and adults. At the end of the scene, a close-up of the father's face is juxtaposed with a set of reaction shots in which the mother's face is overcome with grief. For both the teacher and the father, encountering the grief-stricken mother implies their guilt. The teacher expresses this through gestures. In the father's case, it is prepared in the scenes leading up to the encounter: during the search, the father vows to continue until his son is found, only to be immediately dissuaded from continuing by his fellow settlers. Guilt also plays a role in the children's sub-plot, and is mentioned in the caption when Micha's timid attempt to approach Yigal is rejected.

In all those scenes, through movement, dramaturgical arrangement, and the composition of images, the viewer is conditioned to closely observe individual figures. There is much use of close-ups, with solemn figures repeatedly exchanging glances. The mother's face, in particular, is captured by the camera in a variety of sorrowful expressions. The melodramatic effect is enhanced by the constant danger Oded faces. He is repeatedly depicted as overwhelmed by circumstances, making him seem ever more fragile. Exhausted, he walks away from the camera, dragging his backpack on the ground. A minute later he collapses to the ground and helplessly lifts his empty canister to indicate his thirst. Extreme close-ups and swift camera movements are used when he falls and injures his knee, causing him to lose consciousness once more. He collapses from hunger and exhaustion twice more, the second time just as he is being rescued. He follows the kite Yigal and Micha fly for him, and collapses behind their backs, appearing frail when he is finally safe.

The subjective perspective is heightened by the integration of hallucinations, attributed both to Oded and his mother. Oded's first hallucination is of a stream of water. The second is more "collective". He envisions his settlement's agricultural abundance: cows, chickens, sheep, beehives, a tractor, and orange trees bearing fruit that Oded helps pick. Strangely, the settlement's achievements are presented as mirages of a despairing boy in the wasteland. The mother's hallucination is a matter of anxiety, not wishful thinking. Tending to a calf, she suddenly halts, envisioning her son superimposed on the endless horizon of the desert.

Unlike the pioneer who sacrifices his life in THIS IS THE LAND, Oded survives. This survival is orchestrated as an emotional peak. Earlier help has always come to Oded at the last minute, from an unexpected source. In his thirst, he falls into a delirium in which he sees a stream of water. He awakens alarmed and determined to continue. Having fallen, Oded awakens in a cave with a spring. Lying on the ground, exhausted from hunger, he encounters a stray goat and sucks on its udder.

Ultimately, the melodramatic representation of trouble and despair increases the film's emotional weight. This turns into elation in the final scene, where his parents and the other members of the community run forward to greet the returning son. There is no question that personal agony is central in ODED THE WANDERER. It is also articulated in the poems quoted above, which connect the binding of Isaac to the War of Independence. But it is not verbalised in the original Biblical text they evoke. The tale's melodramatic effect is heightened by God's allusion to Isaac as Abraham's only beloved son (Genesis 22:2), and by the description of Abraham reaching for the knife to slaughter his son before the angel stops him (Genesis 22:11). Abraham and Isaac's emotions are not mentioned at all. This is in absolute contrast to the preceding chapter's narration of the expulsion of Ismael and Hagar (Peri, 2005). In this Biblical narrative, Sarah's slave, Hagar, bears Abraham a son, Ismael, because her mistress is childless (Genesis 15:1–16). After Sarah celebrates the birth of her own son, she insists on the expulsion of Hagar and Ismael. Abraham disapproves of the demand, but is directed by God to fulfil his wife's wishes, and banishes the maid and her son to the desert. As their water runs out, Hagar despairs. An angel reassures her that her son will live and become the father of a nation. He instructs her to continue, and she comes upon a well, saving her son's life (Genesis 21:9–20).

Both the writer Meir Shalev and the literary scholar Menachem Peri point out the parallel structure of the tales of the binding of Isaac and the expulsion of Ishmael (Shalev, 2010, p. 126; Peri, 2005). For Shalev, the most important feature of this repetition is Abraham's conduct as he follows God's horrendous order without protest or resistance (Shalev, 2010, p. 126). Peri, on the other hand, argues that the parallel created in the text is between Abraham and Hagar. In the binding of Isaac, Abraham is faced with an impossible trial in which both his loyalty to God and his parenthood are put to the test. By exhibiting impeccable faith in God, Abraham fails as a father. In her concern for her son, Hagar demonstrates the parental skills Abraham lacks (Peri, 2005). The general cause, equated with God's plan, conflicts with the personal realm and family relations.

Hagar is non-compliant in her plight, and it is instrumental in giving her a voice of her own, which materialises first and foremost through her conduct. She does not abide by Abraham's actions, and he has to load her provisions and her son on her shoulder before he sends her away (Shalev, 2010, p. 127). Her desperate tears are the first to be shed in the Bible (ibid., p. 123). It is the first instance in which human emotions are expressed in this way. Ismael's name is not mentioned throughout the story. As Shalev writes, it is as though the writer adopts Sarah and God's perspectives, and all three deprive Ismael of a name, an identity, and his birth rights (ibid., p. 125). On the other hand, this semantic strategy further emphasises Hagar's perspective. Hagar refers to Ismael, who is at least fourteen, as the *child* (King James Version, Genesis 21:15), while God refers to him as the *lad* (Genesis 21:12). Through the greater part of the story, Ismael is referred to as the *lad*. But when Abraham loads Ismael on Hagar's shoulder, when she casts him under one of the shrubs after the water runs out, when she weeps for his anticipated death, he is referred to as the *child*, which demarcates Hagar's perspective (Peri, 2000). Her anguish breaks through the Biblical text, accentuating her presence.

Agony, loss, and bereavement become means to assert and legitimise the position of the individual. The significance of this is best understood in relation to the communal perceptions described above: the inherent subordinate status of the individual (section 7.2 – the comic figure), and the ambivalence and intrusiveness which characterise relations between the individual and her environment (section 7.1). Particularly when individual affirmation is subject to such social moral restrictions and scrutiny, it is limited to the mitigation of a few practices, like grief, which are legitimised by the community. Paradoxically, the individual makes a claim to an otherwise unacceptable primary status at the very moment of her own deprivation and demise. In that respect, the culture of commemoration, which assists a community in coping with death, also enables a manifestation of subjectivity which is otherwise restrained by the moral code. This concept offers an additional perspective on customary practices of grief, like the idealisation of the deceased in popular commemorative songs. As Meira Weiss and Michael Gluzman demonstrate, the lyrics of these songs describe the fallen soldiers in ideal form: young, determined, tanned, tall, strong, with Hebrew names and "high-rise" hair (Weiss, 2002, p. 70; Gluzman, 2007, pp. 184–185). The euphemisms and unrestrainedly ideal forms ascribed to the departed would be considered inappropriate for any living being.

While the fallen are seen as ideal figures, the bereaved, like Hagar, are given centre stage. Their situation is of utmost importance, something compellingly demonstrated in Weiss' personal account of her work volunteering and conducting research with bereaved families:

> It was as if I were possessed by the experience, as if I knew this was my place, a place of death that had in it the essence of life. Homes where the walls did not just break down

> but rather opened up like flower petals. All secrets were in the open. There was no point hiding anything at a time like this. [...]
>
> A few years later, when a colleague told me about her academic work, which dealt with children's everyday games [...] I was really surprised: how she could deal with such "banal" things while I was immersed in human tragedies? (Weiss, 2002, pp. 79–80)

This state of utter importance is also reflected in the status of bereaved families in public discourse. As Weiss shows, parents of fallen soldiers may employ the uniqueness of the bereavement experience as an argument, cementing their individual distinctiveness into communal convention (ibid., p. 75). Such importance could be attributed to the fact that these sons not only died, but died in battle, elevating victimhood to sacrifice. In its expression, however, it is victimhood rather than heroism which provides this awe-inspiring distinction. This is also evident in ODED THE WANDERER, which revolves around personal and communal victimhood, centred on the loss of Oded in the wilderness. The significance of Oded, his parents, and the community is rendered by means of the potential loss hovering over each of them.

A tradition of martyrdom and commemoration has served Jewish communities for generations in coping with the adversities and losses they had to endure. It created a possible outlet for indulging in the type of individual affirmation that is otherwise perceived as improper within Judeo-Christian moral codes. In adopting the tradition of commemoration, Zionist culture took on this form of individual justification. Loss and agony are associated in the Israeli culture with individual assertion, with implications that reach beyond its commemorative culture. As Loshitzky argues, Israeli identity politics is dominated by victimhood:

> To a large extent, Israeli society has become a society that thrives on victimhood and elevates it to the level of "civil religion". [... The] struggle for hegemony, or at least recognition, is in most cases a struggle for the recognition of suffering and victimhood rather than voluntary sacrifice. (Loshitzky, 2001, p. xiv)

Loshitzky's connection between victimhood and public recognition is significant. But while she regards it as a divergence from the legacy of voluntary sacrifice, my claim is that it descends directly from this lineage. Beginning with Hagar, suffering became a pretext for individual affirmation, and continues to be so in Israeli culture. Contrary to Zanger's argument, this tradition is not maintained by an early acceptance and later rejection of the myth of the binding (Zanger, 2003, p. 95), but by a continued association between suffering and validation. The connection between victimhood and affirmation will therefore be central in my discussion of the victim's entry into the sex scene in chapter 11 and its decline in public discourse of the 1970s in part III.

"Whose Son is *This Youth*?": The Child

Childhood and youth have always had symbolic value in Israeli society. The character most associated with youth is a child in a round brimless hat, named Srulik, an invention of the cartoonish Dosh. As early as the 1930s, Israeli society had been embodied by characters who were children, or at least childlike (Broshi, 2007, p. 67). Srulik appeared regularly in the daily newspaper *Maariv* from the 1950s to the 1970s. At the height of his popularity, he was adopted as a symbol of Israeli identity by the state (ibid., pp. 46–48). Even after he became less broadly popular in Israeli society, Srulik sustained his symbolic status, and no other character replaced him (ibid., p. 30).

His youth represented a new reality, a new society, and a new generation to a generation of immigrants – including Dosh himself (Gurevitz, 2007, pp. 6–7). Something similar occurred with ODED THE WANDERER and the new immigrants of that decade. In the film, children, and Oded specifically, are the object of a sentimental parental gaze, the most prized products of the parent's new life in new settlements within a new land. This is brought into play early in the film, in Oded's interactions with his parents. Before Oded enters, his father shows his mother the gift he is about to put in his son's backpack, a diary with a dedication, and they smile with delight. When Oded finds the diary, he smiles just as emotionally. When Oded appears, his parents stand on both his sides as though posing for a family photograph, loading the backpack on his shoulders, giving him his breakfast, and debating the safety of the trip. There is an exchange of tender looks between the parents, from a higher position, and the child below. When Oded sets off, his mother follows him down the road, expressing her maternal care by buttoning his shirt, straightening his collar, and fastening his backpack. This parental fondness is echoed in the following scene, as the class leaves the settlement. A man appears in close-up, watching the children. His eyes glow in recognition and he begins to motion. In the next shot, a mischievous girl in the crowd – evidently his daughter – responds to him and approaches. As she enters his frame, they embrace, and she immediately begins to indicate that she needs to go. As she leaves he smiles tenderly, and she is seen in the crowd once more, enthusiastically waving goodbye.

Beyond the display of parental care, the film produces an infatuated gaze in its depiction of the children. Oded's depiction before he meets his parents implies sentimentality. The camera focuses on him as he is awakened by sunlight, stretching and getting up to wash under a tap in the garden. Throughout the film, the camera captures the children in a similar manner, and follows them in a variety of close-ups as they march together, sit together, play, rest and eat. They perform for the camera, signalling their awareness that they are being observed by friendly eyes. The sentimental gaze is implied even beyond the plot. Shots of toddlers are used as prelude and postlude as the film leaves the settlement and later returns to it. The first toddler stands at the edge of a plot, barely keeping upright. The second is seated, and pounding a hammer on a wooden section of a wagon's wheel. Beyond these young children's symbolic affiliation with the new settlement, these images also carry the gaze of their proud parents, who cannot help but withdraw from the story to direct an enchanted glance at their little ones.

Aside from the symbolic value of youth in Israeli culture, Talmon points out that youth culture was heavily cultivated in the new society. Invested with the hopes and dreams of their immigrant parents, those born in the new nation were adorned with the crown of eternal youth, both because the culture honoured the many soldiers who died in their youth, and because they were seen as privileged, towering over their immigrant parents, questioning their authority and refusing to grow up (Talmon, 2001, p. 113).

One of the outlets of this vibrant youth culture was the Palmach, an elite force of the Haganah underground movement. The organisation, which existed between 1941 and 1948, was based on young volunteers, and its youthful practices quickly became mythical – a myth that outlasted its existence (ibid., p. 114). The writer and former Palmach member, Poochoo, immortalised it in a popular trilogy published between the 1950s to the 1970s. Poochoo emphasised the group's giddy, youthful spirit: the pranks, practical jokes, and general sense of chaos they brought to the kibbutz where they were training. Their innocence and the difficulty they experienced in dealing with death was another central trope (ibid., p. 115). The importance of the tasks members of the Palmach were entrusted with – assisting illegal immigration, fighting the War of Independence, establishing new settlements – seem almost inconsequential in Poochoo's novels (interview with Eshed, 2009). Youth culture, however, did not remain associated only with the Palmach generation. As Talmon points out, the mischievous Sabra gang remained a favoured agent of self-reflection in the Israeli society and an object of nostalgic yearning well into the 1990s (Talmon, 2001, p. 121). Fashions and music changed, but the youth group formation remained steady (ibid., pp. 69–70).

The question arises: what associations and affects do the figures of the child and adolescent carry into the Israeli cultural realm, and consequently into Israeli film? Some of the connotations these figures bore can be traced back to early Jewish culture, as reflected in Biblical texts. Two prominent examples are the tales of Ismael and Isaac discussed in the part of section 7.2 dedicated to the victim. The fact that both potential victims are in their early youth is explicit in both stories (Genesis 21:12, 14–20 and 22:5). The actions are all the more deplorable for being committed against young people.

In another Biblical tale that circulates in modern Israeli culture, a young David wins in battle against Goliath the warrior (1 Samuel 17:1–54). His youth is emphasised on multiple occasions. When he is introduced, it is stated that he is the youngest of eight children, and that he stays behind while his three older brothers go out to battle, making it clear that he is too young to be mobilised (1 Samuel 17:12–14). Later, when David proposes to that he fight Goliath, King Saul cautions him that he is but a youth (KJV 1 Samuel 17:33). As he approaches Goliath in battle the latter despises him because he is a youth (1 Samuel 17:43). Having won the battle, and having carried Goliath's head to Jerusalem, the King asks him three times whose son he is:

> And when Saul saw David go forth against the Philistine, he said unto Abner, the captain of the host, Abner, whose son is *this youth*? And Abner said, As thy soul liveth, O king, I cannot tell.
>
> And the king said, Enquire thou whose son *the stripling* is. [...]
>
> And Saul said to him, Whose son art thou, *thou young man*? And David answered, I am the son of thy servant Jesse the Bethlehemite. (KJV 1 Samuel 17:55–56, 58, emphasis mine)

David's youth is also clear in his approach to combat. He declines to go to battle with the armour, helmet, coat of mail, and sword that Saul gives him, because he has no experience with such things. Instead, he arms himself with a staff and five smooth stones (1 Samuel 17:38–40). He does not appear in the battle as a warrior, but as an adolescent shepherd – something that provokes Goliath (1 Samuel 17:42–43).

As with Ismael and Isaac, David's youth enhances the effect of the narrative. In their case, it is the horror that is enhanced; in David's, it is the miraculous nature of his victory over Goliath. This victory – over an experienced warrior, six cubits and a span tall, and heavily armed (1 Samuel 17:4–7) – is all the more outstanding because of David's youth and inexperience in the battlefield. There are also particular attributes associated with the child and the youth. These have been identified by the journalists Amos Elon and Dan Pattir, by the anthropologist Zeli Gurevitz, and by the curator Michal Broshi in their analysis of Srulik as a national character. Compared to another caricature from the time, Israel Saba (Grandpa Israel), Srulik is quick, sharp, and cheeky – not old and tired, not dragging behind him a long history of persecution (Pattir, 2007, p. 130). He lives here and now, not entangled in the past (Elon, 1971, p. 261).

Being a youngster, Srulik is innocent and childish, a bearer of a great dream in a petty, aggressive world (Broshi, 2007, p. 61). He is vulnerable and helpless, a child who is often surrounded by ugly, hostile adults (Gurevitz, 2007, p. 18). He reflects Israel's fragile status in the international arena, as perceived by its citizens, and represents an innocent sanity which is constantly confronted by madness (Broshi, 2007, p. 87). He is inexperienced, unprepared for the perils that await him in the sunny landscape, and so is always on edge (Elon, 1971, p. 262). On the other hand, because he is a youngster, his troubles are also portrayed as juvenile, trivial, and laughable. He vacillates between worship and ridicule (Gurevitz, 2007, p. 13). In addition, Srulik embodies an adolescent nation. He does not validate, but seeks validation (ibid., p. 15). He sways from one extreme to the other, from overconfidence to underconfidence, from optimism to pessimism. As a teenager, he is temperamental and suffers from a crisis of identity. Wondering who he is, Srulik is in constant need of love, support, and approval (Broshi, 2007, p. 80; Pattir, 2007, p. 130). His mischief attracts no criticism: he is not evil, and he is not responsible. He is disarming, and cannot be harshly or even seriously judged (Gurevitz, 2007, p. 15).

Srulik is a reflexive caricature, repeatedly interacting with a world of caricatures associated with Israel and the Jews. Dosh was particularly engaged in the battle against anti-Semitism (Pattir, 2007, p. 108). In many drawings, Srulik incredulously faces a mirror reflecting a monstrous image he never recognises as his own (Broshi, 2007, pp. 87–88). His very appearance is meant to counteract the prevailing stereotypes of the tragic, pitiful Wandering Jew, or of the hunchbacked Jew with a crooked nose, fleshy lips, and money in his pockets – stereotypes adopted by many caricaturists in contemporary Arab press (Pattir, 2007, p. 130).

In her discussion of youth culture, Talmon discusses another central attribute in the depiction of youthful groups in Israeli culture and film: the orchestration of what she defines as liminality. Talmon is not the only one to apply the term to Israeli film (see, for instance Munk, 2004, pp. i, 7–9). However, she is the only one to avoid using it in a sheerly metaphorical sense. She does so by applying the term to existence on the borderline, to crossing borders, and to the cinematic enactment of youth and youth rituals. In the liminal phase, as part of an initiation process, one social identity and status is traded for another. The transition is typically between childhood and adulthood. In that phase, boundaries are blurred and social hierarchies are deactivated, solidarity among peers increases, and rituals and myths are employed (Talmon, 2001, p. 47n10).

The performance of liminal rituals in Israeli film makes it possible for adolescent figures to enact a position which undermines social structure, rebels against it, and at the same time accepts and reaffirms its norms (ibid., pp. 58–59). Talmon suggests that such scenes articulate, delegate, and legitimise social changes, and particularly changes in values. The representation of the cinematic group expresses collective yearning for, and fear of, integration. And its repeated localisation in liminal, anarchic contexts signifies a cultural difficulty in determining the components and boundaries of Israeli identity. It reveals the general tendency towards "immaturity" and ambiguous relations to collective identity (ibid., pp. 59–60).

It should be clear by now that the figures of the child and adolescent contain elements associated with the victim, and elements associated with the comic figure. They are vulnerable, which enhances their status as victims, and yet they represent small subjectivities, autonomous but harmless, which are exempt from seriousness. Furthermore, like the comic figure, they are subordinate to social order but not identified with it. The specificity of the child and adolescent as figures lies in the way they fluctuate between the comic figure and the victim. It is in the newcomer's sharp awareness of the world, and the estrangement it harbours – the liminality of a subjectivity which is both included and excluded, both joined and detached from the environment in which it develops. The presence of the child and adolescent sets out a challenge to communal identity.

ODED THE WANDERER embodies all this. Oded is as much a comic figure as a victim. The other children are just as much participants in a comedy as a melodrama. For much of the film, Oded is the object rather than the subject of observation. He serves as the focal point for his parents' loving gaze and the tourist's enthusiastic picture-taking. He is even unobservant: from his first appearance in school, he is oblivious of the environment, fully immersed in a book, which is replaced by his diary during the field trip. Alone in nature, however, Oded becomes an observing subject. As he lifts up his eyes from the diary, a set of reaction shots captures his enthralled interaction with a chameleon. After he discovers that he is alone, the unfamiliar environment is captured through his increasingly alarmed process of cognition – a small figure in extreme long shot, running in the vast desert, shouting into the empty landscape. When confronted by an eagle, Oded quickly retreats. He reacts with gestures of alarm – typical of the silent film era – when he witnesses the tourist's capture by the Bedouins. Just as the environment unfolds through Oded's presence, his agency as an observing subject expands through interaction with the unfamiliar.

It is also crucial that the film revolves around the group dynamic of children, who move easily between structure and chaos, between subordinate participation in their school, camp, and field trip and playful unruliness. Within this dynamic, Oded the individual both belongs and does not belong to this community of his peers. He stands out, trails behind, and secludes himself. Immersed in his diary, he does not take part in the children's antics. In his absence, nonetheless, the community of children and adults comes to a halt. His own "initiation" into the wilderness accentuates how fragile he is outside this community, and his hallucinations express his uncontested place within it. As for the victim and the comic figure, Oded represents only one facet of what children came to embody in Israeli film. In chapter 12 and part III, I demonstrate just how instrumental the child and adolescent are in negotiating various aspects of Israeli identity and the changes it undergoes in Israeli film.

7.3 Where is My John Wayne? Where is My Muscle Jew?

At the end of chapter 5, I challenged the claim that early Israeli cinema was utopian, ideal, mythic, and inhabited by heroic, muscular Jews. Before closing this chapter, I want to test this assertion by examining the manifestation of muscular, sovereign manliness in ODED THE WANDERER more closely. My argument is not that there is a shortage of muscular men, acts of courage and demonstrations of dominance and sovereignty in early, as well as contemporary, Israeli films, but that their function is more ambiguous and complex than has been recognised in academic discourse.

Indeed, ODED THE WANDERER offers its viewers instances in which masculinity is shown as a dynamic spectacle. After Oded disappears, the film returns to the settlement, and the effect of the news of Oded's disappearance. After the exposition featuring the toddler with a hammer, the scene changes to an empty road. It lies still for fifteen seconds, and then the frame is filled with settlers, predominantly but not exclusively male, who run toward the camera. Title captions announce Oded's disappearance, and his distraught parents are shown, each reacting to the news. The father, quickly mounts a horse and takes leave of his wife. After another unidentified settler is shown fastening the saddle and riding away, the father's departure becomes part of a dynamic flow. The father is then seen leading a party of male settlers on horseback. As the camera moves backward, the father disappears to the left of the frame, and the men continue to gallop towards the camera for half a minute in unified rhythm. After the mother is seen in close-up inspecting the riding party, the camera returns to the men that ride past it.

For the next seven minutes, the men's search of Oded in the wilderness is interwoven with the children's return to the settlement, Oded's misfortunes, and his mother's agony. The search party provides a dynamic motif. They are seen from a high angle, flowing through the scenery, or else riding past the camera. Individual riders sometimes halt, dismount, search in caves, and then continue. The sense of movement is not encumbered but enhanced by the speed of their actions. The collective body of men and horses, in constant action, maintains an important effect. But the spectacular search party is unsuccessful. The men stand still, without their horses, heads hanging down, surrounding the agonised father. Laying a hand on his shoulder, a man talks the father into returning to the settlement to comfort his wife. The men then walk slowly towards the camera. A caption explains that only the teacher and another man are left to search for the boy. The party on horseback returns to the settlement in slow strides. Reaction shots reveal dispirited children looking at the men, emphasising the weight of disappointment. There are close-ups of Yigal and Micha, both dejected.

It is childish initiative, not muscular heroism, that saves the day in ODED THE WANDERER. Micha makes amends with Yigal. They set out into the desert and fly a kite inscribed with Oded's name, which attracts both him and the men searching for him, bringing the escapade to a happy end. Their guilt is obviated, the solution coming from the very source that caused the crisis: youthful mischief. The same pattern is reproduced as the conflict between the tourist and the Bedouin tribe is resolved. A minute after being captured, he is sitting in a tent, chained and gagged. After Oded tells the adults of the tourist's situations, a settler named Simon goes to the Bedouin camp. He rides swiftly from the horizon into the camp. As he arrives at the centre of the frame, he dismounts, and is greeted by the men. He sits down, and the men follow suit. He is familiar with the Bedouins and their customs, and his posture reflects assurance, dominance, and authority. He talks them into releasing the tourist, but as they turn to the tent where he is imprisoned, they discover that he is no longer there. While the men negotiate, the viewer sees him cut his way out of the tent's fabric, and hastening away on the back of his donkey. A male authority figure rushes to the rescue, and demonstrates abilities to solve the problem. But the tourist, who got into trouble through a comic mishap, frees himself in his own comic way.

Men of authority and strength have a role in the fictional universe of ODED THE WANDERER, but they are systematically separated from the forces that advance and resolve the plot. To my mind, this contradicts the claim that the muscle Jew simply emerged as the protagonist of early Israeli film. It testifies to the ambivalence of this very first Israeli film when reflecting the utopian image of heroic manliness. This ambivalence is in line with the moral standpoint I described in this chapter, where the boundaries between private and public are not settled, and are perpetually checked for imbalance; where the individual is bound to a subordination which is negotiated through comic disobedience and childish liminality; and where the personal sense of importance is mitigated through victimhood.

ODED THE WANDERER does not disavow the complexities of Jewish identity which were inherited from the Diasporic tradition during Zionism's mobilised phase. Rather, it shows how these were continued and developed within the Zionist context – which was passed on to following generations, which continued to articulate and re-inscribe Israeli cultural self-perception. In short, it is a part of a historical continuum.

8 Concluding Words

I began part I by discussing the perception that sexuality is central to subjectivity, and that sex scenes are a manifestation of this concept. Examining existing studies of Israeli film, the main problem I encountered was not the sporadic, elusive nature of existing discourse on sex scenes. Rather, it was the prevalent assumption that Israeli film and Israeli film history are a perpetual manifestation of historical disjunction and Otherness.

Against this, I argue for historical continuity, and for the emancipation of subjectivity from the constraints of Otherness. I presented four elements that are crucial for any attempt to chart cultural continuity in Israeli film. My discussion of these four elements – the enactment of disruption, the comic figure, the victim, and the child – located their significance in the Israeli perception of human subjectivity and its relation to the social environment.

Since the sex scene is an arena in which the individual and their relationship with the environment is characterised and explored, it provides a medium in which the four elements I presented take concrete cinematic form. In my analyses, I demonstrated how all four elements are manifested in various mediums, including an early film that has no sex scenes in it. This demonstrates that the patterns I describe occur independently of the sex scene.

In part II I analyse the four elements as they manifest themselves in the early sex scenes of the 1960s. I argue that, while the elements and communal perceptions that shaped them exist outside sex scenes, they are fundamental to such scenes, and to the role they play in the construction of subjectivity in film. The core of these scenes lies within the specificity of Israeli culture.

Part II: **The 1960s: Comedy, Victimhood and Paradise Lost**

9 The Introduction of Sex through the Prism of the Type Figure

Part I presented the theoretical foundations of my work: I started by arguing that sex scenes are the arena in which the personal and the interrelated – subjectivity and identity – are enacted, bringing into view an individual and community that are culturally specific. I ended part I with a comprehensive presentation of four specific elements of Israeli culture and tradition which are primary in its construction of subjectivity: the disruption of space, the comic figure, the victim, and the child. Using film analysis, I will now provide the material basis for my argument, and draw a connection between my opening claim and these four elements. My discussion of films of the 1960s focuses on the interplay of each element in the construction of the sex scene, as well as its function within the film.

The next three sections each focus on a single type figure, beginning with the comical figure, continuing with the victim, and ending with the child. Cinematic figures cannot be reduced to prototypes, and most represent a combination of several type figures. Nonetheless, my aim is to demonstrate the cinematic realisation of the elements described in chapter 7, and the historical configurations particular to the 1960s. I therefore discuss each type separately. Spatial disruption is the dominant element, and is so pervasive that it will not be examined separately. Instead, it features throughout the analysis, both in part II and part III. While discussing the victim and the child, I also touch on a fifth element, addressed in chapters 4, 5, and section 7.3: the tentative representation of male dominance and assertiveness in Israeli cinema. By demonstrating how this corresponds to the main motifs I discuss, I establish in addition how eroticism and the uncanny are evoked in Israeli cinema.

Part II will further strengthen my argument, first made in chapter 6, that there is no dominant rift in Israeli culture between Hegemony and Otherness. It is only in the third part, however, that I will be able to observe the dynamics of continuity and change described in chapter 5. Part II deals with the emergence of the sex scene in the 1960s, from which the sex scenes of the 1970s later evolved.

The scenes of the 1960s will be discussed thematically, rather than chronologically. As I argued in chapter 2, I make no attempt to explain why sex scenes began to appear in Israeli films from approximately 1963, or why they became commonplace. Such an explanation would involve numerous historical factors, something I have chosen not to touch upon here. My approach also requires me to disregard most historical aspects of the film industry. Note, however, that all the productions I discuss were low-budget, which is typical of 1960s Israeli film. All but three – 999 Aliza the Policeman (1967, D: Menahem Golan), The Dybbuk (1968, D: Ilan Eldad), and Every Bastard a King (1968, D: Uri Zohar) – were shot in black and white. In addition, many films of the time employed a relatively consistent cast and crew, with the result that a small number of actors and actresses appeared in different roles in the films I discuss.

Despite economic constraints, a homogeneous cast and crew, and institutional pressures placed on the industry by the state through the Board for the Review of Films and Plays (described in chapter 2), the films analysed in part II use a wide range of aesthetic means of expression, and a wide range of strategies to formulate sexual representation. Even at its birth, the Israeli sex scene was a pluralistic arena. In the next chapters, I discuss three different contexts in which it was conceived.

10 "We Have a Little Sister and She Hath no Breasts": The Comic Figure and the Deterioration of Eroticism in MOTIVE TO MURDER

Our first type is the comical figure. As I have shown in my discussion of the comic type figure in section 7.2, comedy was dominant at the outset of the Israeli cinema. This remained true as the industry went into regular production in the 1960s. Nonetheless, our central case study in this chapter is not a comedy but a crime thriller, MOTIVE TO MURDER (1966, D: Peter Freistadt). Like ODED THE WANDERER, MOTIVE TO MURDER uses comic figures and conventions, which make up an essential part of its repertoire of poetic gestures. As I will show, MOTIVE TO MURDER's elaborate use of comic patterns, Israeli cultural codes, and sex scenes make it very useful for outlining the broader discussion.

10.1 MOTIVE TO MURDER

The corpse of a young woman, Naomi Hausdorf, is discovered in her home on the eve of Independence Day. A police detective, a sergeant, and a police physician spend the night in the house with Naomi's father, Dr. Hausdorf, a shocked female witness, and four suspects (three male associates and a lodger). At dawn, the murder mystery is solved, as the father unexpectedly confesses to having murdered his daughter.

This thriller was the first of its kind (Rapaport, 1966), and for many years was the sole attempt at this genre on the Israeli screen. Gertz and Schnitzer speculate that it was censored due to its association with a national holiday (Gertz, 1993, p. 21; Schnitzer, 1994a, p. 16). As is typical of thrillers, MOTIVE TO MURDER connects an annual national celebration with a sensual experience of disenchantment and mistrust, which evolves through the construction of an enclosed cinematic space, full of suspicion, lies, aggression, resentment, and sinister motives. Although the genre could be considered "foreign", the film employs local topoi in its construction of space and figures, bringing the heavy atmosphere carried by the crime thriller "home". The thematic link to historical events is most obvious here: as Dr. Hausdorf's confession reveals, he murdered his daughter because she taunted him for having failed to rescue her and her mother from the Holocaust. While very prominent, this element is the least significant of the Israeli cultural codes the film deploys.

Through the Entrance Hall: The Disrupted Space

One element that MOTIVE TO MURDER enacts heavily, both spatially and dramaturgically, is the disruption of space (described in chapter 7). Individual characters are depicted both as intruding and being intruded upon. The boundaries between one individual and another, and between the intimacy of privacy and the propriety of the public domain, are constantly emphasised as they are violated.

In the beginning of the film, the witness-to-be, Mona Zilber, is seen walking the streets before arriving at the Hausdorf home. From that point, the film becomes a chamber play, set within the confines of the house. As the contemporary critic Azaria Rapaport complained, this confinement evokes a sense of suffocation, rather than intimacy (Rapaport, 1966).

Much of the sense of intrusiveness is constructed through the criminal investigation. Its depiction emphasises breaches of privacy. As it progresses, the film and the team of investigators gradually penetrate almost every space in the house. They move from the living room (which also contains the study, the dining room, and a music corner) to the hall, the kitchen, the lodger's bedroom, Naomi's bedroom, and the veranda. These spaces are not reconstructed as the scene of the crime. Rather, they become a stage for interrogating the suspects, during which the truth is reluctantly revealed.

The penetrative act of interrogation itself is magnified by camera work. Shlomo Sh'hori and Yerach Halperin, both assertive suspects, sustain their sovereign space by appearing alone in the frame, or part of the frame. The more vulnerable suspects, Moshe Harpaz and Ze'evik Ashkenazi, are seen in close-up during their respective interrogations, sharing the frame with the blurred back of the investigating officer, and the investigator in turn with theirs. This implies their inability to fend off the pressure exerted by the investigators, marked visually by the physical presence of the latter.

As time goes on, the house and the interrogations become more crowded. The living room is filled with silent participants: Mona, the shocked witness (who is also Ze'evik's girlfriend), Dr. Hausdorf, and Naomi's body. The body remains in place for a markedly long time, and is only removed fifty-two minutes into the film, observed by a silent crowd in front of the house.

Only a few questions are asked and answered discreetly. Most of the investigations take place in the presence of others, whether the silent figures in the living room, members of the investigating team, or the other suspects. This is made ever more conspicuous as the frame becomes increasingly crowded. This process is gradual, reaching a peak in the final investigation, where all are present and visible, and participate both as defendants and witnesses. The camera movements and chosen frames bring the active and inactive participants into constant view.

The way the investigation occupies the space, the visual emphasis on the penetrative nature of the investigation, and the increasing crowding of the screen all enact the repossession of the private space by the public one. But this does not mean that the film "recollects" a private sphere, one that was intact before the murder and investigation. Flashbacks reveal a constant assault on privacy through the incongruities between daughter and father, and the presence of witnesses. Before I return to this aspect, which is constituted through sex scenes, I turn to another cultural factor which plays a major role in the film.

The Podium: Comedy

In accordance with the rules of the crime thriller, the suspects and their associates are displayed to the viewer for scrutiny. This goes beyond any conceivable role they may play as perpetrators: they become objects of harsh judgment, and the judgmental perspective levelled against them gives the sense that something is inherently wrong with the norms and social structure these figures inhabit. The murderous act is on trial, and so too are the human relations surrounding it. This is true in MOTIVE TO MURDER. The characters' aggression and dishonesty offer a possible link to the murder, and serve as the main source of the viewer's judgements. At the same time, the characters' comic qualities produce a very different effect within the local cultural context, one which is incongruous with the genre.

These comical qualities are discussed by Elliott Oring in his study of a phenomenon called the *Chizbat*, a practice of humorous storytelling combining biographical truths, hyperbole, and fantasy. This became widespread through the Palmach, an elite fighting force in the Haganah underground movement which continued to play a role in Israeli culture long after it was disbanded in 1948. Oring shows that these qualities, which he calls "values", were used in the *Chizbat* to determine self-image, and remained relevant in this respect during the 1960s (Oring, 1981, p. 123).

Oring identifies two conflicting sets of values – that is, attributes and linguistic traits – represented in the *Chizbat*. One is associated with native Israelis (the Sabra, discussed in part I). The attributes involved are: Levantine; secular; primitive; boorish; dirty; slovenly; unregimented; unemotional; self-assured; improvising. The linguistic traits are slang and terseness. The other set is associated with immigrant Jews. The attributes involved are: European; traditional; civilised; cultured; clean; disciplined, regimented; emotional. The linguistic traits are literary language and rhetoric (ibid.). According to Oring, no set of values predominates. Moreover, each is used in the *Chizbat* to undermine the other (ibid., pp. 125–126), meaning that "audience identification can never be totally congruent with either set of values" (ibid., p. 125). This humorous construction does not confirm one set of values, but undercuts both, setting them off against each other and rendering each inadequate.

In MOTIVE TO MURDER, this division is reinstituted in the form of a generation gap between the older suspects, who are interrogated first (including the lodger, Moshe Harpaz, and a businessman, Shlomo Sh'hori), and the younger ones who arrive later (including the roguish Yerach Halperin, and the naïve clerk, Ze'evik Ashkenazi). The first group, dressed in white shirts and suits, is identified with Oring's immigrant qualities. To some degree, the connection to immigration is established by the father, Dr. Hausdorf, who has a heavy foreign accent, European manners, and a constant preoccupation with classical music, a chess set, cigars, and liquor – thereby constituting the ultimate immigrant. The suspects, on the other hand, are identified with the values mentioned above, but not as immigrants (although repeated references to Harpaz's original name suggest that he was also an immigrant). The second group of younger men, in colourful shirts and sandals, are identified with the native values.

Both groups are distinguished by their use of language (literary vs. slang), and each character displays attributes from the associated repertoire. They are confronted with alternative values, but never by confronting each other. Harpaz's overstressed literary language is countered by the police sergeant's slang. Sh'hori's pretence of civility is overturned by Naomi's open insolence (in the flashback), and the detective's direct inquiries (in the "present"). Within his flashback, Ze'evik is seen talking to Dr. Housdorf. During this dialogue, which is made up of close-ups, the former's boorish and primitive nature is contrasted with the latter's exaggeratedly cultured habits. Furthermore, Yerach's display of cheeky self-confidence during his first interrogation takes place in Dr. Hausdorf's music corner, the objects in which – a tapestry, a harp, a note stand, a chest with a decorative mantelpiece – contrast with his unrefined performance, creating a discrepancy between figure and environment.

In presenting these sets of qualities, the film departs from the affective scope of the crime thriller. When the characters display dishonesty and aggression, they attract the suspicion which is typical of the genre, but their association with immigrant/native qualities makes them objects of mockery, in the humorous tradition of the *Chizbat*. The comic effect comes out most fully in the interrogations of Moshe Harpaz and Yerach Halperin, during which the sergeant serves as an agent of the comedy.

Harpaz's first testimony depicts both himself and the victim in socially acceptable colours. After his police record as a Peeping Tom is brought to light, he is interrogated again under duress by the sergeant. The scene offers no new information, and its sole function is to bring about a change: as a result of the sergeant's assault on Harpaz's pretence of respectability, his gestures and speech become irritated, and he is exposed, not as a villain, but as a character in the comic sketch tradition performed on Israeli stages since the 1920s. This association is complete by the end of the interrogation, when he delivers the punchline:

> "Mr Harpaz, I'm sick of hearing about your showers. Just tell me what you did after your last shower!"
> "Yes ... I dried myself."[1]

From this point onward Harpaz largely maintains his irritable gestures and tone of voice. He does not just provide the truth, the whole truth, and nothing but the truth. As a newly appointed jester, he uses his omnipresence as a Peeping Tom to expose facts which other characters try to conceal, and to confront them about their own morality.

Unlike Harpaz, Yerach is not forced into his comic role. His performance is comic from the outset, and his humour remains his stronghold. Though his comic act is constantly interrupted by the detective's lack of cooperation and the sergeant's hostility, he dominates the space around him with extravagant mimicry and gestures. Like Harpaz, he takes on the role of the jester, exposing truths and confronting other characters in moral terms. While the other suspects are revealed to have lied about some matter or other in relation to the victim and their own whereabouts, Yerach's account remains solid. Lest he be presented as a pillar of truth, however, his last piece of comedy undermines him, exposing him, too, as a fabricator and an exaggerator. In that scene, he brags to the sergeant of his exploits during a stay in Hamburg. Chewing a toothpick, rubbing his hands over his body, and bursting into laughter occasionally, he describes his sexual conquests. His less-than-seductive performance belies his self-portrayal as a Casanova. He boasts of having received golden watches, new suits, and "live crocodile" shoes from a beautiful German lover, while pointing to his naked arm, his simple shirt, and his bare feet, bringing down the sergeant's scorn.

---

[1] My translation. As a general rule for film quotes in this book, when no translation was available, as is the case with MOTIVE TO MURDER, translations of dialog are my own. In cases in which a translation was available, it was used, and at times slightly modified in order to more accurately reflect the original Hebrew.

Paradoxically, Yerach's dignity, like Harpaz's, is both enhanced and undercut by his comic performance. As jesters, they tell "truths" and ridicule others, while at the same time serving as targets of ridicule. Their performance boosts their dominance on the screen and prevents the audience from viewing them with esteem. In this respect, they embody the comic principle described in section 7.2. As subjectivities, they present both a subjugation to the investigators and the viewer's scorn which demeans them, and a rebellious independence which elevates their cinematic presence.

The Boudoir: Eros Disarmed and the Question of Female Promiscuity

In the scene described above – where the denigration of Yerach reaches its peak – the point of the comedy is his delusional self-image: what Yerach lacks is not just material wealth, but erotic allure. It unravels after Yerach has delivered his anti-erotic performance in the bedroom. But the link between comedy and malfunctioning eroticism goes well beyond Yerach. It is at the very core of an entire process within the film. The murder investigation leads repeatedly back to an arena in which sexual performance is debased as a farce – motivated by malice, lacking in harmony, and ending in ridicule. As the comedy increases, the eroticism diminishes. Thalia disarms Eros.

There are four flashbacks from the suspects' perspectives, in which each reconstructs their encounter with Naomi. Through these scenes, her character and motivations are materialised and transformed. Although represented from different perspectives, they complement each other, forming a coherent narrative. Three are sex scenes, and sex therefore becomes an essential part of the investigation. A source of secrets and the basis for the victim's "dirty" games, sex provides the investigators with their main line of inquiry.

A dominant factor is that Naomi had more than one lover. This is certainly not the first or last time in Israeli cinema that a female figure is shown with several male partners. Such situations were hinted at in films from the 1950s, and became more conspicuous in the 1960s. In BLAZING SAND and DALIA AND THE SAILORS, the female character is desired by several male counterparts. In THEY WERE TEN (1961, D: Baruch Dienar) and SABINA (1966, D: Peter Freistadt), the female character has a partner, but is coveted by others. Talmon comments on this pattern, which she labels "two men and the woman between them" (Talmon, 2001, p. 98). She sees it as a manifestation of the woman's objectification by a male collective (ibid., pp. 103–104). But this is not the pattern's inevitable effect. If anything, as in MOTIVE TO MURDER, the male characters often do not form a durable collective. In any case, Talmon's argument is that, when a woman fulfils a cultural or interpersonal function, she is objectified. Any depiction of a woman as "being-with", then, is objectification. By contrast, I argue that when a female figure is depicted as manifold and as an active, dominant character, as in MOTIVE TO MURDER, she is not objectified. Rather, she could be described as subjectified.

In MOTIVE TO MURDER, three suitors voice public condemnation of the promiscuous female character: the disappointed Harpaz ("I didn't lie in her filthy bed"; "Who would marry a girl ... like her?"), Sh'hori ("Aside from the payment, the difference between her and a common streetwalker was very small. The girl was dirty down to her soul"), and Yerach ("With her, one went to one place: to bed"; "[Ze'evik] was here ... ? Well done! ... He must have been at the end of the line, I didn't see him"). But the film's main source of authority, the detective in charge of the investigation, defies this judgement. A tall, middle-aged man, his tone of voice and posture convey authority and paternal gentleness. His gestures express his displeasure at each deprecating remark about Naomi, and he says only positive things about her ("Strange business ... a beautiful intelligent girl is murdered ... "). His judgements of the other participants are uniformly negative.

Beyond the moral amnesty granted to the film's sexually promiscuous female protagonist, the suitors' harsh words are undermined by Naomi's dominant performance in their flashbacks. She remains in audio-visual focus in each scene, and exerts control over the very suitors who condemn her. In more than one way, the demeaning social category in which convention seeks to pigeon-hole Naomi is transcended.

The Bedchamber: Sex Scenes

In her discussion of the pattern of multiple sexual partners in Israeli film, Talmon correctly associates it with a general disruption of the private sphere by the collective (Talmon, 2001, pp. 103–104). In MOTIVE TO MURDER, this is manifested not only by the multiple male participants, but by the constant presence of Naomi's father, Dr. Hausdorf – an unwilling witness. The main revelation of the flashbacks is that the performances are deliberately designed to intrude on him. This comes to light gradually, as does their farcical nature.

At almost nine minutes, the first flashback is the longest, and contains several modal shifts determined by Naomi's performance. It is told from the perspective of Sh'hori, the least comic figure, and does not begin comically, but as a subtle seduction scene. Naomi and Sh'hori stroll along a suburban street to the house, close to each other, but still maintaining distance. She gently convinces him to enter the house.

Inside, in the father's presence, the mood changes. Naomi becomes increasingly verbally abusive to him. Her expression darkens, having been open and bright, and expresses mockery and scorn. With her back to her father part of the time, she repeatedly interrupts the polite conversation between him and the suitor. Their civility stands in sharp contrast to her insolence.

Everything that earlier provided sexual undertones – harmony, implicitness, playfulness – has vanished. The sexual tension now revolves around the fact that the courtship takes place behind the old man's back – a farcical frame of reference. Vulgarity is at play. The sexual gestures become more direct. The two grope each other and steal kisses. Naomi entices Sh'hori and pushes him away. She smiles, holding her tongue between her teeth, and then laughs loudly as she evades him.

When it is time to consummate the relationship, Naomi sends her father out of the house. Sh'hori, who stands up to bid him farewell, remains with a wondering gaze in the middle of the frame. Entering from the side, Naomi extinguishes her cigarette and turns Sh'hori towards her. They kiss, embracing ever tighter as the camera moves from medium shot to close-up. In this synchronised movement, Sh'hori is passive and Naomi active. The end of the sexual act is signified by the record on the gramophone coming to an end. Naomi appears again, lying on her belly, covered by the sheet, with a soft expression on her face and a cigarette in her hand. She is not only the active party, having initiated the act, but is the one gratified by it. She is alone in the frame, implying that her bliss is not related to any spiritual or physical proximity to her partner.

Her alienation continues to take farcical form, now directed at Sh'hori. She alternates between looking at him mockingly and making playful gestures, stroking him with her foot and kicking him gently. At the sound of a whistle, she turns her head and begins to whistle back at someone through the bedroom window. She swiftly sends her new lover on his way, deflecting his attempt at a passionate embrace with a light kiss. She smiles at him, but behind his back her expression is stern.

At the beginning of the flashback, Naomi was a lady, but by its end the farce has transformed her into an adolescent. It has not yet taken possession of the sexual act itself – which is all passion and pleasure, having been suggested by a subtle seduction, materialised in a passionate embrace, and ended with her pensive expression. Sex is influenced by aggression laced with farce, turned against the father in the pre-coital stage and against the lover in the post-coital one – simultaneously determining, tainting, and enflaming the sexual act. For now, it is not an integral part of it. Later in the film this will no longer be the case. The erotic undertones vanish, the sexual act becomes a farce, and the viewer experiences a process of deterioration.

In parallel, the comic aspect intensifies. In the first flashback the comedy is unanticipated, as are the cruel, disturbing, and decidedly un-funny relations between daughter and father. In the second flashback and the second (unsuccessful) sex scene, however, the viewer is in on the joke from the beginning. The male participant, Harpaz, has already become comical. His last shred of dignity vanishes during the scene, even before Naomi enters.

Harpaz appears on his bed, barefoot, his shirt half unbuttoned and his sleeves rolled up, looking at pornographic images of a woman in a crumpled magazine. His expression as he presses his lips with lust and satisfaction is the most vivid yet. This character, who stated just before the flashback that he is over fifty, acts like an adolescent. He quickly hides the magazine under the pillow when Naomi knocks at the door. During a banal exchange, she repeats many of the gestures from Sh'hori's flashback. But in this scene, which is almost half the length of the previous one, the gestures lack their earlier, orderly temporal and logical progression: in a short span, Naomi puts on a bright smile, glances behind her, bites and licks her lips, smiles with her tongue between her teeth, and gestures playfully at him with her legs. Such gestures are stripped of their previous erotic plausibility, and signify only comedy.

Mostly shown at the edge of the frame, Harpaz plays his part through increasingly irritated and excited passivity. When he finally reacts actively to Naomi's solicitation, he rapidly becomes forceful, attempting to pin her down. His aggressiveness is an escalation of Sh'hori's passionate embrace. Naomi roars when Harpaz attacks her, bursting into laughter – something that transports the whole act to the realm of the ludicrous.

He chases her as she runs out of the room and down the hallway. She ends the chase by the side of the gramophone, behind her father, who greets Harpaz. The latter refrains from entering, remaining at the end of the hall. Sh'hori entered the living room and was forced to listen to Dr. Hausdorf's apologetic monologue, whereas Harpaz only eavesdrops on the bitter conversation between father and daughter.

The scene functions independently, but its true effect lies in its correspondence with the previous sex scene. There are several parallels between them: Naomi's gestures, the act of seduction, the male figure's display of passion, and Dr. Hausdorf's presence at the end. Through these parallels, the second scene serves as a comic variation of the first, accentuating what the earlier scene revealed only partially and gradually: the lack of symmetry between Naomi and her suitors, the farcical nature of her sexual exploits, and their true addressee, her father. More importantly, it nullifies the erotic content of the earlier scene, something the viewer experiences as a decline.

The next sex scene, the fourth flashback, is from Yerach's perspective. At three minutes and forty-five seconds, it is the shortest of all. Its main section is structured as a comic sketch, based on what seems to be an improvisation by the two main participants – notable, given that the film's predominant acting style is theatrical.

The scene begins in bed, with Naomi and Yerach emerging from the sheets. Smiling, she expresses her dissatisfaction: she wants "attention" and "romance". The two then enact several parodies of conventional Israeli representations of eroticism.

The source of their parody is described in Ben-Ari's study of the suppression of the erotic in Israeli culture. As mentioned in chapter 3, Ben-Ari portrays the culture that developed in Israel during the ideological phase as essentially puritanical. An erotic vocabulary and forms of expression developed between the 1930s and 1970s in the cultural margins, through translated literature, popular light fiction, and medical and pseudo-medical texts (Ben-Ari, 2006, pp. 134–188). This domain was marginal, leading to conservative standards in light fiction: rarefied, outdated language, metaphors rather than direct expressions, and clichés and stereotypes (ibid., pp. 277–290). Medical guidebooks used a mixture of foreign terminology, Biblical and Talmudic expressions, linguistic innovations, and literary quotations (ibid., pp. 293–312). This is the repertoire Yerach and Naomi explore.

His hairy chest exposed, Yerach begins with a variation of a Biblical phrase from the Song of Songs, well known as the earliest Hebrew source of erotica. However, the phrase he chooses and his performance lack any sensuality: "What shall we do to our sister who hath no breasts?" "We shall give her hormones", retorts Naomi, drawing from the medical lexicon.

Naomi, on the pretence of showing Yerach how things should be done, presents a literary cliché, speaking low and precisely: "I am an empty vessel, fill me!" "Madam, I'm the National Water Carrier – without water", Yerach responds, extending the metaphor to the domain of national engineering and eradicating any eroticism.[2] The parody doesn't stop at the verbal level. They proceed to satirise cinematic representation of the passionate sex scene. As Naomi leans over Yerach for a kiss, his eyes are appropriately soft, but his mouth rebels: he shows his teeth and grimaces. Naomi, too, repeatedly interrupts her enactment of passion with winks.

---

[2] The National Water Carrier, a monumental project for carrying water from the Jordan River to southern Israel, was completed in 1964.

Figure 1: The decline of eroticism in MOTIVE TO MURDER: Naomi with Sh'hori, Harpaz and Yerach.

In the earlier sex scenes, such farce targeted enticement and desire. Here, the "thing" itself – or rather its depiction – is the focus. Lacking appropriate means, and with inappropriate means readily available, the sex in this final exposition is kept non-erotic and therefore barren. This is done with glee, and is celebrated rather than bemoaned. In the earlier scenes, the farce remained specific to the characters, but here the constant use of cultural codes and conventions makes the figures and their refusal or failure to produce eroticism representative of something larger: a cultural lacuna, a shared deficiency.

As Ben-Ari demonstrates, a tradition of reference to inferior smut culture quickly developed in Israel. Humorous allusions were naturally a part of this (ibid., pp. 163–167). But comic sex scenes of the period did not often allow for such cultural references: each comic figure entered the sex scene on its own terms, lacking obvious intertextuality. Yet the result was always the same, and therefore repetitive. As a general rule, the incorporation of comedy and sex was a sign of the decline of eroticism.

In the tradition of Jewish comedy, this deficit arises from the male character's naivety, his lack of basic knowledge. In THE FLYING MATCHMAKER (1966, D: Israel Becker), based on one of the earliest Yiddish plays, the naive limping male is taken aback by a sophisticated woman's advances, and becomes so enraged that he attempts to flee town. A POUND A PIECE (1963, D: Yoram Gross) and GIRLS' PARADISE EILAT (1964, D: Nathan Axelrod and Leo Filler) each transpose this structure to a contemporary frame. In the first, a vagabond misunderstands a housewife's aggressive advances. In the second, a resident of Eilat lands in a cheap hotel in Tel Aviv, and escapes when he realises it is a brothel.

Heartthrobs like Yaron Zinder, a side-character in the comedy 999 ALIZA THE POLICEMAN, and the comic protagonist of ERVINKA (1967, D: Ephraim Kishon), deserve closer attention, because they appear at first sight to overcome the traditional divide, combining eroticism and comedy. Nonetheless, their erotic charms serve as a basis for parody.

Zinder is repeatedly shown in passionate embrace with two different women. The other characters frequently recount his nonexclusive sexual exploits. He becomes so synonymous with erotic appeal that, when the film's protagonist, Aliza the cleaning woman, has a short scuffle with him, she treasures it as an erotic experience.

The sexual magnetism of Ervinka, who is not as conventionally handsome as Zinder, is made tangible by even more exaggerated compositional means. As a magnet for women, he is shown generating desire wherever he goes, caressing and kissing any woman within reach of the frame. His presence engenders various forms of sensual ecstasy in the women he meets. All this is deflated when Ervinka reaches the intimate sphere of his dilapidated home. For the benefit of his next-door neighbours, an infuriated husband and an enchanted wife, he vocally enacts a seduction scene, pretending to seduce a young woman he has brought home for the first time. At the same time, he physically enacts his own fantasy, winning the lottery and shaking hands with the lottery representative. Both are suddenly interrupted by the peeved woman who had been waiting for him in bed all along. His eroticism remains a fantasy, and does not amount to a concrete sexual act with an available partner.

With a woman at his side in the next scene, Ervinka dreams of winning the lottery. Swaying in elation, he greets, hugs, and kisses all the film's characters. This all-embracing fantasy reflects something fundamental, visualised by a character who is never alone and possesses no private sphere. The scene of Ervinka's homecoming expresses exactly this extreme breach of privacy: he is the product of constant existence in a shared space.

Zinder, too, exists in a public sphere, without any real possibility of retreating into the private. He is constantly fending off public attention to his

Figure 2: Two comic variations: The naïve vagabond in A POUND A PIECE and the heartthrob in ERVINKA.

deeds by sneaking around, hiding, making excuses, and instigating extravagant brawls. His home is not a sanctuary. In the course of the film it is invaded by a police sergeant, lead by a female associate who quite clearly knows her way around the apartment. They are met by a housekeeper, also well informed about everything that takes place there.

Ervinka and Zinder are not the only ones constantly within the public sphere. The same is true for the characters in Girls' Paradise Eilat, A Pound a Piece, and The Flying Matchmaker. Whatever the pretext for these characters' lack of erotic fulfilment, they always combine it with the disarming effect of a comic figure, and with a chronic lack of private space.

Returning to Motive to Murder, and to the fourth flashback in particular: it is not incidental that this scene, which marks a comic turn, has the least privacy and the greatest number of intrusions. Unlike in comedies, however, intrusion terminates the laughter. During the exchange between Naomi and Yerach, the camera cuts twice to the morose father in the living room. Sh'hori furiously barges into the bedroom, shouting. The tone becomes increasingly serious. Yerach retreats after Naomi rejects his efforts to protect her from Sh'hori's fury. A drunk, staggering Dr. Hausdorf collapses into his arms in the hall, and Naomi orders him gravely to leave her father alone.

On the Veranda: The Meaning of a Damaged Private Sphere

All three sex scenes in Motive to Murder end solemnly. Merriment and sex mask the true essence of what "in fact" takes place in the film, and what "in fact" motivates Naomi's character. The key is in the third flashback, which involves neither sex nor comedy.

It is recalled by Ze'evik, the only suspect/witness without a sexual relationship with Naomi. Comedy in the scene is restricted to a few self-deprecating comments by Ze'evik about his academic failures. Naomi, for once, does not dominate the sequence. The longer part of the scene is dedicated to Ze'evik's cheerful interaction with Dr. Hausdorf. With no humour or sex to serve her as weapons, Naomi barges in on them angrily, and then runs back to her room. What follows is the longest of a very few moments in the film where a character is shown alone in a room. For twenty seconds, we observe Naomi in medium close-up, weeping. The viewer understands that, behind the comedy, sex, and cruelty, there is only pain and distress.

Motive to Murder employs comic figures, blending them with an acute sense of cruelty and suffering. It explores the Israeli phenomenon of self-recrimination in the aftermath of the Holocaust. But to reduce the film's content to that theme alone would render excessive all that I described above: the violation of the private sphere, the irruption of comedy, and the consequent decline of eroticism. As in contemporary comedy, these elements mount an assault on individual coherence. What comedy presents more softly is accentuated in a crime thriller: in both genres, the viewer is confronted with a ruptured individual space, dominated by dissonance.

These elements are consistent enough to act as seismographs. The level of cruelty in a comedy, the degradation of the private sphere, and the debasement of eroticism are indicators of the acuteness of the phenomenon discussed in section 7.1: unresolved cultural uncertainties about the boundaries between private and public. As I show in chapters 15 and 16, the rise of these features in films from the 1970s affectively articulates continuing paradoxes over relations between individual and society in Israel.

11 "We Are Both Crippled": Victimhood, Status, and Sex in Dramas and Melodramas

> Look! Acting out a scene of lovemaking on the stage isn't the problem. You get used to that. But to talk like this about the Holocaust, after it happened to a large part of your family, and to identify with that part – that's embarrassing! (Gideon Shemer, actor, in an interview 1965)[1]

I now leave the sphere of comedy for that of drama and melodrama, and the figure of the victim. But this is not entirely unknown territory, for the victim shares common ground with the comic figure.

Having examined damage to the private sphere and the debasement of eroticism in the comedy of the 1960s, I now examine these themes in relation to the role and representation of sex in melodramas and dramas of the same period. I show that the cultural association of loss and suffering with individual validation is translated, in Israeli cinema, into the eroticisation of the victim. In all the films I discuss in this chapter, this is manifested through the accentuation of the physical presence and cinematic centrality of figures that are subjected to danger, pain, loss, and death. I demonstrate how attractiveness, sensuality, and even erotic fulfilment are constructed as intrinsic to the essence of the victim.

11.1 THE DYBBUK and FORTUNA – Me Against Us: Victims of the Community

The least complex variation of victimhood comes in films where the individual's position is contrasted that of the community. One example is THE DYBBUK, a German-Israeli television co-production. The film is an adaptation of the Russian/Yiddish play from 1913–20 which was foundational for modern Jewish theatre (Konigsberg, 1997, pp. 23–24). It tells the story of the love between Chanan, a young Talmudic scholar, and Leah'le, the daughter of a rich merchant. When Leah's father arranges her marriage to another man, Chanan dies suddenly. On her wedding day, his spirit possesses her. It transpires that they were promised to one another by their fathers before their birth. Even after the matter is settled by a rabbinical court and the father pays for his wrongdoings, Chanan's spirit refuses to leave Leah'le, and she chooses to follow him into death.

---

[1] Bashan, 1965, my translation.

There are no sex scenes in the original play, and none were added in the 1968 production. In every other respect, however, the adaptation sexualises the story. In the beginning of the film, the two are shown looking at each other longingly in the synagogue. Leah'le kisses the velvet curtain in sensual intoxication. Later, when Chanan turns into a spirit, his physical presence is accentuated – unlike in the original play, where he had no physical presence at all, and could only be experienced through the possessed Leah'le. Traditionally, Leah'le appears aloof during the possession, "pale as a ghost" and speaking in a monotone.[2] This matches popular depictions of ghosts as ethereal. In the 1968 film, Chanan, as a spirit, appears in superimposition, in a space of his own. His lips do not move, but his voice is heard. He is not pale, is sweating visibly, and his eyes and rich voice are piercing. The couple's sensuality is contrasted with a grotesque depiction of tradition and community, expressed in the play's only moment of celebration. On the eve of her wedding, Leah'le's family offers a charity meal for the poor of the community. The beggars lead the bride in a dance. In the film, the beggars are particularly hideous. Their dance becomes wilder and wilder, spinning into violence, and Leah'le, unprotected, is overwhelmed.[3]

A similar dynamic occurs in FORTUNA (1966, D: Menahem Golan), which, unlike THE DYBBUK, takes place in a contemporary setting: the town of Dimona, in southern Israel. The film features a patriarchal immigrant family from Algeria. It revolves around a forbidden affair between the youngest daughter, Fortuna, and a non-Jewish French engineer, Pierre, who works for the factory where the men of the family are employed. This gentile lover is unacceptable to Fortuna's family; in any case, they object to any attachment on her part, as she has been betrothed to one Monsieur Simon, from Paris, since early childhood. The father and brothers attempt to kill Pierre. Fortuna is punished. When her groom-to-be arrives, he turns out to be as old as her father. During the engagement celebrations, Fortuna escapes and rides away with Pierre in his Jeep. Her brother Chaim chases them, and in the ensuing car duel between the two men, Fortuna is killed.

In her first medium close-up during the credits, Fortuna, a young, dark beauty, lightly caresses herself and slips off her shoulder strap. From that moment onward until much later in the film, Fortuna personifies erotic allure in every shot she appears in, whether bathing, laughing, dancing, running, walking or standing – what Laura Mulvey calls "to-be-looked-at-ness" (Mulvey, 1985

---

[2] This applies to any prominent production of the play, like the Polish film directed by Michal Waszynski (1937), or the Bimah theatre group's production from 1922, which lasted over a thousand runs.
[3] Salcia Landmann criticises the film's interpretation of this scene (Landmann, 1989, p. 137).

(1975), p. 309). Pierre's slim muscular body is also tangible to the viewer in the many scenes showing him in action. When the two come together – first in the desert, and then by a waterfall – they kiss passionately, in the type of imagery satirised by Naomi and Yerach in MOTIVE TO MURDER. The two figures' mutual immersion intensifies their erotic magnetism.[4] Fortuna's loss of virginity is hinted at in the desert scene: the camera focuses on her shoulder strap, which tears against the bark of a tree as the couple sinks to the ground. Otherwise, the sexual act is not present visually or metaphorically, and the scene revolves primarily around the exposure of two attractive bodies to the viewer.

Figure 3: The young couple immersed in passion in FORTUNA.

Beside Fortuna and Pierre, Chaim is also displayed in a way that emphasises his slim, muscular physique. He is as tall as Pierre, and his laughter resembles Fortuna's – all things which fuel incestuous undercurrents throughout the film. Chaim is jealous for his sister and antagonistic towards Pierre. In several scenes, the two siblings are shown in physical proximity which hints lightly at sexual attachment. This escalates at the end of the film, when Chaim holds Fortuna's dead body in agony and nearly kisses her lips.

This incestuous jealousy remains ambiguous. But the result of Fortuna's forbidden affair with a foreigner is quite clear: an attack on her eroticism. The family punishes her by cutting her hair. But the true antidote to erotic charm

---

4 Shohat draws an analogy between the sensuality of the lovemaking scene in the waterfall and SPLENDOR IN THE GRASS (1961, D: Elia Kazan) (Shohat, 1989, p. 159).

comes in the form of Fortuna's flabby, balding, aging fiancé – who, to top it off, informs the family that he lives in Marseilles, not Paris. The engagement party is designed to stimulate disgust, not just through the image of the drunken groom forcing his bride to dance, but through that of a celebrating community. The camera lingers on older people, a row of women spitting shells of sunflower seeds onto the floor, and men dancing, staggering drunkenly, and spilling bottles of arak. An obese man is placed in the front of the room and a dwarf at the back, lending the scene circus-like proportions.[5] With fast-paced editing, these images are integrated those of the struggling newlyweds and the room spinning, heralding Fortuna's imminent escape. FORTUNA and THE DYBBUK maintain the same pattern. The protagonists are distinguished by their physical presence and erotic allure. Their community and family victimise them by suppressing their "natural" erotic choices. Finally, the act of suppression is accompanied by the repulsive spectacle of the community, which counters their eroticism. Since the suppression is external, the victims do not lose their erotic charm as they do in comedies. They only lose their lives.

11.2 Is TEL AVIV BURNING? and EVERY BASTARD A KING – Us Against It: The Victim in the Community

In FORTUNA and THE DYBBUK, victimhood is directly linked to the suppression of individual desire by the community. But even when the concept of victimhood surpasses this frame of reference, and when death, loss and destruction result from something other than the communal suppression of desire, the enactment of social intrusion and the erotic intensification of the victim continue to play a role. We find a variation of this in war films, where both community and individual are threatened by military conflict.

Is TEL AVIV BURNING? (1967, D: Kobi Jaeger) was the first film to portray the events of the Six-Day War. One of the four narratives interwoven into the film revolves around a young couple, Nahum and Rachel. Throughout much of the

---

[5] As a whole, despite the pointed use of ultra-popular artists playing Mediterranean music, the festivities of a North-African family are represented as the peak of vulgarity. Moreover, the family members are depicted as impulsive and hot-blooded on the one hand, and fanatically conservative on the other. They are shamefully uneducated, and yet maintain socially dominance through scheming and manipulation. Considering all this, it seems that the public protests after the release of this film were justified. These are described by Shohat in the Hebrew addition to her book (Shohat, 1991, p. 158–159).

film, before the war, they lie naked in bed, close to one another, talking about their lives, their thoughts, and their plans for the future. These scenes do not contain sexual acts, but their relaxed intimacy implies that they are indeed intimate with one another, before or after – possibly both before and after – they appear on the screen.

As the war begins, Nahum joins the military. The film follows him as he tries to supply his comrades with a case of drinks, during which he nearly gets killed. The inanity of this close call denies Nahum an aura of heroism – a last-minute hindrance that prevents him from becoming a victim. This joins the film's more general diminution of the pathos of war films and melodramas. The idea of Nahum's near-death nonetheless remains central to this strand of the narrative, as his attempt to contact Rachel fails and she is wrongly informed that he has been killed.

The extended scenes in which Nahum is seen bare-skinned and physically close to his spouse, retrospectively support his position as a potential victim. The couple's intertwined bodies set the stage for Nahum's death and Rachel's loss. In Bataille's words: "Mortal anguish does not necessarily make for sensual pleasure, but that pleasure is more deeply felt during mortal anguish" (Bataille, 1962 (1957), p. 105, quoted in Williams, 2008, p. 207). In Is Tel Aviv Burning? this sensuality is granted not to those who die, but to the one who, arbitrarily, survives.

The arbitrariness of death and the survival of the victim were particularly relevant during the Six-Day War. The public atmosphere in Israel during the "waiting period", on the brink of war, was one of anxiety and panic. People anticipated that things would end badly. The swift victory that followed brought a general sense of euphoria and jubilation – an expression of relief that the worst, in fact, didn't materialise (Bregman, 2000, pp. 51–61). No wonder that last-ditch survival and the arbitrariness of death also play a role in Every Bastard a King, the most renowned film portrayal of the Six-Day War. A long sequence shows the survival and rescue of a soldier left on his own to fight a lost battle, and the film ends with the futile death of an American journalist after Israel's victory.

In this context, the sense of individual victimhood perfectly matches that of communal and national victimhood. It is not the community that intrudes so much as harsh communal circumstances. In principle, there is no deviation here from the Biblical archetypes of the book of Genesis: the binding of Isaac and the expulsion of Ismael, discussed in relation to the victim type figure in section 7.2. In both those narratives, the death that threatens the child seems arbitrary, a manifestation of inexplicable cruelty. In both, salvation occurs at the last moment. Through the children's rescue, the promise of a national future is attained. The soldier's rescue in the two films does not carry such a direct outcome, but the very enactment of their survival personifies national salvation.

11.3 Eldorado

No Place for Me: Space and Intrusion

Even before the Six-Day War, ELDORADO presented Israeli audiences with a protagonist as a potential victim who barely survives. This was also one of the first films to include sex scenes. The film largely takes place in a section of Jaffa popularly referred to as *Hashetah Hagadol*, the "Large Area". This suffered severe damage during the Israeli War of Independence, and was considered a hotspot for crime in the 1950s and 1960s.[6] The protagonist, Binyamin Sherman, is a former criminal, just released from prison, who must constantly contend with the authorities. It is significant that the portrayal of a marginal protagonist from a delinquent milieu helped form patterns later applied to the national ethos.

ELDORADO reproduces the absence of private space. The streets, alleys, and ruins of the Large Area are woven into a labyrinth in which the characters constantly follow each other, or else hide. The private sphere does not provide a refuge from the public one. The main protagonist's shabby dwellings are almost completely transparent to the world, and are often penetrated by unexpected visitors. Inside the apartment, the characters are observed and overheard by others lurking outside. Through this careful choreography of movement and settings, the space in Jaffa becomes enclosed and confining.

Neighbouring Tel Aviv presents an alternative. At one point, two small-time criminals and a beggar marvel at its skyline from afar. Later on, its public spaces are integrated into a musical sequence depicting the main character's day out – a cinematic manifestation of freedom and open space. Tel Aviv holds the promise of liberty. But the public sphere in Tel Aviv becomes just as claustrophobic and transparent as that of Jaffa. Members of the Large Area's criminal milieu observe each other there. In one scene, the main protagonist attends a society party and

---

[6] In the opening credits of ELDORADO, a caption assures the viewer that the film reflects the earlier state of the Large Area, before it was rehabilitated by the Governmental Urban Society for the Development of the Old City of Jaffa. Within two years, by 1965, this society had indeed completed a process of renovating and gentrifying the area.

becomes the central attraction: he is looked at, talked about, and finally provoked into a brawl.

It's All About Me: Male Spectacle

In ELDORADO, the construction of intrusion and the absence of a private sphere are closely related to the staging of the individual as the centre of attention. Sherman is the target of both positive and negative attention, and the viewer is first invited to observe the former. During the opening credits, he walks along the coastal road to Jaffa as the theme music plays. He walks, skips, and runs, giving a sense of his fitness and vitality. He continues to dominate the frame in an extreme long shot, even while his body occupies only a fraction of the frame. Approaching the market and alleys of Jaffa, multiple shots show Sherman being greeted by crowds of people. Their attention establishes his persona as a star.

This introduction matches Paul Willemen's description of the male spectacle in Anthony Mann's films, often quoted as a prototype in academic discussions of male cinematic eroticism: "The viewer's experience is predicated on the pleasure of seeing the male 'exist' (that is walk, move, ride, fight), in or through the cityscape, landscape, or, more abstractly, history" (Willemen, 1981, p. 16). Willemen also described a subsequent "unquiet pleasure of seeing the male mutilated" (ibid.). The question arises whether Sherman's cinematic figure subscribes to this popular paradigm. Indeed, sixty-seven minutes into the film, the viewer sees him overwhelmed and beaten by thugs. However, Sherman's body is never genuinely mortified in front of the camera. Through most of the scuffle Sherman maintains the upper hand. When beaten up, his body is obscured by the assailants or left out of the frame. He then lies, passive and defeated, at the lower part of the screen as Margo the prostitute tends to him. During this segment it is her body rather than his that is put on display. The "unquiet pleasure" of a sadistic spectacle is hardly granted to the viewer. I argue that a different pattern is at play here, one by which Sherman – the star, the bearer of eroticism – is endowed with the role of the victim.

However, before I demonstrate how victimhood and eroticism correspond in ELDORADO, some attention is owed to the tradition of academic discourse on the erotic spectacle of masculinity. This particular discussion followed discourse on female spectacle in the 1970s, and proliferated in the 1980s and 1990s. As in earlier discourse, the participants focused on the varying identities of the viewers and on the axes of male-female and heterosexual-homosexual. What complicated the discussion from the outset was that it began with a denial of its core element: the male's role as a sex object. This resulted from the principles outlined by Mulvey, a pioneer in the field. As Peter Lehman notes:

> Laura Mulvey's work was primarily concerned with women and the representation of the female body, but it has strong implications for understanding the male body. For Mulvey the male did not serve an erotic function but served as an active point of identification [...] for both male and female spectators. (Lehman, 1993, p. 20)

The implication was that scholars theoretically interested in erotic male spectacle often resorted to the claim that this objectification was suppressed, or nonexistent.[7] Another way to overcome the gap between the male sex object and his hypothetical absence was to point out the effeminising effects of the spectacle on the cinematic figure.[8] Subsequent academic discussion turned energetically around the affirmation and disavowal of these assertions. In any case, suppression and feminisation constitute only a small fraction of an array of sexual pathologies which the male erotic spectacle had come to be associated with. This, too, is the inheritance of the discourse of female spectacle, which was rooted in psycho-semiotics. Typically of the 1980s, Steve Neale, for instance, diagnoses the viewer of the male erotic spectacle with narcissistic identification laced with the threat of symbolic castration, and an alternation between repressed homosexual voyeurism, which involves sadomasochistic fantasies, and fetishistic scopophilia (Neale, 1983, pp. 4–14). Writing a decade later, Paul Smith attempted to break loose from many of the assumptions of this paradigm, introducing an alternative in the spirit of the 1990s – one that is nonetheless just as pathological. On the assumption that eroticisation and destruction are interrelated, and that "the destructibility of the male body is to be grasped as a masochistic trope" (Smith, 1993, pp. 156–157), he focuses on the (action) film figure rather than the viewer, and accordingly shifts the diagnosis from the sadistic to the masochistic/exhibitionist potential of objectification (ibid., pp. 155–159). Smith denies the subversive value of masochism as a perversion (ibid., p. 164), and claims that the male masochist serves and obeys "the phallic law" (ibid., p. 166). The "masochistic trope" is temporary (ibid., p. 162), and is part of the film figure's progression "from eroticization, through destruction, to re-emergence and regeneration" (ibid., p. 156). Masochism serves masculinity in a "struggle to maintain in a pleasurable tension the stage of

---

[7] An example of the former is given by Steve Neale, discussed below (Neale, 1983). An example of the latter is given by Richard Dyer (Dyer, 1982).
[8] Peter Lehman and Paul Smith both provide a historical summary of the discussion and challenge the hypotheses of suppression and feminisation (Lehman, 1993, pp. 20–23; Smith, 1993, pp. 151–169).

symbolic relations to the father" (ibid., p. 166). And while "[the] male access to control is marked as a symbolic or metaphorical matter, a process of forgetting the body" (ibid., p. 168), the physical then re-emerges in male hysterical excess (ibid., pp. 170–171).

The two case studies mentioned above well represent how the sadomasochistic paradigm of viewer-film figure relations had served since the 1970s as a fertile basis for endless film analyses – or, rather, diagnoses which make heavy use of pathological language.[9] As Peter Lehman observes: "The history of psychoanalytic film theory is as much, if not more, a history of misreading Freud and Lacan as it is of reading them" (Lehman, 1993, p. 34). Lehman also points out that, beyond Freud and Lacan, there is a vast psychoanalytic literature on the issues in question which is seldom referred to (ibid.). Moreover, the true weakness of most psycho-semiotic theories is their dependence on assumptions drawn from psychoanalysis. If those are proven wrong, the whole model topples (ibid., p. 32). If we accept that Sherman attracts the erotic but not the sadistic gaze, both the models of Neale and Smith become inoperative.[10] Since all figures I discuss in this segment are eroticised on the one hand, and placed in danger on the other, it would be tempting to adopt the very effective assumption that an intrinsically sadistic gaze is cast on the male erotic spectacle. I claim, however, that this obscures the alternative viewing practices the films offer.

Discovering those practices hinges not only on the assumption that erotica may exist outside the sado-masochistic axis, but also that it is universal and non-exclusive, that "all men and women are in some way objectified in the cinema", and "while watching the movie everyone is looking at representations of bodies in ways that include, but are not limited to, objectification" (ibid., p. 21). Eroticism, therefore, may be evoked independently and be associated with all possible cultural contexts.

Essentially, the eroticism manifested by the films I discuss in this chapter is evoked through various cinematic means, but it is repeatedly associated with a common cultural denominator: the characters' potential and actual victimhood. Chanan and Lea'le in THE DYBBUK, Fortuna and Pierre in FORTUNA, Nachum and

---

9 There are a few exceptions to this practice, which nonetheless prove its dominance: Richard Dyer, for instance, avoids all psychoanalytic vocabulary, but still adopts the sadistic paradigm (Dyer, 1993). Williams uses such language extensively, but introduces a whole different paradigm (Williams, 1991). Gaylyn Studlar discusses male eroticism, and avoids both psychoanalytic vocabulary and the sado-masochistic paradigm – but we sense their echo in her conscious effort to present an alternative (Studlar, 1993).

10 Lehman challenges Neale's theory on this point (Lehman, 1993, p. 32).

Rachel in IS TEL AVIV BURNING? are all depicted with heightened sensuality and eroticism, and they all suffer loss. The sadistic gaze is not involved in this bond between eroticism and victimhood. Instead, eroticism and victimhood enhance each other. Danger elevates each of these film characters; this elevation justifies enhanced eroticism; and this in turn makes the sense of their loss more poignant. This is also the case with Sherman, his companions, and the rest of the characters discussed here.[11]

Poor Me: Victimhood Stardom

As I have shown above, Sherman's stardom and erotic appeal are established during the credits in the beginning of the film. Even before that, however, his victimhood is determined during the opening sequence.

The film begins in a Tel Aviv courtroom, where Sherman is acquitted of murder for lack of evidence. As he is released from jail, Bugdanov, the police sergeant who assisted the prosecution, declares he will make sure that "Sherman pays". Sherman-Will-Pay turns out to be the protagonist's nickname,[12] and throughout the film the threat hangs over his head. He will pay for his neglectful upbringing; for his past crimes and mistakes; for the antagonism and sympathy he arouses; for his fame and infamy; and for his attempt to make it all better. He is in danger of failing in his attempt to rehabilitate, in danger of being falsely incriminated, and in danger of losing his life. Sherman is both a star and a

---

11 A WOMAN'S CASE (1969, D: Jacques Katmor) presents an exception to the cinematic rule outlined here. In the beginning of the film, the body of a beautiful young woman appears as it is being prepared for an autopsy. Through the rest of the film the woman is depicted on the day preceding her death, which she spends with the man who turns out to be her murderer. The camera is focused on her a great deal more than on her companion, and during the film variations of her sensuality unfold. The film refrains from the emotional affectation of using her sensuality to enhance the effect of her death, and vice-versa. Instead, it communicates sensually to the viewer the sadistic gaze attributed to the male protagonist. Long series of images appear to the sound of psychedelic rock music, in which female bodies are objectified, sexualised, constrained, subjugated, and suggestively positioned for imaginary acts of violence – although no act of violence is ever depicted. A WOMAN'S CASE does not lead the viewer to relate to the woman's victimhood, but rather to sense the tension between her dominance, movement, and "independence", and the sadistic gaze upon her. This tension is resolved at the end of the film, when she is strangled. Such dominant sadistic motifs are unique in Israeli film history.
12 The nickname is actually based on an expression that would have been well known to Israeli moviegoers in 1963: "Shulman will pay" (*Shulman yeshalem*), "it's on the house".

victim, something complemented by his permanent position as a target of interest. He is constantly followed by petty criminals and beggars. He is sought out by Bugdanov and the police; by his former partner Schneider, who wants to renew business and who fears betrayal; by his ex-girlfriend, the prostitute Margo, and his new flame, a legal assistant and lawyer's daughter, Naomi; by police sergeant Cohen, who believes he was wrongfully incriminated; and by his lawyer, who wants to sever Sherman's connection with his daughter. Many of these visits to Sherman are witnessed: both criminals and his respectable new employers see him with the police, while Margo, the beggars, and the petty criminals see him with Naomi, and Naomi's father sees him with Margo.

Sherman's star and victim persona are unified in his active willingness to "pick up the tab". As the film progresses, his inclination for self-sacrifice intensifies. Halfway through the film, it becomes clear that he stood trial for murder to cover up for the real perpetrator, Margo. He puts his reputation, health, and life in danger to keep other criminals safe from unsavoury dealings and from police raids. In the last action scene in the film, Sherman's self-sacrifice is manifested in a spectacle of his body. On a mission to warn a former smuggling partner, Moussa, he runs to Jaffa harbour. He gets caught up in a police raid, which risks incriminating him, and is chased by Schneider, who believes he has been betrayed. All through the sequence, Sherman runs, climbs, jumps, and swims – activities that accentuate his physique. His body is gradually exposed. He begins shirtless, later disposing of his jacket and shoes.

The climax of the sequence comes with the suggestion of Sherman's death: we hear gunshots and assume he has been hit. Seventy seconds go by before we learn of his survival and Bugdanov's death. Witnesses express anxious concern, and then relief when they hear he is still alive. Only then does Sherman appear – exposing his body one last time.

Gain and Loss: The Sex Scenes

Sherman's erotic allure materialises in this sequence through his motions as an action figure, but it is ultimately linked to the notion of his victimhood and possible loss. The association of his body with victimhood and loss begins early in the film, and serves as a dominant feature in his sex scenes with Naomi and Margo.

Sherman's affair with Naomi unfolds in the first half of the film. She first appears as an intruder, waiting for Sherman on his doorstep. This is the only scene in which she intrudes and he poses an implicit threat to her, placing his hands around her neck before they kiss. As they come to form a unity, all

Figure 4: The sensual victim: The eroticism of Sherman's body, in movement and action in ELDORADO.

intrusions, threats, and difficulties come from the "outside", from their respective environments. Sherman takes on the role of victim and Naomi that of saviour. Their second passionate kiss, for instance, occurs after a policeman calls in on Sherman in his home. Sherman is questioned as a suspect in a car theft, and is defended by Naomi. After the policeman leaves, an agitated Sherman expresses his frustration. Naomi consoles him with comforting words, and they embrace. Their next intimate scene also involves Sherman's troubles. It takes place on the beach in front of a hotel. Sherman's entry to the society party was unsuccessful. They lie on the sand, and Sherman talks about police persecution, and having never received trust or opportunities. Her manicured hand lightly strokes his face:

> "Nobody ever believed I could do any good. Not even one thing. They didn't even see me. They all have eyes of glass."
> "Do I have eyes of glass? [He shakes his head]"

This final exchange is sealed with a kiss. The camera captures them in long shot as they put their arms around each other. The next scene returns to the beach at dawn, where they have spent the night in their evening clothes. The ensuing sequence follows them through various locations in Tel Aviv, still wearing the same clothes, which are finally removed at the end of the sequence, at sunset. They are seen through the window in Sherman's apartment – first in long shot, dressed up and embracing, and later in extreme long shot in their undergarments. Until this point, the question of whether Sherman and Naomi had gone "all the way" has been left open. At the moment it becomes most obvious, the camera draws away, as though to leave the couple alone in their newly obtained, short-lived privacy. Sherman and Naomi's progression into intimacy is connected to the creation of a cinematic space free of intrusion. They possess the frame with their embraced bodies, and ultimately step out of the frame of social conventions to conquer Tel Aviv's public space and enact freedom. Their physical proximity is continually associated with Sherman's victimisation – a token of reparation for his afflictions.

In the second half of the film, contrasting dynamics occur between Sherman and Margo. Margo, like Sherman, is represented as the target of attention. Before appearing, she is described to a potential client by the small-time criminals as "the hottest chick in Jaffa". To confirm this, the viewer first sees her bare legs leaning against the wall, before the camera moves to reveal her in a negligée which accentuates her breasts. As she walks through the streets of Jaffa, she is followed by Schneider and the beggars, each proclaiming their affection for her. In her moment of sorrow, she sits in the bar and narrates the story of her downfall, stretching and gesturing at her legs and body – attracting

Figure 5: Sherman, the erotic target of Naomi's care and Margo's sense of loss in ELDORADO.

the gaze of every man present. In the encounters between Sherman and Margo, she, rather than he, is the victim, and her loss of Sherman becomes the central theme.

Margo follows Sherman in Jaffa and Tel Aviv, but their first direct exchange takes place fifty-one minutes into the film, when he finds her waiting for him in his apartment. This tête-à-tête is the reverse of the encounters between Sherman and Naomi. The latter manifested the creation of unity, whereas Sherman and Margo spiral into growing discord. The codes of communication change accordingly: they use slang, their intonation is exaggerated, they raise their voices, and she bursts into tears. He is increasingly aggressive towards her, pushes, grabs, and finally slaps her. With his growing aggression she becomes increasingly tender. She strokes his shoulder, then his chest and face, and finally holds him and lays her head on his chest, as she sobbingly confesses her love for him. Each time she touches him, his undershirt-clad upper body is put on display. The viewer witnesses her touching a body which is lost to her.

After Sherman is beaten unconscious by Schneider and his thugs, Margo rescues him from the bar and nurses him at his home. The sex scene which ensues upon his recovery is constructed as the exact aesthetic opposite to the scene with Naomi, with the viewer drawn closer rather than pushed away. The camera draws near as Sherman pulls Margo to him and she lightly bites her lips and bends over to kiss him. An extreme close-up of her cleavage is followed by an extreme close-up of his face as he returns her kiss. Another close-up captures his hand dropping a burning cigarette on the floor. The sex act itself remains out of sight, but unlike the previous sex scene, the camera returns to the couple after the cigarette on the floor has turned into ash. Her back bare, Margo lies over Sherman. She passes a cigarette between his lips and her own. Both their hands move, caressing one another. But this is not a display of bliss: according to Margo, Sherman stared at the ceiling with "eyes of glass" during sex. He is contemplating his other lover, and is not "with her" as he used to be, she concludes. The exposure of their bodies, their physical proximity, and the gestures of familiarity enhance a sense of intimacy which, at the same time, is declared gone. It extends the sense of loss present in Sherman's and Margo's first turbulent scene.

Like Sherman, Margo – a victim of him and her loss of him – evolves from victimhood to self-sacrifice, where the film ends. As Sherman performs his last spectacle, she invites her former rival, Naomi, to rescue him. In a final melodramatic gesture, she turns herself in to the police for the murder Sherman was accused of.

11.4 HE WALKED THROUGH THE FIELDS – Me Too: Following Sherman's Footsteps

Sherman and Margo are labelled marginal characters, outside the national ethos, but the melodramatic pathos invested in them, the accentuation of their physical presence, the enactment of their agony, and the active sacrifice each undergoes all place them within the framework of the Israeli victim figure. Parallels can easily be drawn with HE WALKED THROUGH THE FIELDS, based on a novel by the same name and once considered the epitome of the Israeli national ethos.[13] The film takes place in a kibbutz before the establishment of the State of Israel, and revolves around the youthful affair between Mika, an adolescent immigrant from Europe in the care of the kibbutz, and Uri, the kibbutz's first son.

Like Sherman, Uri returns home after having been away – in his case, at agricultural school. Like Sherman, the film begins with him walking back home through the landscape. Like Jaffa, the kibbutz is depicted as a transparent labyrinth in which the characters are in constant search of one another, and where encounters and interactions are witnessed and commented on. While Sherman lives in a hovel, Uri's home is a tent, similarly beset by unwanted visitors. Like Sherman, Uri faces a predicament which inhibits the stability he strives for. The problem is, however, of a different nature. Sherman struggles to rehabilitate in an environment that has always been harsh. Uri, on the other hand, confronts a changed reality. He returns to the kibbutz to be with his father, Willie, and become part of the community. Upon his return he encounters his mother, Ruth'ke, with her new boyfriend, and hears of his father's plan to leave for Europe on a national mission. His parents are neglectful. It is his father's girlfriend, not his mother, who leaves him a welcome note and chocolate on his bed. It is his mother's boyfriend, not his father, who asks him about his achievements at school.[14] The job he is assigned to by the kibbutz – overseeing the young immigrants at work in the fields – is hindered by their misbehaviour.

---

[13] See Schnitzer, 1994a, p. 81. The director of the film, Yosef Millo, was instrumental in popularising the novel and establishing its cultural status, by creating two stage productions of it in 1948 and in 1956. The film was his third and final adaptation, and was still popular with contemporary audience (Oren, 1967). According to Gertz, the mixture of "old" national values and "new" individualist ones distinguishes the film from the novel, demonstrating a change in communal values (Gertz, 1993, pp. 63–65).

[14] Talmon correctly recognises influences from American films of the 1950s in the representation of familial alienation and angry youth (Talmon, 2001, pp. 137–138).

Uri's growing frustration is expressed through a spectacle of motion which occurs twenty-five minutes into the film. In this scene, as his father leaves the kibbutz, he finds his mother's boyfriend loading a truck in the fields. Without a word he joins in loading the truck, breaking into sweat and taking off his shirt. Unlike Sherman, Uri's body, which is leaner, does not play a major role in this spectacle. Rather, the notion of movement does. The pace is set by the editing, which becomes faster and faster. Boxes are captured as they slide across the floor of the truck. Uri's movements become sharper, as do those of the mother's boyfriend, as he catches and then dodges the boxes thrown at him. Shots of both men from extreme angles indicate Uri's volatile state of mind. The segment, however, ends in an "objective" straight angle, depicting Uri in medium shot, sweating, and breathing heavily.[15] Mika is present and begins to follow him. Just as Naomi intrudes on Sherman, Mika intrudes on Uri. And Uri, like Sherman, poses an implicit threat to her as he chases her in the fields. They too eventually unite, creating a space of their own which also serves as compensation for Uri's grievance. This space first comes into being through two scenes which the couple spends in dialogue, and later when they appear together in the community. The direct causal connection between ailment and cure, between Uri's emotional pain and his involvement with Mika, is indicated in the sex scene which leads from their dialogue to the couple's public appearance.

The young immigrants who have been stacking hay leave Uri and Mika at the top of the stack, a temporary fortress. Uri, bare chested, is breathing heavily and sweating in the burning sun. Mika takes off her hat, breathing heavily and sweating as she looks at him. The use of extreme close-ups, cutting from his mouth to her eyes, from his eyes to her mouth, gives a sexual connotation to an image that previously signified anger. The sexual act is divided between five close-up shots which capture them from the neck up (briefly descending, once, to their shoulders) as they kiss, caress, and then press against each other. A hand grasps the hay and finally scatters it to the wind, marking climax and the end of the scene. Notably, the visual centre of the close-up composition is Mika, rather than Uri. The experience on view is hers as she closes her eyes and opens her mouth to gasp and bite – denoting that her body has been penetrated.

He Walked through the Fields is divided into two halves, using the same organizing principle as Eldorado. The first half follows the development of a sexual bond, and the second is dedicated to its loss. Uri does what his father

---

15 Talmon identifies here a quotation from East of Eden (1955, D: Elia Kazan), in which the frustrated son pushes large ice chunks out of his father's new icehouse (Talmon, 2001, p. 137). There are in addition formal similarities between this scene and one in The Hero's Wife, discussed below.

had done before him, leaving the kibbutz to serve the cause of the nation – in his case, by undertaking paramilitary training in the Palmach. Mika, left behind, is placed in the same position as Margo, suffering abandonment and loss. But while Margo is in Sherman's physical presence, Mika's loss is articulated in Uri's absence. Nevertheless, she carries the marks of their intimacy into this experience, during which we see her open mouthed and breathing heavily. This occurs as she hears of Uri's approaching departure; later, when being examined for her pregnancy in the clinic, as she closes her eyes and sobs in anguish and regret; and in another scene, which develops in parallel to Uri's flirtations with a woman in the training camp: Mika drops the cup of tea Ruth'ke serves her, and is shown in close-up, leaning forward and opening her mouth, her heavy breathing a sign of pregnancy-related nausea. The sex scene transfigures Uri's frustration into the erotic realm; and, through Mika's physical experience, eroticism is translated into its consequences: pregnancy and the fear and pain of loss.

Both Gertz and Talmon see Uri's final military actions and death as heroic (Gertz, 1993, p. 90; Talmon, 2001, pp. 136–137). However, as Steir-Livny points out, the film undermines this conception (Steir-Livny, 2007, pp. 297–298). Uri is portrayed in the beginning of the film as the fastest among his peers at assembling a weapon blindfolded. But later, when he is in command, his performance is flawed. At the camp, he fails to listen to the plight of his elderly subordinate. During the field mission, he applies water discipline,[16] runs his troops to exhaustion, and miscalculates the route. His self-sacrificing decision to take on the mission that ends his life is disapproved of by his second-in-command, who claims it would endanger the whole force. He exceeds the time allotted for the mission, and spends a moment staggering in bewilderment. Before his image freezes, indicating his death, he lies in the field in wide-eyed passivity, opening his mouth and sweating. His performance has nothing of the physical spectacle Sherman delivers. Sherman, the criminal from Jaffa, is unabashedly heroic, whereas Uri – a son of the kibbutz and a member of the Palmach, a supposedly ideal figure – cannot be seen as such. The mission he dies on is just a diversion to distract the British troops from the real action – Willie's mission, not fighting, but smuggling refugees. Uri's final frozen image, open mouthed, wide eyed, and sweating, indicates that the figure perpetuated in loss is the frustrated son, the youthful lover, the spouse who abandons his partner. Uri is not a hero but a victim who dies an arbitrary death, like his

---

16 Water discipline, involving the strict rationing of water to soldiers, was a common practice in the Israeli army (Epstein, 2011). It was abolished in 1959, eight years before the film was released, which would make it familiar to most contemporary viewers as a harmful, even sometimes fatal policy.

cinematic contemporaries after the Six-Day War. In Eldorado, the viewer is held in suspense by the suggestion of Sherman's death. In He Walked through the Fields, on the contrary, the pathos of loss is enhanced as the viewer bears the knowledge of Uri's death for four minutes in which his community remains ignorant of it.

In Uri's absence, Mika decides to abort his child. After learning of his son's death, Willie rushes after her and finds that she had changed her mind. Uri's loss is intertwined with the rescue of his son. Unaware of Uri's death, Mika utters: "Uri will return and everything will be wonderful for us all, Willie. You'll see. You'll see". Her words echo as a young soldier in Israeli military uniform is seen driving a jeep. This anonymous young soldier of the Six-Day War turns out to be Uri's son, named after him. The sentimental value in this segment lies in the fact that Mika's prophecy is both true and false. In the swift transition from "past" to "present", Willie, who was weeping at his son's death, now greets his grandson, another Uri. The pathos of the film, like that of the mourning poems cited in section 7.2, does not come from heroism or an idealised depiction of a character, but from the expression of painful loss.

11.5 The Hero's Wife

I am in Pieces: The Fragmented Individual

As the last example, I now discuss The Hero's Wife. Not only does this offer one of the first sex scenes on the Israeli screen, but it does so within one of the most complex cinematic reflections on victimhood in the Israeli communal environment yet produced.

The Hero's Wife takes place in a kibbutz by the Sea of Galilee. It revolves around a romantic triangle between Rachel and Yosef, two kibbutz members, and Jerry, a rebel who attends the kibbutz's *ulpan*, or Hebrew programme. Victimhood is dominant in the film, not dramaturgically but as a biographical fact, the backdrop for all that transpires. Rachel, the main protagonist, is the ultimate victim: a Holocaust survivor and a war widow, having lost her husband, Eli, in the War of Independence.[17] In this respect, she is an older version of Mika in He Walked Through the Fields. Jerry justifies his rebellious

---

[17] Both Yael Zerubavel and Steir-Livny refer to Rachel as a prototypical victim. Each of them, however, alludes to only one aspect of her victimhood. While Zerubavel only examines her depiction as a war widow, Steir-Livny concentrates on her representation as a Holocaust survivor (Zerubavel, 2003, pp. 243–244; Steir-Livny, 2009, pp. 89–91).

behaviour by his traumatic experience in the Korean War. Rachel and Jerry draw closer by comparing their inner wounds:

"There was so much noise in the hell of Korea that I still hear it to this day."
"There was so much silence in the hell of Mauthausen that it disturbs my sleep to this day."

But the actual experience of loss, grief, and trauma are not the focus of the film, which instead centres on Rachel's identity crisis. Her struggle with approaching old age, loneliness, and childlessness are expressed in diegetic scenes and inner monologues. The film operates within the aesthetics of the Nouvelle Vague,[18] however, and uses this to convey more than the inner world of the protagonist. Following Nouvelle Vague tradition, it challenges the viewer in the exposition, which includes the opening credits and first sequence, by exposing him to more details than he can decipher. The imagery during the opening credits oscillates between lush landscapes in which Rachel moves to harmonious music, and more abstract representations backed by music which echoes the score of NIGHT AND FOG (1956, D: Alain Resnais). The exposition includes elements central to the film: Rachel's middle-aged elegance; her internal conflict; her bereavement; her traumatic past and her method of containing it; her sensual relations with nature; and her lost sense of selfhood within her environment. But not enough is conveyed for the viewer to grasp what she sees. The next sequence thrusts the viewer into a large Purim celebration in the kibbutz.[19] The viewer is encumbered by a flow of multiple characters, details, and events, with gaps in information further complicating the experience. While Rachel's authority is immediately apparent, her role as *ulpan* teacher becomes clear much later, twenty minutes into the film. Rachel and Jerry's first exchange on the screen indicates tension, the roots of which are only revealed later.

The film maintains this tension further on by means of fragmentation, through repeated breaches in the progression of events which mar the link between cause and effect. Several narrative threads are intertwined in simultaneity, but without direct thematic or expressive association. Consequently, the film goes back and forth between events which are not tightly linked to one another. As the scenes are juxtaposed with no causal or expressive correlation, viewers are required to constantly reorient themselves. We leave Rachel's

---

18 Interestingly, Ariel Schweitzer, who works on Israeli films influenced by the Nouvelle Vague, refers to THE HERO'S WIFE as a counterexample to this film corpus (Schweitzer, 2003, pp. 39–42). He does not discuss the Nouvelle Vague's clear influence on it.
19 Purim is a Jewish holiday based on the story of Esther. The festivities take place at the same time of year as carnival in parts of the Christian world, and shares many of its attributes.

experience after class in the cemetery and rejoin Yosef on his days out tending to the sheep – a sharp turn from her poetic inner monologue about her life without Eli to his prosaic concerns over a fatal disease affecting his sheep.

As a result of this structure, matters that are causally connected are placed at a remove from one another. In the eighteenth minute of the film, for instance, Rivka, Rachel's next-door neighbour, commands her husband, Dubi, to have a "man to man" talk with Yosef and convince him to propose to Rachel. This narrative thread only continues ten minutes later, when Dubi finds Yosef in the mountains. Several powerful sequences unfold in the intervening period, wholly unrelated to this thread, giving a sense of disrupted continuity.

Due to its fragmentation, THE HERO'S WIFE fits David Bordwell's description of art-cinema narrative.[20] Bordwell describes the disturbance of the viewer's sense of coherence as a means of promoting ambiguity and a relativistic notion of truth (Bordwell, 1988, p. 212). In THE HERO'S WIFE, however, these means facilitate a somewhat different effect. As the figures are placed in constant simultaneity, and expressive unity is avoided, a space is created which never belongs just to one figure and just one mood – not even to Rachel, the protagonist. The repeated discord between characters makes their multiple subjectivities evident. This is enhanced through the repeated enactment of division between characters, as in the encounter between an exalted Rachel and a cerebral Yosef forty-two minutes into the film, and the conflict between an enraged Rachel and a drunk Jerry seven minutes later. Along with the representation of discrepancies between individuals, the film reflects upon society through the portrayal of groups and crowds. In scenes with the children Rachel cares for and the *ulpan* group, the camera alternates between the group and individuals. Close-ups also characterise the film's mass scenes in which the entire kibbutz assembles.[21] The

---

20 This correlation goes beyond the structural patterns. Along with what David Bordwell defines as the "loosening of cause and effect, an episodic construction of the syuzhet", and the "subjective or 'expressive' notion of realism", he also describes "an enhancement of the film's symbolic dimension through an emphasis on fluctuations of character psychology". "Protagonists may act inconsistently [...] or they may question themselves about their purposes". This is "an effect of the narration, which can play down the character's causal projects, keep silent about their motivations" and provide "overt narrational 'commentary' [...] in which the the narrational act interrupts the transmission of the fabula information and highlights its own role" (Bordwell, 1988, pp. 206–209). All these attributes can be identified in THE HERO'S WIFE.

21 Actual members of eight kibbutzim from the region take part in these scenes. The camera lingers on them, and details that are completely immaterial to the plot, style, and rhythm of the film are often captured – signalling an awareness of the film's second role as a historical document of these people and their environment.

film pointedly portrays public events in the collective: a commemoration, a grand assembly, and a Purim party which appears in an elaborate nine-minute scene at the very beginning.

Purim is a central motif in early Israeli film. It featured in a score of early Israeli documentaries like THIS IS THE LAND, and in the first Israeli short feature film, ONCE UPON A TIME. The carnival as an event evokes, among other things, the relations between individual and community. On the one hand, it relies on a large crowd. Bakhtin refers to carnival as an ultimate collectivist event: "Carnival laughter is the laughter of all the people [...] [I]t is universal in scope; it is directed at all and everyone, including the carnival's participants" (Bakhtin, 1968, p. 11). For Bakhtin, it is a realm in which degradation leads to the transcendence of individuality (ibid., pp. 18–24). On the other hand, the participants in a carnival distinguish themselves through extravagant performance and costume, articulating their individuality. For Bakhtin, any expression of individuality is the source of negativity and divergence from the utopian carnival (ibid., and also pp. 36–42). One may, however, read it more favourably as a symbolic performance of the democratic public realm, the dominion of equal individuals. According to Arendt, in ancient Greece

> the public realm itself, the *polis*, was permeated by a fiercely agonal spirit, where everybody had constantly to distinguish himself from all others, to show through unique deeds or achievements that he was the best of all (*aien aristeuein*). The public realm [...] was reserved for individuality; it was the only place where men could show who they really and inexchangeably were. (Arendt, 1998 (1958), p. 41)

In other words, along with Bakhtin's dynamics of degradation, which pulls the individual into the collective, we can see the opposite in the carnival: an elevation from the equal sphere into distinction. Indeed, the carnival sequence in THE HERO'S WIFE contains elements of both paradigms. The festival is represented as a continuous stream of processions, dances, games, and performances, in which the masses move harmoniously. With the exception of one passage with a stage routine, performers and audience share a space and alternate roles, and spectatorship receives as much attention as performance. There are close-ups of individual participants. In bird-eye long shots which capture the magnitude of the event, the engagement and elaborate costumes of individual participants stand out. To that extent, and in keeping with the rest of the film, the carnival is a democratic spectacle of multiple individualities.

On the other hand, Bakhtinian elements keep it from becoming a utopian vision of egalitarian individual expression. Extreme close-ups blur individual figures and distort their appearance. At one point, the lights are turned off, obscuring individual performance for the sake of uniform movement. Visitors who dare arrive without a costume are subjected to a quick compulsory dress and makeup session. Conformity is also expressed by numerous participants that appear in similar costumes. The pluralistic microcosm depicted in the party maintains a subtle measure of suspense regarding the sovereignty of its individual members.

Me, Not Us: Eroticism Rebels

The subtle suspense between the collective and the individual at the Purim party comes to a screeching halt: during a dance, Jerry forces himself on Rachel, locking her in an embrace and kissing her until the crowd stops singing and stares in silence. Rachel frees herself and escapes. As in the other films discussed here, the private sphere in THE HERO'S WIFE does not remain intact. In this case, however, the clash between private and public also results in the disruption of communal space. Breaches of privacy in the film are enacted through a chorus of kibbutz members who repeatedly comment on the comings and goings of Rachel, Jerry, and Yosef. Unlike a Greek chorus, they voice contradictory views, as befits a democratic ensemble. In addition, Rachel's neighbours, Dubi and Rivka, appear to hear everything that takes place in her home, and meddle in her relationships with the two men throughout the film.

Communal space is violated twice in the film during public events: Jerry's scandalous conduct at the beginning of the film, and the public turmoil caused by Rachel towards the end. An assembly is convened to decide whether to expel Jerry for his disruptive behaviour. Rachel delivers a speech in his defence. Her plea is accepted, but at the end of the meeting she unexpectedly asks to be discharged from her duties as a teacher. Some of those present react with anger. To the viewer who has witnessed Rachel's emotional crisis, her resignation is more coherent. Rachel expresses this crisis in a series of scenes where her yearning takes the form of increasing sensual intoxication. The roots of both public disturbances are sexual in nature.

The incongruity of eroticism with the community is embodied most potently through Jerry, whose defiance is associated with his sexual appeal. Jerry's position as an outsider to any community is determined at the beginning of the film. All through the film, he positions himself outside of the crowd, on doorsteps and window ledges. In most scenes, he provokes and challenges those around him, with each act of rebellion accompanied by jazz music. Throughout the film, Jerry's physical attractiveness is emphasised. His perpetual outfit of jeans and jacket accentuate his muscular body and serves as a reference to another rebel – Marlon Brando in THE WILD ONE (1953, D: Laslo

Benedek). His body is accentuated even further when he dances and works, actions which are always accompanied by rebellion.

One scene, for instance, begins like the sort of ideological documentary on pioneer work which proliferated in Israeli cinema from the 1930s. Jerry hands down heavy logs to his colleagues in the field. His movements are a vital part of the whole and are in synchrony with the arduous music playing on the soundtrack. He then begins throwing logs at the men, putting a twist on the initial imagery; at the same time, a jazz theme overtakes the original music. There are structural similarities between this scene and the one in HE WALKED THROUGH THE FIELDS where Uri loads the truck. But while Uri expresses anger, Jerry's rebellion is more universal, unattached to emotional distress. Uri's tantrum is productive – at the end of it the boxes are neatly stacked in the truck – whereas Jerry's actions are destructive and interrupt the work in the fields. This constitutes the essence of Jerry's rebellion.

The cinematic display of Jerry's body often occurs just before or while he romances – in today's terms, sexually harasses – female figures who are always partially responsive. Bodily spectacle is associated by proxy with these female figures' gaze. But it is never associated with Rachel's point of view. Her attraction to Jerry is made tangible through other means during a scene that depicts their excursion in Tiberias. In this sequence, Jerry and Rachel's voices are heard discussing personal experience and ideological conviction, while the images change at an accelerating pace. This engages the viewer sensually. The height of the process captures the motions of a motorboat ride on the Sea of Galilee, but much of the effect is achieved through editing. The images change in synchrony with the dialogue, almost with every phrase. It corresponds, not only with the rhythm of the conversation, but also with its content, which is Jerry's anti-social manifesto. Jerry's erotic allure is also constructed through an affective display of his discourse, by which rebellion is made sexually attractive. This does not induce identification with Jerry's position and views but gives substance to Rachel's attraction to him. Rachel's position is ambivalent inasmuch as she rejects Jerry numerous times and simultaneously expresses attraction towards him. When she berates him in one scene, for instance, he grabs hold of her. Close-ups reveal that she returns his embrace, and her hands wander from his arms to his thighs before she escapes.

It's not You, It's Us: Yosef and The Unattractiveness of Community

Jerry's rival, Yosef, is not unattractive. His outfits compliment his taut body and his stately presence. He possesses the aura of a romantic hero and an object of desire. In addition, his resemblance to Rachel places him on a par with her. They appear to be the same (middle) age, and share the same elegance, the same composure, and the same oratorical style of speaking. His blond mane matches her carefully shaped blond chignon. Shots of them in front of breath-taking scenery associate them both with the landscape. In addition, he shares her bereavement. At the beginning of the film he is presented as her late husband's best friend, who takes part in her commemorative rituals. The eroticisation of the widow-friend bond is uncommon for the era,[22] and Yosef's open infatuation is distinctive. But the sense of taboo associated with such situations in Israeli films of the 1980s is absent.[23] In fact, as I shall demonstrate, the attachment is plagued by social acceptability. Like Rachel, Yosef is a figure of authority. He fulfils social functions, conducts the kibbutz's commemoration service, and teaches at the *ulpan*. When Jerry and later Rachel disrupt social events, Yosef restores social order. In the first case, he restarts the public dance; in the second, he publically volunteers to take over Rachel's responsibilities.

Yosef's sexual allure is not enhanced as Jerry's is. His body is not put on display, and he is not associated with movement or upbeat music. Most of all, his eroticism is undermined by the presence of his comrades, Dubi and Rivka. Rachel's neighbours are a short, ageing couple with slightly foreign accents. Early in the film they discuss a possible liaison between Rachel and Yosef while performing their bedtime rituals with unerotic familiarity. Repeating each other's phrases, their performance is comic. Rivka reaches her conclusion in the most unromantic and unerotic terms: they should help Yosef and Rachel "finish the business" and get married. When Dubi delivers the message to Yosef, it remains unappetising. He sits with him on the side of the hill, with the Sea of Galilee in the backdrop. Laying a friendly hand on his shoulder, he delivers an oration which enhances his East European accent – an arrangement often been used for ideological speeches in propaganda films.[24] After the commemoration service, Yosef attempts to approach Rachel. His actions are subjected to the community's scrutinising gaze and Rivka's sarcastic remarks. The commentary has a distancing effect. Yosef's erotic allure is tainted by his proximity to Rivka and Dubi, and through them to the community.

---

22 It appears in BLAZING SAND, and is hinted at in SIEGE (1969, D: Gilberto Tofano).
23 In films such as THE VULTURE (1981, D: Yaky Yosha), REPEAT DIVE, THE LAST WINTER (1984, D: Riki Shelach Nissimoff), ATALIA (1984, D: Tzvika Kertzner and Akiva Tevet), and THE VALLEY TRAIN (1989, D: Jonathan Paz).
24 One example is a scene with two pioneers in THIS IS THE LAND, discussed by Bursztyn (Bursztyn, 1990, pp. 46–47).

Compared to THE DYBBUK and FORTUNA, THE HERO'S WIFE presents a very mild version of the suppression of individual desire by the community. It is portrayed not by action, but by presence – reminiscent of a phenomenon characteristic of the kibbutz which Ben-Ari describes. According to her, under the liberal approach of the education system in kibbutzim, sex and eroticism were not encouraged, but instead demystified and sublimated (Ben-Ari, 2006, pp. 77–83). Sex was not taboo, but also not something to indulge in. This may clarify why the kibbutz community in THE HERO'S WIFE is open and liberal, and at the same time fatal to any erotic mystique.

The *ulpan* Jerry is enrolled in poses similar dangers for eroticism. In class, students repeat Hebrew sentences with heavy foreign accents and grammatical mistakes. They make exaggerated gestures and expressions as they struggle with the new language. In one scene, as an exercise, they practice marriage proposals. The erotic connotations are harnessed for comic effect. The class often bursts into laughter. Jerry participates in the comedy, but this does not undermine his eroticism. While Yosef belongs to a society that undercuts his erotic pull, Jerry remains autonomous.

The Third Rival: Casualties of War

The rivalry between Yosef and Jerry over Rachel signifies the conflict between individualism and conformity. The third rival, one that challenges them both, is Rachel's dead and idealised husband, Eli – another powerful alternative, a figure enhanced to mythical dimensions by sheer loss. Jerry articulates this in a drunken rage: "Rachel, the hero's wife. And his hands are upon you, and under your dress. He's allowed, because he's in a [picture] frame."

Eli never appears, and only materialises in Rachel's internal monologue. His absent presence aligns Jerry and Yosef in their defeat. In a scene at the cemetery, Yosef repeats Jerry's actions from an earlier scene at the club. Both appear in medium close-up as they grab hold of Rachel. Their plea is almost identical. In the earlier scene, Jerry calls out: "I'm alive! Not dead, not sacred, not a hero. They can't put me in a [picture] frame!" Yosef rephrases this: "You are a living woman, and he [Eli] is a dead hero!" The mourning process the viewer experiences is not over the dead spouse, but rather the new alternative. Rachel's relinquishment of Jerry is melancholy. It reaches its conclusion at the *ulpan*'s farewell party, where both are shown in corresponding shots with gloomy expressions complemented by the mellow theme song. In the dead of night, the kibbutz is shelled, and the tables are turned. The erotic attachment between Rachel and Jerry finally yields a sex scene – not because the rebel overpowers the mythic victim, but rather because he steps into his shoes.

War Time: The Synchronisation of the Communal Body

The attack on the kibbutz occurs over a sequence of ten minutes. It changes the pace and structure of the film. Although it is encompassed in many short simultaneous segments, taking place in various locations in and outside the kibbutz, it maintains a unified structure. The sequence shows both the raid and the defensive measures that follow. Despite the diffusion, there is no room for incoherence – not just because everyone is affected by the same event, but because they are depicted as part of a cohesive body. Members of the kibbutz all take a functional part in the operation. Yosef, Rachel, and Eitan, the kibbutz's secretary, form a headquarters and supervise operations by radio.

Jerry's integration into this coherent collective begins through an association with victimhood. Earlier in the film, during his excursion to Tiberias with Rachel, they walk in front of archaeological ruins. When she conveys that she had been in the camps, a quick succession of images appear, combining well known Holocaust imagery with images from the ruins in Tiberias and a modern ruin, which will later turn out to be a shelled house in the kibbutz. Jerry sardonically remarks:

> "Yes, yes, this we know how to do."
> "What?"
> "Ruins." [He turns around and motions at the direction of the fortress.]

When Jerry the rebel adopts the plural form "we", he positions himself in a tradition of agony – a meta-historical amalgam of debris in which the Holocaust serves as the centrepiece.

During the attack, Jerry enters a bomb shelter with other students, a confined space with narrow walls, low ceiling, and rows of occupied bunks. As Ariel Schweitzer observes, this is reminiscent of images from the concentration camps (Schweitzer, 2003, pp. 40–41). His image freezes as explosions and machine guns are heard, accompanied by the image of a pile of military boots. The image incorporates Holocaust and military imagery, fusing Jerry's traumatic experience as a soldier and that of a victim of genocide.

Jerry later becomes active: he entreats Dubi for orders and, unsatisfied with the instruction to hold back, runs to the smoke-filled woods. He observes the kibbutz members trying to pull fuel barrels away from the fire and begins to act as part of the whole. After helping to harness a cart with barrels to a tractor, he rolls other barrels away from the fire, providing yet another spectacle of his muscular body. Unlike the previous spectacles, it is not complemented with a jazz tune. Moreover, the act does not constitute rebellion, although Jerry disregards the order given through the loudspeaker to step away. This is an act of self-sacrifice rather than mutiny. He becomes dirty from the smoke, the flames, and the water sprayed at him. Unlike the previous spectacles, part of the viewer's fascination derives from danger. His life is at risk. The spectacle resembles that of Sherman in ELDORADO, his rebellious eroticism now harnessed to the ethos of self-sacrifice. Like Sherman, he is shamelessly heroic.

The sense of danger is also expressed through Rachel, who arrives at the scene. Her terrified expression matches Jerry's deeds. When his jacket catches fire, she runs forward. Held back by Yosef, she loses her composure, distraught and dishevelled, and struggles and cries out, repeating: "Jerry!" "Get him out of the fire!" "He will burn!" "Move away from the fire!" The sense of fear turns into one loss, when she begins calling out for her husband, Eli.

The flames on the screen relate to the Jewish tradition of lamentation, in which fire plays a central role. The Holocaust, Jerry's trauma in the Korean War, and Rachel's bereavement in the War of Independence are fused into an all-encompassing event, as the scene transgresses the limits of an isolated incident to render a primary constellation. Jerry's activity and Rachel's outburst are two sides of the same ailment. Together, they enact a sense of victimhood, and this is what finally brings them together. Returning to her room, Rachel finds Jerry, a shadow in the dark room. He greets her with the words: "Rachel, we are both crippled. Help me."

Finally in the Frame: Sexual Climax

Sexual suspense has been built gradually all through the film. But the fulfilment only takes place after both Jerry and Rachel perform their roles as victims. To paraphrase Jerry's remark earlier in the film, by performing their victimhood, they have entered the frame and gained permission. Their sexual act is accordingly dramatic and supplemented with orchestral music.

They begin slowly and ceremoniously. She caresses his face. The blanket falls off his naked back as he kneels before her and moves his hands up her body. Her eyes close and her head moves in intoxication. Their gradual descent to the floor is followed by the camera, which remains elevated. The act itself is performed through caresses that enhances the tactile sensation of skin against skin. It is captured from the waist up, progressing through close-ups and medium close-ups as the couple enter the missionary position. This arrangement allows a view of Jerry's broad back and Rachel's ecstatic expression. His body has been displayed all through the film, just as her increasing emotional burden was articulated through her face. Integrated into the sex scene, the trait which personifies each of them is enhanced. Like Mika in HE WALKED THROUGH THE FIELDS, Rachel is the centre of the composition.

This sexual act is not only constitutive, but also serves as a remedy for Rachel and Jerry's suffering. A metaphor takes over: fire is superimposed on the screen, and the couple appears and disappears through the flames, a musical peak marks their final disappearance. The music becomes lighter, and the flames are replaced by treetops and a series of daylit nature scenes. The lovers return, embracing and caressing on Rachel's bed. The once dark scene is now fully lit. The progression is marked by increasing light and by a transformation from consuming fire to natural revival.[25] The series of scenic landscapes end with bombarded kibbutz structures in daylight. Trauma is not suppressed and denied but integrated into the landscape. The segment ends with a tractor toiling at the blackened ruins, indicating reconstruction. The couple appear in Rachel's bed. They caress and kiss each other, regenerating the tactility of their bare skin. He declares his love for her and his intention to stay. She, in return, compassionately takes leave of him, sending him back to his family and son. The physical proximity the viewer witnesses is being relinquished. The final pathos of the sex scene is reserved for Rachel's act of self-sacrifice.

Back to Life: The Return to Democratic Space

Like Naomi and Sherman in ELDORADO, and Uri and Mika in HE WALKED THROUGH THE FIELDS, Rachel and Jerry reached momentary autonomy through their act of passion. Unlike the other couples, their unity ends there.

The community returns with a sequence that depicts the kibbutz awakening: members gathering in the early morning, preparing for work, and going out to the fields, and children in pyjamas cheering as they leave the shelter. It ends with Rachel's preparations for the new day. Various tableaux follow, mostly associated with preparations for the *ulpan*'s departure. Jerry hangs back gloomily, but this becomes part of an otherwise jubilant sequence celebrating friendship and continuity.

---

25 This is reminiscent of the cyclic revival Bakhtin describes (Bakhtin, 1968, pp. 24–25). However, it is associated with an intensification, rather than a destruction, of what Bakhtin deemed the isolated bourgeois individual.

Figure 6: Jerry performing self-sacrifice, Rachel performing grief, and the couple's sensual farewell in THE HERO'S WIFE.

Rachel and Jerry's central position in the film does not dissolve but resurfaces in melodrama. Tension builds as Jerry arrives at the bus that will take him away, looking with anticipation, and finally boarding. Yosef, the white knight, finds a depressed Rachel, cajoles her to take her leave, and holds her as she bursts into tears. The simultaneity of these scenes creates the opposite effect from the one it served throughout most of the film. It generates melodramatic suspense, amplifying the individuals' centrality. The final takeover occurs as Rachel and Jerry kiss goodbye in front of the bus, and the crowd feigns protest.

But the final shot is reserved for a different couple. As the bus pulls out, Yosef and Rachel take centre frame. He watches her tilt her head and lays a firm hand on her shoulder. She strokes his hand and pets it lightly, indicating that she will continue to accept and evade his romantic offerings. The smiles on their faces as they leave the frame suggest that they are resigned to their roles.

One may draw a parallel to the state in which the viewer is left at the end of the film. On the affective level, the fragmentation with which the film begins is replaced by two coherencies: that of the community, beginning with the bombardment, and that of the singular individual, manifested in the sex scene. Both are temporary. Communal unity is only restored in emergency, and the celebration of the individual endures only for a short spell, intensified by the prospect of its ending. Seduced by the lucidity of the last twenty minutes of the film, however, the viewer is prevented from experiencing resolution. Yosef, Rachel, and Jerry remain within view – but never within reach – of their prospective desires. The viewer, likewise, is allowed to enjoy temporary climaxes in which all falls into place. But what in fact endures beyond it is a cinematic space which frustrates such unity: a democratic space which persistently gives rise to incongruities between individuals, and within which the public and the private sphere are in constant threat of intruding on one another. The viewer must reconcile themselves to this space.

11.6 Shining Through: Conclusion and Commentary

Gender plays a significant role in the interplay of victimhood and sex in the films discussed here. However, in keeping with Peter Lehman's warning about the rigid binary distribution of male and female roles (Lehman, 1993, pp. 7–8), each film's flexibility in this matter should also be taken into account. Visual erotic spectacle can be generated by female figures, but it is overwhelmingly upheld by the male figure. The affective experience of sexual exaltation and the agony of loss could be associated with male figures but is predominantly attributed to women. Contrary to traditional claims about Israeli cinema, viewers of these films are presented with a cinematic experience which, in its construction of victimhood, largely validates female subjectivity and male objectification.

This chapter opened with a quote by actor Gideon Shemer suggesting that the display of sexual activity and the treatment of the ultimate form of victimhood are both potential sources of embarrassment. The sense of shame each may evoke is not the result of exposure but of active enactment, the execution of a role.

My discussion of the films in this chapter shows that the display of victimhood and eroticism is negotiated with care. For instance, eroticism and heroism are more easily attributed to an "outsider" like Jerry, or a marginal character like Sherman, than to characters considered central to the national ethos of the era. Within the cultural restrictions, the bond between eroticism and victimhood is empowering. Eroticism enhances the sense of victimhood, and victimhood legitimises eroticism. Both place an emphasis on the individual. In my concluding example, THE HERO'S WIFE, this is translated into an affective experience allowing unity and coherence to shine temporarily through the fragmentation of the democratic realm. This is an expression of what, in effect, cinematic victimhood always stands for: a momentary enhancement of the individual as above, beyond, and in spite of communal order.

12 Where is the Child? Where is the Adult? The Child Enters the Sex Scene in A NIGHT IN TIBERIAS, NOT MINE TO LOVE, and IRIS

Between ODED THE WANDERER and the consolidation of the film industry, children featured frequently in Israeli films, most of them facing dangers of some sort. Oded is lost in the Palestinian wilderness, and the children in OVER THE RUINS (1938, D: Nathan Axelrod) are left without parents to start a life in that wilderness during the Roman occupation. The child in LACKING A HOMELAND, on the other hand, must survive the hardships of an exodus from Yemen before he even arrives in Palestine. Similarly, in MY FATHER'S HOUSE (1947, D: Herbert Kline), children who have survived the Holocaust must make the dangerous journey to Palestine, and come to terms with the loss of their family. Other children put their lives at risk fighting in the War of Independence in THE FAITHFUL CITY (1952, D: Józef Lejtes) and DAN QUIXOTE AND SA'AD PANCHA (1956, D: Nathan Axelrod).

In some of these films, a secular variation of the myth of David and Goliath is revived. More importantly, in all of them, the endangered child embodies the sense of fragility in all stages of the pioneer venture. This does not mean that these characters are reduced to expressions of fragility. The other traits associated with children and adolescents in section 7.2 – intelligence, simultaneous liminality and centrality, simultaneous affiliation with and estrangement from the community, frivolity and playfulness – are all embodied in the films mentioned here, and continue to feature in those I now turn to. Nonetheless, fragility is their predominant attribute.

This sense of fragility is present not just after the establishment of the State, but during the quiet of the early 1960s. In CLOUDS OVER ISRAEL (1962, D: Ilan Eldad), it is transferred to the figure of a Bedouin baby whose life is saved by Israeli soldiers in the Sinai War of 1956. In EIGHT AGAINST ONE (1964, D: Menahem Golan), international politics replaces the wilderness as the site of danger. The parents are not absent in this film, but absentminded, and a defenceless group of children must battle a dangerous international spy. The threats faced by the baby in CLOUDS OVER ISRAEL and the children in EIGHT AGAINST ONE no longer just reflect dangers to the Zionist project and the state, but the moral questions involved in it.

After sex entered the scene, in the second half of the 1960s, children were to face a new peril: adult sexuality. Paedophilia and child abuse were not explored at this point. Instead, the unsettling associating of childhood and sex was used within the existing tradition of cinematic representations of fragility, which was translated into a contemporary context.

12.1 A NIGHT IN TIBERIAS – Paradise Lost: The Clash between Childhood and Adulthood

The first child casualty of adult sexuality on the Israeli screen was Catherine Bronti in A NIGHT IN TIBERIAS (1966, D: Hervé Bromberger).[1] The daughter of a French water engineer disappears. At first, the police suspects political abduction, as Catherine's father is employed by the Israeli government. However, the investigation reveals the girl escaped from her dysfunctional home. The Brontis neglect not just their daughter but their marriage, both of them entertaining potential lovers. Early in the film, during a sex scene, the wife arouses the husband by referring to the other woman, working her into a light erotic fantasy. Progressively, the daughter appears indignant over both her mother's infidelity and the cruelty and neglect directed towards her. The search for the missing girl brings about "correction". The daughter turns into the centre of attention, and the adults' indiscretions are cleared away. Catherine's parents are discharged of all erotic tension, and their surrogate partners lose their extramarital roles.

Beyond the family drama, the film seduces the viewer with action. The opening segment of the film builds up suspense with a successful terrorist attack on a water tower. It compensates for this guerrilla assault with a display of power by the security forces. The local fleet of police cars is displayed, as well as the coastguards, police dog unit, and Bedouin scouts. Police intelligence plays a considerable role in the plot. The superintendent in charge of the investigation embodies pure competence, undermined only by a representative of the secret services who involves himself in the case.

In this respect, erotic allure is replaced with the appeal of continuous potency demonstrated by the security forces. But even this blatant display does not present resolution and closure. Towards the end of the film, the girl escapes from the police forces into a mine field on the border. When rescued, she declares: "I don't feel like playing war anymore, sir." Military potency is no more appropriate for a little girl than erotic seduction. Innocence goes amiss not only through the Brontis' unstable marriage, their pursuit of sexual thrills, but through the game of war, which Israel is shown to play so well. Paradise is lost

---

[1] The film was first released in early 1966. A re-edited version with added scenes appeared in late 1967 (Gross, 1967). French and English are the two main languages in the film.

on more than one front, and the blamelessness and fragility of the child is no longer fully identified with the state.

Specific historical facts could account for the fissure that appears between the child's identity and that of the state even before the Six-Day War. Mr. Bronti's project, which is infiltrated by the enemy, involves water engineering – a likely reference to the National Water Carrier, Israel's most remarkable such project. But another grand engineering project of the same period, assisted by the French government, quickly became a more obvious symbol of Israeli power, and a more likely target for espionage and attack: the nuclear reactor whose construction started in the south of Israel in 1957. Officially a research centre, by 1968 it was producing nuclear weapons (Aftergood and Kristensen, 2007). It was a strictly guarded national secret, but widely known to the Israeli public. The censors would never allow a direct cinematic reference, but the association is likely – not only because of the references in the film to security risks, spying, and French engineering, but also because of its manifestation of the threat to innocence presented by Israel's entry into the nuclear race.

Nevertheless, no strategic development in the country's military or foreign policy, however dramatic, could be fully explained as a clash between childhood and adulthood. In A NIGHT IN TIBERIAS, it is paralleled by a fascination with the armed forces, but this clash soon becomes a regular pattern in Israeli film, appearing in many films with no such association.[2] In particular, it is central in the two films discussed in the following segments: NOT MINE TO LOVE and IRIS. The repeated re-enactment of this clash in these films and many to follow, the portrayal of child abuse and the inaptitude of adults, serve as a hallmark for ambivalence in the transition away from the ideological era, from a compulsory mobilised standpoint to a critical one. More dramatic than the material changes Israeli society was about to undergo in the next two decades was the change in how it perceived itself.

---

[2] Relevant films in the decade between the mid-1960s and mid-1970s vary greatly in style and origin: THE BOY ACROSS THE STREET (1965, D: Yosef Shalhin), THE PRODIGAL SON (1968, D: Yosef Shalhin), A BOY AND A CAMEL (1968, D: Osamu Takahashi), IRIS, BLAZE ON THE WATER, THE DREAMER (1970, D: Dan Wolman), GET ZORKIN (1971, D: Joel Silberg), THE PILL (1972, D: David Perlov), I LOVE YOU ROSA (1972, D: Moshé Mizrahi), PEEPING TOMS (1972, D: Uri Zohar), FLOCH (1972, D: Dan Wolman), LIGHT OUT OF NOWHERE (1973, D: Nissim Dayan), THE HOUSE ON CHELOUCHE STREET (1973, D: Moshé Mizrahi), and JUDGEMENT DAY (1974, D: George Obadiah). I refer to some of these films in this and the next chapters.

A second revival of the theme came between the late 1970s and mid-1980s, with films like LEMON POPSICLE, ROCKING HORSE (1978, D: Yaky Yosha), THE WOODEN GUN (1979, D: Ilan Moshenson), GROWING PAINS (1980, D: Ze'ev Revach), THE THIN LINE (1980, D: Michal Bat-Adam), NOA AT 17 (1982, D: Isaac Zepel Yeshurun), and FORCED TESTIMONY (1984, D: Raphael Rebibo).

This observation required the premise that a communal change of perspective can be infused and cinematically rendered in the structural form of interpersonal relations among individuals. This basic supposition should be mentioned because of the tradition in which NOT MINE TO LOVE, IRIS, and other Israeli auteur films of the late 1960s and early 1970s – generally referred to as the "new sensibility" or "personal cinema" – were regarded academically. Film scholars who discuss the evolution of these films note a change of perspective they express, but tend to define them as apolitical, as failed attempts to form an experience isolated from Israeli reality. In this spirit, Gertz criticises NOT MINE TO LOVE for its lack of political bearing, and for limiting itself to bourgeois references to love and relationships (Gertz, 1993, pp. 129–130) while passing over the social and national causes for the discontent it expresses (ibid., pp. 131–132). By contrast, Shohat (who does not discuss NOT MINE TO LOVE or IRIS directly, and who is just as critical of "personal cinema") locates in such films the political content which is supposedly missing in the form of "implicit, unconscious and even inadvertent allegories", allegories that lie "less in the intention than in the reading as well as inhering in the context from which the films emerge" (Shohat, 1989, p. 11). In her view,

> [t]he apparently apolitical films of the self-designated "personal cinema" [...] can be read as projecting allegories of solitude and displacement in which anguished personal destinies, inadvertently and perhaps despite the intentions of the authors, come to "figure" the displacement of the milieu and the solitude of the nation state as a whole. (ibid.)

Yet the premise that NOT MINE TO LOVE and IRIS "limit their scope" to the bourgeois and the personal, and that they are apolitical in content and intent, is questionable. It is true that, in comparison to A NIGHT IN TIBERIAS, they are more subtle in their use of political context. The ample references to regional political and the military settings which form an emphatic part of A NIGHT IN TIBERIAS are tuned down. There are no spies, no terrorists, no brave security forces, and no international intrigue. The arena is indeed the private one. But we need not seek some subconscious allegory to find the historical and political underpinnings of these films. Contextualising it as such would also not go against their grain, for this context arises from their use of the cityscape, and from their dramaturgical edifice.

There is no coincidence, for instance, that in one of the main scenes of NOT MINE TO LOVE a boy who is about to be removed from the kibbutz by his parents is left alone in a deserted Muslim graveyard in West Jerusalem, calling out to Eli in a frail voice: "Comrade! Comrade!" The traditional imagery of children in danger is deployed here, in the new context of a fairly obvious ideological predicament. This is not an isolated scene that carries a fleeting "allegory," or a shrouded message. Both NOT MINE TO LOVE and IRIS employ elements of historical and political significance in their affective gesture, making these perceptible on an emotional level. Beyond a sense of solitude and displacement, both approach the clash between old and new, youth and maturity, from various directions, stimulating growing discomfort, which is less relevant to the "solitude of the nation state" and more in line with a contemporary change of perspective which they make physically and emotionally tangible for the viewer. Both make use of the tradition which had developed around the child, while seemingly focusing on adults. They thereby pave the way for a change in pattern.

12.2 NOT MINE TO LOVE

Jerusalem Personified: Internal and External Cityscapes

Zohar was one of the most influential directors to explore the clash between childhood and adulthood extensively, and NOT MINE TO LOVE presents a major example of this tendency. An adaptation of A. B. Yehoshua's story *Three Days and a Child*, it follows Eli, a maths student in Jerusalem, over the course of three days in which he takes on the task of looking after Shai, the three-year-old son of his old flame from the kibbutz. The clash between childhood and adulthood is enacted both by the increasing threat that Eli poses to Shai in the present. It also materialises in the Eli's youthful trauma of failed initiation, which is recounted over the course of the film.

The clash between young and old is hinted at in the title sequence, in which shots of new buildings – primarily the newly completed Hebrew University campus – are contrasted with shots of older parts of Jerusalem, from before the establishment of the state in 1948, and the division of the city the following year.[3] The sequence also introduces the protagonist and his companion, who move through the cityscape to an upbeat bossa nova percussion soundtrack. They appear cheerful, engaged, and energetic.

The sensual experience of the viewer in the opening sequence is carried onward through the film on two levels. On the one hand, the city's busy roads and specks of untamed nature, recreational spaces, old constructions, and new

---

3 In that context, the depiction of Jerusalem in NOT MINE TO LOVE does not include the historic, symbolic dimensions referred to by Zanger. At no point is it magnified into a sacred space or the centre of the world. Instead it remains what Zanger calls an "ordinary city", transmitted to the viewer through its material existence, removed from any tradition's mystical inscriptions (Zanger, 2012, pp. 153–164).

boundaries continue to play an important role. On the other hand, the disparity between old and new shifts into the plot and materialises in the fragments of the past, appearing in flashbacks that express Eli's yearning and ambivalence and contrast with the present. It also expresses the gap between Eli's position, marred by dark urges, bitterness, rivalries, and memories, and that of Shai: the lucid perspective of the child responding to the existential present.

Thorny Routine: Eli's Perforated World

After the title sequence, a voiceover by the protagonist opens the film, describing the events to come in the past tense:

> "I thought I'd have to apologise, but it's as if things turned around. The three years old son of a beloved woman was brought to me to care for in the last days of the summer vacation. At first I cared about the child, and then I wanted to kill him. But … I still have to understand what prevented my doing so, since the time and place were right for it. The time: end of summer. The place: Jerusalem, a quiet city."[4]

The viewer is confronted with a disturbing plot, the protagonist's murderous urges, and his unemotional tone.

As these words unfold, Yael, Eli's girlfriend, appears nude on the screen, inspecting an array of thorny plants that seem to fill the apartment. It indicates that she studies botany. On a visceral level, the proximity of her bare skin to so many thorns implies potential injury and vulnerability. On the other hand, her nudity is casual and private. As the film progresses, nudity and part-nudity distinguish the apartment, which will become a central location in the film, from the public sphere. When Eli's voice disappears he comes into view, bare chested and lying down. Without his thick-framed glasses, and with a gentle expression on his face, he appears almost childlike. Sounds from the street and the neighbouring apartments become audible: a car horn sounds, a baby cries. The private sphere is not entirely isolated from the outside.

Yael and Eli's interaction appears positive: she wishes him good morning; he motions for her with his hand; she smiles at him. As she approaches him, one would expect them to unite in a frame. Instead, she sits over him and puts her feet on his chest. The reaction shots continue, with Yael in the superior position and Eli at her feet, and their exchange now moves between erotic tension

---

4 As Hakak points out, this text comes from the first paragraph of the novel the film is based on (Hakak, 2001, p. 136). Hakak and Gertz analyse this film extensively in relation to the novel.

and open animosity. He makes sexual advances at her and she reacts with displeasure. She strikes him lightly with a large thorn and finally presses it against his skin. He, in turn, reacts sarcastically, speaking with a hard expression and his teeth exposed. The metaphor is complete: like the vegetation decorating their room, their relationship appears to be quite thorny.

After his advance is met with resistance, Eli announces his capitulation and retreats into passivity. This triggers an instant change in Yael's conduct. To the sound of light guitar and flute music she proceeds with the actions expected before the onset of animosity. Eli's blank expression occupies two thirds of the screen. Yael fills the rest with her profile. She smiles, kisses him, and gently moves her finger over his body. Whispering in his ear, she makes him smile. She climbs on top of him, and is about to kiss his lips, but stops shortly and bites her thumb. After a short wait he smiles, ends his passivity, and lays a hand on her head. They kiss tenderly. Their conflict is not reversed but complemented by their erotic relations. Yael maintains her defiance in both, and navigates Eli through both conflict and sexual engagement.

The sexual act continues as the music stops. But the voices and sounds from outside penetrate their environment, as does the creaking of their own bed. As Gertz observes, the noises are the first sign of the intrusion of the public onto the private (Gertz, 1993, p. 125). Soon, a voice calls out: "Eli! Phone call!" He continues to kiss Yael, but then stops, puts on his glasses, and climbs out of bed. Yael doesn't change her position, and Eli's movements are met with resistance. When he finally leaves the frame, she remains in medium close-up, lying on her side with a gloomy expression.

The sexual act that opens the film creates an elusive, short-lived harmony, which is intercepted by the outside world and comes to an abrupt end. As he alternates between sarcasm and passivity, Eli seems the opposite of the cheerful version of himself that appeared in the title sequence. This remains his dominant modus throughout the film. The following fifteen minutes portray his daily life, conduct, past, and motivations. What is predominantly communicated is the extent to which Eli intrudes and is intruded upon. Wearing nothing but boxer shorts, he enters his neighbours' bedroom to answer the phone. He watches them in their morning rituals, and doesn't take offence at his neighbour's probing question. They share intimate details about their lives. As he leaves the apartment he is accosted by Zvi, Yael's friend. He reacts with animosity, as though Zvi is his romantic rival. Zvi then enters Eli and Yael's home and interrupts their thorny exchanges. Later, when he appears at their dinner table, bursting into a monologue about the wonder of nature, it becomes clear that he is a dominant "third wheel" in their lives. Eli makes aggressive remarks throughout the sequence.

The Memory of the Mother, the Presence of the Son: Absence of Sovereignty

Eli's first recollection of Noa, his youthful love, seems to offer a refuge from this perforated existence. It is instigated by her phone call. When he hears her voice on the receiver, music begins to play, the "present" vanishes, and images from the "past" of Noa in the kibbutz flood the screen. She is seen from a variety of angles, in various locations, wearing different clothes. Her dissimilarity to Yael is striking. Noa's face is more delicate and pleasant. On the other hand, Yael's femininity is contrasted with the manliness of Noa's deep voice and stalk which she chews on in most images.

In Eli's second recollection of the "past" he becomes an active participant. It mixes nostalgia with ambivalence and reveals a more complex relationship between "past" and "present". As a soldier, three years previously, Eli is missing his thick glasses and his sarcastic expression. He seems less stolid, walking a fair distance to see his beloved Noa. But Noa is pregnant and, in the presence of her older husband Ze'ev, Eli is in the position of the intruder and third wheel – Zvi's present position.

The parallel between the Ze'ev-Noa-Eli triangle and the Eli-Yael-Zvi triangle is evoked both visually and dramaturgically,[5] with a slight difference between them. While "past" Eli is a passive participant in Noa's joke on her husband, in the present he actively encourages Yael to laugh at Zvi. The viewer is in on both jokes. The sounds Ze'ev makes as he cuts his food and eats are enhanced. We understand why Noa looks at Eli meaningfully, smiling and laughing. At his own kitchen table, Eli attempts to repeat Ze'ev's performance by loudly slurping his yogurt. Yael's gaze is stern, her smile bitter. It is his sarcastic remark to Zvi that finally draws out a furtive laugh.

These scenes call to mind Freud's tendentious joke. Like smut, Freud says, the tendentious joke is a libidinal process which requires three people: the one who makes the joke, the second who is the object of the hostile or sexual aggressiveness, and a third who takes pleasure in it (Freud, 1960, p. 100). The joke is meant to evade social restrictions and release aggressions (ibid., p. 103):

> By making our enemy small, inferior, despicable or comic, we achieve in a roundabout way the enjoyment of overcoming him – to which the third person, who has made no efforts, bears witness by his laughter. (ibid.)

---

[5] Both Gertz and Hakak point out various compositional similarities (Gertz, 1993, pp. 127–128; Hakak, 2001, pp. 137–138).

The most plausible target for a tendentious joke is therefore "the dignified and the mighty, who are protected by internal inhibitions and external circumstances from direct disparagement" (ibid., p. 105). The key to what takes place in the two triangular scenes lies in the question of who is supposed to be the joker, the listener, and the target. By targeting her husband, Noa is offering Eli the libidinal pact of an unsophisticated tendentious joke. Eli, however, remains solemn, and does not enter this pact. In the company of Yael and Zvi, Eli attempts to adopt the role of the target, which would validate his dominant position. He is, however, granted the mischievous role of the joker, and a fleeting libidinal connection with Yael at Zvi's expense.

Eli's reality both in the past and the present lacks sovereignty, not only because he intrudes, and is intruded upon, but also because within these circumstances he is only offered and can only master the position of the jester rather than the king. This will turn out to be the main difficulty with the arrival of the boy.

One would expect Eli's new guest, Shai, to complement the established pattern and present a form of intrusion. But the roles are reversed, and it is Eli who intrudes upon the boy. Eli wistfully expects the boy's mother, but when he answers the door he finds her husband, Ze'ev, and the little boy who greets him with a grimace. Eli begins to relate directly to the boy only after Ze'ev leaves. As Hakak says, "without words, Eli projects on Shai his love and yearning for No'ah, in a most tender, yet sensual and possibly perverse manner" (Hakak, 2001, p. 138). Eli's "loving" reaction toward the boy takes the form of molestation. In the beginning of the film, Eli gestured to Yael for sex. From the same bed, he now gestures to the boy with his finger for a caress. With his face to the camera, the kiss Eli gives the boy is all too fleshy. With his back to the camera, he seems too engrossed in his caresses. The potential menace and subsequent discomfort are diffused when, in a series of reaction shots, Eli makes Shai laugh with grimaces of his own.

What follows corresponds with the pattern established since the beginning of the film: a short harmonious phase followed by an increasingly discordant and disturbing progression. Harmony is portrayed in an eighty-four second sequence in which Eli explores Jerusalem with Shai to a bossa nova tune. Even a protective wall against snipers serves as harmless scenery. There is no crisis when Eli has to chase Shai as he runs toward the border.

The situation changes when Eli returns to his role as jester, rather than caretaker. He abandons Shai during a game of hide and seek in a deserted Muslim graveyard, only to save him at the last minute as he runs into the busy street. He goes to Yael's parents, and despite their animosity, uses their garden swing, but the boy suffers vertigo and vomits.

Mischief, Guilt, and Menace: Unsovereign Affairs

Both of the times in which Shai shows signs of distress, it is accentuated through cinematic means. In addition, Eli is confronted by the accusing gazes of Yael's parents. Later, he tries to feed the sobbing boy in a restaurant and is confronted by the gazes of the other costumers. At home, Zvi tends him, displaying the parenting skills Eli lacks. The lies Eli tells Noa on the phone about her son further underline his failure. The sense of guilt that colours all these scenes is introduced through another flashback, depicting another sex scene.

Yael's mother poses Eli an insolent question: "You don't love Yael. Why don't you leave her alone?" It serves as a catalyst for Eli's recollection of his first encounter with Yael, which was propelled by intrusion and defiance. Eli intrudes on Yael and Zvi during a field trip, positioning himself between them, pursuing Yael aggressively and treating Zvi as though he is the trespasser. The sex scene that follows begins suddenly and unexpectedly. Daylight switches to darkness, and Eli lies on top of Yael on the floor of a moving truck, surrounded by sleeping companions.

Yael's cleavage is a signifier of the erotic context, but the couple does not engage in sexual activity until the very end of the scene. Their cheerful conversation revolves around the disturbance that objects pose to them, and the extent to which they impose on their travel companions. They giggle and whisper like children. Nobody else appears with them in the frame until they embrace. A wide shot from the top captures not only her hands sensually caressing his back, but also fellow travellers lying close by. A close-up of Eli embraced by Yael is followed by a close-up of Zvi, lying with his eyes wide open, sharing a frame with a sleeping companion and listening to Eli and Yael.

Despite having most of the frames for themselves, Eli and Yael aren't alone. The segment closes with Eli looking over his shoulder into the camera, slowly sinking his head behind his shoulder, and in doing so obscuring Yael. The voice of Yael's mother is heard: "If only she would have come home just to sleep." Eli's past guilt toward Zvi for bursting into his relationship with Yael blends with his current guilt toward Yael's parents for barging into their family, and defines his dealings with the child.

Mischief has turned into guilt. Guilt then turns into malice. The second transition is expressed in Eli's voiceover, in the passage from the restaurant during the day to Eli's private apartment at night: "I think he feels bad already. Actually, I don't mind. I'm not responsible. I didn't ask her to send him over to me, her one and only child. I know they have no other friends in Jerusalem. But I'm not a friend either." The last sentences are spoken harshly, and Eli moves toward Shai, who is leaning on the rail of the balcony. It seems like Eli is about to throw the boy over the rail. Instead, he picks him up and carries him in. Later, indeed, Eli will put the boy's life at risk. But his most open act of aggression toward Shai takes place beforehand, as part of a sex scene.

In the morning, Eli is woken up from a nightmare by his neighbour and inadvertently pulls her to him. When she begins to touch and kiss him, he remains passive. Only after he notices the boy had woken up, he becomes active and makes love to her. The ferocity of his action is clear when the woman, who discovers she is being watched by the child, pleads and fights to free herself from Eli's embrace.

Gertz notes analogies between this and the other sex scenes in the film. To her, this repetitiveness marks universal alienation and a negation of the romantic notion of love (Gertz, 1993, p. 127). However, such correlations may also reflect Eli's development as a figure. His shift from passivity to activity, from complacence to control, is consistent with his conduct during the very first sex scene. The glances he directs toward Shai during sex are continuous with those he directs toward Zvi in the second sex scene. But whereas a sense of guilt epitomised his glance at Zvi, he now shows defiance.

Just as telling as the similarities are the elements which set the sex scene with the neighbour apart. This scene is more grotesque than the others, partly a feature of the age difference between the young Eli and his middle-aged partner. This effect is enhanced by the couple's facial expressions. Eli grimaces, first in disgust and then in sexual exertion. The neighbour displays a variety of animated facial expressions, from desire and ecstasy, to exertion and then struggle. While the camera angles in the previous sex scenes are limited to the upper body, this scene includes a medium shot of her lap as she tries to rebuff his attempt to remove her robe. Moreover, the slight tremor captured in their next close-up indicates that he is pleasuring her roughly with his hand. When she pulls him to her, his imperfect, naked back stretches over most of the screen, adding to their hectic and increasingly violent movements.

Most prominent are the boy's five reaction shots. During the previous sex scene with Yael, Zvi only appeared at the end. Here, the camera keeps returning to Shai, whose sheer presence affects events. The "realistic" nature of this scene, compared to the others, arises from the fact that it constitutes an exhibitionistic display of adult sexuality, for Shai to witness and internalise. Shai, who is lively during the scene, becomes lethargic and low spirited immediately afterwards. The scene becomes an act of violence against the child.

Once Upon a Time: The Recollection of Youth

Having "initiated" the boy into the world of sexuality, Eli's final flashbacks return to his own youthful sexual initiation. This develops in a secondary narrative, parallel to the primary one, in which Eli's volatile relations with the boy continue to unfold. The connection between the two tropes is not clear until the end of the film, particularly because they seem to differ in atmosphere. As the relations with the boy become darker, Eli's recollections of youth apparently offer a brighter ambiance.

One recollection comes when Eli and Shai are at the municipal swimming pool. Eli is greeted by a group of teenage girls to whom he teaches math. They appear in several group shots, talking, giggling, and holding on to each other. As they dominate the screen, their cheerful, indiscernible voices take over the soundscape. Eli, leisurely conversing with the girls, is captured from a higher angle, surrounded by adolescent torsos and backsides clad in bathing suits. Their lack of maturity is just as palpable as the flirtation and excitement with which they interact with Eli and the camera.

His flashback recalls an encounter with Noa in Eli's youth. Hakak notes the sharp contrast between the loud encounter with the girls and the tender melody that accompanies the flashback, as well as the mute interaction between Eli and Noa (Hakak, 2001, p. 139). However, it is just as important that the flashback returns to a time in which Eli and Noa were the age of the school girls before him. The sight of youth before this memory unfolds is a reminder of its imperfection, a transitory state between childhood and adulthood – something not manifested in the sentimental projection of Eli's memory.

In the flashback, Noa is walking in a vineyard. As she steps out to a clearing, she sits down and gets some water from a canister, and Eli steps into the picture. In the following reaction shots, she watches as he removes grapes and vine leaves from her muddy feet, gently strokes them, and inscribes her name in water on one foot, and his on the other. Looking at him, she draws her feet together and begins to softly rub them against each other. Then a male voice calls out her name and she rises, turns, and runs. As her feet hit a puddle, Eli is taken aback. This scene bears more erotic weight than any other in the film. In its suggestive magnetism it holds a promise of continuation – a future which in fact lies in the past.

The next recollection flashes suddenly, unexpectedly and briefly, eight minutes later, in the dead of night. A soft bell tune heralds the sight of the shimmering sunlight, reflected from the lake. Noa is wearing a dress. She turns to Eli, who approaches her with the same desiring, wondering expression as in the previous flashback, as she takes the piece of straw he hands her. The vision heightens the erotic promise of the vineyard. From such a peak, the fall is all the more profound.

The thread is picked up again five minutes later. It returns to the same point, after Noa takes Eli's offering of a straw. Eli comments in voiceover: "Only once did I sleep with her." She turns around and tells him to come. This is the moment both past and present Eli seem to yearn for. However, as the setting changes to the scene of their "crime" – a deserted shed – the atmosphere darkens. The door looms through the shaky frame of a hand-held camera. The shed is dark and disorderly. Noa and Eli are in separate frames. She appears intimidated, he embarrassed. Eli's voiceover continues: "That one time. It was terrible. She ... I didn't ... I ... " As a narrator, Eli introduces several scenes. This is the only time his voice breaks.

The scene is fragmented, cut down to many shots and camera angles. There are gaps in the actions that disrupt the sense of continuity. Some of the frames defy classical perspective. Additionally, both Noa and Eli are rigid and awkward, which adds a surreal quality to the scene. Far from the ease of their earlier erotic tension, Noa and Eli are now two intimidated youngsters. Lying naked, Noa appears detached, her eyes staring into in space. Eli sweats, and his movements as he kisses and strokes Noa are quivering and clumsy. Halfway through the scene, Eli lies on top of Noa. They are captured from the top down to their waist. He begins to stir above her, evidently penetrating her. A close-up captures Noa's expression over Eli's shoulder blade. Her eyes move toward him, but his head, only partially in the frame, is turned the other way. Her countenance softens, a reaction to his movement inside her. She turns her eyes and head toward him again. It seems that all would be well if he turned his head and kissed her lips, but his head remains unturned, and the image fades to black. They reappear, sweating and out of breath. He removes himself from her and she turns her back to him. With her face to the camera, Noa wears a gloomy expression, much like Yael at the beginning of the film. When the shed door opens back to the lake, it offers relief.

This scene is central: the film builds up to it and it serves as a kind of retrospective resolution. It reveals Eli's youthful trauma, in which he is too petrified to function, to be properly initiated into adulthood. However, even this failure is somewhat ambiguous – something well reflected in the scene's soundtrack. Gertz discusses the sound of the tin shed in the wind, mentioning the various other screeching sound that lead up to this scene, and arguing that it signifies discomfort and disharmony (Gertz, 1993, pp. 119–120). Indeed, the noise of the shed emphasises dissonance, and the wailing wind gives voice to desolation. But there is a third element that is increasingly audible, ultimately ending synchronically with the sexual act: the sound of percussion playing a bossa nova beat, which balances out the sense of stagnation in the scene. When Eli penetrates

12 The Child Enters the Sex Scene — 161

Figure 7: Eli's evolution through sex scenes with Yael, the neighbour, and Noa in NOT MINE TO LOVE.

Noa, the rhythm becomes louder. His movements are in perfect synchrony with the percussion, as though he is dancing to it. The beat functions as it would in a more positive context, in a "successful" sex scene. Moreover, it recalls the beat played at the opening title sequence, and during Eli and Shai's harmonious excursion in the city – two dynamic scenes in which Eli appears vibrant, fulfilling his role as a man, a friend, and a caretaker.

One may associate this with the fact that Eli's failure in the sex scene is not absolute. Eli does not fail to have sex with Noa, but to connect with her. He is functional and dysfunctional at the same time. This is not only the essence of his youthful trauma, but his major characteristic.

Dysfunctionality: The Non-Sovereign Murderer and Unredeemed Rescuer

I have demonstrated how Eli fails as a caretaker to Shai. It becomes clear that he is also an incompetent murderer. The first "murder" attempt happens in the municipal swimming pool, when Eli sees Shai crawling towards the edge of a roof. He does not leap to his rescue. Instead, he attempts to break his own glasses to provide himself an alibi when the boy does fall. The boy is then rescued by strangers. This incident is given a dramatic accent, creating suspense around the danger to the boy. The other "murder" attempt lacks such dramatic substance. Returning home with Shai, Eli finds Zvi frantically looking for a poisonous snake in the apartment. He had brought it the previous night in a box. The viewer witnessed Eli open the box and look at the snake, and then take a few steps to observe Shai in his sleep. It becomes clear in retrospect that the snake had been released, risking everyone's lives.

One murder attempt is pursued through inaction, the other through distraction. Eli is a rather passive murderer. All the while, his failure as a caretaker continues to be manifest in the boy's dejection. On the iconic level, this lack is contradicted. Eli repeatedly displays affection to the boy, petting, caressing, kissing, and especially carrying him. Again and again he holds the boy in his arms. Again and again, Shai, who otherwise shows increasing alienation toward Eli, holds on to him, and lays his head on his shoulder. These gestures do not palliate the crisis, but rather emphasise it.

This iconic aspect takes on a different dimension when Eli is rehabilitated by a rescue mission. Zvi and Eli search the apartment for the snake, leaving it in disarray. The snake appears and bites Zvi. Eli lingers before helping Zvi, but finally takes on the role of saviour and carries him through the olive groves in the Valley of the Cross. Not only is the environment Eli moves through evocative, reminiscent of the deeper past, but he also carries a heavier weight (Zvi, rather than Shai), and has a more serious mission (saving rather than tending). For a short moment he defies the apathy and truculence he had embodied.

The operation ends unspectacularly when Eli loads his patient onto a moped, which rushes to the hospital. It soon becomes clear that the rescue did not redeem him. After recalling his youthful trauma, Eli returns home to find that all has been brought into order in his absence. The apartment is tidy again, and Shai, washed, combed and dressed, is seated with a picture magazine. Seeing Eli, the boy steals over to his new protector, Yael, who has returned home and is standing in the kitchen, a model of maternal authority. In this environment, Eli's weary, unshaven appearance stands out. He dutifully returns to his incompliant, passive role: he pretends to sleep when Noa and Ze'ev pick up their son, and fails to explain himself to Yael. His epilogue is short and vague. With a melancholy expression he turns to lie on his side, facing the camera, evoking the images of both Yael and Noa as they appeared in their post-coital discontent.

Post-coital discontent expresses the frustration of expectations, which reflects upon the viewing process of the film. The film prompts the viewer to expect both an awful event which never materialises and a substantial change which never comes about. The boy remains unharmed, the man unsaved.

See Me, Feel Me: Male Anti-Spectacle

In the course of the film, the viewer is familiarised with Eli's body, which is unearthed but unaltered by the viewing process. A better understanding of this experience is gained when compared with the viewing process generated by the figure types discussed in part II.

Like the comic figures in MOTIVE TO MURDER, Eli appears in a succession of sex scenes of decreasing eroticism: a thorny yet harmonious engagement which ends abruptly, followed by a cheerful act of defiance which closes with an expression of guilt, then a grotesque moment of violence, and ending with an imposing act of failed initiation. Unlike a comic figure, however, Eli's eroticism is not debased and quenched. A sensual scene two thirds of the way into the film maintains its vitality.

Like the victim figures, Eli's body is put on display. Through most of the scenes that take place in the intimate sphere of his home, he appears predominantly without a shirt and/or trousers, his body exposed. However, unlike the male spectacle, Eli's body is not exhibited in extravagant motion, but in a docile state – a sort of anti-spectacle. This produces the opposite effect to the erotic allure of the male spectacle. It does not obliterate erotic potential, but rather makes the viewer acutely aware of its atrophy.

Figure 8: Eli, exposed and docile in a thorny home and relationship in Not Mine to Love.

Both Lubin and Bursztyn pay tribute to various aspects of anti-spectacle in other films by Zohar. Lubin discusses Gutte, the protagonist in Peeping Toms (1972), whose physical neglect and lack of purpose and action are displayed in an endless succession of brutal episodes (Lubin, 2001, pp. 104–105). Writing on Boys Will Never Believe It (1971), Bursztyn discusses male bodily exposure, which he sees as a recurrent premise in Zohar's films. He alludes to a succession of sexual acts in which the participating male is a passive object, aware of and collaborating with his objectification. Whether the protagonist embodies failure or success, he is pathetic, expressing deep yearning for passivity (Bursztyn, 1990, pp. 115–118).

While Lubin sees every aspect of such anti-spectacle as resistance to the Zionist metanarrative (Lubin, 2001, pp. 103–135), Bursztyn interprets it as a consumerist gesture of reification, legitimising the egoism of the new bourgeoisie (Bursztyn, 1990, pp. 118–119). However, what we principally gather from their respective analyses is that Zohar uses various means to recreate a consistent sensation of anti-spectacle, which he attached to a wide range of characters. The growing sense of unease that Zohar aroused in the viewer toward the film figure had no consistent source. In Boys Will Never Believe It, it counters the festive atmosphere that dominates the film. In PEEPING TOMS and NOT MINE TO LOVE, it is used to indicate arrested development. The weight of anti-spectacle plagues an aging beach bum in PEEPING TOMS, and a troubled young student in NOT MINE TO LOVE. In both cases, it hovers over a fusion of old and new, age and youth. In PEEPING TOMS, it lends a bitter taste to an ongoing procession of juvenile endeavours performed by grown men. In NOT MINE TO LOVE, it darkens the protagonist's aura in the presence of the child he endangers, and invalidates the scenes in which he appears to be dynamic, and to bear the promise of a new generation of young adults.

Anti-spectacle is used both in PEEPING TOMS and NOT MINE TO LOVE to indicate that something has gone strikingly wrong in the developmental process of the subjectivities the films fabricate, and that they are fundamentally inadequate. This is the sense expressed by several films from the late 1960s and early 1970s.[6] In each of these, the characters bear the symptoms of childhood into adulthood and old age.

12.3 IRIS

Past Present: Untimeliness

IRIS is the only fiction film produced by David Greenberg, a pioneering advocate of art films in Israel (Gertz, 1993, p. 15; Schnitzer, 1994a, p. 87; Schweitzer, 2003, p. 97). It evokes childhood, rather than representing it, and is an exemplary cinematic depiction of arrested development. IRIS portrays the May-December romance between Yoel, a journalist in his forties, and Iris, an adolescent girl,[7] at the brink of Yoel's divorce. Their romance begins as a quasi-platonic alliance forged over Romain Rolland's novel *Jean Christophe*, and ends with the very first rape performed on the Israeli screen.

IRIS, which was produced two years after NOT MINE TO LOVE, shares some of its features. Both were conceived and perceived as auteur films. In both the cityscape is central. Both stimulate unease in the viewer, and include sexual assault. Both focus on an unequal, intergenerational relationship. While Eli in NOT MINE TO LOVE becomes a temporary caretaker to a little boy, Yoel in IRIS provides the adolescent with books, stories of the past, and

---

6 Including BLAZE ON THE WATER, TAKE OFF, THE DREAMER, GET ZORKIN, and THE PILL.
7 Their exact ages are not mentioned in the film. Some references put Yoel's age at forty, and Iris' at sixteen (Katzir, 2013; Schnitzer, 1994a, p. 87; Gross and Gross, 1991, pp. 261–262).

companionship, and thus becomes a mentor of sorts. Both films explore the relationship between past and present. Not Mine to Love makes use of flashbacks, while Iris evokes the past only through spoken memory. Both films revolve around a traumatic experience. Not Mine to Love locates trauma in the past, while Iris generates it in the present. While Not Mine to Love closes with ambivalent peace, Iris ends in a storm of violence.

Both Not Mine to Love and Iris integrate the protagonist's ominous, non-diegetic prologue into their openings. Yoel's monologue occurs before the credits. It is heard in voiceover as Yoel is shown running through residential and industrial parts of Tel Aviv:

> "I beat him. I beat him until he was unconscious. Perhaps he even died. Karin was with him, on the couch, in the apartment. She jumped, scared, and hid behind the curtain. 'Leave him alone', she cried, 'he lied, he lied'. What happened to Iris? Will you ever forgive me, Iris? It is unforgivable. He lied. She was innocent. She was mine."

This is repeated with rock music accompaniment. It ends when Yoel runs into an apartment building and violently knocks on a door. Three short visual excerpts from the rape scene are inserted into this segment, in which Iris is seen "headless" from the neck down. The viewer sees her naked body in the midst of a tussle. In the second insert, Yoel is exposed as the perpetrator. The full context of all this is brought to the viewer at the end of the film. Yoel rapes Iris, and after he passes through the door, he does what he describes in the prologue, assaulting his best friend, Yoram.

Yoel's monologue is more opaque than Eli's. While the latter provides a summary of the film, Yoel simply offers an abrupt description of the film's last scene, which is to some extent incoherent. However, as Ariel Schweitzer notes, this is the only sequence in the film that challenges the linear narrative structure (Schweitzer, 2003, p. 124). As a venture at disjointedness, it is rather timid – certainly in comparison to The Hero's Wife. The purpose is not to disorient the viewer. The scene even contains cues to help the viewer overcome any confusion. The monologue is repeated twice, and the inserts indicate exactly what "happened to Iris" and what is "unforgivable". Rather, this opening is directed at the effect of temporal disorder as a form of untimely disruption. It is the very first manifestation of untimeliness, which, as I shall demonstrate, is the driving force behind every facet of Iris. It will surface through interactions between present and past and in discordant relationships, particularly between Yoel and Iris.

The Winter of Our Content: The Abhorrence of the Present and the Celebration of the Past

Much of IRIS revolves around the chasm between past and present, rather than present and future. In this respect, the age gap between Yoel and Iris has very little importance. The generational incongruities are between Yoel's generation and their predecessors, which reflect on Tel Aviv as it is and as it once was. Yoel conceals his divorce from his mother, and tells her instead that he and his wife might be expecting a child. When his ex-wife, Shuli, finally confronts the mother with the truth, the latter enters a state of shock. Yoel's friend Yoram, also a journalist, is seemingly engaged in a professional dispute with the elderly chief editor of the newspaper, Mishori. The conflict turns out to be a bitter quarrel over Mishori's daughter, Mira'le, who commits suicide after Yoram refused to marry her. In both cases, information is withheld from the older generation about a crisis which could not be reconciled with its expectations.

The visual exposition of new public spaces conveys unease over the present. Three fashionable locations – a model party, a bowling alley, and a fashion show – are shot with a moving camera from unconventional angles, generating a sense of vertigo. The pop tunes that accompany each exposition functions as ironic commentary, and the atmosphere is tense. Yoram dominates the party scene with an objectifying commentary on the women present. A confrontation between Yoel and Shuli is only narrowly defused in the bowling alley. Shuli escapes the fashion show after modelling a bridal dress in front of Yoel and his new flame, Iris. The trendy present, in short, is portrayed as negative and alienating. Schweitzer reads this scene and others like it as an emulation of European cinema's critique of capitalism (Schweitzer, 2003, pp. 149–150). Indeed, as he points out, Tel Aviv remained too quaint and Mediterranean to justify its portrayal as an urban jungle. However, Schweizer also points out that the city was changing rapidly in the period (ibid., p. 146). The sense of alienation in IRIS stems not so much from the economic implications of this new culture of consumerism, but the change it brought to the urban landscape. Tel Aviv had ceased to be what it once was.

Yoel and Iris' three wandering scenes unfold in this context, as they walk together to the soothing melody of the film's theme. Typical of the genre, these scenes slow the film's pace and display the hidden beauty of the cityscape (ibid., p. 126–129). These scenes have been criticised for their intertextual reference to European cinema (Schnitzer, 1994a, p. 87; Schweitzer, 2003, p. 166) and their wintery European weather and atmosphere (Schweitzer, 2003, p. 148).

Most critics hold that the frequent use of winter by the "new sensibility" attests to the makers' desire to escape the Israeli sphere altogether and pretend they are somewhere else (Shohat, 1989, pp. 200–202; and, in wider context, Schweitzer, 2003, pp. 146–153). However, Iris makes accentuated use of winter weather, depicting Tel Aviv as more overcast and drizzly than it typically is, even during this season. This expresses untimeliness.

In one scene, Yoel and Iris roam Tel Aviv's dilapidated promenade. A central location in the city's life in the 1920s, by the time Iris was made, the promenade was in dire need of renovation, and the businesses around it had bad reputations (Ravid-Hameiri et al., 2008). An off-season aesthetic dominates the scene: the wet surfaces of a wide empty promenade, pieces of torn nylon blown by the stormy wind. The two jump over a locked gate into a large promenade café, which is evidently closed. In mock ceremony, they pretend to interact with the non-existent staff and waltz across the dilapidated terrace. Their playful movements are suggestive of the way it must have looked during the season in its heyday: bathing in sunlight and brimming with crowds that came to swim during the day and dance in the sweltering evenings. In this off-season cosmos, Yoel and Iris celebrate being in the wrong place and time.

The opening of the second wandering scene, at the Yarkon River, prepares the viewer for a nostalgic mode. Yoel and Iris are flipping through his photo album. As he speaks of the Yarkon in past tense, naming landmarks that no longer exist, they are seen on the river bank, playing among racks of boats. Yoel's voiceover reminds the viewer that boats once sailed on this water. The couple appear in a small boat on the river. Yoel rows it back and forth as Iris spins her umbrella like a parasol. They appear in a very long shot, partially obscured by a layer of vegetation and out-of-focus fishing nets in the foreground which undermine their position. Thunder strikes; the camera zooms in on the couple in the boat struggling with the wind and the rain, a reminder that their excursion is taking place in the wrong season.

In these two scenes, Yoel and Iris visit spaces still partially occupied by the past. In the next scene of wandering, however, the present and the future loom behind them. The couple shares a romantic walk through a landscape of dunes and open fields. However, in two major instances the horizon is dominated by edifices: first by a large factory, and then by high rise apartment blocks. A crane rising behind a dune indicates that urban development is in progress. Like those before it, the scene marks a space in transition. The film does more than favour the past over the present: it places Yoel and Iris in the rift between eras.

"I Once Looked After Him ... A Little": Yoel's Misogyny, Lack of Mastery, and Sexual Surrender

Yoel, the film's protagonist, is first seen in spatial and temporal discord. He opens the film in a frenzy. Stout, with thick glasses, he then appears unshaven at the rabbinical divorce court, and cannot find his identity card until his ex-wife-to-be produces it from his front pocket. When he arrives at his new dwellings, a shabby extension built on a windy rooftop, his belongings lie in disarray. Yoel is a man in crisis, who lacks control over his life. He hides from his mother the fact that he is childless and divorced. Throughout the film, he is shown being manipulated by his close circle. To his trusted friend Yoram, he describes how his ex-wife coaxed him into marriage. Later, it becomes clear that Yoram himself dreamt up this manipulation.

Yoel's absent sovereignty extends to his relationship with the singles market. His lack of resolve is demonstrated shortly after the divorce scene. Immediately after he declares his intention to be a recluse, he appears at a crowded model party.[8] All through the film, Yoram directs demeaning and objectifying remarks at women, using crude terms designed to arouse the viewer's abhorrence. Yoel protests, but not against Yoram's misogyny or demeaning conduct. In a separate misogynist undercurrent, Yoel objects to the sexual entanglements Yoram promotes by directing pejorative comments towards the female party goers.

When Karin, Yoel's devotee, is introduced at the crowded model party, she makes a vulgar remark that hints that Yoel has also yielded to the very thing he claims to despise: "I once looked after him ... a little." Her final assault halfway through the film illustrates this more clearly. Karin walks into Yoel's roof apartment at night, while he is typing at his desk. As she talks, switching between snide remarks and puzzled questions, she takes off her fur coat to reveal a skimpy black dress underneath, and then grabs a dagger from the coffee table and dangles it over its sheath. This is done to no avail behind Yoel's back. Yoel is only engaged through touch, which begins when she leans over the desk beside him and taps him on the shoulder to the rhythm of his typing. Yoel glances at her and loses his composure. As he stands up, the frame captures him from the chest to his buttocks, allowing the viewer to gaze at his chubby body. Yoel turns his back on Karin and tucks his shirt into his trousers. Karin pulls the shirt out of his trousers and rubs his undershirt. His movements become

---

8 Similar parties – known as "Mesibot Heshek", or lust parties – are shown in A Woman's Case and Boys Will Never Believe It. In all three films, it is visually indicated that the women who partake in such gatherings are younger than the men.

hesitant. For a brief moment, they struggle over his shirt. When the camera moves to a long shot the pair are turning, his arms already around her, and his head is sunk in her shoulder. The erotic tension leading up to the sex scene is not associated with sensuality but with Yoel's lack of sovereignty. Ineptitude leads to sexual performance, rather than a failure to perform.

Yoel's weakness is not manifested in passivity. He undresses Karin down to her trendy undergarments and lies on top of her. The intensity with which he embraces, kisses, and pushes up against her sustains sexual tension. The camera zooms in as his head moves to reveal her closed eyes and vivid smile. However, the scene cuts abruptly. Karin, who was lying in the rightmost quarter of the screen, is suddenly seen on the left, motionless, her hand holding her head and her expression severe. The promise of pleasure is abruptly transformed into displeasure. A wider medium shot reveals Yoel on a rocking chair. Spent, fully clothed, and covered with Karin's fur coat, he rocks back and forth. Karin is sprawled naked on the bed, a pair of glasses on her thigh like a garter. Both Karin and Yoel avert their gaze several times during the segment, looking grim. Schweizer points out that Karin in this scene resembles Ingres' *La Grande Odalisque* (Schweitzer, 2003). As in Ingres' painting, the sensuality of Karin's curves and impeccable soft skin are accentuated. Like the painting, this is countered by the figure's averted eyes. The promise of pleasure is presented through Karin's body and, simultaneously, quenched by the expressions on the faces of Yoel and Karin, which manifest a contradiction present in Yoel himself.

Icon and Spectre: The Spectacle of Girlhood

Yoel first encounters Iris when he slips out of the crowded model party and sees her silhouette hunched over a book under the street light. From the beginning, she poses a contrast to the trendy and licentious environment. He approaches her. Shuv observes that, during their interaction, the camera relates to Iris differently than to Yoel. While he remains in medium shot, she is captured in close-up, her face appearing flat and depthless. Shuv points out that within Hollywood conventions such a close-up attributes iconic value to female figures. Because Israeli films lack female glamour, she claims that such shots cannot play the same role within them (Shuv, 1998, pp. 220–221). In Iris' case however, the figure is raised to iconic levels precisely because she is devoid of glamour.

The camera explores Iris' face several times in the film, primarily in moments related to Yoel's consciousness. On all these occasions, her unruly hair is braided into two plaits and her eyes are often turned up, enhancing her girlish appearance and lending her smile a mischievous quality. In all but one instance, Iris is shown in clothes which hang loosely on her body. This lax style is played up against glamour. When she appears one night in fashionable clothes and a high hairdo, the shadows in Yoel's terrace obscure her stylish appearance. Yoel quickly changes her hairstyle back to plaits, and in the next scene he parades her as his companion to a fashion show, where models exhibit the voguish womanhood she stands in contrast to.

Glamour is also embodied in Iris' two female "rivals", Shuli, the ex-wife, and Karin, Yoel's devotee. Both appear in a variety of fashionable outfits which highlight their stature. They wear meticulous make up, their hair piled high. Karin, British and blond – with the allure of a foreign beauty – often wears sparkling earrings and a fur coat which enhance her glamour.[9] Shuli's and Karin's female charms are brought to view in extended scenes of flirtation each has with Yoram. The film, however, favours Iris. She is featured at length, idolised by Yoel and the camera, and her "rivals" are shown at a disadvantage during their encounters, during which they gaze at her.

Iris' youthful appearance is central, as is her conduct, which resembles that of a child more than a teenager. Iris is first seen with a lollipop in her mouth, playing hopscotch. In most of her appearances, she ventures into childlike play. She often hops rather than walks. In several scenes, she hides for no apparent reason. On occasion she also uses childish speech, and Yoel refers to her as a child. When she discloses that she knows exactly where he has been and what he had done, he smiles and playfully grabs hold of the edge of her braids while reciting what could easily pass for a children's verse: "Everything is known to Iris / Everything is seen by her." The traditional imagery of childhood is evoked. But Iris is portrayed as a young woman, not a child: in her overt display of juvenility, Iris does not embody childhood, but regression.

The complexity of Iris' role is located in the sexual dimension. She poses an alternative to the world of parties and its modern sexual mores, and nevertheless still bears eroticism. This is only possible as long as she and Yoel display but do not consummate their desire. Twice in the film, the viewer is made to expect Yoel and Iris to kiss. In both cases they draw together and their lips almost meet, but a kiss does not follow. Once, Iris places her injured finger in front of Yoel's mouth in a juvenile gesture, to kiss it "all better". Their suggestive glances are captured as their playful movements become slower and more

---

[9] The actress, Mandy Rice-Davies, gained notoriety in England with the Profumo Affair of 1963. In Israeli culture of the period she was seen as glamorous and fashionable.

sensual. The gesture becomes erotic, but then Iris slips away from Yoel, and he is left holding a branch to his lips. Sexual realisation is not only avoided, but candidly frustrated – until the next scene, where Yoel carries out the sexual act, this time with Karin.

Iris is not presented as devoid of sexual motivation. Like Karin, she initiates sexual contact with Yoel. But this act ends with a decline in erotic power. Yoel and Iris are covered with soot, Yoel having put out a fire on his roof. In a matter-of-fact manner, with her back to Yoel and the audience, Iris takes off her blouse and heads to the shower. Yoel, sitting on the bed, shows signs of silent excitement. With only the shower curtain to cover her body, Iris gives Yoel further instructions. She sends him to the barber for a shave, signalling her sexual readiness. Earlier in the film she told Yoel he needs to go to the barber so that his cheeks wouldn't scratch her. Naked, she now indicates to Yoel that he should prepare himself to approach her. Yoel and the viewer expect that matters will progress – which they do, in an untimely and unanticipated manner. Yoel sees Iris showing her breasts, but in a drawing on the wall at the barber shop. Having recognised the nude drawing of Iris, and having learnt that it is by Izzi, the Bohemian artist who hosted the model party, the camera follows Yoel as he runs down the street and through the roof into his apartment. Wearing nothing but a blouse, Iris gets ready to begin, and throws her arms around Yoel. Yoel, however enters a different mode, and grows increasingly aggressive toward Iris, finally grabbing her hands and throwing her onto the bed.

Iris regresses in the full sense of the word. She grabs the cat sitting next to her and, like a child, crawls underneath the bed. Appeased and appeasing, Yoel crawls underneath as well to offer his apologies. The extent to which the scene loses its sexual force becomes clear from a third perspective. Shuli, Yoel's former wife, enters the apartment. She sees Iris' clothes thrown on the floor, and directs an apprehensive look further into the apartment, where Iris' naked feet and Yoel's legs pop out from underneath the bed. Had she walked in on a passionate sex scene, her reaction would have been negative. Instead, she smiles and giggles as Yoel impersonates a cat. Then she turns away and leaves. The sexual tension is discharged, but the tranquillity achieved in its place does not last. Iris escapes the apartment after Yoel asks in good humour how Iris knows Izzi. For the next eight minutes of the film, she is declared missing. Iris' attempt to come together with Yoel deteriorates in a complete loss of eroticism. She can only regain her erotic allure and idolised status through temporary disappearance.

The frustration of the long-awaited sexual incarnation of Yoel and Iris' bond occurs through exposure to the public sphere and the present time.

More accurately, in the very moment that Yoel and Iris are to consummate their erotic attachment, the film transfers Iris to the public, promiscuous sphere so reviled by Yoel. It takes an overt performance of a child in danger on Iris' part, and the consequent eradication of eroticism, to drive this spectre away.

Beside the connection between sexual materialisation and debasement, a major factor in this calamitous scenario is the fact that Iris, in contrast to Yoel, does not have a biography. The circumstances of her life remain obscure, communicated through conversations and rumours but never consolidated into images and facts. The question of how Izzi came to draw her portrait, for instance, is never answered. The gaps make Iris a fertile vessel for projection, and Yoel credibly changes his impression of her entirely twice in the course of the four-minute scene.

Yoram, too, crafts a projection on Iris in his final monologue – which brings Yoel to carry out the rape. During a conflict between Yoram and Yoel, Iris becomes the main target of Yoram's verbal assault. He depicts her as an imposter, a disaffected sex fiend with emasculating views of Yoel and a pathological drive for sex with many partners. This version of Iris, told by an unreliable character, in contradiction to many details seen and heard in the film, does not sway the viewer as it does Yoel. Nor does Yoram's subsequent sermon in favour of loveless, exploitative attitudes towards women. Nevertheless, Yoram associates his barrage with the sense of loss of the past is instilled in the film: "But I feel worse for you. Someone who still wants to hold hands, and sing the old homeland songs. Listen, those days are over. The blue shirt, the youth movement. It's time you stop dreaming of ideal love."

Socio-political allegiance and private emotional allegiance are compressed into one. They are placed in the past tense – both society's past, which is no longer so committed and committing, and the individual's past, who cannot retrieve the unswerving passion of youth. The film has shown that both communal and individual pasts are irretrievably gone. Most discomforting is that the present which replaces this past is ambiguous and unclear, subject to projection and speculation. In this context, Iris plays a dual role. On the iconic level, she is reminiscent of the irretrievable past. Her plaits are not only a feature of childhood but emblematic of the youth movement, like the blue shirt Yoram mentions, indicative of a period which was both individually and nationally formative. On the narrative level, this ideological stance is absent and Iris is aligned with the present: frisky, obscure, and elusive.

Violence and Confusion: The Turbulent End

After Yoram ends his speech the camera moves closer to Yoel, who appears grief-stricken and disenchanted. In the next two scenes he tips the scale, ending the film with violence. The danger that had been lurking is finally manifested not through a villain or a cynic, but through the "good guy", the starry-eyed protagonist. Yoel's ultimate transformation into the aggressor is part of the destruction. In contrast to THE HERO'S WIFE, in which the sex scene was a culmination of the film's atmosphere, a resolution of the existential dilemmas surging through it, in IRIS the two last scenes contradict and destroy all that has been built up during the film.

The breakdown is not completely sudden, and is not only heralded by Yoram's words. The sense of impending upheaval is constructed in the last third of the film, beginning with the breakdown which hinders Yoel and Iris' expected sex scene. Running and chasing become major motifs in a chain reaction. Yoel searches for Iris, growing increasingly impatient and aggressive. When they unite and appear publicly together at the fashion show, it is Shuli who runs away in the middle of the show. Shuli then confronts Yoel's mother and informs her of the marital breakup, which heightens the crisis. In the hospital, Yoel assures his paralysed mother that he is still married and will bring a child to the world. Iris, who witnesses this, runs frantically through the hospital corridors with Yoel chasing her.

At the end of the film Yoel brings violence in dual form, in two successive, stylistically contrasting scenes. The scene in which he rapes Iris lasts 145 seconds – twice as long as the one in which he beats up Yoram. While the rape scene is surreal, taking place in a boat-wreck on the bank of the Yarkon River, the beating takes place in the very mundane environment of Yoram's apartment. The rape scene is almost completely silent, with only one line uttered by Iris ("I knitted you a sweater"). Otherwise, it begins with the sounds of singing birds and croaking frogs, complemented by quiet sounds of squeaking from the boat. In contrast, the beating scene is loud, starting with the sound of car traffic, continuing with Yoel's accusing murmurs, the pop tune played from the transistor that falls on the floor, and Karin's worried cries. In both scenes, the act of violence is seen predominantly up close and in full screen, with sporadic use of non-conventional angles in which objects obscure the violence. Both acts of violence are placed upfront for the viewer to experience. However, in the rape scene, most of the shots capture both perpetrator and victim in a single frame, whereas in the beating scene they are separated through reaction shots. Despite these differences, the beating complements the rape scene. On the face of it, it serves as a reaction to the injustice of the rape, and an act of liberation from the manipulative force which caused it. The beating continues the violence which began with the rape, and sustains Yoel's role as violator. The source of the violence is one and the same, and none of the acts offer release.

The rape scene is distinguished by the destabilisation of the viewer's perspective. For the first time in the film, there is no "realistic" pretext to the event and location. Having earlier searched for Iris in vain, Yoel locates her easily in the uncanny ruins of stranded boats that they visited in an earlier scene. The boat where he finds her is sloped at a high angle, which complicates the viewer's visual perception. At times, the image is presented upside down. For instance, when Yoel peers into the boat, he is shown in an upright position, but the unnatural position of his hair and swollen cheeks indicates that the image has been inverted. The camera tilts several times during the scene, and as a result the viewer must ask whether what seemed to be vertical was actually horizontal, and vice versa – so that, by the end of the scene, it is no longer clear where the top and bottom are.

The rape is partitioned into a succession of shots. Yoel peers into the boat where Iris is hunched. She hands him a sweater which he discards. He pulls off her blouse and bra, exposing her torso, lies on top of her, kisses her body while forcing her down, pulls off her pants, and pushes against her. A violent act is depicted, but the imagery itself is not particularly intrusive, revealing, or shocking. The camera ventures below the waist only once, revealing Iris' pelvis as Yoel pulls her pants down. Brutality occurs through action. During the struggle, the centre of the frame switches back and forth between assaulter and victim. At first, Yoel's ferocious movements are depicted as he pulls Iris' clothes off and then pushes up against her. His face is tense with exertion. After he presumably penetrates Iris, the composition centres on her as she struggles, clenches her teeth, and wriggles. The viewer sees her fail to get away, fail to release herself from Yoel's embrace, and fail to pull him off her as he pushes against her. Her face expressed sorrow and awe. She repeatedly shakes her head. Her vulnerability is emphasised not only through her delicate face and figure, which are exposed, but also in her disparity from Yoel, who remains fully clothed, in a woollen sweater that accentuates the heaviness of his body.

Less than halfway into the scene, the camera tilts and the situation turns. Yoel's movements and expressions soften. Iris closes her eyes and her countenance becomes soft and absorbed. She returns Yoel's kiss and holds the back of his head. She alternates between attempts to push him away and sensual caresses. His movements come slowly to a halt, marking the end of coitus. The camera remains on Iris' face, expressing both exhaustion and awe. The film makes use of a pattern which was internationally common in that period: of a rape victim collaborating with the act, turning coercion to ravishment – "lying back and enjoying it", in Williams' words (Williams, 1999 (1989), pp. 164–165). Academic

Figure 9: Yoel's violation of Iris in IRIS.

discussions of such depictions in mainstream and pornographic films describe unambiguous instances of this pattern. Williams sums up the established hypotheses: that this pattern manifests a patriarchal fantasy, expressing at the loss of male power; that it constitutes a nostalgic utopia in which rape, ravishment, and the abuse of women goes uncensored; that it relies on a reality in which women are held responsible for crimes that victimise them, on the suspicion that the victim wants to be victimised and the idea that women's pleasure is damning. She adds that, since the crime of rape depends on the victim's mental state, consent nullifies it. The depiction of woman's pleasure therefore vindicates the man's coercion. The assumption behind such scenarios is that rape is a form of education in which a woman learns that she wants to be ravished. The distance from "no" to "yes" becomes a measure of female desire (ibid., pp. 160–166).

The rape scene in IRIS, however, does not conform to any of the configurations Williams and others describe. It departs from the film's sense of reality, but never amounts to a patriarchal fantasy. Iris never "shouts for more", never completes her "education". For most of the scene, the viewer sees her struggle to rebuff the attack. Her cooperation is short lived and partial. In the aftermath of the rape, the focus remains on her sorrowful expression. Both men involved in the rape, the manipulating Yoram and the manipulated Yoel, hold weak positions. The act of rape could plausibly be perceived as a way of venting their weakness, but not as a way of resolving it. In the thirty-two seconds during which Iris embraces Yoel, he is not vindicated and she is not condemned. In addition, female desire is articulated in active form earlier in the film, both by Iris and Karin. The rape, then, does not represent its "unmasking".

The question of the function played by Iris' submission cannot be answered using existing academic discourse. The poetic structure of the rape scene provides a more plausible explanation. As shown above, the viewer's position in the scene is constantly undermined. In more than one way, the viewer is made to doubt her own perception. For a short instance this continues in the beating scene which follows. Yoel overcomes Yoram, bangs his head on the floor until his eyes close – in Yoel's words from the opening monologue, until he is unconscious, perhaps dead. This is then reversed, with a short close-up showing Yoram looking back at Yoel, lightly twitching his eyes. Neither of the assaults remain complete and unchallenged. The severity of each act of violence is never put into question, and Yoel is never exonerated, but ambiguity is nevertheless generated. The abuse of Iris is not erased or reversed. But the sense of certitude that could be drawn from her initial resistance evaporates by the end of the scene because of her change of conduct and conflicting reactions. Rather than ending the scene with perseverance or horror, Iris' expression is one of mournful confusion.

It would seem that Yoel ends the film with an assurance and resolution Iris lacks. But his performance conveys no less confusion. Having overwhelmed Yoram, he looks at Karin in defiance and calls out, in English, "You are a liar too!", and then, in Hebrew, "Like him!" Sustaining the defiant glare toward Karin he walks backward, and accidentally knocks the entrance door shut, before he manages to exit. The unstable camera and Yoel's clear agitation undercut the decisiveness of his words and actions. More crucial than both is the fact that his conduct is more suited to a rebellious teenager. The film, which began with a teenager emulating a child, ends with a middle-aged man emulating an adolescent. Regression is the final expression of untimeliness which closes the film. The call of defiance – so visible in on the international arena, with all its revolutionary movements – loses its eminence when expressed by a non-youth who had just perpetrated a vicious rape. Throughout the film, regression has been accompanied by a sense of yearning for an irretrievable past, poetic ardour, tenderness, innocence, and juvenility. In the violence of its final acts of destruction, regression loses its romantic mantle. It offers no solace, no prospect for the future – just a sense that, in the transition from past to present, something has gone fundamentally wrong.

12.4 Children in Danger, Men in Crisis: Conclusion and Commentary

Of the three films discussed in this chapter, only the first, A Night in Tiberias, has the endangered child at its centre. The other two, Not Mine to Love and Iris, revolve around grown men in crisis. Nonetheless, I have shown that the traditional image of the endangered child plays a major role in both films. So too does the menacing role of adult sexuality in that context. In Not Mine to Love, the caretaker entrusted with the child grows increasingly harmful toward him. In parallel to the growing danger the boy faces, the film returns to the man's own youth, revealing the traumatic events at the heart of his arrested development. In Iris, the traditional imagery of childhood is evoked by and through a pubescent girl whose incongruous romantic partner transforms into a predator.

Furthermore, in Not Mine to Love and Iris, the transition between private and public spheres plays a part in the dramaturgical evolution of the crisis. In Not Mine to Love, Eli frequently returns to passivity and resistance. His lack of sovereignty is epitomised by the intrusion of the public sphere into the private, and his chronic lack of privacy. Eli's impropriety with the boy is also judged in the public arena. Similarly, Yoel's lack of control in Iris is associated with the intrusion of his social circle into his private space and affairs. Exposure to and in the public sphere frustrates his affair, causing anger, upheaval, and violence.

Indeed, the two dangerous men, disempowered and lacking sovereignty, embody a crisis of masculinity, as Talmon argues (Talmon, 2001, p. 160). I have demonstrated that this crisis is communicated through the traditional image of the child, simultaneously vital and endangered, and the chronic mutual intrusion of the public and the private sphere. This challenges the assumption, typical of Israeli film studies, that portrayals of disempowerment necessarily correspond to an earlier pattern in which a masculine idyll reigns supreme.[10] Barry K. Grant, who discusses the representation of masculinity in American film, cautions against the idea that a mythic, stable, monolithic concept of masculinity has ever existed, and that any diversion from this pattern constitutes a crisis in this heteronormative ideal (Grant, 2011, pp. 5–7).

---

[10] Such hypotheses are not exclusive to the Israeli case. Since the representation of men was discovered as a topic, crises of masculinity have been systematically detected and mapped by film scholars in many national cinemas and almost every era. Some of their titles are already telling: Constance Penley's *Male Trouble* (1993), which echoes Butler's 1990 *Gender Trouble*; Gaylyn Studlar's *This Mad Masquerade* (1996); Steve Cohan's *Masked Men* (1997); Russell West's edited volume, *Subverting Masculinity* (2000); Raya Morag's *Defeated Masculinities* (2009); and Elahe Haschemi Yekani's *The Privilege of Crisis* (2011).

As I have shown in section 7.3, male dominance, competence, and strength provide spectacle in the first Israeli feature film, but were not the dominant motif of this or later films. The common patterns Not Mine to Love, Iris, and A Night in Tiberias use to formulate their respective crisis provide the key to a different interpretation.

Instead of regarding figures like Eli and Yoel as counter-products of a positive ideal of the New Jew, I suggest that they appeared in a more pluralistic realm, in which all the complexities of Jewish identity were being negotiated. I demonstrated in chapter 11 that, around the time Eli and Yoel were playing out their broken masculinity, male spectacle was assigned to the figures of the victims, whose pain and loss justify and enhance their physical presence. The juxtaposition of Eli and Yoel with images of childhood embeds those contemporaneous, ominous manifestations of identity in the existing tradition of communal self-reflection in Israeli society. In this context, the introduction of sexual assault and rape mirrored the fears emerging in Israeli society in the second half of the 1960s about what it was becoming.

My discussion of Israeli films of the 1960s has shown that, within the pluralistic realm they reflected, male and female identities were being negotiated. Comedy was probing the borders between individuals and their environment, and eroticism and victimhood were cautiously being used to legitimise an emphasis on the individual. Figures of children were repeatedly used to explore the themes of fragility and inadequacy. Part III discusses how these factors were renegotiated in the decade that followed, in relation to contemporary events.

Part III: **The 1970s: War, Protest and Youth**

13 Same Same, But Different: The Politics of Sex and Identity

In part II I analysed the early Israeli sex scenes of the 1960s, demonstrating the role played by the disruption of space, the comic figure, the victim, and the child, their utility in the performance of subjectivity, and the identities they correspond to within Israeli culture. As historical cultural continuity is essential to my argument, in part III I demonstrate how the same elements continued to nourish a communal self-image as the turbulences of the 1970s found cinematic expression – a self-image negotiated through sex scenes.

This was a decade in which both the Israeli state and the film industry experienced prosperity, crisis, and change. The industry developed, with new filmmakers and actors joining its ranks. While in the 1960s films were shot, as a rule, in black and white, the majority of those made in the 1970s were in colour (including all those discussed in part III, with the exception of LIGHT OUT OF NOWHERE). Despite rapid changes in Israeli cinema over the period, it was not until the late 1970s that there was any discussion of an emerging Israeli "new wave". This reflects the general perception that the 1970s largely represented a continuation of the films and genres conceived in the 1960s. Another contributing factor was that semi-academic discourse about the history of Israeli cinema only emerged in the late 1970s.

During the 1970s, Israel experienced a major war (1973), its first democratic change of governing party (1977), a peace treaty with a nation which had once been its bitter enemy (1979), and the rise of civil protest movements. I discuss all of these in greater detail in the following chapters. Meanwhile, culturally, major developments took place in the depiction and discussion of sex and sexuality: According to Almog, the belated arrival of the sexual revolution in Israeli society occurred in the late 1960s and early 1970s. This manifested itself in a number of anthropological phenomena: the public legitimisation of premarital sex, liberalised attitudes towards it, increasing eroticism in fashion, the incorporation of sexual idioms into everyday language, and the popularisation of sexualised humour (Almog, 2004, pp. 1053–1059). In newspaper advertising, sexualised imagery became dominant during the late 1960s, and correspondingly suggestive language came to prevail in the mid-1970s (ibid., p. 1113).

The 1970s saw the proliferation and progress of sex education literature for teenagers (ibid., p. 1075), children (ibid., p. 1081), and adults (ibid., p. 1083). Sexual therapy clinics were established at the end of the decade, offering practical medical assistance (ibid., p. 1087). Progress was evident not only on the medical and educational level, but also in fiction and art. Almog notes an increase in depictions of sex in literature and the theatre in the 1970s (ibid., pp. 1121–1136). According to Ben-Ari, until the late 1970s, official censorship was accompanied by self-censorship on the part of writers and publishers. This does not mean that erotic literature was non-existent, but that it was relegated to the cultural margins. The late 1970s saw a reduction in marginal literary practices, like erotic pulp fiction, and the emergence of mainstream erotic literature. Such literature ceased to be "parentless": writers and translators of erotic literature no longer used pseudonyms, and women joined their circle (Ben-Ari, 2006, pp. 62, 127).

Both Ben-Ari and Almog cite Dahn Ben-Amotz's popular novel *Screwing Isn't Everything* as the first Hebrew literary work in mainstream culture to revolved around explicit sexual content, integrated within a distinctively local cultural context (Ben-Ari, 2006, pp. 313–331; Almog, 2004, pp. 1110–1129). The novel – which, according Ben-Ari and Almog, was not only successful, but also had an impact on public discourse – was published in 1979, the year in which the films discussed in chapter 16 were released.

Within the general cultural context, then, it is no wonder that the number and frequency of sex scenes in Israeli cinema significantly increased in the 1970s. The film censorship committee continued its work, sustaining a harsher line towards local productions compared to international ones (Shalit, 2006, pp. 111–112, 140–144). In 1979, the director Avi Nesher was forced into intensive discussions with the committee over Dizengoff 99, just as Zohar had been twelve years earlier with Not Mine to Love (compare Nuriel and Ben Ari, 2009, p. 7; and Shalit, 2006, p. 144). Still, the sheer number of sex scenes produced in the decade make it clear that the premises according to which films represented sexual content were shifting.

When Williams describes the public impact of sex scenes on the American screen in the 1970s, the transformation she outlines is a "drawing back of curtains" on more than one level. In her analysis of two popular X-rated films, The Last Tango in Paris (1972, D: Bernardo Bertolucci) and Deep Throat (1972, D: Gerard Damiano), Williams shows how more explicit content appeared on screens, European conventions entered American cinema, and pornography entered popular culture (Williams, 2008, p. 114, 120). She underlines that, in flocking to see both movies, American viewers publicly recognised their own interest in observing sex, and in films that made sex their main feature (ibid.). The context in which sex was perceived also changed. The sex act in The Last

TANGO IN PARIS was imbued with powerful emotions (ibid., p. 119–120), and both films arouse lust, intermixed with other emotions (ibid., p. 122). This, and the fact that screenings were no longer confined to the arthouse, integrated them into the fabric of cultural life (ibid., p. 123). The change Williams describes in the United States during the early 1970s includes both an increase in explicit content and growing public exposure to it.

The surge in the number and frequency of sex scenes on the Israeli screen suggests something similar, although the parameters were different. Nothing as extraordinary as the acceptance of a pornographic film into mainstream culture occurred, in the 1970s or any time after. Furthermore, there was never such a clear division between national and foreign conventions used in the representation of sex, or a similar distinction between commercial and art cinema. Only four years passed between the emergence of the sex scene in 1963, in ELDORADO and THE HERO'S WIFE, and the onscreen enactment of intercourse in NOT MINE TO LOVE. The oblique approach to representing sex had not been established for long before more explicit forms were deployed. Ultimately, both elusive and explicit forms of representation were inspired by foreign sources.[1] The first local filmmaker to challenge the authority of the film censorship committee before the High Court was the poet David Avidan, who clashed with censors when his artistic trio of short films, SEX (1970), was banned (Almog, 2004, p. 1152).[2] Generally, however, as we saw in part II, and as we will see again here, commercial and non-commercial Israeli films were united in keeping their sex scenes within the formal limits of the industry. Both commercial and art films explored new contexts and forms for representing sex scenes. Both contributed to the increasing variety of emotions and perceptions associated with cinematic sex.

Within this diversity, in the 1970s, sex also came to be associated with violence, in films like HIGHWAY QUEEN, LIGHT OUT OF NOWHERE, and THREE AND ONE (1974, D: Mikhail Kalik).[3] Most of the emotions explored in Israeli sex scenes during the 1970s, in both commercial and non-commercial productions, were distinctly unharmonious. In addition, as the number and frequency of sex scenes increased, films like TZANANI FAMILY (1976, D: Boaz Davidson) and SWEET AND SOUR (1979, D: Ze'ev Revach) made the presentation of sex artless, even

---

1 See my discussion in chapter 2.
2 SEX (1970, D: David Avidan) is a short experimental film, and therefore lies outside the scope of this study.
3 HIGHWAY QUEEN and THREE AND ONE will be analysed in depth in this chapter.

mundane. As a result, Israeli sex scenes in the 1970s went through a demystification, which, Maiberg and Lord note, resulted in a great deal of sweat in the typical Israeli sex scene, and a complete lack of eroticism (Maiberg, 1982, p. 98; Lord, 1994, p. 66).

In part II, I showed that, in the course of the 1960s, the enactment of intrusion challenged both private and public space, creating the tension within which sex scenes were constructed. The appearance of the comic figure and its toll on individuality eroded the eroticism of the sex scene; the appearance of the child did the same, by underlining its potential for threat. The enactment of victimhood provided a context in which eroticism could be constructed and enhanced. In part III, I argue that, in the 1970s, the effects created by the enactment of intrusion, the comic figure, and the child were all maintained, but that the facilitation of eroticism through victimhood became less prominent. In the following chapters, I connect this change of pattern with the political context. As I show, erotic scenes and the sensual presentation of the human body did not cease, but the context in which they were presented changed. The legitimacy victimhood bestowed on eroticism in the 1960s was utilised far less in the 1970s, and was complicated by other factors.

My aim in part III is to demonstrate the discursive continuity in perceptions of communal identity during a decade marked by dramatic structural and conceptual changes in the political, social, and cultural spheres. I show that this perceptual transformation was carried out using existing terms.

One focus of part III is the interplay of spatial disruption, the comic type figure, the victim, and the child with the events and trends of the 1970s. In chapter 14, I compare the first two films that deal with the Yom Kippur War. In chapter 15, I analyse the construction of Oriental Jewish identities. In chapter 16, I examine two popular films identified with a new wave of youth films. While chapters 14 and 15 discuss the materialisation of political discourse through the affective realm of the sex scene, chapter 16 examines more closely changes in filmic representation of sex and sexuality.

Each chapter challenges the existing academic discourse on Israeli film from a different angle. Chapter 14 is dedicated to two films that have received very little academic attention. My discussion of them is also an attempt to reintegrate them into Israeli film history. By contrast, chapter 16 challenges an existing academic discourse on two films. Chapter 15 is dedicated to one of the central themes in academic discourse on Israeli film, Jewish Oriental identity, offering a different methodological perspective.

Many sex scenes were shot in the 1970s, and for my purposes I concentrate on a small number of them. This study does not offer a complete ontology of

Israeli sex scenes from the 1970s, although it includes some major instances.[4] The following chapters offer a broad perspective on events and social changes in Israel during the 1970s. I demonstrate how a society that underwent so many transformations did so in continuity with its history, within the boundaries of a communal self-image forged over preceding decades.

---

4 The most prominent sex scenes from the period that are not included in the discussion are in Zohar's Tel Aviv trilogy: PEEPING TOMS, BIG EYES (1974), and SAVE THE LIFEGUARD (1977). The representation of sex and the male physique in PEEPING TOMS has received some academic interest, as seen in chapter 12. All three films are worthy case studies, as are BOYS WILL NEVER BELIEVE IT and TAKE OFF. Since I have examined Zohar's poetic approach in my analysis of NOT MINE TO LOVE, however, my study will benefit more from an analysis of the work of other filmmakers.

There are many other films which exceed the scope of my discussion, but which would serve as valuable case studies: THE DREAMER; THE CONTRACT (1971, D: Menahem Golan); FISHKE GOES TO WAR (1971, D: George Obadiah); TWO HEARTBEATS (1972, D: Shmuel Imberman); ESCAPE TO THE SUN (1972, D: Menahem Golan); SALOMONICO (1972, D: Alfred Steinhardt); DAUGHTERS, DAUGHTERS! (1973, D: Moshé Mizrahi); MARRIAGE GAMES (1973, D: Joel Silberg); ADAM (1973, D: Yona Day); SAINT COHEN (1975, D: Assi Dayan); MY MICHAEL (1975, D: Dan Wolman); TZANANI FAMILY; ONLY TODAY (1976, D: Ze'ev Revach); A MOVIE AND BREAKFAST (1977, D: Alfred Steinhardt); ROCKING HORSE; THE FOX IN THE CHICKEN COOP (1978, D: Ephraim Kishon); COVER STORY (1979, D: Avraham Heffner); WRONG NUMBER (1979, D: Ze'ev Revach); and SWEET AND SOUR.

14 Past/Present/Future: The Yom Kippur War in Melodramas

I begin my examination of the 1970s with the Yom Kippur War. Along with the War of Independence and the Six-Day War, the Yom Kippur War (1973) is seen as a watershed in the Israeli-Arab conflict (Karsh, 2000, p. ix). In particular, the Six-Day War and the Yom Kippur War are often perceived as reflections of each other.

The Israeli public anticipated the Six-Day War (discussed in chapter 10) with anxiety, panic, and premonitions of defeat. After a swift victory, this changed to euphoria, relief, and a sense of triumph (Bregman, 2000, pp. 51–61). In comparison, the Syrian and Egyptian attack in October 1973 – which took place on Yom Kippur, the Day of Atonement – was unanticipated, coming as a complete surprise to the Israeli forces and public. As P. R. Kumaraswamy puts it, the euphoria that followed the war of 1967 was suddenly transmuted into Israel's worst nightmares. The initial failure of the counter-attack led to apocalyptic expectations among the Israeli public (Kumaraswamy, 2000, p. 2). The general feeling was that the state's existence hung in the balance (Karsh, 2000, p. ix).

Israel did ultimately gain the upper hand, but, while the Six-Day War underscored the inability of the Arab states to eradicate Israel, the Yom Kippur War redeemed Arab dignity and self-esteem, humbling Israel profoundly (ibid.). The end of the Six-Day War was marked with celebrations, whereas the Yom Kippur War ended on a far more sombre tone. The war's lasting effects were profoundly different: The Six-Day War brought economic prosperity to Israel, while the Yom Kippur War was followed by a deep recession (Bruno, 1986, pp. 276–277). The trauma of 1973 is often seen as the price for the complacency and conceit that took hold in the Israeli psyche after the victory of 1967 (Karsh, 2000 p. ix; Kumaraswamy, 2000, p. 3; Hattis Rolef, 2000, p. 178; Katsnelson, 2008, p. 130).

With the largest number of casualties since the War of Independence, the Yom Kippur War had a heavy price. For many, it came at a steep personal cost (Kumaraswamy, 2000, p. 2). The economic toll was high (Bruno, 1986, pp. 276–277), and Israel emerged diplomatically weakened, becoming more dependent on the United States (Inbar, 2008, p. 3). The greatest cost, and the largest consequences, however, were psychological. The acute sense of crisis did not revolve around the external threat, but the internal failure.

The surprise attack had caught the Israeli army unprepared, and the mobilisation of military reservists was chaotic (Hattis Rolef, 2000, p. 177). The war has come to be remembered and discussed primarily for this initial "unpreparedness" (Kumaraswamy, 2000, p. 2). Myths about the quality and morale of the Israeli Defence Force were shattered. Political and military leaders failed to anticipate the attack, and, as a result, their competence in preparing for and fighting the war were placed in doubt – a situation aggravated by internal conflicts (Hattis Rolef, 2000, pp. 177–178). In the public arena, a number of protest movements emerged in the war's immediate aftermath. Along with protests at the war, political movements by Oriental Jews, Arab minorities, feminists, and religious groups all gained leverage. Within a year, there was a "changing of the guard" in the ruling Labour Party, in favour of a younger generation of political leaders. Three and a half years later, the Labour Party lost its first election since the establishment of the state, with the right-wing Likud party emerging victorious (ibid., pp. 178–184). The Yom Kippur War was a catalyst rather than a source of the many social and political changes of the years that followed (ibid., p. 190), and contributed incalculably to the negative atmosphere in which those changes took place.

14.1 THREE AND ONE and JUDGEMENT DAY

Cry, the Beloved Country: The Political Deployment of Melodrama

Given the events of the Yom Kippur War and the public atmosphere surrounding it, it is not surprising that the two first cinematic attempts to deal with the war, JUDGEMENT DAY and THREE AND ONE, are melodramas that portray expressive forms of lamentation, translating national upheaval into family crises and emphasising internal breakdown over external conflict.

Each of the directors approached melodrama from a different perspective. Obadiah, previously active in the Iranian film industry, specialised in commercial melodramas (Iskovitz, 2015), while Kalik was an acclaimed new-wave director in the USSR before migrating to Israel in 1971 (Katsnelson, 2008, p. 127). While Obadiah focused on the emotional effect of his films, and argued for the commercial viability of melodramas that would make the audience "laugh a little and cry a lot" (Iskovitz, 2015), Kalik selected the genre in the spirit of the Soviet ideological tradition, basing his film on Maxim Gorki's *Malva* (Katsnelson, 2008, p. 143n13). According to Anna Waxler Katsnelson, melodrama had been adopted in the USSR following its influential reconceptualisation by French author Romain Rolland as a highly legible, popular form, "common to the philosopher and the labourer", and therefore ideally suited for revolutionary theatre (ibid., p. 145n27).

The fact that both JUDGEMENT DAY and THREE AND ONE are melodramas was probably why they were almost entirely dismissed as representations of the war,[1] receiving viciously negative reviews and little academic attention.[2] Scholars may have disregarded the melodrama of ODED THE WANDERER, but they ignored JUDGEMENT DAY and THREE AND ONE altogether because of the genre they belonged to.

This attitude is not unique to Israel. In Western culture, melodrama is a discredited genre. As the film scholar Christine Gledhill explains:

> Emerging out of and drawing on the proscribed and marginalised folk and early urban entertainment, melodrama provokes, much as today, anxiety of the establishment as to the cultural degeneration and insubordination of the lower order. (Gledhill, 2000, p. 230)

In Western film studies, until the 1960s, melodrama was an "anti-value" from which "high" cultural values were to be protected (Williams, 1998, p. 43). In the early 1970s, it was "redeemed" as a genre through the work of director Douglas Sirk. Even then, Sirk's melodramas were read as ironic (ibid., pp. 43–44). Williams argues that, as late as the mid-1980s, academic discussions of melodrama did not acknowledge the powerful appeal its use of pathos could generate (ibid., pp. 44–47).

As if to make amends for years of academic disregard, both Gledhill and Williams concentrate much of their argument on the assertion that melodrama is central to Anglo-American culture, and that the melodramatic gesture is present in mainstream cinema of the past and the present (Gledhill, 2000, pp. 225–241; Williams, 1998, pp. 51–82). But this inclusive approach is of little use when handling such "unabashed" melodramas as JUDGEMENT DAY and THREE AND ONE. The contention that dramas and action films are also melodramas is unhelpful in understanding films that do not conceal their heavy emotional qualities behind the dignified mask of a "respectable" genre.

---

[1] Ben-Shaul for instance overlooks both films when he claims that THE VULTURE from 1981 is the first reference to the war in Israeli cinema (Ben-Shaul, 1997, p. 33).

[2] JUDGEMENT DAY has received very little academic discussion (Rolef, 2016), and THREE AND ONE even less (Katsnelson, 2008, p. 142n7). The only extensive reference to the latter seems to be an article by Anna Waxler Katsnelson (Katsnelson, 2008). I have given an extensive analysis of JUDGEMENT DAY in an article of my own (Rolef, 2016).

As stated above, this academic oblivion followed a negative response to the films in the contemporary press. Obadiah's films, mainly commercial melodramas and comedies, were typically panned, and JUDGEMENT DAY was no exception (Iskovitz, 2015). Despite his art-house credentials, Kalik's reception was likewise overwhelmingly negative, and THREE AND ONE remained his only Israeli production (Katsnelson, 2008, p. 127). The critical attitude toward both films is reflected in Schnitzer's anthology, which remains dismissive of them twenty years after they appeared (Schnitzer, 1994a, pp. 149, 152).

Both JUDGEMENT DAY and THREE AND ONE unfold their melodrama using what Katsnelson calls the "faults" of Kalik's film: blatant, explicitly didactic allegorical narratives, heavy-handed symbolism, emphatically emotive acting, expansive panoramas, and warm, strongly lit locations (Katsnelson, 2008, p. 130). The accentuated use of colour in both films, the iconic stylisation of the figures, and their declamatory speeches, made while facing the camera, all establish a static temporal-spatial form akin to fotonovelas and soap operas. More importantly, both films are invested in what Williams called "the sensation of overwhelming pathos in the 'weepie'" (Williams, 1991, p. 4). Pathos is the main form of expression. Not only do the protagonists sob and weep at key moments of both films, as Naomi does in MOTIVE TO MURDER; the atmosphere, too, is emotionally loaded, and the viewers are expected to share the gesture, watching the films through a screen of tears. Emotions are central, and, as Kappelhoff argues, instead of conventional "meaning", melodramas communicate emotive values and affective tones (Kappelhoff, 2004, p. 239).

These emotions are not abstract, incoherent, or isolated from political reality. In a sense, melodramas contain an emotional formula directed at communal crisis. According to Williams, melodramas seize on social problems. Using a combination of realism, sentiment, spectacle, and action, they reveal moral good in a world where virtue has become hard to read (Williams, 1998, pp. 53–54). As Gledhill puts it, melodrama articulates social and aesthetic questions. Bodies, gestures, looks, and the grain of the voice all perform affective scenarios whose aesthetic involves moral and social drama (Gledhill, 2000, p. 238). The use of heightened contrasts and polar oppositions in melodrama aim to make the world morally legible (ibid., p. 234).

Kappelhoff's work on melodrama bears out Williams' claim that emotional "excess" may itself be organised as a system (Williams, 1991, p. 3). Cinematic compositions like JUDGEMENT DAY and THREE AND ONE are, from Kappelhoff's perspective, emotion machines which lead the viewer through an emotional process.

My claim, then, is that both Obadiah and Kalik construct their films as highly saturated emotional experiences specifically affiliated with the Yom Kippur War. Although they deal with the same war, using many of the same associations and motifs, each constructs a completely different process, with a different outcome. While THREE AND ONE ends in tears of grief and devastation, JUDGEMENT DAY ends in tears of relief. My focus here is not on the enactment of lamentation in JUDGEMENT DAY and THREE AND ONE, but on the context in which this occurs, and the meaning it produces. A close comparative analysis of the films, and their construction and employment of sex scenes, shows that war and social crisis can be inscribed in two very different experiences, but that this difference is embedded throughout the two films.

Common Ground: Family Crisis, Intergenerational Difference, and Men Behaving Badly

It is obvious that the plots of both JUDGEMENT DAY and THREE AND ONE revolve around the disintegration of the nuclear family and the loss of the father. THREE AND ONE takes place over five days in October 1973, up to the eve of Yom Kippur, several hours before the war begins. Absalom Ben-Dor, a man in his early twenties, travels to Eilat in the south of Israel to find his father, Yosef, nicknamed Palmachov, who has left behind his family and his career as an executive in Tel Aviv. The father lives in a tent, earns his living as a tour guide, and wallows in memories of the War of Independence, when he and his Palmach comrades conquered the region. Absalom finds Palmachov with his young girlfriend, Marva, who he immediately begins to pursue. Marva also receives the attentions of a hippie, Eli. Marva's vacillation between the three men leads to conflict, and she finally chooses Absalom. The two are about to leave Eilat, but return to Palmachov's campsite to find that he had set his tent on fire and had sailed out to sea to die. Their cries blend with the sirens that announce the beginning of the Day of Atonement.

In JUDGEMENT DAY, David Chen, a hotel manager and a father, neglects his family in favour of his sexual exploits. His wife, Shoshana, divorces him, severing all connection between him and his daughter, Vered, who suffers the consequences. She grows up to marry a family friend, Nissim, a nightclub singer, becoming a singer as well. David, who moved with his girlfriend Helen to the United States after the divorce, learns of the outbreak of the Yom Kippur War and returns to Israel to participate. He is wounded, and brought to the hospital where his daughter volunteers. Only after she saves his life with a blood donation do they meet and recognise each other. At his request, Shoshana comes to the hospital, and the family is reunited (Rolef, 2016).

What Gledhill calls "the axis of polar oppositions" is constructed in the form of a fraught generational divide introduced at the very beginning of each film. The opening sequence of THREE AND ONE revolves around this rupture. Contemporary Eilat is embodied by water-skiers off the coast, in front of the desert hills and the new hotels. In another shot, an airplane passes modern buildings to land at the city's new airport. The camera captures Absalom as he exits the plane, moving as it follows his energetic steps. The past is represented by black and white stills of Palmach soldiers, the last of which is a famous photograph of soldiers hoisting an improvised Israeli flag after the battle for Eilat. Palmachov appears alongside the photos in his provisional camp, with a boat, a tent, a makeshift pier, and fishing nets. His link with the soldiers in the still photo is clear, not just because of his beige outfit, which resembles a military uniform, but because of the shot's lack of colour, and the lack of movement of and within the frame. He is not completely still, but his movements are slow. He often gazes beyond the camera, looking reflective or expectant. His stillness is contrasted with dynamic shots of contemporary Eilat, a disparity reinforced in dialogue throughout the film: the father is associated with past myths, humble material existence, and idealism, while the son is associated with the present and materialistic pragmatism.

The rupture in JUDGMENT DAY is of a different nature, residing in the spaces father and daughter occupy (Rolef, 2016). The two are not seen together. Vered opens the film in a residential area, leading a group of peers on bicycles and singing. In her next scene, she is the lead singer in a school performance. Both melodies resemble children's music of the period, and their lyrics emphasise childhood and naivety. Between these scenes, David is introduced. He appears naked in a hotel bed, passionately embracing a woman while an "adult" pop song plays in the background. The woman breaks away from him, breathless and exhausted. She pushes him away as he attempts to engage her again. She gets up and puts on her stewardess uniform while they talk about his sexual insatiability. The stewardess is then seen descending the stairs into the hotel lobby, walking past Helen, an American tourist, who David then woos in turn. David is presented as an insatiable philanderer, his world, actions, and sexuality contrasted with Vered's innocence. As the film progresses, the disparity deepens. Vered collapses during her school performance and is rushed to a hospital, brightly lit with neon lights, while David escorts his new date to a nightclub, dimly lit with red lights. Vered's pale, sickly, motionless face contrasts with the voluptuous bodies of the two go-go dancers that dominate the screen during Nissim's nightclub performance. Vered conveys the same fragility as the children in A NIGHT IN TIBERIAS and NOT MINE TO LOVE.

In both films, the rupture is expressed through a clash. In JUDGEMENT DAY, the domains of the father and the daughter are mutually alien – which eventually tears them apart when Shoshana enters David's space, catches him with his new conquest, and leaves him. In THREE AND ONE, the incompatibility is dramatised through the son's intrusion into his father's realm. The emphasis in both films is not on intrusion into private space, but on egotistical, even agonistic acts which lead to conflict. It is the abandoned wife and the abandoned son who walk in on the fathers, and yet, in both films, the individual ultimately intrudes on the family as a community, rather than the community intruding on the individual. In THREE AND ONE, the contemporary mentality is contrasted with the myth of the past, whereas in JUDGEMENT DAY it is contrasted with innocence. In the former, it is a question of incompatibility with past ideals, while in the latter the issue is hedonism. As I showed in chapter 12, past films had already drawn a link between childish innocence and the austere past, and between the fear of change and the fear of hedonism. Both films therefore address the same predicament.

As in NOT MINE TO LOVE and IRIS, the contemporary landscape is associated with the loss of innocence. In THREE AND ONE, Eilat's current status as a holiday resort contrasts with the battle for it twenty-five years earlier. Palmachov, who tells the story of the battle with great passion in his own abode, repeats it in a far more subdued manner later for an elderly American couple taking a tour in his boat. Their questions dampen his narrative. The photo of the flag being raised appears once more, and is contrasted with the tourist's request for a new role of film for their snapshots. JUDGEMENT DAY also makes more implicit use of changed environments. It primarily uses locations marked by transformations that took place after 1967. During David and Helen's vacation in Eilat, the new northern promenade is shown from every possible angle. The bay of Taba in Sinai, which came into Israeli possession in 1967, is also included. The family's home is located in Ramat Aviv, a neighbourhood which was being turned into a symbol of the new middle class through development projects. Jerusalem, where Shoshana's parents live, is depicted exclusively using locations which lie along the border that, until the war in 1967, divided the city (Rolef, 2016). The melodrama is associated with new terrain. In both films, the outbreak of the Yom Kippur War is the final mark of contemporary times.

Like THREE AND ONE, JUDGEMENT DAY does not simply use redemption to resolve the moral tale it constructs around the Yom Kippur War. The men who inherit the earth are morally questionable. In this allegory, David is paralleled not with Palmachov – even though the two are father figures who have abandoned their families – but with Palmachov's son. Both are associated with material wealth and unquenched sexual lust. David is well dressed, and his surroundings are mostly lavish. Absalom stands out because, unlike his rivals, Palmachov and Eli, he does not denounce the material world. He wears neat clothes, drives around in a jeep, and identifies with the middle-class world his father left behind. This takes on performative guise after he pursues Marva in the water, throwing away his flashy watch without hesitation, and spreading what he calls his "father's money" on the sand to dry.

Throughout both films, David and Absalom pursue women. This pursuit makes up the majority of David's performance. He philanders; abandoned by his wife, he enters a five-and-a-half-minute romantic sequence with Helen; leaving her, he goes back to pursuing his wife. Absalom advocates for family unity, petitioning over and again for his father to return home. More durable, however, are the long scenes in THREE AND ONE dedicated to his pursuit of Marva, swimming with her in the sea, driving together on empty roads, and strolling among ruins. Immediately after a conflict with Marva, Absalom pursues another woman, a prostitute – an action that sets him apart yet again from his rivals, who only have eyes for Marva. In a scene designed to underline Absalom's impulsiveness, he drives a jeep at sunset. A close-up of the woman's rear end appears, from her waist to her knees, as she walks slowly in a short dress. Absalom stops the car, shakes his head, and reverses back to her to start negotiations. The image is frozen as he looks back at the prostitute lifting her leg to get into the jeep, suggesting he is catching a glimpse beneath her dress.

The negative association of material wealth and sexual lust recalls Bursztyn's criticism of the protagonist in I DON'T GIVE A DAMN (1987, D: Shmuel Imberman), who, he argues, embodies the self-infatuated, shallow, materialistic values which associate capitalist consumption with sexual objectification (Bursztyn, 1990, pp. 175–177). Rather than submit to the sheer moral condemnation that melodrama constructs, however, we can use it to reflect on the context it makes manifest. In the case of David and Absalom, their fiscal and sexual promiscuity is designed to repel rather than appeal to the viewer, and may well be associated with a specific historical perspective, reflecting the prosperity that followed the Six-Day War as seen in the hindsight of the post-1973 recession. The moral condemnation which, in accordance with melodramatic conventions, is levelled at Absalom and David is also manifested in the fact that both their victories at the end of each film are marred. Absalom follows Marva as she runs frantically to Palmachov's burning compound, and then to the sea. He ends the film on his father's pier, shouting and then whispering "father". David ends the film with a visible limp, supported by his ex-wife as he climbs into the back of Nissim's car. Sitting next to him, Shoshana does not turn her head to return his intense gaze. The camera moves down to show him taking hold of her right hand with the same intensity. Four seconds go by before she lifts her left hand to caress him. The camera moves back to catch him advancing to kiss her – not her mouth, but her cheek. Although her face expresses sentimental excitement, this scene falls short of a complete reconciliation.

Differences: Circular vs. Linear Progression, Exterior vs. Interior Space, Desperation vs. Healing

Although JUDGEMENT DAY and THREE AND ONE operate on a similar melodramatic terrain of sharp disparities, there are clear differences between the two films. THREE AND ONE ends in death and regret, while JUDGEMENT DAY ends in resurrection and reintegration. Both films pursue their conclusions through their respective poetic structures. A comparative analysis reveals the viewing process each film creates.

Although the two films are of similar length (85 and 83 minutes), their sense of time and space differs. THREE AND ONE, which reduces the plot to five days and one geographic location, maintains a circular structure, while JUDGEMENT DAY, which stretches over several years and several geographic locations, remains linear. In THREE AND ONE, the characters move in loops, from one confrontation to another. Many of their interactions recur at different stages. Again and again, Palmachov waits for Marva, musing over her. Again and again, Absalom gives Marva lifts in his jeep. Absalom and Marva's flirtation is a repeated ritual, in which he continually attempts to kiss her and she evades him at the last moment. Palmachov keeps asking Absalom to leave, and, when Marva decides to go with him, she says farewell twice, both to Palmachov and Eli. Instead of leaving, Marva returns in a rush to Palmachov's compound, after Eli hints that something has happened to him. Like Vladimir and Estragon in *Waiting for Godot*, despite much leave-taking, Absalom and Marva never go.

JUDGEMENT DAY, in contrast, complements its linear structure with abrupt editing, transitioning swiftly from one scene to the next,[3] which generates a rapid pace. At times, the transitions are so abrupt that the scenes seem to intrude on each other. A scene in which David makes love crowds in on another showing his wife's interaction with their daughter; Vered's pale, unconscious face intrudes on her father's nightclub outing; the eruption of war interrupts Shoshana's emotional conversation with her parents. Furthermore, the rapid editing creates a sense that the circumstances develop instantaneously. Shoshana's conversation with a divorce lawyer is immediately followed by David's subsequent phone call with him. Her discussion with her parents about their daughter's unhappiness is quickly followed by Vered's therapeutic music lessons with Nissim. Shoshana and Vered's argument about the latter's plan to become a singer segues immediately into Vered's nightclub performance. David's announcement to Helen that he will return to Israel is promptly followed by his plane landing (Rolef, 2016). THREE AND ONE leads viewers through an absurd maze of dead ends; JUDGEMENT DAY, by contrast, rushes them through a decisive series of events.

Each film creates a sense of space which complements its structure. All of THREE AND ONE takes place outdoors. The mountains, beaches, and sea provide settings, with permanent structures, mostly hotels, appearing occasionally in

---

[3] I argue elsewhere that this abrupt editing also echoes the sudden outbreak of the Yom Kippur War (Rolef, 2016).

the background. The city of Eilat is characterised by temporary beach facilities, railings, boats, and swings. Palmachov has a preliminary "showdown" with his son in Nelson's village, a holiday resort that did indeed existed in Taba. This beach resort is presented in a stylised manner, with wagons and saloon music, recalling a Western. More typically, however, the film lingers more in provisional locations: isolated beaches, Palmachov's compound, Eli's hippie colony. Both Palmachov and Eli have "homes" that are neither steadier nor sturdier than Absalom's jeep. The only community that appears on the screen are the hippies that surround Eli. The only social structure we are presented with, then, belongs to a group which rejects society. In general terms, the space in which the film takes place is depicted as an outpost – not just on the geographical fringes, but on the social fringes, as befits the theatre of the absurd. Palmachov makes the connection between the social structure he rejects and permanent buildings: "The villa is a good thing. Everything is modern, but heavy. You can't move it. Here you can move things."

His wife and his friends, he continues, have all become strangers, suffocating in villas and air-conditioned offices. In a symbolically fraught scene, Marva and Absalom walk through the ruins of an ancient city. Marva mockingly suggests that Absalom, who is studying to be an engineer, will build a happy home for them all: Palmachov, Absalom, Marva, Eli, Absalom's girlfriend, his mother, and her potential new life partner. This implies that no permanent construction can contain the human web that has replaced the broken nuclear family. There is no "home" for the family members to return to.

Interiors, completely absent in THREE AND ONE, are the hallmark of JUDGEMENT DAY, where progress through different spaces is part of a process of change. Residential interiors accompany the family crisis. The inside of the Chen family's home is first seen when Shoshana and David fight and separate. Its meticulous modern design, lavish but crisp, gives a sense of cool. Shoshana moves with her daughter to her parents' home in Jerusalem, a modest apartment with whitewashed walls and old-fashioned furniture, which provides the background for a warm domestic scene: Vered, in pyjamas, wins a game of checkers against her grandfather, while her grandmother works at her sewing machine and serves tea. The couple pokes fun at one another, obeying the conventions of comic sketches, and Vered and Shoshana speak gently and lovingly. The old house, with its old-fashioned chairs and the oilcloth on the table, is associated with warmth.

Vered hears of her parent's separation by chance, and flees back to Tel Aviv. Wandering the streets of the city at night – the space once occupied by her father – she runs into a friend, Nissim, who invites her home. He makes tea for her in his kitchen, and plays her music in his living room. Both the wallpaper and the couch have flamboyant patterns, and decorative cloths are spread on the furniture. Nissim's home is less elegant and less cool than the Chen's. His interiors are more conventional and homely.

Warm, domesticated interiors, then, provide the setting for the start of the healing process. Where the grandparents introduced comedy, Nissim ushers in the musical. In a series of four songs, performed by Nissim and Vered, he consoles her, educates her, brings her onstage, and marries her. Vered enters the nightclub stage, "domesticating" it (ibid.). The family gathering in Jerusalem, on the eve of Yom Kippur, is the peak of this musical interval, and of the healing process. As in THREE AND ONE, the broken nuclear family is replaced by an alternative. This expansion of the nuclear family is more traditional, bringing three generations and a son-in-law together around a single table. From this strong foundation, the characters can face the war that erupts suddenly, represented through documentary images.

The state of emergency in THE HERO'S WIFE, A NIGHT IN TIBERIAS, and NOT MINE TO LOVE is a healing process, in which the protagonists are saved through mobilisation. In JUDGEMENT DAY, David, who betrayed his role as a father, returns to the film and to his country to fight. Vered, too, shows engagement and self-sacrifice in the hospital, reversing her father's abandonment (Rolef, 2016). But such mobilisation is secondary to domestication, which remains central to the work of recovery. The film's final arena is not the battlefield, but a hospital on the home front. Rather than conflict, the emphasis is on healing. In this context, THREE AND ONE takes after IRIS: it does not enact a state of emergency to save its protagonists, but locates the ideal in the past, nostalgically, and grieves over its irretrievable loss.

As is the rule with melodrama, both films portray victimhood, amplifying its affective impact. THREE AND ONE associates this partly with Eli, who enacts his misery in encounters with Marva and Palmachov, and mainly with Palmachov. Long scenes are dedicated to Palmachov's dejection, building up to his final grand exit, in which he plays the role of sacrificial lamb.

JUDGEMENT DAY builds up the melodramatic pathos through emotional scenes involving female figures, from Vered's onstage collapse to the breakdown of the Chen family. But the melodrama is repeatedly softened by other modes of performance: level-headed discussions, the grandparent's comic sketches, David's holiday spectacle, and Nissim's performances. Melodrama, Gledhill argues, is a hybrid genre that "plagiarises" from every possible source (Gledhill, 2000, p. 225). JUDGEMENT DAY uses this hybridity for relief and emotional elevation. Approaching the film through the prism of our four central elements, we can say that the problems in JUDGEMENT DAY are caused by intrusion and victimhood, while Vered's childish charm, and her grandparents' comic performances, are used as contrasting, generative forces. In the first stage of the healing process, the melodramatic return to innocence and virtue occurs through the construction of the child and comic figures – that is, through modest, blameless subjectivities.

While JUDGEMENT DAY depicts a healing process, THREE AND ONE portrays escalating conflict. In JUDGEMENT DAY, harmony begins when each family member finds their proper place. In THREE AND ONE, by contrast, there is no such option. The three men represent three alternatives forms of Israeli identity: old ideology, new pragmatism, and anarchic protest (Katsnelson, 2008, p. 129). The film allows for no reconciliation between them, and sets them in sexual rivalry over a single woman, the endless source of antagonism and conflict. In JUDGEMENT DAY, conflict between husband and wife, mother and daughter, is sporadic and brief, ending in division, whereas it forms a primary motif in THREE AND ONE. When Marva teases Palmachov, or introduces Absalom to Eli, she sets the men against each other like gladiators. Conflict runs deep in the film, driving every interaction. Each moment of communication reveals a difference between the protagonists, who are pursuing contradictory goals. Conflict and rivalry are the means by which all the characters, including Marva, become performative, hold their postures, and make their voices heard. In JUDGEMENT DAY, music contributes to the process of healing. By contrast, the songs Eli sings in THREE AND ONE express an antagonistic spirit of protest.

When documentary imagery of battle appears in JUDGEMENT DAY, it is accompanied by footage of protective measures taken by civilians, and the evacuation of the wounded. The war is organised into a series of actions and reactions, setting the mood of mobilisation that envelops the protagonists. In THREE AND ONE, it is the War of Independence, not the Yom Kippur War, which appears in documentary footage at the end the film. The still photos used in the opening sequence come alive as Palmachov's tent is set ablaze. A black-and-white image of an explosion suddenly appears onscreen, followed by images of armoured vehicles and men fighting. This is the business of war, materialised both in the distant events Palmachov refuses to part with, and in the nation's sustaining myth. In THREE AND ONE, Israel is a nation of soldiers who, like the characters in the film, thrive on everlasting conflict.

In short, the two films pursue contradictory approaches. JUDGEMENT DAY engages its characters and viewers in a process of mobilisation, one that reshapes trust and the family unit. THREE AND ONE exposes both of these, not only to increasing aggression, but to the realisation that the destruction runs deep.

Tenderness vs. Violence: Sexual Economies and the Dissipation of the Victim's Sensuality

I turn now to the fine grain of subjectivity and human relations which runs through the sexual economies of JUDGEMENT DAY and THREE AND ONE.

JUDGEMENT DAY presents David as sexually insatiable, in constant erotic pursuit. Neither male nor female pleasures are depicted in his first sex scene, but rather David's relentlessness. There is no eroticism in his interactions with Helen as he pursues her. Instead, it is mediated through the bodies of the two go-go dancers accompanying Nissim's performance. Brightly lit, moving constantly, they dominate the scene. As the camera alternates between them and the other characters, it fixates on their quivering bellies, moving down to their pelvises and capturing their breasts from a lower angle. As their bodies provoke erotic stimulation, we hear Nissim's lyrics about the frosty end of an affair, and see Helen's pointed rejections of David's advances.

David's conquest of Helen in his office coincides with Shoshana's discovery of the affair. After he hastily follows his wife, the camera lingers for a full twenty seconds on Helen, standing in agitation, melancholic piano music playing. Their first tryst is marked by guilt, rather than sexual allure. During the holiday David and Helen spend in Eilat, walking through tourist attractions, fashionably dressed, the settings are romantic. The expressions and body language of the two are easygoing and playful, but not passionate. This does not change even at the end of the sequence, on the seashore, as David takes Helen's hand and, to her clear surprise, confesses his love, and that he intends to follow her to America. When they begin to embrace each other, the camera moves upward and evades them.

Erotic stimulation is associated with David's world, and it seems to disappear with him from the film. The sheer presence of Shoshana's comical parents has an anti-erotic effect, as strong as that generated by Dubi and Rivka in THE HERO'S WIFE. They, too, speak in a foreign accent, switching to Yiddish. The grandfather, in particular, uses exaggerated body language and facial expression. His lecture to his daughter on finding herself a partner has the same unappetising effect as Dubi's speech to Yosef in THE HERO'S WIFE.

When Vered sings at the nightclub, there is no erotic stimulation offered to the viewer which can compete with the go-go dancers. Vered's version of adulthood is devoid of sexual implications, although she does take part in a brief sex scene. At the end of the wedding song, Vered's mother strokes her cheek, leading her from right to left to the rhythm of the song. The camera zooms in on the white curtain between them. The picture then changes to another curtain, in the newlyweds' bedroom. Vered, wearing a nightgown, is in the same spot, on the right-hand side of the bed. Nissim is to her left, bare chested. They hold hands, look gently at one another, and move into the missionary position. The second sex scene in the film takes place in a domestic setting, and Vered, who has already taken possession of the nightclub, now also takes over the bed. Sex receives the family blessing, and is presented to the viewer with a tenderness that had been absent. Significantly, it is tenderness, rather than passion, that dominates the sequence.

This sense of family union doesn't end with Vered's marriage. In hospital, she discovers her father. David, pale and drained, wipes a tear from his cheek and extends his hand to her. The image changes to a sequence in the park – fantasy or memory? – in which Vered, still a child, jumps into his outstretched arms, while Shoshana looks on and laughs. The daughter runs along the side of a river, followed by her father and mother. Next, David and Shoshana walk together in the park, joyful, tender, laughing, and caressing each other. Shoshana appears in close-up, reading in bed. A small cloud of cigarette smoke draws her attention. She smiles and turns to her right. A reaction shot shows David in the bed, bare chested. He returns her smile. As she puts down her magazine and turns to him, the film returns to David, pale, lying in the hospital bed, his daughter to his right as her mother had just been. She holds his hand, and he asks to see Shoshana. The scene, which emphasises the tenderness associated with the domestic bed, cuts the reunion short, creating an expectation that Shoshana and David will complete the action – something that occurs at the very end of the film, as they embrace in the car. Sex is not abolished by the new domestic sphere, but is appropriated, taken over not just by social propriety but by emotion.

The opposite process takes place in THREE AND ONE, in which sexual relations become increasingly disharmonious. Marva's sexual encounters with the three men complement one another, forming a unity. The first encounter is with Palmachov. With Absalom present, he and Marva have no privacy in the tent. They walk on the beach in the pale light of the setting sun. Marva taunts Palmachov into a rage, tickling his insecurity and jealousy. He slaps her, and she reacts by moving away, mocking him with his son's advantage – his youth. Palmachov stands still, defeated. She returns and apologises. He strokes her arms, still angry, puts his hands around her neck as if to choke her. He turns her around and kisses her neck passionately, seizing her breasts, which reveals the wedding ring on his hand. The camera follows his hands as they caress her body, feeling between her legs and travelling back to her breasts. As the camera moves up again to their faces, their kisses resemble bites. They drop to the sand, out of sight of the camera. The agonistic nature of their relations is clear. The aggression between them inflames their desire.

Figure 10: Sex returning home. David's sexual exploits, Vered's wedding night and the marital reconciliation in Judgement Day.

When Absalom wakes from his drunken sleep, Palmachov and Marva are seen lying on the beach. Her dress is lifted above her knees, but she is fully dressed. His shirt is open, as are his flies. Exposed, he acknowledges his aging body, his fear of losing his youth, and his dependence on Marva. She kisses his chest, lays her head on it, and strokes his body, making it tangible to the viewer. This is almost a replication of the night-time scene with Sherman and Naomi on the beach in ELDORADO (discussed in chapter 11). Like Sherman, Palmachov laments his victimhood; like Naomi's caresses, Marva's sensual gestures carry erotic energy into the act of comforting. Like a score of victims before him, Palmachov is marked as an erotic figure. As in earlier films, this enhances the sense of loss in the final scene, when he ends his life. Unlike the victims discussed in chapter 11, however, sensuality does not remain the exclusive possession of Palmachov, the sacrificial lamb.

Ten minutes after Palmachov and Marva's scene on the beach, she returns from scuba diving to find Absalom waiting for her on the shore. The sexual tension is maintained in their flirtatious conversation, as she apparently rejects him out of love for his father. She laughs when he grabs hold of her, throws her into the water, and follows her. As they swim together, their movements become perfectly synchronised. The camera focuses mostly on Absalom's taut body. His clothes, transparent from the water, move against his skin. When Marva steps out of the water, she sits next to Absalom, but quickly steps away from him and out of the frame. She lies on the sand, and the camera moves from her feet upwards, revealing that she has taken off her dress. As though challenged, Absalom takes off his clothes, revealing the first fully nude male body in Israeli film, and lies on the sand. She looks at him intensely, establishing the erotic tension that will determine their relations.

Marva's sexual encounter with Eli begins thirty minutes later. While Palmachov waits for her, she takes refuge with Eli in the shadow of the boat, smoking marijuana and poking fun at both father and son. After Palmachov confronts Absalom at the bar, the camera returns to Eli and Marva. He wants to be Marva's only love, and she wants to end her indecision and choose one man. As he sings to her, she stands up, walks away from him, and takes off her dress, repeating the gesture she made to Absalom. He continues to sing until her legs enter his frame. She smiles down at him. He gets up and caresses her bare chest. Her hand proceeds to undo the buttons of his jeans. He moves his head to kiss her, but she lowers her head and kisses his neck, chest and belly. A long shot reveals that she positioned herself for fellatio. The camera cuts to him looking grim, averting his eyes. She looks earnestly at his body at the edge of her frame, and then gives his groin a long hard look before turning her eyes to the ground. The anarchist, the rebel, is impotent. More

Figure 11: Eroticism split in three: Marva with Palmachov, Absalom and Eli in THREE AND ONE.

importantly, the relationship between Marva and Eli fails because they display no mutual antagonism. Instead, they share their antagonism towards Eli's rivals. Sex and the performance of subjectivity are only possible with the antagonism and aggression which increase as the film progresses.

A few minutes later, Absalom turns on Marva with male vengeance. After Palmachov attempts to kill him, he rushes to Marva, who stands in a gloomy haze while tending to flowers in a run-down greenhouse. Absalom enters, out of breath, and blames her for his father's violent rage. He blames her promiscuity, then grabs her. Struggling, they fall into the flowers. The camera becomes unsteady. He tears her apron, exposing her breasts. Her body wriggles under his weight, and he pushes himself between her thighs. The camera zooms in to her face, breathing heavily as she sobs. The camera switches to the watering can, fallen on the flowers and dripping water. Absalom shakes his head and retreats. Katsnelson associates Absalom with his Biblical character, "the rebellious son of King David who attempted to seal his palace coup by usurping his father's concubines" (Katsnelson, 2008, p. 129). If we equate Marva with the king's concubine, the greenhouse is the palace. In this case, it is a vivid symbol of the Zionist ideal: flowers made to bloom in the desert. Marva is brutally violated by Absalom, and so is the Zionist dream. Nonetheless, the scene does not end in total devastation. In her desperation, Marva seeks a solution from Absalom, who suggests that she leave his father and join him.

JUDGEMENT DAY transforms unbridled lust into tender affection, whereas THREE AND ONE turns eroticism into brutality. But these contradictory processes lead to the same result: a connection between victimhood and eroticism, which, as I demonstrated in chapter 11, is complicated and broken. Although David's life is endangered, and Palmachov dies, their eroticism only partially increases the imminent sense of their loss.

In JUDGEMENT DAY, David's flashback evokes past marital bliss. Wounded, he is rushed to surgery. David's "past" sensuality and vitality are contrasted with his pale, weakened body, and with the threat of death. However, during the first third of the film, David's sexuality is emphasised as the negative element in the melodramatic moral equation. His relentless sexual pursuits are contrasted with his daughter's innocence, and lead to the destruction of the family unit. The short spell of "redeemed" family sensuality does not erase this. David's status as the sinner endures, even as he becomes a self-sacrificing victim.

Palmachov's victimhood is enhanced by his eroticism, and vice versa. But eroticism is not his exclusive domain, and is shared by his rivals. The viewer enjoys Absalom's attractive body as he swims with Marva, and when he undresses. The father's aging body, displayed shortly beforehand, suffers from the comparison. Because Palmachov, Absalom, and Eli are all shown interacting sensually with Marva, eroticism is distributed among them. It is intertwined with the melodrama's sense of moral sin, and as a result its effect on the display of victimhood is reduced.

JUDGEMENT DAY and THREE AND ONE share the idea that the most crucial battle in the Yom Kippur War was the struggle over national identity. In their contrasting melodramatic approaches, both reflect the fact that, in the war's aftermath, communal and individual identities were tainted as never before. They provide cinematic expression of the sense that the nation had lost its own innocence, and loosened the moral grip which had allowed it to mourn its dead and wounded. Victimhood and eroticism are now blended with guilt.

15 "They're Not Nice Guys": Oriental Jewish Identity Enters the Political Arena in the 1970s

The key to reflections on Oriental Jewish identity in films of the 1970s lies in the political significance that identity had accumulated over the course of the decade. The term "Oriental Jewish" refers to Jews from Muslim (Hattis Rolef, 1998, p. 209) or Middle Eastern regions (Goldberg and Bram, 2007, p. 227). As is often the case with ethnic distinctions among pluralistic populations, the very names of these groups, and their boundaries, are subject to extensive debate (ibid., pp. 230–235; Kimchi, 2012, pp. 13–29). The history of the term and its nuances will not be part of the discussion here, except to note that the term "Sephardi" ("Spanish", an expression originating in Spanish Jewry), which Shohat uses in her 1989 study, has been replaced in the dominant idiom by "Mizrahi" ("Oriental"), which all other scholars use.

When Israel was established in 1948, 23% of its Jewish population was of Oriental decent. By 1960, a little short of half a million immigrants had arrived from North Africa and the Arabian Peninsula (Hattis Rolef, 1998, p. 209), constituting 51.6% of the new arrivals (Bernstein, 1984, p. 130). Beyond the harsh employment, resettlement and housing conditions all new immigrants faced, and the state of general austerity, Oriental immigrants had to endure discrimination and patronisation on the part of the authorities. The establishment made no secret about its desire to do away with the traditional, "primitive" social structures of Oriental communities (Hattis Rolef, 1998, p. 209). Members of those communities found themselves subordinate and dependent, economically, politically, and culturally. The overlap between class position and ethnic origin which emerged was to the disadvantage of Oriental Jews, and remained in force in the subsequent generation (Bernstein, 1984, pp. 130–131). All this contributed to a sense of alienation and growing frustration among Oriental communities, with considerable political implications in later years (Hattis Rolef, 1998, p. 209).

Major protests took place in the first two decades after the establishment of the State of Israel (Hattis Rolef, 1998, p. 209). Still, the Oriental cause played only a minor role in the democratic process during this period (Bernstein, 1984, p. 131). The 1970s are generally regarded as a turning point in both the public and the political arena, beginning with the protest movement of 1971, which had a substantial public impact, and ending after the elections of 1977, when the Oriental agenda finally tilted the political scale.

In 1971, the Israeli Black Panthers were formed, a protest movement of young people of Moroccan origin from Jerusalem's slums. Named after their African-American counterpart, the group organised numerous demonstrations and protests. Their main demand was for a full and equal social, political, and cultural share for Orientals (ibid., pp. 133–138). While they never formed a broad grassroots organisation, and failed to consolidate into an electoral force, they had a strong public impact, provoking a wide range of responses (ibid., p. 133).[1] On an iconographic level, they were important for their emphasis on "assertiveness instead of compliance" (ibid., p. 138), which forged a connection between protest and public self-affirmation. This plays a role in the repeated allusions to the group in discussions of Oriental identity within film studies (Ne'eman, 1979, p. 23; Shohat, 1989, p. 129; Shohat, 2001, pp. 194–196; Yosef, 2004, pp. 94–98; Yosef, 2010, pp. 118–121; Kimchi, 2012, pp. 21–22).

Dramatic political change was finally achieved a few years later, in 1977, by a right-liberal bloc which successfully translated protests by Oriental communities into electoral gains. The Likud party triumphed for the first time, with the support of Oriental voters, whose socio-economic and cultural deprivation the party had made a campaign issue (Hattis Rolef, 1998, p. 209).

15.1 From History to Theory: Oriental Jewish Identity in Israeli Film Theory

As a result of these political changes, the authorities moved to address the growing presence of Oriental Jews in politics and the media (ibid., pp. 209–210). In addition, the protest movement led to a new generation of Oriental writers in the 1970s (Kimchi, 2012, p. 22). The most remarkable changes, however, took place in academia, where the terms in which scholars discussed Oriental communities and their struggles were redefined. Until the 1970s, dominant sociologists in Israel had adopted the American paradigm of modernisation, on which Oriental Jews were seen as "traditional", in need of modernisation if they were to be successfully "absorbed" into Israel's European-oriented, "modern" society. There was no discussion of the distinctive features of their culture and identity, or the discrimination and prejudice they were subjected to (Goldberg and Bram, 2007, pp. 227–228; Kimchi, 2012, pp. 14–15). The 1970s, however, saw the rise of "critical sociology", based on a critique of the old paradigm. The new sociologists

---

[1] The title of this chapter refers to an infamous remark that Prime Minister Golda Meir made about this protest group in 1971.

focused on conflicts and power struggles within Israeli society, even while maintaining a binary perception of Oriental vs. European (Goldberg and Bram, 2007, p. 228; Kimchi, 2012, pp. 15–16). In this context, Oriental identity became a central theme for film scholars. The representation of ethnicity became the dominant theme in academic discourse. At the same time, attention turned to the only genre ever associated exclusively with Israeli cinema, *bourekas* – low-budget, ethnic entertainment films, named after a Balkan pastry. Kimchi identifies two ideological diagnoses film scholars attach to bourekas films, involving two contrasting approaches to Oriental identity: Shohat's post-colonial approach, and that of Ne'eman and Ben-Shaul, which he calls "modern" (Kimchi, 2012, pp. 61–67).

In a 1979 article, Ne'eman attributes a political agenda to bourekas films that can only be identified with the newly elected Likud party: capitalism, Oriental culture, and go-getting, which Ne'eman criticises in neo-Marxist terms (Ne'eman, 1979, pp. 20–22). Ben-Shaul's articles, written twenty or thirty years later, do not contain the same moral indignation (Kimchi, 2012, p. 62). He argues that Israeli films in general reflect the national mood. Both commercial and art films of the 1970s express an autonomous, liberal ideology. To that extent, they are harbingers of the rise of Likud (Ben-Shaul, 1998, pp. 128–129). By contrast, films of the 1980s express anxiety and increasing political and ethnic tension (Ben-Shaul, 2008, pp. 159–162). Ben-Shaul associates Oriental identity with contemporary political agendas and the emotions associated with these.

Shohat, who heavily influenced discourse on Oriental identity in Israeli film, concentrated on the representation of Oriental Jews. She makes a distinction between Sephardi and Ashkenazi filmmakers of both art and commercial films, and refers to the former positively and the latter negatively (Shohat, 1989, pp. 133–178, 205–216). Yosef and Kimchi continued this tradition of discrimination (Kimchi, 2012, pp. 68–143; Yosef, 2004, pp. 98–117; Yosef, 2010, pp. 121–163). While Shohat's analysis of commercial films focuses on what she argues to be negative portrayals of Oriental Jews by Ashkenazi filmmakers (ibid., pp. 135–166), later researchers have generally focused on positive forms of representation, echoing Shohat's analysis of art films by Oriental filmmakers (Lubin, 1991; Loshitzky, 2001, pp. 72–89; Shemer, 2011, p. 131; Yosef, 2004, pp. 84–163; Yosef, 2010, pp. 109–163). These scholars often use bourekas films as the negative paradigm which later films react against (Loshitzky, 2001, pp. 74–76; Shemer, 2011, pp. 120–122). Any positive aspect of this supposedly negative form is interpreted as an act of subversion (Lubin, 1991; Padva, 2008).

I believe that the complexity of the representation of Oriental Jews in the 1970s has yet to be fully explored. The conflation of Oriental identity and bourekas, the distinction between art and commercial films, and the division of filmmakers according to ethnic background has been counterproductive. Researchers have failed to take into account the pluralistic forms used to represent Oriental characters, the cultural sphere and system of production in which commercial and art films were made, and the vibrant cross-genre interactions between these films. My hypothesis is that, in the 1970s, the cinematic manifestation of Oriental Jewish identity was influenced by contemporary events which affected every part of the industry. This does not mean that these films mirrored political events involving the Oriental cause, but that Jewish Oriental identity became a more central locus of subjectivity to be explored. In this respect, I agree with Ne'eman and Ben-Shaul that the representation of Oriental Jewish identity reflected its evolving currency in the political field. Rather than trying to identify a manifestation of the governing ideology in this reflection, however, I will demonstrate how socio-economic turbulence defines cinematic subjectivity. I also argue that the construction and reflexion of Oriental consciousness in these films relied on the existing patterns I have discussed in earlier chapters.

The representation of Oriental Jews in films of the 1970s was diverse. They were sometimes portrayed as representatives of the lower class, but also as members of the middle and upper classes.[2] They were mostly, but not exclusively, presented in a context of socio-economic struggle and ethnic difference. They appeared in comedies, dramas, and melodramas, at times embodying erotic victims, disarming comic figures, and endangered adolescents.[3] The two films discussed here are not art films, and are not bourekas films: Menahem Golan's 1971 melodrama HIGHWAY QUEEN is sometimes mistaken for a bourekas film, although it was a high-end commercial production. Ze'ev Revach, who directed LITTLE MAN in 1978, was a renowned actor and director of bourekas films, but LITTLE MAN marked a venture into drama. HIGHWAY QUEEN was released at the same time as the first demonstration by the Israeli Black Panthers, and LITTLE MAN was released a year after the elections which brought Likud to power. As I will show, both films revolve around Oriental protagonists and the social restrictions they are subjected to. Both represent the apparatus of social ascendancy as an intricate, volatile system. In making social injustice tangible to the viewer, each film constitutes a manifesto against oppression.

---

[2] Lower-class Oriental figures appeared, for instance, in the art film LIGHT FROM NOWHERE, the musical KAZABLAN (1973, D: Menahem Golan), the melodrama MARRIAGE GAMES, and the comedy ONLY TODAY. Middle- and upper-class figures starred in the comedies THE CONTRACT, DAUGHTERS, DAUGHTERS! and THE TZANANI FAMILY.

[3] THE HOUSE ON CHELOUCHE STREET, for instance, contained both the erotic self-sacrificing victim, Nisso, and the overburdened adolescent Sami. The many comic Oriental figures in Israeli film include the protagonists in THE POLICEMAN (1971, D: Ephraim Kishon) and CHARLIE AND A HALF (1974, D: Boaz Davidson).

15.2 LITTLE MAN and HIGHWAY QUEEN

"He Who Fucks Alone, Dies Alone": Liberation from Comedy

The first film I will discuss is LITTLE MAN (1978, D: Ze'ev Revach), in which the protagonists revolt against long-established social structures and loyalties. It expressed a new sense of Oriental self-assertion after the Likud's electoral victory. As in many of the films Revach directed and starred in, social mobility is a central motif. Yosef made this point about his comedies:

> Revach's male body is always in relation to the world, to the social reality of deprivation and poverty that the Ashkenazi hegemony enforced on Mizrahim. His grotesque body is a result of, but also a critical response to and a weapon against, the ethno-economic discrimination in Israeli society, and the specific implications it has for the Mizrahi man. He manifests a male subjectivity that is always deauthorized by its attempt to maintain mastery. (Yosef, 2004, p. 114)

I argue that this also holds true within the subtle conventions of Revach's drama.

In LITTLE MAN, the Oriental protagonist, Shraga Katan, commands an army reserve crew of five in an armoured manoeuvre on Israel's northern border. At night, a local girl, Sophie Dahan, arrives to entertain them with an amateur singing performance, which ends in group sex. After Sophie discovers that she is pregnant, she travels to Tel Aviv to confront the men. By the end of the film, Shraga breaks his engagement with the beautiful daughter of his rich employer, takes responsibility for Sophie's pregnancy, and enters into a loving relationship with her.

The romantic affair in the film, which bridges a socio-economic gap, resembles that of FORTUNA, as well as MARRIAGE GAMES, a melodrama released in 1973. In all three, the immediate attraction between the protagonists is presented as an act of nature. The male protagonist is at an economic and educational advantage, and, as the film progresses, the couple must overcome social conventions, taboos, and prior entanglements. The major difference that sets LITTLE MAN apart from the other two films is the male protagonist's ethnicity. While Pierre (in FORTUNA) and Uzi (in MARRIAGE GAMES) are blond and blue-eyed, marked as "European", Shraga's complexion is dark. The difference is not just skin deep, as he appears to be familiar with Sophie's social and cultural situation.

In the opening of the film, Shraga is portrayed as a man who has made it. He is shown in the title sequence, in London with his fiancée, an elegant air stewardess. In the following sequence, back in Israel, he drives a new car to the factory, where he holds a position of authority. Between these two sequences, however, his mother is seen toiling in his kitchen. Her headscarf and foreign, Oriental accent reveal Shraga's humble origins. He is a successful social climber. The male protagonists in FORTUNA and MARRIAGE GAMES are secure in their social position, whereas Shraga's status is more tenuous. His conflict with his fiancée and her father over his connection to Sophie revolves around the question of whether he owes them his success.

After she arrives in Tel Aviv and confronts the crew halfway through the film, Sophie appears at Shraga's doorstep unsolicited. She invades his bohemian apartment three times. He rebukes her each time, but grants her immediate admission. Like Shraga's mother, Sophie introduces herself to his household through domestic work: she leaves him breakfast at his bedside, vacuums, hangs his laundry, and irons his shirts. This nurturing is mutual: Shraga gives Sophie his bed and moves to the couch, leaves her a key to the apartment, and tends to her when she is ill. The film implies that their reciprocal care is rooted in a shared social code.

The connection between Shraga and Sophie is not set up in contrast to his engagement, but to another social affiliation – the company of military reservists Shraga serves with which is introduced at the beginning of the film. This is made up of four men: Abner, Freddie, Chiby, a young, chubby soldier, and Eli, a reporter from the military radio station. Both of the latter join the unit at the last moment. Shraga is their commander. The precariousness of his authority is subtly introduced early in the film by the use of his surname, Katan, which attests to his Iraqi origins, and literally means "little" in Hebrew. As the tank crew prepares for mobilisation, the name "Katan" is repeated by the angry troop commander, and by Chiby and Eli. Shraga reacts with irritation, particularly when the reporter calls his name. Explicitly, the negative connotations only involve the surname's literal meaning, but the ethnic association subtly colours the sequence.

In this military context, Sophie, a Moroccan Jewish girl from a small northern Israeli town, becomes a unifying object. Until she arrives at the tank, the team of men are shown as heterogeneous and uncoordinated. Her entry brings them into unison. They all glare at her, flirt with her, laugh at and with her, and join in with her singing. She is lifted onto the tank for her performance, as though it were a pedestal. Shraga's relationship with her becomes a team project. During her performance, Abner, Eli and Freddie surround Shraga, who is at the centre of the frame, gazing up intensely at Sophie. Abner begins by noting Sophie's interest in Shraga, but goes on to say that she wants them to "screw" her. As he says this, he hugs Shraga and presses his forehead against the side of his head. The men hold on to Shraga, and then cheer for him to join Sophie on the tank. The military crew invades the initial, erotic exchange of glances between Shraga and Sophie.

The couple's intimacy materialises in isolation from the group. There is a sudden thunderstorm, and the two escape into the tank. As Sophie slides through the narrow entrance, her skirt lifts, and Shraga's hand glides up her exposed thigh. They lie together, sprawled horizontally in this confined space. He looks apprehensive as she snuggles up to him. He checks if no one else is present before embracing her intensely. The couple's privacy is short-lived, ending when Chiby peers through the entrance. His perspective reveals their lower bodies. Sophie's skirt is drawn back, revealing her knee-high boots, as she wraps her legs around Shraga's uniformed thighs. After the other soldiers join the scene, the camera returns to a more "respectable" perspective, capturing them from the chest up, locked in a kiss that radiates not just passion but warmth.

Figure 12: Shraga looks out for invaders in a rare moment of intimacy in LITTLE MAN.

The invasion begins with Freddie's lewd variation of a proverb: "He who fucks alone, dies alone." The camera remains on the tank's entrance as the men slide inside, one by one. Shraga's protests die down, replaced by the men's chatter and Sophie's cheerful shrieks. As Chiby enters, he turns on the tank's radio, and the sounds penetrate the troop commander's staff meeting. The commander is furious, but his staff members can hardly hold back their smiles. The collective takeover of the pair's intimacy goes public, gaining a sniggering audience.

When she is just in Shraga's company, Sophie does not appear in the nude. After the men enter, however, she is shown in four shots, naked, fully exposed from the shoulder up. She is in the centre of the frame, her bare knee lifted so that it appears in the shot, indicating that she is sexually accessible. Abner and Eli are on both her sides, just as they stood by Shraga's side earlier. Freddie and Chiby, alternately, appear in front of her, and all of them touch, grab and kiss her. In the first shot she looks bewildered, calling for Shraga. In the other shots, she laughs. The cheerful tone, the light comments, and the laughter all draw this scene toward the comic, but Shraga's presence works against this, offering an alienated experience of the comedy. He is not among the men surrounding Sophie, but is positioned alone on top of the tank, where he expresses his displeasure and shuts off the wire. When the tank reappears in the light of dawn, Shraga stands at its foot, his face to the ground. His melancholic disposition is contrasted to the men's cheerful mood as they step out of the tank. Shraga helps Sophie off the tank, and along with the viewer, beholds her – a woman who has been "had" several times over. He alternates between looking unhappy and putting on a smile for her. He hugs her, and becomes despondent when she proclaims that she is not a loose woman.

At no point does Sophie's portrayal become comic. Nor does she become a sacrificial victim, used up and defeated. She places herself at the centre of the frame, in front of Shraga and the viewer in long shot, smiling and hesitating, soliciting Shraga's and the viewer's empathy, which Shraga reinforces with his reaction. The fact that their intimate encounter is seized by the collective and becomes public shows them both to be on shaky ground with the group.

But this military collective is also shown to hold a reward for Shraga. The whole crew must face the consequences of the sexual act, and not he alone. The team's multiple fatherhood becomes a force which unifies the crew, and a source of comedy for the rest of the film, in which Shraga is given an equal part to the others. The men are summoned back to the base in the north, where the commander, gesturing at a map of northern Israel, opens with a great deal of pathos, before revealing their task: to take responsibility for the "mishap" with Sophie. Together, they decide that Chiby, the underdog, should take the fall. Together, they receive the news that Chiby has been rejected by Sophie. Together, they are summoned by Sophie to a restaurant in Tel Aviv. Together, they take her on an emergency visit to the gynaecologist, standing nervously in his waiting room and entering his office to hear the results. In all except the meeting in the restaurant, Shraga is filmed as part of the group. He is not positioned at the centre of the collective frame, and receives the same length of close-up as the others.

But the group structure does not prevail. The early meetings have an aim, and results, but this purposefulness comes to a halt after the gynaecological

Figure 13: The military collective of potential fathers in LITTLE MAN.

inspection ends, off-camera, in a shouting match. The two last gatherings, in Shraga's home and on the beach, conclude without resolution, establishing a sense of futility and immobility. As Talmon writes in relation to other films of the period, a group formed for the sake of a mission loses hold of its task (Talmon, 2001, p. 64).

Sophie singles Shraga out, visually isolating him from the group. In the scene at the restaurant, Sophie communicates solely by whispering to him. In the resulting composition, Shraga shares Sophie's frame, separated from the others. After the others arrive at his apartment and find Sophie there, they gather on his couch while he hovers nervously around them. Instead of leading to the expected resolution, the group only repeats its invasion of Shraga's private sphere.

During the last quarter of the film, the failed collective is absent, and comedy, too, is discarded. When Shraga quarrels with his fiancée and her father over his right to act independently from them, he does so with dramatic gravity. Shraga and Sophie then salvage their private intimate sphere, in a sex scene laden with the pathos that was stolen from them by the comic collective. To the quiet sound of the theme music, Sophie looks at Shraga asleep on the couch, walks over to him, and drops the towel wrapped around her. The back of her slim body is revealed as she squats in front of the sofa and lays her head on it with an earnest expression. Shraga sits up and looks at her, and she slowly joins him under the covers. They look intensely at each other before she puts her head on his chest and tearfully confesses her love. Their embrace is long and tender. Even during this scene, in which Sophie and Shraga recreate their sovereign space, the military crew invades the screen. When he embraces her, an image is superimposed of Sophie in the tank, laughing, surrounded and being touched by men. Two additional shots show her embracing Eli and Abner. Compositionally, these harmonise with the couple's embrace in the present. The comparison makes their relative tenderness tangible. The film also depicts a fantasy, an alternative version of their first encounter in which Sophie takes her leave of the group and Shraga helps her down from the tank. He holds her briefly and lightly, and she asks him his name. The film then returns to the naked couple, embracing in bed. Their familiarity grows as they now behold each other. Sophie slowly sinks to the couch, out of sight. Shraga's gaze remains in the air for a moment before he sinks toward her, his back arched. Sophie's light-skinned hand, her nails painted red, slides over his dark back. Beyond this sensuality and tenderness, the couple's presence is enhanced through their victimisation by the group.

The music continues as the film cuts abruptly to Sophie picking up her suitcase and quietly leaving Shraga's apartment, throwing one last glance at him as he sleeps. She goes to the left of the screen, a movement complemented by an image of a bus, traveling across a northern landscape, heading leftwards. With her departure, Sophie sacrifices herself, waiving her demands and facing her predicament alone. The connection between eroticism and victimhood is revived and cemented. Shraga, too, exercises self-sacrifice. In the next scene, he announces to the men that he is going to take responsibility for Sophie. He does not join in their laughter, and leaves them in contempt. Having travelled to the north, Shraga also undergoes physical martyrdom. When he shows up in Sophie's factory, he is beaten up by her brother and his three companions – a macho echo of the lost military camaraderie. As with Sherman in ELDORADO, this violence is not designed to elicit sadistic pleasure in the mutilation of his body, which is obscured by those of his assailants, but to establish his status, along with Sophie, as a legitimate victim.

In the last shot, Shraga and Sophie are seen at night, standing in a crowded bus going back to Tel Aviv. He holds her to his chest. Both their expressions are sombre as the radio broadcasts Eli's field report – a recording of their first encounter, in which the men cheer Sophie and laugh at Shraga's name. The discrepancy between the visual and the audible brings out the central motif: the distance between Shraga and Sophie, on the one hand, and the collective spirit which defines them on the other.

Shraga's individualism is assigned to the genre of drama, and his collectivism to comedy. From the oppression of collective comedy, the film salvages

Shraga and Sophie as dramatic, sensual victims. Victimhood, individualism, virtue, and pathos are inscribed into Oriental identity, to which the rejected collective remains foreign. Shraga and Sophie's subjugation is made palpable by the collective invasion of their sexual bond. Their new autonomy is manifested in the reinstatement of eroticism, tenderness, and intimacy, in a sex scene free of laughter. Ultimately, the transition from comedy to drama, away from the comic figure to the victim, is represented as an Oriental Jewish act of liberation.

"It's Written All Over Your Face": Elevation and Degradation

Like LITTLE MAN, HIGHWAY QUEEN elevates its protagonist from a comic figure to a victim. The film depicts Margalit Hasson, a prostitute of Moroccan Jewish origin in Tel Aviv. When she meets a friendly client, Arik, a truck driver and a kibbutz member of European Jewish decent, she is preparing to retire from the profession, get pregnant, and become a single mother. She uses Arik to father her child and returns to her mother in Dimona, a small southern town. One evening she meets four young men from Tel Aviv who violently rape her, setting off a broader calamity in her life.

Whereas in LITTLE MAN Shraga and Sophie rise from the status of non-sovereign figures in a comedy to sovereign, self-sacrificing victims, in HIGHWAY QUEEN Margalit rises from prostitution only to descend into calamity. This process of elevation and degradation is quite different from the dynamic of LITTLE MAN, and from the process of decline traditionally associated with prostitution.

An archetypical example of the depiction of prostitution as a continuous process of degradation is William Hogarth's *Harlot's Progress*. This series of six engravings, made in 1732, outlines the life and career of a prostitute as a continuous process of deterioration, as she gradually loses her wealth, health, and dignity. One Israeli film that operates within this convention is JACKO AND THE PROSTITUTES (1972, D: Paul L. Smith). Helen, a minor character, is an innocent young woman, lured into prostitution in Haifa's club strip by Jacko, a pimp. Her evolution into a full-fledged prostitute is organised into stages, each depicted in a scene accompanied by its own distinct jazz theme. Helen begins as an unsuspecting backpacker, picked up by Jacko in his convertible. A lengthy scene shows a trip to a secluded cave, at the end of which they make love passionately. The next time they make love, it is in the lewd environment of Jacko's club. He begins to have sex with Helen, and then leaves her with another man, who carries on. She is then bluntly informed that she had just performed an act of prostitution. She reacts violently. Afterwards, the viewer is informed that she has begun working at the club. Two years later, she appears for the first time in a skimpy outfit, drawing eyes with a long, erotic dance. The viewer sees her drunk once, and then "on the job". A truck driver picks her up at a gas station. They go to the back seat of a car, which is raised up by a car lift, activating a visual pun – uplift in Hebrew is a coarse slang word for intercourse. Helen is then shown in two brief scenes, wearing scanty outfits on the street and interacting with her employers. She goes from romantic engagement to debauchery, subjugation, titillating others, suffering abuse, and, finally, settling into routine. While at the beginning she is featured in a long, sensual scene, her sexual engagement in the last part of the film is not erotic, but comic. As the film progresses, she becomes indistinct, an ill-respected cog in a machine.

In comparison with JACKO AND THE PROSTITUTES – and, indeed, most contemporary productions – HIGHWAY QUEEN was an upscale production, set apart by its use of the cinematic methods of New Hollywood: heavy use of non-classical camera angles, an expressive editing tempo, and a challenging viewing process. Unlike JACKO AND THE PROSTITUTES, it presents a multifaceted, rather than a linear process, with Margalit continually oscillating between elevation and degradation. I argue that these extremes are poetically linked: The alternation between ascent and decline is not only the central motif around which Margalit's subjectivity is constructed, but the main principle that unravels the oppressive social structure confining her.

When Margalit first appears, in the title sequence, she is in a scrapyard, wearing a blond wig, miniskirt, and high boots, which she zips up as she scrambles behind a client. He drives away as she tries to enter his car. In this first appearance, Margalit is being treated with less than common courtesy, and struggling to keep up. Throughout the rest of the title sequence, the camera continues to follow her as she leaves the scrap yard, gets a taxi, and returns home to a rooftop apartment furnished in feminine style. Her movements are weary, but she no longer appears to have lost control. Her entrance is captured in an unusually steep bird's-eye shot. She immediately takes off the blond wig, revealing her brown hair, and her boots, and spreads bank notes over the pillow. The film implies that the prostitute's uniform, her mask, can be removed, and that the viewer is being offered a glimpse behind the scenes.

In the next eight minutes, until she is back on the job, the film elevates Margalit's status by attributing ever greater strength to her – a trait implied by her Oriental surname, Hasson, which literally means "strong" or "sturdy" in Hebrew. She enters the chaotic home of her neighbour, who is absent, and, despite initial resistance from the children, manages to impose temporary harmony. During a friendly conversation with the neighbour, who has returned home, the film uses reaction shots to pursue a comparison. The blond neighbour is older and not as pretty, and Margalit points out that she is younger, fresher, less burdened by life, and financially more secure than her neighbour. With her colleagues at the gas station, Margalit manages to draw a john's attention away from a younger prostitute. A colleague informs the viewer that she is hard, determined, competitive and independent, working without a pimp.

The camera then captures her walking seductively by the roadside, as a john follows her in his car. With a golden aura of sunlight, she leans on his door. This is the height of her elevation, which is followed by a decline. As soon as she enters the car, her price quickly falls, from double what her younger colleague had demanded, to seventy Israeli pounds (in a hotel) to thirty (in the car). Thus, prostitution and her interaction with johns continue to have a debasing connotation. Margalit soon transitions into a comic figure.

This sequence, in which she has sex with the john, is the opening of a four-and-a-half-minute segment depicting Margalit's working life. As in JACKO AND THE PROSTITUTES, purchased sex is directly associated with comedy. Whereas the humour surrounding Helen's prostitution is completely dependent on a visual pun, Margalit, like the children in ODED THE WANDERER, is a comic performer. With lighthearted comic music playing in the background, the camera moves up and down to simulate the thrust of penetration. The car is seen shaking from Margalit's movements. Medium close-ups show her in motion, resisting the john's embrace, wearing an expression of unconcealed disinterest, and glancing at the man's watch. She is then shown in long shot, straightening her skirt, and stepping out of a slightly different car, in a slightly different outfit, at a different location. Waiting for more customers, she appears in yet another outfit by the train tracks, waving her hands and dancing at a passing train, reminiscent of a comic figure in a silent film.

The sounds of the train provide an opening to a new, quicker musical score, and the screen splits into five sections, showing different scenes from Margalit's routine. Two of these feature sexual acts, characterised by the setting of the scrapyard and by Margalit's indifferent expression. Others show money changing hands in close-up, and Margalit making a deposit at the bank, standing on the strip, walking with colleagues, scuffling with them, and then with the police, who arrests her and the others. During the fight, Margalit's exaggerated expressions and body movement increase the comic effect. Later in the sequence, the screen splits into nine sections, showing variations of the same procedure. She is seen in an extreme long shot at the entrance to a hotel, entering with a john, then in close-up as she has sex with him, moving up and down with a disengaged expression, then in long shot again, leaving the hotel. In some of the sections, she is approached by another john, and walks back in. In the central section, a client's naked back appears, moving up and down, while Margalit, who faces the camera, plays with her nails behind his back. We then see a close-up of her hands counting banknotes. The facade of the hotel is white, while the close-up shots are darker. This creates a play of colours between the nine sections, with the central one serving as the centrepiece. This visual composition has a distancing effect: on the divided screen, the many acts of penetration appear small, contained, and mechanical, something matched by Margalit's comic gestures. The increasing pace of the music, the sight and sound of the train, and the complex movement across the different panels all create an industrious atmosphere. Prostitution takes on the nature of a mass-produced, hasty, comic act.

Arik's arrival, some ninety seconds after this sequence, is marked by a deceleration and diminishment in the comedy. His interest in Margalit and interactions with her are accompanied by a slow, quiet theme. Arik is a newcomer to the sex industry, and, as in VIVRE SA VIE (1962, D: Jean-Luc Godard), the novice's unfamiliarity with the process of transaction undermines its automatic mechanism. When Margalit and Arik first meet, he does not recognise that she is a prostitute. As they discuss the price, he remarks that seventy pounds is his annual wage. As a member of the kibbutz, he exists outside Margalit's monetary system. A whole segment is dedicated to his efforts to raise the money.

Arik finally obtains the sum of thirty-five pounds, and arrives at the gas station with evident delight to purchase Margalit's services. When they get to the scrap yard, the camera slowly rises, until they are seen in extreme long shot. It captures the surroundings as Arik looks at them, slowly walking behind Margalit for two and a half minutes. These lengthy shots compel a more acute perception of the crumbling landscape the viewer was introduced to at the beginning of the film. They arrive at a shack. Reaction shots show Arik's low-spirited glance at the ragged old man Margalit evacuates from the building and its chaotic interior. She urges him to come in and close the door. The transaction, which had recurred so repetitively fifteen minutes earlier, is slowed down, broken into smaller details that increase the viewer's resistance, along with Arik's.

As the film's pace decelerates, the viewer must take a more concentrated look at Margalit, her actions, gestures, and expressions. There are more close-ups of her. This is paralleled by a diminishment in her strength. As the sequence begins, she appears vulnerable. Before Arik finds her, she is robbed by two johns. When they meet, she is bruised and low-spirited. The spatial chaos and wreckage of the scrap yard is a manifestation of her inner state. Instead of the anticipated sexual transaction, Arik takes on a chivalrous, nurturing role. On the way to the scrapyard, he stops the truck to disinfect Margalit's injured knee. When Margalit suddenly rushes out of the shack and vomits, Arik tends to her, drives her home, and lets her keep the money for the next encounter. Margalit's figure not only gains depth, but is made to seem more vulnerable.

The sexual transaction is delayed, and when it finally takes place, it sustains the bond between Margalit's enhancement and her tangible vulnerability.

The sex scene between Arik and Margalit has a different aesthetic quality to the earlier sexual acts. They are shown through the bars of Margalit's bed, from the shoulder up, in medium close-up. Unlike the other sexual encounters, both are bare-skinned and horizontal. The camera zooms out and the theme tune plays as Arik orgasms. For part of the time, Margalit closes her eyes, opens her mouth, and licks her upper lip, succumbing to sexual pleasure. She also looks away, upwards, but not with the same detached expression she wore in previous encounters. Reaction shots show various trinkets that decorate Margalit's room, some of which move as the bed rocks. They all depict children and animals, and most regard Margalit and the viewer with big eyes, their childish nature emphasising vulnerability.

By the norm established in the film, sex takes place in a vertical position outside the private sphere. Paradoxically, the sexual act in the private bedroom, with both partners naked, is an unusual, precarious event. Margalit's bare skin, her trinkets, and the glances she casts at them signal how exposed she is by this intimacy. The sensualising effect of the sex scene on Margalit elevates her figure. But this same sensuality gives a sense of exposure and endangerment.

The conversation that follows makes the source of Margalit's vulnerability clear. Arik's presence brings her socio-economic disadvantages into play. Among other things, when she tells Arik her name, she pronounces it with the stress on the penultimate syllable, a pronunciation associated with lower social status. He insists on correcting her, placing it instead on the final syllable – the grammatically correct pronunciation, associated with the privileged milieu of the kibbutz. Margalit, however, does not remain defenceless. Rather, she reinstates her power through her performance in the dialogue. Seated at the dresser, in front of a set of three mirrors, she puts on her jewellery and rotates back and forth on her swivel chair as she talks with Arik, who asks her if she means to leave the profession. She responds with a parody of the woeful life story of the victimised prostitute.[4] Although Arik shares her frame in the over-the-shoulder shots used in this scene, the focus alternates between the two of them, demarcating a distance between them which signifies Margalit's protective shield. Arik leaves the frame before she commences her final assertive monologue, in which she rejects the

---

4 This is a clear parody of the prostitute's monologue in ELDORADO, which, I argued in chapter 11, enhances her status as a victim. The effect relies on the intertextual reference, on the fact that both films are by the same director, and that both prostitutes are portrayed by the same actress.

narrative of subjugation. She is free, independent, has made her fortune, and will soon retire. From across the room, Arik again corrects her pronunciation of her name, reasserting her inferiority.

The encounter between Margalit and Arik sets off two processes. In the first of these, their connection continues to be disentangled from the monetary system, resembling a transaction less and less. Arik makes opulent gifts of fruit, which Margalit shares with her colleagues and neighbour. Margalit opens Arik's wallet to look at pictures of his children, and makes a gift of her teddybear to his daughter. In the second process, by contrast, the comedy plays off Margalit's socio-economic status. Throughout the film, she speaks with a heavy Oriental accent. Only after her encounter with Arik, however, does the comedy revolve predominantly around her linguistic inadequacy. Dressed as elegantly as a stewardess, she is approached by an American john. The comedy revolves around their communication, which breaks down because of her limited English. Another linguistic breach is created when Margalit is picked up by a john whose profession she cannot pronounce – he is a veterinarian – and who answers her question about (human) medicine in a pedantically erudite, declamatory way.

However, the ultimate comic verbal discrepancy occurs when Margalit appears in Arik's kibbutz. She is inappropriately dressed for the agricultural community in a shiny green suit, nervously chewing gum and playing with an amber chain of Oriental prayer beads. Not only does she perform poorly within the social codes of the community, but she also enters it as an imposter. She pretends to be a former employee of the dairy distributer Arik delivers to, and claims to have come to the kibbutz as a volunteer. Margalit's basic unfamiliarity with her alleged prior employer and the institute that recruited her to the kibbutz becomes the source of abundant grammatical blunders. Whereas in LITTLE MAN the dominant collective culture is the source of comedy, in HIGHWAY QUEEN, humour arises from the shadow cast on the marginal protagonist by the dominant culture. Margalit becomes an awkward bungler.

The comic effect evaporates when Margalit and Arik are left alone and he introduces her to his two young children. She swings Arik's two-year-old blond son in the air; the camera continues the swing, returning to show Arik on top of Margalit, horizontal, naked, making love to the sound of their theme tune. In this sex scene, their nakedness strips them bare of socio-economical difference. It does not constitute exposure, but liberation. The brightness of their skins is enhanced by the soft, rosy background and the fluffy white surface that surrounds them. An extreme long shot reveals that they are in a barn, on a stack of cotton. The camera captures the sensual interaction of their smooth bodies from unusual angles. During most of the scene, Margalit remains at the centre of the frame, engaging actively with Arik. She does not look away. Margalit is elevated to the film's sensual peak.

But this cinematic pinnacle is not represented as a manifestation of unbridled eroticism that overcomes all socio-economic boundaries. Margalit is not romantically motivated; rather, she is interested in having a child. Before the scene, Margalit has herself checked by a fertility specialist to find out if she could bear a child. Arik and Margalit's interaction with his children do not contrast with the sex scene, then, but complements it. Eroticism materialises through a male-female, European-Oriental encounter, but it does not promote a heterosexual relationship or an inter-ethnic bond. Rather, it is for a higher cause, which further empowers Margalit. Just as the erotic allure in this scene is greater than in the first sex scene between the two, so is the gap between them at its conclusion. Arik rolls off Margalit. They lie side by side. Their faces are captured in close-up, the focus alternating between them, as after their first sex scene. The out-of-focus part of the frame, however, is far more blurred. Arik suggests that Margalit wants to have a child, but she refuses to explain her actions. Her empowerment is not created only through her bond with him, but also through her detachment.

By refusing the relationship but obtaining the child, Margalit maintains an autonomy that is only perceptible from the standpoint of her marginality. As she prepares for motherhood, however, it becomes evident that her autonomy is not all-embracing, for there is an element of emulation in her actions. In the kibbutz, Margalit meets Arik's wife, a blond beauty with short hair. On the train to the small southern town and her new vocation as a mother, Margalit appears with a new short haircut of her own, playing with it repeatedly. Arik and her blond neighbour serve as authority figures, speaking in favour of childrearing. Their predominantly blond children are the ones that Margalit looks at and cares for. When Margalit prepares for motherhood, she decorates her room with magazine cut-outs of blond toddlers. The film shows Margalit's model of parenthood to be an external frame of reference, one constructed from European elements.

Eighteen minutes of the film are then dedicated to Margalit's encounter with and assault by a gang of four young men. Shohat claims that they are portrayed as Oriental, and that their brutality contrasted with Arik's gentleness (Shohat, 1989, p. 159). It is central to the poetic structure of the film, however, that they are depicted as middle-class rogues of European Jewish origin. In that sense, they serve as an extension of Arik's socio-economic superiority.

The four, who arrive in a convertible, are fashionably dressed. Two have baby faces, and three have fair hair, light complexions, and light-coloured eyes. The tallest of them wears a moustache which echoes Arik's own. Whereas the johns that robbed Margalit earlier shouted insults at her in strong Oriental accents, the gang speak meticulous Hebrew, without any foreign expressions. In the conversation at the gas station, where Margalit, working as a waitress, serves them behind the counter, much of the exchange relies on the fact that the men come from the centre of Israel and are unfamiliar with the south. When Margalit lists the evening venues available, they sarcastically marvel the possibilities: billiards, television, and the "scotheque", mimicking her mispronunciation of the word "discotheque". They underline her Achilles heel throughout the film: her humble origins and linguistic inferiority.

Before the viewer witnesses Margalit's fall, she is elevated one last time. She joins the men at the club. A succession of psychedelic rock tunes plays as she smokes, drinks, plays billiards, and dances with them. She remains at the centre of the composition through most of the sequence. The camera zooms in on her when she makes a successful shot in the game. Reaction shots show three men looking at her as she dances with a fourth, another series of shots shows the fourth man looking at her as she dances with the other three, who move energetically, encouraging her with their movements.

Margalit is enticed to go with the men to Sodom, the site of the Biblical city destroyed by God (Genesis 19) – a symbol of impenitent sin. As the car arrives at the site, the wide lens distorts the perspective. The men jump out of the car, while Margalit stays inside. They and the camera move in circles around Margalit, like the jackals audible in the background. The space is broken into single medium shots and close-ups that maintain the spatial sense of a circle enclosing Margalit.

The men's intentions are stated explicitly. The tallest of them pulls Margalit out of the car, saying that he recognises her from Tel Aviv. The new hairdo doesn't change a thing, as "it's written all over your face". Margalit's inadequate vocabulary is used for the last time, now wholly detached from comedy. One of the baby-faced men smiles pleasantly and utters sympathetic words. She pleads with him in broken language as he nods his head. The attack begins when she lays his hand on her belly and he moves it to her breasts. Linguistic elements which, earlier in the film, served the elevating purposes of comedy, now return in melodramatic earnest. In the absence of comedy, both Margalit and the viewer lack a protective shield. At first, Margalit fends off the men. Compositionally, the chase resembles the dance at the club: she remains at the centre and they move energetically around her. The final attack on the protagonist is remarkably similar to the scene which elevated her shortly before. Margalit repeatedly shouts "The child!" The camera moves restlessly, and the editing accelerates as the men pin her down on a dune. It returns several times to her distorted face as she screams. She is punched twice in the stomach. Her body is captured from above as her dress is torn, her breasts and belly, exposed and her bare legs pulled apart. The tall man pulls down his trousers. Penetration is shown by a close-up of his frantic movements, and a reaction shot of her distorted face as she screams. The baby-faced man takes his place. Margalit is captured from a canted angle as she turns her head, apparently losing consciousness. The film moves abruptly to the sight of her at dawn, lying alone on the dune, in an extreme long shot, the Dead Sea shining in the background.

Earlier in the film, the viewer observed Margalit being sexually penetrated repeatedly. But the screen was split, the settings were comic, and Margalit was disinterested and emotionally unaffected. The rape scene constitutes quite the opposite: the camera draws near, Margalit's body stretches out before the viewer, and the horror of the scene is unmistakable. Its brutality resides not only in the "realistic" details of the assault, but in the transition from the protagonist's subjectification to objectification. Margalit is transformed from a central figure, in the dance scene, to a target for violence. Her body, once erotically exposed in the barn with Arik, now quivers under a collective act of penetration. The first time the viewer encountered her exposure, it increased her eroticism. The collective attack is a violent materialisation of danger. As in previous films, Margalit's sensuality enhances the sense of her loss, and vice versa. Importantly, however, HIGHWAY QUEEN goes further: eroticism, subject enhancement, and victimhood are causally connected.

Margalit's victimhood is constructed around the fragility traditionally connected with the type figure of the child. The victim, then, is enhanced by sensuality, but the melodramatic gesture is brought to its peak through the child's vulnerability. The physical attack centres on her womb, and her screams direct the viewer's horror towards the embryo she carries. This is supported by her concerns over pregnancy before the rape, and by the long sequences that follow, showing its aftermath.

Earlier in the film, Margalit's fears about childbirth were associated with scenes showing her close to a mysterious castle-shaped building, in a compound by the sea. In the waiting room of the fertility clinic, she is haunted by horrific fantasies of giving birth. A sense of danger, then, is already present before the rape. In its aftermath, as Margalit crawls, and then walks, in the bright sunlight, images appear, all of them coloured yellow: her doctors' warnings about external injuries to the foetus, the gates of the castle swinging open, a dwarf smiling hideously between its bars, and the assault itself. The physical injury materialises in all these forms. This is followed by a sequence in the hospital, showing Margalit lying with a blank expression in the maternity ward, her mother beside her. The other women receive flowers from male visitors, and a smiling nurse brings in a baby for another young woman to breastfeed.

Figure 14: Margalit's rise and fall: with a john, with Arik, and during the attack, in HIGHWAY QUEEN.

Margalit's loss of the child is intensified by the fact that she has been denied what the others are receiving. Motherhood had been presented as a domain in which Margalit emulated an external model. In this scene, motherhood remains outside her reach. The camera zooms in on her expression, cutting directly to her brown eyes.

Until this point, the castle has played an abstract, emblematic role. In the next scene, however, it materialises into "realistic" space, as Margalit stands at its gates and is admitted. It is a nursing facility, and she is there to visit her first son, born before the events of the film, and whom she has not visited for eight years: a small, shy child, slightly deformed. The higher angle from which he is shot makes him appear not only small, but also as though he has been compressed – a position related associatively with the violent penetration of the rape scene. The fact that this child existed prior to the assault raises the physical attack that the viewer witnesses from a single event to a general state of Margalit's being. The brutal attack extends to the past, present and future of her injured existence.

After a sequence in which Margalit attends to the child, drawing him out from complete passivity to timid responses, she returns him to the institute. The last aspect of her calamity then unfolds. She walks from the institute to a convertible, driven by a pimp. As he drives away, she pulls out her blond wig and purse. She is back on the job, having given up her independence. In the last sequence, Arik's truck stops by her on the strip. Reaction shots reveal his friendly and then apprehensive reaction as she resentfully gives him the cold shoulder. The camera lingers on his slow change of demeanour before he drives away. The film's emotional trajectory compels the viewer to identify, in this last encounter, both with Arik's dismay and Margalit's alienation.

In HIGHWAY QUEEN, the sex industry is not the cause of the Oriental prostitute's calamity. Rather, it is the whole social structure which marginalises her, descends upon her, and destroys any shred of autonomy. In that respect, Arik is not the exception, but part of the system. While Shraga and Sophie released themselves from the shackles of comedy, Margalit's own comedy is not presented as a form of subjugation, but as the last available shield against it. Her extension beyond the realm of comedy not only enhances her erotic presence, but exposes her to attack. Margalit's victimhood – extending over twenty-two minutes, from her assault until the end of the film – is not just a bad omen attached to eroticism, but outlines a social structure that suppresses the protagonist. Margalit's marginal existence, like her son's disability, is the result of external circumstances – not a hereditary defect, but the outcome of social injustice.

Social Oppression and the Struggle for Sovereignty

My purpose in this chapter was to offer an alternative analysis of the representation of Oriental Jewish figures in Israeli films of the 1970s. I focused on two films constructed as manifestos about the injustice perpetrated on their Oriental protagonists by the class system.

In LITTLE MAN and HIGHWAY QUEEN, Oriental subjects and the world around them were constructed using traditional patterns. The instability of the boundaries between public and private, the insignificance and autonomy of the comic figure, and the pathos and sensuality of the victim are all integral to the films' poetic structure. HIGHWAY QUEEN also uses the fragility of the child to heighten its melodrama. All these elements provide structures of meaning, embedding the cinematic representation of Oriental subjectivities within established communal perceptions of subject and environment.

Both films use comedy in a reflective manner that allows the viewer to contemplate its mechanism. In LITTLE MAN, the evolution of the main protagonists into victims rescues them from comedy. In HIGHWAY QUEEN, sensuality is not only associated with victimhood, but presented as its source. In both films, social oppression is translated at an affective level by repeated penetration. The viewer experiences inequality through the sexual act. HIGHWAY QUEEN reflects the depth of social injustice. As a melodrama, it constructs an affective world in which redemption is impossible. Seven years later, after the change of government, this redemption was finally enacted in LITTLE MAN.

16 We Are Young, We're Not Free: The Face of a New Generation in Youth Films

Unlike the national political developments discussed in the previous two chapters, we find little reflection in recent historiography of what was celebrated, in the late 1970s, as a new cinematic era. Between 1977 and 1978, word spread of a "New Israeli Wave", heavily praised in the Israeli press (Gertz, 1993, p. 175). Gross and Gross attribute this wave to new participants in the industry, as well as new contents and attitudes in the films themselves (Gross and Gross, 1991, p. 346). In part, they argue, the new wave arose with the disappearance of the three filmmakers who had previously dominated the industry: Ephraim Kishon, Uri Zohar, and Menahem Golan (ibid., pp. 342–343). Writing in 1978, the critic Uri Klein attributed the commercial success of LEMON POPSICLE and THE TROUPE (1978, D: Avi Nesher) to the "external gloss" which they possessed as American-style films (Klein, 1978, p. 6). Fifteen years later, Gertz notes that these films, along with others, created new genres that would come to dominate the Israeli screen (Gertz, 1993, p. 175). Most researchers see the main feature of this trend as a thematic common denominator – youth – which continued to dominate well into the 1980s (Bursztyn, 1990, pp. 206–207; Gross and Gross, 1991, p. 342–344; Gertz, 1993, p. 244; Hetsroni and Duvdevani, 2000, p. 101; Talmon, 2001, pp. 146–148; Almog, 2004, p. 1158).

According to Gertz, all the films of the era express ambivalence. In commercial productions, young people rebel against middle class values while simultaneously adopting them; in political films, the prevailing norms are undermined, but the protagonists do not discard them, and no alternatives are offered (Gertz, 1993, pp. 244–246). Both commercial and political films convey a sense of adolescent discontent. Talmon also identifies an inherent contradiction in these films, which she attributes to a transition from collectivism to individualism. In youth films of the late 1970s, male alliances and solidarity evoke nostalgia and the emotional lure of the collective (Talmon, 2001, p. 160). At the same time – specifically in the LEMON POPSICLE series – they establish new norms of hedonistic and egotistic individualism (ibid., p. 59). Gertz and Bursztyn also subscribe to this view (Gertz, 1993, p. 246; Bursztyn, 1990, pp. 206–207). Hetsroni and Duvdevani, writing about Nesher's early productions, agree that these youth films possess individualistic tendencies, but offer a more positive perspective, arguing that the films reflect a departure from old-fashioned idealism, expressing an excessive pursuit of pleasure and a lax sexual morality (Hetsroni and Duvdevani, 2000, pp. 108–109).

Contrary to the scholars just mentioned, I argue that the films in question are far from libertarian expressions of hedonism and egotism. Rather than celebrating individual sovereignty, they return to and explore the borders between individual and community – features of Israeli cinema from its very beginning. The intrusion of the individual upon the community, and of the community upon the individual, is enacted in them with an intensity that leaves no room for individualistic displays of personal autonomy.

Hetsroni and Duvdevani review the broadly negative response Nesher's films received when initially released, pointing out that much of this criticism focused on their lack of political content (Hetsroni and Duvdevani, 2000, pp. 103–104) – something which held true for the LEMON POPSICLE series. They therefore define Nesher's early films as post-ideological (ibid., p. 106), a label which applies to the LEMON POPSICLE series and the youth films that followed. But Israeli cinema's lack of ideological commitments did not originate in the late 1970s, and was already prevalent when the industry was established in the early 1960s. Why did such a conventional posture generate such reactions at that particular point in history?

Our focus turns, then, to the conditions in which this wave of youth films materialised. Talmon cites Haim Lapid's argument that representations of youth in the late 1970s reveal a social crisis arising from the Yom Kippur War and the Labour Alignment's electoral defeat. This crisis shattered the parental authority of the founding fathers, and left the social elite powerless – which, Lapid argues, led to cinematic expressions of egalitarianism, on the one hand, and childish regression on the other. Alongside a general crisis of identity, Talmon diagnoses a crisis of manhood which began pre-1970, and which found its way into representations of young people (Talmon, 2001, pp. 159–161). The depiction of youthful initiation ceremonies in films from this period reflects broader social change (ibid., p. 60).

It is undeniable that, as the sociologist Shmuel Eisenstadt observes, Israel was undergoing deep perceptual and structural changes in the late 1970s. In the aftermath of the Yom Kippur War, the institutional structures which had dominated Israel from its foundation began to disintegrate (Eisenstadt, 1985, p. 401), with the 1977 elections marking the crystallisation of a new institutional framework (ibid., p. 506). Just as importantly, public political disputes escalated, increasing a general sense of polarisation and intolerance. All sides saw the political divide extending into the social and cultural spheres (ibid., pp. 504–505). The growing belligerence of political discourse was the basis for the militant tone critics generally adopted at the time (Hetsroni and Duvdevani, 2000, pp. 103–104), and for their scorn of and indignation towards this new wave of cinematic adolescence.

Like Talmon, I interpret the emergence of youth films as a reflection of major changes in social structures. But these films did not necessarily reflect a major social crisis, particularly because the transformation within Israel during the late 1970s also included happier events. On November 20, 1977, the Egyptian President Anwar Sadat delivered a speech before the Israeli parliament in Jerusalem. After extensive negotiations, the two countries signed a peace agreement on March 26, 1979 (Hattis Rolef, 1998, pp. 229–230). Sadat was the first leader in the Arab world to recognise and sign a peace treaty with Israel. This was all the more significant because, until that time, Egypt was a leading force in the consolidated opposition to Israel, and a major participant in the wars against it (ibid., pp. 228–229). Sadat's diplomacy ended Israel's regional isolation, and offered military relief. His historic visit, and the peace settlement which opened up the border with a nation that had once been Israel's bitter enemy, were celebrated by a hopeful Israeli public.[1]

My premise is that critics of youth films were provoked, not only by the absence of political objectives, but also by a lack of an implicit threat. As Israeli society changed, the moral scales by which it measured itself were affected. Because fragility and victimhood played such a major role in the traditional equilibrium, the depiction of a more mundane, less precarious environment was unsettling for critics. As the contemporary critic Heda Boshes explained, the film (DIZENGOFF 99) itself is not bad, boring, or disappointing. However, it expresses a typical contemporary view, which repulses her (Hetsroni and Duvdevani, 2000, p. 108). Viewers were deprived of the sense of danger and crisis traditionally associated with young people.

When Gertz, Talmon, and Lapid discuss ambivalence, transition, and regression in the new youth films, they are discussing features associated with young people a decade earlier. The appearance of young protagonists in the late 1970s did not, in itself, signal a crisis. Moreover, the young people depicted in the period seem less daunting than their predecessors. As I have argued, in the 1960s, youth was associated with a paradise lost, something that continued into the 1970s in films like JUDGEMENT DAY. By the late 1970s, however, this association was no longer dominant. Another common motif in the 1960s was arrested development, manifested by the gap between a character's age and his

---

[1] Another marked Israeli achievement during the late 1970s came in sports. In April 1977, the Maccabi Tel Aviv basketball team won the European Champions Cup – the first time an Israeli team, in any sport, had reached the finals of any championship (Galily and Bar-Eli, 2005, p. 415). The Israeli public saw this as a politically symbolic event (ibid., p. 413), something made clear by the captain's remarks as he received the Cup: "We're [on] the map, and we'll stay [on] the map – not just in sport, but in everything" (ibid., p. 415).

conduct – middle-aged characters acting as teenagers, and teenagers acting like children. This continued into the 1970s, in films like THE DREAMER, THE PILL, PEEPING TOMS, and FLOCH. During the last quarter of the 1970s, this pattern appears in ROCKING HORSE, but otherwise it practically vanished. The characters were allowed to act their age, and youth was given back to the young.

In short, the wave of youth films at the end of the 1970s was not a manifestation of individualistic ideology or social crisis. The novelty of these films was not their focus on youth, or their lack of political commitment, but the new conditions in which they appeared. Rather than being an arena for endangerment and disappointment, sex scenes increasingly became the grounds on which boundaries were tested – the boundaries of young people's communal identities, and of the sexual practices that were becoming conceivable for the Israeli public in that era (see my historical review in 3.1).

Indeed, sex became central in this new wave of youth films. Scholars have noted that many of them, particularly the LEMON POPSICLE series, focus on their protagonists' sexual exploits (Gertz, 1993, p. 224; Talmon, 2001, p. 164; Hetsroni and Duvdevani, 2000, p. 101). In 1978, Fainaru celebrated LEMON POPSICLE for its sensitive depiction of erotic situations, a first in Israeli cinema, including the seduction of minors by an older woman, the physical and moral exposure of the "good girl" undergoing an abortion, a sordid visit to a prostitute, and a measuring contest between boys. Though more laughable than erotic, these scenes were unprecedented (Fainaru, 1978, p. 18). Nesher's representation of sexual relations was also central to the reception of his early films in academia and the media. Thirty years after the release of DIZENGOFF 99, those who participated in it view it as pioneering. The film's most memorable and heavily discussed scene is a three-way (Nuriel and Ben Ari, 2009, p. 32), which critics described as a somewhat heavy-handed attempt at sexual liberation (ibid.; Hetsroni and Duvdevani, 2000, p. 109).

Through a detailed analysis of the compositional structure of these sex scenes, we can assess the validity of these reviews, and understand the cinematic patterns they respond to. To explore the expression of sexuality in the new wave of youth films, I focus on two defining examples: LEMON POPSICLE 2: GOING STEADY (1979, D: Boaz Davidson) and DIZENGOFF 99. Both were sequels to commercial sensations from the previous year (respectively, LEMON POPSICLE and Nesher's debut, THE TROUPE). GOING STEADY and DIZENGOFF 99 were conceived with the objective of translating a popular formula into serial form. In their cinematic aesthetics and marketing strategies, they maintained the "American gloss" Klein identified in their predecessors. The films competed with each other promotionally, and were released on the same day. They achieved substantial commercial success, although not to the same extent as their predecessors (Nuriel and Ben Ari, 2009, p. 32; Hetsroni and Duvdevani,

2000, p. 100n4, p. 105). They were released in 1979 – the same year as *Screwing Isn't Everything*. I explore how far the two films are cinematic equivalents of Ben-Amotz's novel, and whether their sexual content veers into pornography. Most importantly, I analyse how the sexual content of each film is specifically associated with Israeli culture.

Many of the features which came to be identified with these two films were already present in earlier Israeli films. Their youthful vigour and joie de vivre had its precursor in THE CONTRACT. Despite Fainaru's claims, youthful sexual impropriety had been explored years earlier in LIGHT OUT OF NOWHERE and in HOUSE ON CHELOUCHE STREET. The latter also included immature sexual encounters between adolescents, physical embarrassment, and a seduction by an older woman. BOYS WILL NEVER BELIEVE IT, meanwhile, featured the first Israeli threesome. Before the LEMON POPSICLE series, HOUSE ON CHELOUCHE STREET explored a marginalised urban culture of the past, identified with the dandy and martyr Nisso Hudera. Finally, the style of comic interruptions and confusions that characterise many of the sex scenes in LEMON POPSICLE series was already present in Davidson's TZANANI FAMILY. The two films nevertheless represented a new turn in Israeli film, as we will see.

16.1 LEMON POPSICLE 2: GOING STEADY

"C'mon Everybody": The Perpetual Impertinence of the Gang

GOING STEADY is set in the late 1950s, and opens with the sound of an American rock and roll song. The protagonist, Benzi, and his two friends, Momo and Yudale,[2] appear, cruising at night in a convertible, surrounded by other cars. They are dressed in the Western fashions of the 1950s. They walk into an ice cream parlour, decorated with posters, where a crowd of fashionable teenage boys and girls are dancing to a jukebox.

The scene is reminiscent of AMERICAN GRAFFITI (1973, D: George Lucas), which Gertz, Talmon, and Almog identify as the primary inspiration for LEMON POPSICLE (Gertz, 1993, p. 279n101; Talmon, 2001, p. 163; Almog, 2004, p. 1156). The series as a whole revolves around urban culture: young people dressing in Western fashions, listening to Western music, dancing, and, like their parents,

---

2 Benzi, Momo, and Yudale (all nicknames) were renamed in the international release to Benny, Momo/Bobby, and Johnny/Huey. The character I refer to below as Bracha is called Martha in the international edition.

enjoying a range of leisure activities. As both Gertz and Talmon point out, this urban culture was marginalised and even frowned upon in the Israel of the 1950s. The newly established state, with its mobilised society, expected ideological and practical commitment from its youth. Gertz, Talmon, and Almog argue that the centrality of this middle-class trend, and the absence of the dominant ideological alternative,[3] are historically revisionist (Gertz, 1993, p. 246; Talmon, 2001, p. 163; Almog, 2004, p. 1158).

Like AMERICAN GRAFFITI, GOING STEADY constructs an audio-visual spectacle of the Western youth culture of the past. Unlike its nostalgic American predecessor, however, it uses this past to present a historical revision, erasing the mobilisation that was dominant in the period depicted. Furthermore, GOING STEADY utilises an Americanised backdrop to depict an Israeli narrative of constant conflict between individual and community. The LEMON POPSICLE series employs physical discomfort, conflict over boundaries, and revelations and subsequent humiliations as a source of humour, seasoning this with sometime indecent 1950s slang, partly historical, partly invented. The protagonists are permanently out of alignment with their environment.

Six and a half minutes into the film, it is revealed that the convertible is stolen. Unlike their American counterparts, Benzi, Momo, and Yudale do not own a vehicle. The autonomous space that the cars in AMERICAN GRAFFITI provide is absent. Furthermore, the protagonists in GOING STEADY are more hostile than their American predecessors. As the trio cruises, they catcall a girl on a motorcycle and exchange insults with her male companion. In the ice cream parlour, as they pass the film's proto-nerd, Ronny, each of them pokes him, eliciting a cry of protest. After a short confrontation, they take over a table from a group of girls. Their cheeky, antagonistic behaviour extends to their pursuit of girls. The busty girl they catcalled earlier enters the parlour, leading a pair of identical twins. Reaction shots go back and forth between the girl's proud strides across the floor to their table and the boys' gazes. The three girls are given derogatory nicknames: Tnuva (Israel's largest milk distributor) and the Horny Twins. Momo intensifies the insult by discussing Tnuva's hypothetical

---

[3] The first film of the series, LEMON POPSICLE, contains minor signifiers of this alternative. Young people in youth movement uniforms are part of the crowd, and the protagonist's school sends its students to volunteer in a struggling settlement on the frontier. In GOING STEADY, this frame of reference is reduced even further. Tammy, Benzi's beloved, appears once in a blue shirt that recalls the youth movement uniform. When another character, Shelli, offers Benzi the chance to travel with her to Eilat, she makes no reference to the fact that, in the 1950s, it represented Israel's southern frontier. Her promise of sun, sand and sea instead presents Eilat as the tourist location it had become by the 1970s.

sexual availability in degrading terms. Yudale is sent out, and his exchange with the girls is just as antagonistic as the group's previous interactions; nevertheless, shortly after, the boys have the girls in their car. A verbal conflict ensues almost immediately, as the boys reveal they are headed to the beach, and the girls protest.

On the dark beach, the two trios remain visually and audibly separate. The boys noisily shed their clothes and run into the sea. They call the girls to join them, and the girls shout back for them to return. This is not an act of seduction on the boys' part, but of impertinence, and the tables finally turn when the girls collect the boys' clothes and escape on the back of their boyfriends' motorcycles. The boys' failure and degradation are complete when their car gets stuck in the sand, and they sneak back home with little to cover their bodies. When Benzi gets home, he actively challenges his parents by exhibiting his naked body in their living room to their amused, bewildered guests.

When the boys undress on the beach, displaying their naked bodies to the camera, the exposure is gradual. Momo's beautiful tanned body is the first to appear, followed by Benzi's shorter, paler body, and finally Yudale's untanned, pudgy figure. This order is repeated as they enter the water. In their cooperative sexual exploits, too, Momo's body serves as prelude and Yudale's as finale, as in a seven-minute sex scene which occurs halfway through the film.[4] Momo informs the others that he has arranged a tryst with Tnuva. Unbeknown to her, he allows them to sneak in and have sex with her as well. When they get to Tnuva's room, Momo diverts her attention and sneaks Benzi into her closet and Yudale underneath her bed. The scene is clearly a comic one, backed by the diegetic music on Tnuva's record player, The Coasters' "Yakety Yak". Nevertheless, the eroticism does not diminish, maintained by the display of Momo's body in a tight T-shirt which he takes off. Tnuva kisses him passionately. She lies on the bed and turns off the light. In the darkness, Momo moves into the missionary position, providing yet another glimpse of his figure. The camera moves down, dividing the frame almost equally between the couple and Yudale lying in his underwear and shirt beneath the bed.

The sex scene is constructed to emphasise Yudale's position under the bed, and Benzi's in the closet, as well as their interaction with the act itself. There are no more shots that objectify Momo's body. It disappears into the blind spot where the core of the sexual activity takes place. The beginning of coitus is marked by another change of tune, this time to Chubby Checkers'

---

4 All the scenes described are from the Hebrew version of the film. The German version differs from the Hebrew's visual editing, sound editing, and dialogue.

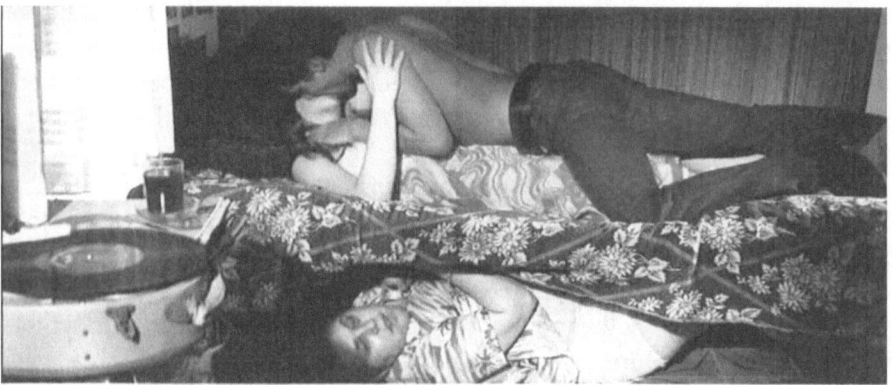

Figure 15: A cooperative sexual adventure: Momo and Tnuva on the bed and Yudale underneath in GOING STEADY.

"Let's Twist Again", whose first line creates a sense of collective action: "C'mon everybody … ". Benzi, with an aroused expression, takes off his jacket. Yudale offers a more grotesque variation, struggling underneath the bed to take off his shirt, and looking attentive as Tnuva begins to moan. She is shown as she closes her eyes and moans in ecstasy. The focus quickly returns to Yudale, trying to shield himself from the wire underside of the bed, which repeatedly presses down on him, turning the act of penetration above into a source of physical excruciation below. Benzi grips a rack in the closet, which collapses. The camera captures Tnuva's reaction to the noise and Momo's dismissal of it. As Benzi slowly straightens up, Tnuva's moans become louder. The camera returns to Yudale under the bed. The increased movements stir up the dust around him. He sneezes. The camera follows Momo's hand as it descends, grabs a shoe, and hits Yudale. This begins a chain reaction, which transpires in accelerated reaction shots. Yudale calls out in pain, Momo calls out to disguise the source of the noise, and Tnuva joins in with pleasure. The movement intensifies, causing Yudale to call out again, and Momo and Tnuva to join him. The cycle is repeated three times, during which Benzi tears down a second rack in the closet, without drawing any more attention to himself. The intensifying sound and movement, alongside the accelerated pace of editing, correlates the comic and sexual peaks.

Yudale finally crawls to the foot of the bed. His face is close to the couple's moving feet, offering a ludicrous perspective on the sexual act. He sits next to the copulating couple, parallel to Momo's pelvis, as he takes off his undershirt – something that directs the viewer to compare his corpulence with Momo's slender figure. Yudale taps on Momo's back, and the two begin to cough to cover up the fact that they are trading places. As Momo signals with his head, Yudale takes off his underwear, completing the exposure of his body to the viewer. Before Yudale takes Momo's place on top of Tnuva, a shot of Benzi is inserted to reaffirm his position as a Peeping Tom. Yudale is shot from the same angle in which Momo was seen when the sex act began. The visible difference is accentuated further by Tnuva's shout of surprise, and Yudale's absurd proclamation that he is Momo. The scene does not end with Tnuva's angry reaction. The boys retreat to the bathroom, where Momo, undaunted, continues to plan with his friends. The trio's impertinence is unrelenting. The scene finally ends when Tnuva's biker friend arrives with two companions. They capture Yudale, who is hanging in mid-air from the bathroom window, having attempted to escape. His rivals expose his buttocks to the viewer, beating him with anything they can lay their hands on.

The sexual act, which begins with an erotic display of Momo's body, ends with the palpable, comic revelation of Yudale's corpulence. In the LEMON POPSICLE series, eroticism is never merely a successful process. It is continually evoked and restrained, bound in a repeated cycle of eroticisation and debasement. Again and again, beautiful young bodies are displayed to the viewer, quickly replaced with grotesque spectacles and unattractive physiques. Sexual fantasies materialise and are played out, but only to soon break down, replaced by a comic celebration of failure and discord. Unlike its comic predecessors, however, the attractive bodies and erotic scenarios continue to appear after their debasement, starting the cycle over again. Eroticism is not defeated but revived.

The attack on Yudale's body is also typical of the LEMON POPSICLE series, providing a conclusion to each collective sexual escapade, and to many of the nonsexual ones. Sadism is directed at the imperfect, unattractive body. Eroticism and sadism operate within a unified framework. But they are not joined together in simple relation of erotic "crime" and sadistic "punishment", but in a more complex sensual process. Eroticism occurs through the display of an attractive male torso (entirely unassociated with victimhood). This is both challenged and enhanced by the ensuing comic spectacle. On the one hand, the comedy that dominates the depiction of sexual activity destroys any sensuality. On the other, the same comedy evokes sexual fantasies associated with acts of intrusion by and upon individuals: voyeurism, changing partners, and coercion. The portrayal of these sustains erotic tension. This mechanism is designed to collapse, with each scene ending in failure and humiliation. Each climaxes with a final display of violence against Yudale's body.

One explanation is that Yudale's body is repeatedly punished for falling short of perfection. Gertz claims that Yudale and the other side characters are placed at the bottom of the social hierarchy, as they lack physical and mental compatibility with Zionist standards (Gertz, 1993, p. 246). Lubin goes a step further in her discussion of Yudale's cinematic predecessor, Gutte, the protagonist of Peeping Toms, whose body is designed to repulse rather than attract the viewer, and who is also subjected to physical violence (Lubin, 2001, pp. 104–105). According to Lubin, the unattractiveness of Gutte's body, and the visual evocation of its tactility and scent, not only mark their divergence from the Zionist ideal, but serve as a form of resistance (Lubin, 2001, pp. 114–118). In that respect, the dominance of Yudale's body during the sex scene and its violent finale is a constant sensual reminder of how flawed reality is in comparison with the ideal.

But the scenes themselves disclose a different logic. They are heavy with impertinence and mutual disturbance, with individuals imposing themselves and being imposed upon. This is the main motif and focal point of the film's sexual energy. From that perspective, the attack on Yudale's body after the depletion of eroticism is a continuation of the sensation, a concentrated peak in which the clash between individual and environment materialises in aggression towards an "expanded", corpulent body. It is also crucial that the level of sadism in this attack remains limited. Yudale is struck, but never penetrated or injured. The limits of his his body are attacked, but not transgressed.

In short, the sexual arousal stimulated by the cooperative sex scene, through the combination of eroticised bodies and intrusive sexual fantasies, feeds into a more general irritation the film generates, involving a constant collision between individual and environment. The exposure and agitation of the unattractive body brings this sexual stimulation to a crushing end, serving as the ultimate metonym for the central motif: the prankster having a taste of his own medicine.

"I'm Singin' in the Rain": The Brazen Act of Self-Assertion and the Fragility of Togetherness

Impertinence does not only apply to the trio but also to the main character, Benzi, specifically. More than in any other film in the series, Benzi's brazenness is particularly emphasised in Going Steady. This is manifested in his relations with his parents. Benzi poses a constant challenge, especially to his mother, Sonja. Early in the film he appears naked in front of her guests, and later disturbs their card game with loud, high-pitched cries from the bathroom as he attempts to soothe his "blue balls" by placing a block of ice on his genitals.

Benzi's impertinence offers him a means of self-assertion, something demonstrated most clearly in a hybrid of two iconic scenes from American film: the title dance scene in Singin' in the Rain (1952, D: Gene Kelly & Stanley Donen) and the domestic scenes in REBEL WITHOUT A CAUSE (1955, D: Nicholas Ray). Like Don Lockwood in SINGIN' IN THE RAIN, Benzi bursts into song and dance after a date with Tammy, mimicking Don's performance. Like Jim Stark in REBEL WITHOUT A CAUSE, he wears blue jeans, a white T-shirt, and a red jacket, and goes into his parents' kitchen, opens the refrigerator, and drinks straight from a glass bottle of milk. In the original scene, Jim is then drawn to a noise to the corridor, where, distressed, he confronts his emasculated father. In GOING STEADY, Benzi, singing loudly, instead draws his pyjama-clad parents to him. His mother reproaches him, and they follow him as he sings and dances through the apartment. Their reaction emphasises and mocks their dogmatism, a trope in Jewish comic literature (Wisse, 1971, pp. 33–35, 44–46). After a short interaction, Benzi closes the scene by dancing with his parents around the room; the sensation resembles that created by Don Lockwood as he twirls with his umbrella across the screen. Benzi's behaviour, like Jim's, is construed as a rebellion against his parents. His defiance recalls Don's defiance of bad weather: light-hearted and fuelled by infatuation. The harmony of SINGIN' IN THE RAIN and the disharmony of REBEL WITHOUT A CAUSE are fused into a mischievous riling of the environment.

In the LEMON POPSICLE series, intrusiveness is not one-sided. In most of the domestic scenes, Sonja denies her son privacy, and, in return, he offends her with his (primarily sexual) vulgarity. When Benzi brings Tammy home for the first time, his mother accidentally barges in on them in the living room. Benzi intercepts his mother's conversation with Tammy and pulls her into his room, where they kiss to the screeching sound of a neighbour practising the violin on a balcony. The couple separates as Sonja enters the room, sweeping the floor with a broom. After Sonja's questions and remarks become increasingly penetrating, Benzi goes out and returns with a tray of raw eggs, which he throws through the window at the boy on the balcony. When the boy's mother comes out, Benzi ducks away and embraces Tammy, while Sonja carries on the conflict with the neighbour.

All through the film, intrusiveness is a persistent component in almost every interaction. Benzi and Tammy's relationship is a harmonious safe haven, a counterpoint to the general dissonance. It develops in a series of long scenes in which they interact warmly, to the gentle sound of pop tunes. In these scenes, Benzi is the active agent, gazing at Tammy and reaching out to caress and kiss her. But even this sanctuary is affected by conflict over personal boundaries. Benzi's pursuit of Tammy is precisely that – a pursuit. She remains mostly silent as he follows her through the streets to her home, and as he invents an excuse for her to leave class. He finally wins her over when he sits in front of her in a library, disturbing the peace by biting noisily into an assortment of crisp vegetables which inexplicably appear in his hands. Reaction shots include not only her silent laughter at his defiant expression, but also the irritated face of the man seated next to him. At the end of the film, Benzi's intrusiveness reaches its climax in his effort to win Tammy over again. He impatiently knocks at her door at five in the morning, confronts her father, screams at the top of his lungs in the street, and breaks a car window and presses the horn, waking the neighbours. He threatens to jump from a building, and appears to do so. When Tammy rushes down to the street and finds Benzi alive and smiling, she slaps him, and then gives in to his embrace.

Even before this crescendo, in every scene that depicts the couple together, Benzi attempts to reach the next base. His hands cover more and more of Tammy's body, and his caresses become increasingly passionate. The couple is repeatedly interrupted, and when Tammy withdraws, it sparks a conflict. The two break up. Disharmony emerges not only from the outside but also from the adolescent relationship itself.

Harmony is established for a short time in the scene in which Benzi and Tammy finally overcome the last physical boundary and have sex. They pretend to be newlyweds looking for an apartment from a real-estate agency, and are given keys for a number of potential homes, something that offers them, temporarily, an isolated space of their own. Unlike other pranks in the film, this deception is acted out solemnly – a tone that is upheld during the sex scene that follows. The scene is exceptionally slow, melancholy, and ceremonial. A pop ballad dominates the sound track. Against the barren, whitewashed walls of the empty apartment, Benzi and Tammy appear naked together for the first and only time. In the earlier scene on the beach, Benzi's slim naked figure served as an intermediary body type between Momo's beauty and Yudale's chubbiness. In this scene, coupled with Tammy's slender figure, it now signifies youthful fragility.

Benzi begins the scene in long shot, seated naked on the floor, beneath a shuttered window, in the right of the frame, which is dominated by the pattern of the tiles on the floor. Tammy is then seen from Benzi's perspective. Sunlight breaks through from behind her. Her shadow gradually covers him as he looks up. Both their expressions are earnest. As she slowly advances, her naked body is revealed. Benzi stands up, and the camera, moving upwards with him, travels over her back from her buttocks.[5] The ceremonial exposure of Tammy's

---

[5] Before this caption, there is a segment of a few seconds containing more nude images of Tammy that were cut from the film. GOING STEADY set a legal precedent when the Israeli Supreme Court granted actress Yvonne Michaels a restraining order, requiring the producers to

nudity emphasises the significance of the moment in which she relinquishes her virginity, and cements Benzi's position as the beholder. He slowly touches her, holds her head, and kisses her eyes and nose as tears appear in her eyes. A tear rolls down as he embraces her. The scene ends with a long shot, similar but not identical to the one that opened the sequence. Standing on the tiled floor, surrounded by the barren walls, the naked bodies of the embracing couple are now situated in the centre of the frame.

In their embrace, they dominate the cold environment of the empty apartment. The whole scene is dedicated, not to the act of penetration, but to the slow, tender process of the two adolescents drawing closer. On an affective level, it represents the opposite of Benzi's impertinent performance throughout the film.

Figure 16: Fragility and harmony: Benny and Tammy's ceremonial sex scene in GOING STEADY.

"Let's Twist Again": The Teenage Clique as a Receptive Network

Togetherness never replaces the film's antagonism, however, and, accordingly, the tenuous harmony achieved in Benzi and Tammy's sex scene is nullified in the very next scene by a conflict that involves the couple, the rest of the male trio, and their female partners. The trio's social circle is depicted as a receptive network: conflicts spread across it, and, when a couple separates, alternative partners are immediately found within it. All this is enacted in the public domain, always in the company of many others.

---

remove nude shots from the film that were in breach of their preliminary agreements with her (Feuer, 1995, p. 44).

On Benzi and Tammy's first date, they dance among their peers for the first time. The looks they exchange generate a sense of romantic fascination. But the scene's composition also underlines the presence of Momo, Yudale, and their girlfriends. During the dance, Momo looks lustfully at Tammy, and Yudale's girlfriend, Bracha, expresses her jealousy. Later, at a pyjama party, she attempts to sleep with Benzi.

At the party, Benzi and Tammy leave the crowd and go to a separate bedroom. She resists as he unbuttons her clothes, and the two begin to argue. Tammy leaves. Yudale pleads with Benzi to walk his girl home, to no avail. After he leaves, Bracha enters the room and finds him drunk and asleep, caressing a bottle of alcohol. She moves slowly, a melancholy pop song playing in the background. She undoes her pony tail and removes her glasses, increasing her resemblance to Tammy. The camera travels up and down Bracha's torso as she unbuttons her blouse and takes off her bra, keeping her pants on. Benzi is unresponsive as she strokes him and pulls away his bottle. Nonetheless, when Momo walks through the door, he sees Benzi lying on his back, and Bracha sprawled naked over him. He smirks and withdraws. When Benzi comes to, he violently rejects Bracha and leaves the room. In a sense, Bracha picks up where Tammy left off, and, at the same time, switches their roles. Benzi's aggressive reaction to her advances echoes his aggression at Tammy's withdrawal. Benzi meets Yudale just after he leaves the room. Yudale did the "right thing" that Benzi failed to do by accompanying Tammy home, whereas Bracha attempted to do the "wrong thing" that Tammy refused to do – the four are bound symmetrically in a predicament that later sets off a crisis.

When Yudale and Benzi confront Momo about an ugly public altercation with his girlfriend, Shelly, Momo implies that Benzi had sex with Bracha. In a series of close-ups, we see the crisis travel through the network. Benzi turns his head to Yudale, who turns and looks at Bracha, who lowers her eyes. Tammy and Benzi exchange looks; she leaves, and Benzi returns his gaze to Momo, who smirks. Benzi punches him. Momo and Shelly's breakup, then, affects the whole group.

Among the crowds at the school dance, the network formed by the friends is reminiscent of the first party they appeared in, although the roles have changed. When Momo and Tammy enter the hall and join the dancing couples, Benzi accepts Shelly's offer to dance. A series of reaction shots capture an intense exchange of gazes between the couples. Yudale, dancing with Bracha, looks on just as fervidly. Soon after, Tammy walks away with Momo, followed by Benzi and Yudale. Yudale sees Tammy reject Momo's advances and confess her love for Benzi. Nevertheless, using coarse slang, he tells Benzi that Tammy and Momo are having sex, which motivates Benzi to accept Shelly's advances.

In short, the interaction of the two "organisms" – the group and the couple – is shown to be increasingly troubled, and potentially destructive for both.

Moreover, the film, the driving forces of which are intrusiveness and the violation of boundaries, also constructs a code of conduct that penalises these. Momo breaks the code with his "bad", egotistical behaviour, and Yudale upholds it with his "good" altruism. Momo makes advances to his friend Benzi's date, is openly unfaithful to his girlfriend, and humiliates her publicly; by contrast, Yudale repeatedly mediates between Benzi and Tammy. Momo's disloyal actions escalate conflicts within the network, while Yudale's faithfulness bring de-escalation. Yudale's vengeful lie in the last party scene dramatises a heavy breach of the code. This is immediately reversed in the next scene, when he confesses to the lie and mediates between Benzi and Tammy for the last time. A communal code of conduct is integrated into the film, as is its corrosion. As a result, the film generates an emotional plea for the undermined code. GOING STEADY marks and celebrates the weakening of prevailing norms, but it does not advocate anarchy; instead, it expresses a measure of yearning for the very sense of community it undermines.

The film uses sex scenes to enact both polarities, intrusiveness and sovereign isolation. It also uses its protagonists' youthful bodies to set new parameters for an eroticism which is unassociated with victimhood. Like its comic predecessors, GOING STEADY portrays an eroticism that is destined to be debased. Unlike them, however, it revives it again and again, continuing to stir the troubled mixture.

16.2 DIZENGOFF 99

"Tell Me You Love Me ... Just for Fun": The Crystallisation of the Group and the Phantom of the Romantic Couple

Like GOING STEADY, DIZENGOFF 99 also includes energetic group scenes of young people expressing their *joie de vivre*. Both films combine a carefully detailed *mise en scène*, stylistically appealing camera work, and a catchy pop soundtrack. They both contrast exclusive romantic bonds with group dynamics, friendship and sex. But while GOING STEADY ends with romantic love triumphant, in DIZENGOFF 99 it is defeated and replaced by the group spirit – a celebration of the very sense of community GOING STEADY yearns for. Both embrace and reject community.

DIZENGOFF 99 – the title is an address in the centre of Tel Aviv – follows a trio of young adult protagonists, Naty (Nathan), Ossi (Osnat), and Mushon (Moshe), as they move into a shared apartment in Tel Aviv and launch an advertising production company together. Talmon remarks on the film's strong gesture of integration, performed through displays of togetherness and the representation of a group effort leading to commercial success – all of which follows the pattern of the backstage musical (Talmon, 2000, p. 172). Teamwork is also directed at "personal" projects: on two occasions, Mushon obtains his romantic interests with help from his roommates.

For Gertz, the communal group is depicted as a liberating alternative to familial and romantic affinities (Gertz, 1993, p. 244). Indeed, the group in DIZENGOFF 99 does not clash with the couple, as in GOING STEADY. Rather, it absorbs it. The group is constituted through the frustration of the romance between Naty and Ossi. The two meet at the beginning of the film, when Naty comes to Ossi's office for a job interview. Close-ups of Ossi's intensifying gaze convey her interest in the newcomer, only interrupted by a slapstick collision with her colleague, Mushon. As befits the romantic genre, they go on a date to a restaurant. Their interaction is flirtatious, establishing a pattern of dialogue that will henceforth dominate the film: light-hearted, humorous, and full of puns. But the date does not remain exclusive: Mushon joins them with his girlfriend, and, from that moment on, Ossi and Naty are engaged in playful interactions with an increasing number of people. The viewer witnesses the crystallisation of the group, not the formation of the couple. At the end of the evening, the two are alone again. Naty leads Ossi through his parents' house and toward his room. Before they reach it, Naty's mother rebukes him in the hallway. In his room, Naty unbuttons Ossi's blouse, but before they can continue, his father knocks on the door. A fight begins, and the couple leave the house. The film establishes an expectation of sex which remains unfulfilled.

Shortly afterwards, a sex scene does indeed take place – but not between Naty and Ossi. In the early hours of the morning, Naty and Ossi knock on the door of an acquaintance of his, Miri. After embracing warmly, Naty and Miri's conversation quickly becomes antagonistic. When Ossi asks for a place to sleep, Miri offers her absent roommate's room. Realising she will be sleeping alone, Ossi appears disappointed. After making Ossi's bed, Miri returns to Naty, continuing the hostile dialogue which makes clear that they were in a relationship until recently. The antagonism is defused with a joke. While the dialogue remains charged with Miri's jealousy, they stand increasingly close to each other, camera drawing nearer to them. They embrace; Naty draws her robe down, and she moves her back sensually. He turns on the stereo, and they kiss passionately. The image then blends gradually into a horizontal shot of them in bed, capturing her ecstatic expression. He kisses her neck and strokes her breasts. Their movements are smooth. She begins a conversation that makes the discrepancy between them even clearer: he likes her, but does not love her. Nevertheless, the mood of the dialogue is light, and the last long shot shows them rolling back and forth in a tight embrace, to the sound of the music. The sex scene offers the viewer a melange of harmonious audio-visual sensuality and a bittersweet verbal subtext of constant discord. The scene does not end with the couple, however, but with Ossi, lying alone, looking increasingly dejected, as the others have sex next door. The sequence does not conclude with the sexual encounter that in fact took place, but with disappointment over the one that was thwarted.

In the sequences that follow, Ossi and Naty look for an apartment to rent, move in with Mushon, start a business, and shoot their first two commercials. The prospect of Ossi and Naty having sex remains in view, but it is repeatedly frustrated and pushed further and further to the margins. Soon after the trio moves into the apartment, Ossi retires to her room, flirtatiously taking her leave of Naty, who stays behind in the kitchen. Hearing her shriek, he runs to her room. Mushon has left a frozen spoon in her bed as a prank. Natty sits beside Ossi on the bed, the blanket slips from her naked upper body, and, comforting her, Naty embraces her. Her expression is open and inviting as they look at each other. Naty tells Ossi to go to sleep, and she lies back. He sighs and holds her bare breasts with both hands. She looks tenderly at him as he covers her with the blanket. He leans over her and turns off the light. She caresses him, but he only responds with a peck on the mouth, and the camera captures her disappointed expression as he leaves. The scene ends in slapstick: trying to leave, he walks into a wall, and she bursts out laughing. The scene builds a powerful anticipation of sex, one that is frustrated.

A more low-key interruption takes place when Naty and Mushon, sweaty, return home from a workout. Mushon enters the bathroom while Ossi is showering. Ossi pulls back the curtain to listen to Mushon's complaints. Naty enters the frame, urging Mushon to return to the workout. Despite Ossi's nudity, the situation is casual, devoid of sexual undertones until Mushon leaves the bathroom. Naty and Ossi then greet each other with a kiss on the mouth, embracing. They separate again after Mushon repeatedly calls Naty to the phone.

Figure 17: Casual nudity among roommates: Naty, Mushon and Ossi in Dizengoff 99.

At the beginning of the film, sexual relations between Naty and Ossi are interrupted by his parents' presence. Later, on their own turf, in their shared apartment, it is suspended by other factors. Naty's relations with his parents are depicted as mutually intrusive, providing the rationale for moving out and establishing a "room of one's own" in the shared apartment. But, as the bathroom scene demonstrates, this new domain is anything but private. The same rule applies to all the scenes in the apartment. Doors do not stay closed, and everyone is in each other's company almost all the time. If intrusion does not take place, it is because boundaries cease to exist.

On two occasions, Naty and Ossi are shown in an intimacy that possibly ends in sex. In one scene, Naty has Miri, a musician, compose and perform the jingle for the company's first commercial. The two flirt in the sound booth, and Ossi leaves, jealous. Naty follows her into a secluded studio and eventually calms her with light-hearted jokes. His joking quickly becomes sexual, as he offers to "rape" her and takes off her shirt. The scene ends at this point. In another, after their first commercial film is rejected by the advertising agency, the three disheartened roommates sit in Mushon's red-lit room, at a conspicuous distance from each other on the bed. Mushon leaves the room and Naty signals Ossi to come closer. She cuddles up to him. They speak of the dire state of affairs, and then kiss. The background music continues as the scenery changes, and Ossi appears with her colleagues in the office. In the three earlier scenes, much dramatic weight is laid on the prospect of sex and its frustration, whereas it becomes immaterial in these last two. Naty and Ossi might or might not have sex. The focus is elsewhere.

Although Naty and Ossi do not enter a relationship, the film continually sketches the contours of the couple that fails to form. They repeatedly display physical affection, caressing each other, kissing, and embracing. In the tradition of Hollywood romantic comedies, Naty appears at Ossi's office after he resigns from it, and asks her boss to let her go with him to the marriage registrar. He whisks her away on her swivel chair; Ossi's expression as she moves smoothly across the screen is bemused. Needless to say, no wedding follows, but the atmosphere is nevertheless energised through this suggestive romantic gesture.

More than affection or flirtation, it is Ossi's jealousy that brings forth the phantom bond. As well as the initial rivalry with Miri, Ossi is typically present when Naty flirts with other women. Almost every time, she frowns at the flirting, and even inflicts pain on two of her rivals. When Naty disappears for three days, a five-minute segment shows Ossi's lamentation, grief, and worry, with Mushon and Miri reduced to minor characters. After he reappears, with the intention of leaving again, Ossi asks him to tell her he loves her, "just for fun".

The film generates grief for the relationship it constantly frustrates. Although a romantic relationship never materialises in Dizengoff 99, its phantom dominates the entire film.

"Did You Get Many Responses to Your Ad in the Paper?": The Swinging Scene

Although Naty and Ossi do not become a couple, they appear in two sex scenes together – both non-exclusive. Halfway through the film, they undertake a partner swap with an older couple; three-quarters of the way into the film, they engage in a spontaneous threesome with Miri. Their erotic energy is directed towards communal intimacy, outside traditional concepts of relationships.

The partner swap is initiated while Ossi and Naty are at a party with friends. They appear bored, and Naty asks Ossi if she has "that letter from that couple". At the beginning of the film, Ossi jokingly reads a couple's personal ad, offering partner swapping and threesomes, to her colleagues. The joke continues later, when she reads her roommates the couple's reply to her letter. This correspondence now become the gateway to a new thrill. Before the scene changes, the film turns to Mushon, who is seated beside a couple on the sofa. The man teasingly asks him if all three roommates sleep in the same bed. Mushon answers, with a blank expression, that Ossi was an uncomfortable bedfellow, and that he now only sleeps with Naty. The friend promptly sends his girlfriend to the other room on an errand, draws closer to Mushon, and smiles at him. Mushon's joke briefly draws homosexuality out of the closet. For a moment, it feels like anything goes.

The transfer to the swingers' apartment is abrupt. No music is playing in the background. Naty and Ossi are in a lavish living room filled with works of art, exchanging courtesies with an elegant middle-aged couple, Dan and Gabi. The couples are seated at a conspicuous distance from each other, at either end of a wide shot. The older couple is handsome and well-dressed, with an erotic aura. Nevertheless, their appeal is somewhat diminished, as Gabi, who described herself in the letter as twenty-eight and blond, with long legs and big breasts, is short, brunette, flat-chested, and substantially older.

As the conversation flows, with Naty asking questions that resemble an interview more than small talk, the husband seats himself next to Ossi, and the wife next to Naty. The two put their arms around Ossi and Naty's shoulders. The young people's naturalistic speech seems clumsy in comparison to the older couple's eloquence, and their awkwardness is out of sync with the others' confident manner. Catching on instantly to Naty and Ossi's inexperience, the couple suggests something lighter, splitting off into two separate rooms. They walk off, giving Naty and Ossi space to decide. The disparity is emphasised in a wide shot, showing Naty and Ossi huddled on the couch in plain, bright clothes, and the other couple standing on a gallery in evening clothes and casual, well-calculated poses. The young couple agrees between themselves to cough if they want to escape.

After Ossi goes off with Dan, the film alternates between the two spaces, where parallel events unfold. Both Naty and Ossi ask questions about the couple's life, and remain passively uncooperative in the face of Gabi and Dan's advances. As a result, Gabi and Dan become the focus of the scene, delivering protracted monologues as they attempt to physically stimulate their partners. Gabi takes centre frame, her movements confident, as though on a stage. After Naty pulls his arms away from her, she stands back, slowly taking off her glossy outfit. Dan sits on the bed and takes off his vest and tie. Ossi remains standing, claiming that her back is stiff, and he offers to loosen it for her. She lies on the bed, and he sits across her, in the centre of the frame, rubbing her back. His tight shirt accentuates his muscular torso. He speaks to Ossi softly. Gabi and Dan's performances have the potential to generate eroticism, but this is obstructed, not only by their unresponsive partners, but also by the cliché of middle class dissatisfaction their monologues disclose, revealing that their sexual adventures are a response to a void in their lives.

The further Gabi and Dan progress, the more invasive their actions seem, which increases the repellent effect. Ossi looks up in discomfort as Dan's hands venture to her upper back. Gabi, sitting topless next to Naty, strokes his head with a heavy hand, unbuttons his shirt, and sits on his lap. Dan then appears with his shirt unbuttoned, laying over Ossi, heavy-handedly unbuttoning her blouse and stroking her chest. Her hands fasten over her breasts to block him. His breathing becomes heavy and his movements seem more forceful, as he pulls up her skirt and presses his body to hers. The film returns to Gabi, who reaches for Naty's crotch and begins to undo his belt. Naty utters a single cough. Ossi, almost smothered underneath Dan, who is moving forcefully back and forth, begins to cough loudly. Both Ossi and Naty push their partners back. On the pretext of a sudden asthma attack, they leave the couple behind. The sexual escapade is made unappealing, and the disparity between the couples marks the divide between Ossi and Naty and the sexual lifestyle Dan and Gabi represent.

The epilogue of this scene takes place back at the party, where their friends are watching an eight-millimetre porn film. A reaction shot to the naked couple projected on the wall shows a small crowd watching it, amused and fascinated, lit by the reflection from projector. Some men have their arms around their female partners. They look attentive, and, at the same time, call out sarcastic remarks:

> "What makeup!"
> "Now he explains to her the complete works of [the national poet] Bialik."
> "Very authentic."
> "Her father works at Reading [power station]."

The first and third jokes are directed at the film's low quality, and the second and fourth draw their parodic effect from the juxtaposition of the sexual spectacle with well-known national assets. This repertoire is not far off the one used by Yerach in MOTIVE TO MURDER. Yerach alludes to the *Song of Songs*; DIZENGOFF 99, to Hayim Nahman Bialik. Yerach mentions the national water carrier; DIZENGOFF 99, the power station in Tel Aviv. Despite the fact that sex had become more prominent in Israel in the thirteen years between the two films, the similar use of comic deprecation attests to a persistent sense of incongruity between communal identity and sexual expression.

The scene also reflects a paradox inherent in the consumption of pornography in Israel at the time. Before VCRs made pornographic films available for discreet use in the mid-1980s, it was practically inaccessible to the greater part of "respectable" society (Almog, 2004, pp. 1159–1160). As in this scene, consumption of pornography took place in the public sphere. The small audience is transfixed, and, at the same time, compelled by the lack of intimacy to make deprecating remarks that strengthen the group, hold sexual arousal in check, and keep eroticism out of reach.

When Ossi and Naty walk in, Ossi looks toward the screen. At the sight of a naked couple taking up an unusual position, Ossi smiles widely, hinting sarcastically at the parallel between the racy film and the scene they just returned from. The attempt to experience alternative sexual practices is finally reduced to a joke, a brush with pornography. With the swinging couple and the private porn screening, the film addresses contemporaneous progressive practices with a sense of alienation. Both appear unliberating – unlike Naty and Ossi's second nonexclusive sexual experience, which is a success.

"The Most Natural Thing in the World": The Threesome

According to Talmon, the spontaneous sex between Ossi, Miri, and Naty is contrasted with the partner swap that precedes it. The latter is a warped version of the sexual revolution, whereas the former is more positive, demonstrating a spontaneous intimacy among young people liberated from social norms (Talmon,

2000, p. 176). The threesome scene is more appealing from every perspective. Whereas the encounter with the older couple is thrill-seeking, the threesome is depicted as the apex of harmony. In the course of the film, Naty repeatedly scolds Miri, culminating in an attack that constitutes the most troubling scene in the film. The scenes in which Ossi and Miri treat each other kindly are fewer and more subtle, but also more central. After Naty's attack, Ossi brings Miri to the set of the second commercial, and Naty's antagonism subsides. This is shown wordlessly, through meaningful close-ups. The three then bond over an attempt to set Mushon up on a date, observing his awkward slapstick performance with his new companion. As Mushon and his date appear increasingly embarrassed, Ossi, Naty, and Miri draw physically closer. The sex scene is a rewarding finale to finishing the commercial and setting Mushon up.

The three are seated on Naty's bed. Naty and Miri are at the centre of the frame, leaning on each other. They sing a duet, with Naty playing a guitar. Ossi watches them from the side of the frame. The camera draws in and locks on to Naty and Miri, who kiss. From her own frame, Ossi smiles at them. They look at her, and Miri smiles widely. Naty leaves her frame, joins Ossi, and kisses her passionately. Ossi reaches for Miri, and she joins them. From this point on, the three are coordinated in their movements. When Naty turns and kisses Miri, both women stroke each other's hair. He disappears behind them as they kiss each other. Ossi's voiceover ensures that the viewer will perceive the scene as Talmon describes it: a spontaneous act of liberation from conventional norms. Ossi says that her partners seemed beautiful, and the experience, which should have felt strange, was pleasurable and exciting. She ends with: "Suddenly we were three, me, little Osnat from Kfar Saba, with another guy and another girl. I was shocked that I wasn't shocked. It looked like the most ... natural thing in the world."

Like the previous sex scene between Naty and Miri, the shots blend into each other gradually, adding to the sense of smoothness. The trio reappear, positioned at some distance from one another. They progressively shed their clothes as they move closer together in ecstasy, as the camera zooms in slowly. All three participate, with constant movement in more than one part of the screen. No one ever stays still. When two are engaged with each other, they keep active physical contact with the third person. Both Naty and Ossi kiss one partner and then immediately the other. They alternate, blend together, and disappear behind one another. The traditional division in the Israeli sex scene, where the man's body is put on display, while the woman faces the camera and enacts rupture, does not apply here. Although Naty takes an active part in the scene, he hardly fulfils either role. The composition centres on the women's naked bodies, and only they stretch their necks and close their eyes in ecstasy. The sensual object and subject are female. The act of penetration does not dominate the scene, nor is it even depicted: instead, all three touch, caress, kiss, and bite each other. Even in the last shot, as they are lying down, they are shown from the shoulders up. It is unclear who is being penetrated, or if penetration takes place at all. This recalls Williams' analysis of the representation of female orgasm in the 1970s (Williams, 2008, pp. 155–180): despite the presence of male agency, the centrality of penetration is deferred here, and female orgasm is thereby liberated from its subjugation to phallocentric norms.

Figure 18: Naty and Ossi escaping a partner swap and in a threesome with Miri in DIZENGOFF 99.

The scene is not just a celebration of female eroticism. It also serves as a harmonious apex by which all dramatic conflicts and differences are transcended.

The tension between Naty and Miri is gone. There is no more rivalry between Miri and Ossi. The flow of images offers nothing but harmony, cooperation, and sensuality. This utopian scene surpasses the tentative harmony presented by Benzi and Tammy's sex scene in GOING STEADY. The absence of discord appears in even sharper contrast when compared to another threesome scene, in MOMENTS, which was released in Israel in the same year. Unlike DIZENGOFF 99, MOMENTS uses the sex scene as a dramatic arena in which the conflicts among the participants are not transcended but expressed.

In MOMENTS, two women – Yola, an Israeli writer, and Ann, a French photographer – meet on the train to Jerusalem, entering into a highly flirtatious, complex relationship while exploring the city. Two-thirds of the way into the film, after Yola's boyfriend, Avi, joins her, the couple invites Ann to their hotel room at the end of a night out. The ensuing sex scene reflects the dynamics that exist between the three characters throughout the film.

As Lubin observes, although sexual tension mounts between the two women, they do not have sex with each other, but, rather, take turns having sex with the male partner. She concludes that the film restricts the constitution of female sexuality to the gratification granted by the penetrating gaze of the voyeuristic Peeping Tom (Lubin, 2005, pp. 301–302). However, the scene offers a different logic. When Ann attempts to engage with Yola, the latter reaches for Avi, and makes love to him. While doing so, Yola alternates between looking intently at Ann and ignoring her. Ann's repeated attempts to touch her are ignored. She is treated, not as a lover, but as an audience, and she in turn looks on longingly. After Yola orgasms, Avi turns to Ann, and they position themselves on Yola's lap. As they begin to have sex, the camera focuses on Yola, who tries unsuccessfully to wriggle out from underneath the two, and becomes despondent. When they finish and turn to her, she rejects them. At that moment, despite their nudity and physical proximity, their isolation from each other is palpable. Ann leaves the room with her head held low and her dress in her hand. The scene dramatises the women's insecurities, and the viewer experiences the growing isolation between the three people. It is not a pornographic realisation of male fantasies, as Lubin would have it (ibid., p. 301).

If pornography is defined as the exhibition of sexual fantasies for the purpose of arousal, this seems a better description of the harmonious threesome scene in DIZENGOFF 99. This is its novelty in Israeli cinema. There is no visual metaphor, as in HE WALKED THROUGH THE FIELDS and THE HERO'S WIFE. There is no discord, as in MOMENTS and NOT MINE TO LOVE. Guilt does not taint eroticism, as in THREE AND ONE. On its surface, the threesome scene in DIZENGOFF 99 offers nothing more and nothing less than an erotic spectacle. However, the film's relation to its erotic display is not as simple as it may seem.

"Don't You See You're Ruining Your Life?": Cinematic Self-Reflection

It may seem incongruous that DIZENGOFF 99 – which, in successive scenes, discredits nonexclusive sexual practices and deprecates the collective consumption of pornography – offers the viewer, half an hour later, a softcore pornographic scene which depicts spontaneous, youthful, nonexclusive sex. A closer analysis clarifies this inconsistency.

The only element that subverts the scene is its soundtrack. Unlike the rest of the film, where contemporary pop music dominates the soundscape, the sound and music in this scene is relatively quiet, and seems to come from outside. Unlike the sex scene that opens NOT MINE TO LOVE, this background "noise" does not emphasise the penetrability of the private sphere by the public. The meaning resides in the content, which the viewer can barely make out. We hear music, TV and radio jingles, whistles and sirens. Naty takes off Miri's clothes to a quiet tune which played a central role in Nesher's debut film, THE TROUPE. The two female bodies begin to move sensually, to a piece that sounds like a generic love song, but is, in fact, about separation. When Ossi displays her naked upper body to the camera and lifts her head in ecstasy, a baby cries, and two men sing the song that was played on the radio earlier as the week's number one hit, which corresponds ironically with the infant's whimper: "I have no time to be sad". While the second piece hints at the coming breakup, the first and third establish an ex- and intra-cinematic association with the question of commercial success. The scene tempts the viewer with its permissive sensuality, while the soundtrack evokes ironic reflection. It is no coincidence that this takes place immediately before Naty, Ossi, and Mushon successfully sell their second commercial.

Earlier in the film, the three were commissioned by an advertising agency to produce a beer commercial, at their own expense. Their first commercial revolves around a chubby young man who undergoes a series of slapstick accidents. They are happy with the film, but the agency rejects it. When Naty asks what they should have included instead, the answer is: music, disco, lots of girls, dancing, and happiness. This is precisely the content of the second commercial the trio produces, depicting young, attractive people at a party. The trio, particularly Naty, hate the commercial, but it is a success, and business takes off. Hence, the use of pop music, youth, female sexual allure, and expressions of joy and happiness is placed on par with inauthenticity, opportunism, and selling-out. As DIZENGOFF 99 itself makes extensive use of all these components – as well as slapstick – the sex scene discreetly elevates this equation to a self-reflective gesture.

As far as its audio-visual gloss is concerned, DIZENGOFF 99 is on par with GOING STEADY. The protagonists and those around them are dressed in the latest fashions. They move from one trendy location to another. The soundtrack plays a succession of catchy tunes, and several scenes show crowds dancing. Youth is a central component. All the rooms in the shared apartment are meticulously designed in a youthful style. The walls are covered with posters containing cinematic references, the film stars constantly peeking at the viewer behind the protagonists' backs. Numerous scenes are dedicated to the trio clowning around, expressing a sense of joy and happiness. These are the means by which the film seduces its viewers. It often incorporates female nudity within its parade of attractive young women, culminating in the final sex scene. Sex sells, and precisely this aspect of the film is used as a metaphor for commercial dubiousness.[6]

After the failure of the first commercial, as Naty contemplates his mistakes, he pays a visit to Miri, and, as mentioned, begins to attack her verbally and physically. He begins by asking if she can count how many men have seen her naked, claiming that her promiscuity endangers her reputation as an artist. He interrogates her about a recent date, becoming increasingly aggressive. She finally breaks down, suggesting that she might have been sexually assaulted. He slaps her, dismisses her claim of assault, and blames her for dressing inappropriately and letting men into her apartment. She sobs. Naty begins to break objects in the room, and shouts that Miri is ruining her life: "Learn to use your head instead of objectifying your body. Don't you see you're being used?" He curses her, tells her to give herself a chance, and leaves the apartment. This sudden outburst is meant to make the viewer uncomfortable. Beyond manifesting male aggression and asymmetric gender relations, it comes at a point in the film where the protagonists are considering submitting to commercial demands. Naty is shouting at Miri – a figure that, like Naty himself, is objectified, sexualised, and so exploited by the film they appear in. At this point, the two have already appeared in a sex scene together. Less than ten minutes later, they appear in the threesome scene, which became the hallmark of the film.

The film negatively reflects on its own commerciality and use of sex, and undermines the model of success and unity it seems to endorse. As Talmon points out, the film's powerful gesture of integration is made through its representation of togetherness and collective effort in achieving a goal (Talmon, 2000, p. 172). As soon as that goal is reached, however, and the trio achieves commercial success, Naty withdraws, and the group begins to disintegrate. The last scene is of a surprise party for Naty's birthday – one last manifestation of

---

6 In reality the incorporation of nudity and sex scenes potentially curbed some of the film's commercial success. Its erotic audacity earned it a rating that limited its access to underage viewers (Nuriel and Ben Ari, 2009, p. 7)

exaltation and joy. The subtitles tell the viewer that Naty tried to stay in the apartment, but eventually left the country. Immediately after this celebration of the group, the film tells us, it dispersed.

DIZENGOFF 99 is built on a paradox in its viewing experience. It constructs expectations for a romantic couple that fail to materialise. It attracts the viewer with lavish displays of togetherness and a drive to succeed, before dismissing the former as unsustainable and the latter as meaningless. It seduces the viewer with a display of sexual liberty, but judges its own gesture to be an inauthentic commercial stunt.

16.3 Tel Aviv, Sex, 1979: Conclusion and Commentary

GOING STEADY and DIZENGOFF 99 were prominent in a new wave of films that revolved around sex and youth. Produced during an era in which the dangers to the Israeli community had receded, both films seek formulae to present an eroticism which goes beyond victimhood. In this sense, they resemble *Screwing Isn't Everything*. GOING STEADY constructs its central erotic paradigm within the realm of comedy, stimulating the viewer through the exhibition of young bodies and the enactment of intrusive sexual fantasies. DIZENGOFF 99 entices its viewer with female nudity and constant scenes of intimacy and joy, culminating in the erotic spectacle of a harmonious sex scene.

However, both films undermine their own erotic gestures. In GOING STEADY, every comic scene ends with a clash, and every moment of intimacy remains on unsteady ground. Any sensuality that does not deteriorate into comedy is endangered by conflict and discord. In DIZENGOFF 99, the viewer's constant arousal relies on the unsustainable relations which induce it. Eroticism is presented alongside criticism of the cinematic exploitation of eroticism.

This contradiction, or ambivalence, attests to a difficulty in constructing an alternative to the existing set of concepts, and to the use of victimhood as the primary locus of self-assertion and eroticism. The absence of victimhood from the equilibrium lasted for only a decade, returning in the 1990s. The other type figures – the comic figure and the adolescent – remained integral, and the lack of clear boundaries between private and public became more dominant than ever.

While the political context of JUDGEMENT DAY, THREE AND ONE, LITTLE MAN, and HIGHWAY QUEEN was never in question, GOING STEADY and DIZENGOFF 99 were criticised for their lack of ideological commitment. My analysis suggests that the latter responded to current events just as much as the films that more conspicuously reflected the aftermath of war and the protest movement. All six films contemplated human subjectivity within the new reality that unfolded in the 1970s, and all made use of traditional means to express these developments. Even through the dramatic changes Israel underwent the 1970s, the victim, the comic figure, the child, and the discordance between the private and the public sphere remained the elements through which national identity was communicated in film.

Epilogue

My aim in this book has been to describe a historiography of Israeli film which offers a renewed, broader perspective on this ever-growing body of cinema. I have done so through an in-depth study of sex scenes in Israeli cinema in the 1960s and 1970s. In examining the sex scene, I have focused on a cinematic experience in which the viewer interacts with what Cavell termed *something human* (Cavell, 1979, pp. 26–27). It is a history of subjectivity materialised in physical sensations – a history which always reflects the presence of others. As I have shown, in each and every case study, the sex scene is part of a cinematic flow, woven into the poetic structure of the film as a whole.

By exploring the films I selected outside a pathological frame of reference, I have demonstrated the various ways in which eroticism is generated, stimulating the viewer and enhancing the presence of the cinematic figure, and the ways in which unattractiveness, aversion, threat, and violation are deployed. I have shown how victimhood, comedy, and youth play an instrumental role in all these scenarios in which subjectivity is either enhanced or reduced.

My survey has taken in two decades in Israeli film history – a period of crucial change, as Israeli society renegotiated its identity. I have demonstrated the connection between current events and the cinematic patterns which consolidated in these films.

In film after film, the characters have little room to retreat into privacy, and intrude on others. In film after film, interpersonal encounters are precarious, and harmonious alliances made precious by their transience and constant endangerment. I have demonstrated that the fundamental instability between the public and the private spheres, consistently re-enacted in these films, was not the result of a change from one ideology and its associated values to another, but, rather, a consistent principle of communal Israeli self-perception.

The motif of intrusion established historical continuity, while the other three expressed the cultural change brought on by the repatterning and restructuring of the old order. The type figures of the child, the adolescent, and the comic figure remained largely consistent in the cinematic negotiation of subjectivity. Furthermore, the sense of victimhood which had served as a source of individual affirmation and cinematic eroticism in the 1960s declined during the 1970s. Progressively, the eroticism generated in connection with loss began to diminish, and other patterns of erotic appeal were explored. These alternatives did not simply replace the traditional patterns. They were subjected to and restrained by traditional values, which complicated any new form of eroticism and individual affirmation.

This historiography returned to the era in which the Israeli film industry consolidated and the Israeli sex scene emerged. My theoretical model has been crucial for delineating the specific cultural context in which such scenes were conceived. I have applied it here to films produced in Israel in the 1960s and 1970s, but its utility does not end there. I would like to conclude with the promise of what is yet to be explored, for the theoretical framework presented in this book is just as relevant to films released in the decades that followed, all the way to the present.

Bibliography

Aftergood, Steven and Hans M. Kristensen. "Nuclear Weapons – Israel", *Federation of American Scientists* (2007), http://www.fas.org/nuke/guide/israel/nuke/ (last retrieved 12 October 2020).
Almog, Oz. *The Sabra: The Creation of the New Jew*. Berkeley / Los Angeles / London: University of California Press, 2000.
Almog, Oz. "Eroticism and Promiscuity: Milestones". In id. *Farewell to 'Srulik': Changing Values Among the Israeli Elite*. Haifa / Or Yehuda: Haifa University Press / Zmora Bitan Publishing House, 2004, pp. 1043–1167. [Hebrew]
Alterman, Nathan. "I Shall Come to Your Threshold" [1938]. In id. *Shirim Shemikvar*. Tel Aviv: Hakibbutz Hameuchad, 1972, p. 56. [Hebrew]
Anderman, Nirit. "Why was the First All Israeli Film Forbidden for Screening?", *Haaretz – Gallery* (29 March 2010), https://www.haaretz.co.il/gallery/1.3314626 (last retrieved 12 October 2020). [Hebrew]
Arendt, Hannah. *The Origins of Totalitarianism*. New York: Harcourt, Brace and Company, 1951.
Arendt, Hannah. *The Human Condition* [1958]. Chicago: The University of Chicago Press, 1998.
Arendt, Hannah. "Die verborgene Tradition" [1948]. In id. *Die verborgene Tradition*. Frankfurt a. M.: Jüdischer Verlag im Suhrkamp Verlag, 2000, pp. 50–79.
Aristotle. *Poetics*, with the Tractatus Coislinianus, reconstruction of Poetics II, and the fragments of the On Poets, translation by Richard Janko. Indianapolis / Cambridge: Hackett Publishing Company, 1987.
Ashkenazi, Ofer. "The Symphony of a Great Heimat: Zionism as a Cure for Weimar Crisis in Lerski's Avodah". In Geller, Howard and Leslie Morris (eds.) *Three-Way Street: Jews, Germans, and the Transnational*. Ann Arbor: University of Michigan Press, 2016, pp. 91–124.
Ashkenazi, Ofer. "Improbable Twins: The Bifurcating Heritage of Weimar Culture in Helmar Lerski and Walter Frentz's Kulturfilms", *German Studies Review* 40.3 (2017), pp. 527–548.
Ashkenazi, Ofer. "Strategies of Exile Photography: Hans Casparius and Helmar Lerski in Palestine". In Silberman, Marc (ed.) *Back to the Future: Traditions and Innovations in German Studies*. Bern: Peter Lang, 2018, pp. 87–119.
Attorney General's Commission on Pornography. *Final Report*. Washington D.C.: U.S. Department of Justice, 1986.
Augé, Marc. "Anthropological Place" [1992]. In id. *Non-Places: Introduction to an Anthropology of Supermodernity*. London / New York: Verso, 1995, pp. 42–74.
Avisar, Ilan. "The National and the Popular in Israeli Cinema", *Shofar: An Interdisciplinary Journal of Jewish Studies* 24.1 (2005), pp. 125–143.
Bakhtin, Mikhail. *Rabelais and His World* [1965]. Cambridge MA / London: Massachusetts Institute of Technology, 1968.
Bar-Haim, Gabi. "Sex at Risk of Extinction", *Yedioth Ahronoth – 7 Leilot* (13 December 2013), pp. 10–11, 34. [Hebrew]
Bashan, Rafael. "Gideon Shemer's Monologue: I Didn't Want to Act – I Wanted to Direct", *Maariv* (12 March 1965). [Hebrew]
Bataille, Georges. *Death and Sensuality: A Study of Eroticism and the Taboo* [1957]. New York: Walker, 1962.
Ben-Amos, Dan. "Jewish Folklore Studies", *Modern Judaism*, 11.1 (1991), pp. 17–66.

Ben-Ari, Nitsa. *Suppression of the Erotic: Censorship and Self-Censorship in Hebrew Literature 1930–1980*. Tel Aviv: Tel Aviv University Press, 2006. [Hebrew]
Ben David, Benny. "How did the Zionist Meta-Narrative Turned into Cliché in Writing about Israeli Cinema", *Maarvon* 3–4 (2008), pp. 18–23. [Hebrew]
Ben-Shaul, Nitzan. "Siege", *Sratim* 4 (1989), pp. 2–9. [Hebrew]
Ben-Shaul, Nitzan. *Mythical Expressions of Siege in Israeli Films*. Lewiston / Queenston / Lampeter: The Edwin Mellen Press, 1997.
Ben-Shaul, Nitzan. "The Inconspicuous Bond between Bourekas Films and Personal Films". In Gertz, Nurith, Orly Lubin and Yehuda-Judd Ne'eman (eds.) *Fictive Looks – On Israeli Cinema*. Tel Aviv: Open University Publications, 1998, pp. 128–134. [Hebrew]
Ben-Shaul, Nitzan. "Tensions between Ethnicity and Nationality and their Spatial Representation in Israeli Film", *Israel: Journal for Research of Zionism and the State of Israel* 14 (2008), pp. 151–166. [Hebrew]
Bergson, Henri, "Laughter – The Comic Element in Situations and the Comic Element in Words" [1900]. In Sypher, Wylie (ed.) *Comedy*. Baltimore / London: The John Hopkins University Press, 1980, pp. 104–145.
Bernstein, Deborah. "Conflict and Protest in Israeli Society: The Case of the Black Panthers of Israel", *Youth and Society* 16.12 (1984), pp. 129–152.
The Bible, authorized King James version, with an introduction and notes by Robert Carroll and Stephen Prickett. Oxford / New York: Oxford University Press, 2008.
Bordwell, David. "Art-Cinema Narration". In id. *Narration in the Fiction Film*. London: Routledge, 1988, pp. 203–233.
Boyarin, Daniel. *Carnal Israel: Reading Sex in Talmudic Culture*. Berkley / Los Angeles / Oxford: University of California Press, 1993.
Bregman, Ahron. *Israel's Wars, 1947–93*. London / New York: Routledge, 2000.
Broshi, Michal. "Dosh – Native to the Country of his Dreams". In id. *Dosh – Caricaturist, 1921–2000*. Tel Aviv / Jerusalem: Eretz Israel Museum / Ben Zvi Institute, 2007, pp. 24–99. [Hebrew]
Bruno, Michael. "External Shocks and Domestic Response: Macroeconomic Performance, 1965–1982". In Ben-Porath, Yoram (ed.) *The Israeli Economy: Maturing through Crises*. Cambridge MA / London: Harvard University Press, 1986, pp. 276–301.
Bursztyn, Igal. *Face as Battlefield*. Tel Aviv: Hakibbutz Hameuhad, 1990. [Hebrew]
Butler, Judith. *The Psychic Life of Power*. Stanford, CA: Stanford University Press, 1997.
Butler, Judith. *Precarious Life*. London / New York: Verso, 2004.
Butler, Judith. *Giving an Account of Oneself*. New York: Fordham University Press, 2005.
Butler, Judith. *Parting Ways: Jewishness and the Critique of Zionism*. New York: Columbia University Press, 2012.
Butler Judith and Gayatri Chakravorty Spivak. *Who Sings the Nation-State? Language, Politics, Belonging*. London / New York / Calcutta: Seagull Books, 2007.
Canetti, Jonathan. "And in the First Place", *Zman Tel Aviv* (27 April 2007), pp. 56–57. [Hebrew]
Carroll, Noël. *Mystifying Movies: Fads & Fallacies in Contemporary Film Theory*. New York: Columbia University Press, 1988.
Cavell, Stanley. *The World Viewed*. Cambridge, MA / London: Harvard University Press, 1979.
Cohen, Ayelet. "The Beginning of Israeli Cinema as a Reflection of Contemporary Thought", *Cathedra* 61 (1991), pp. 141–155. [Hebrew]
Cohen, Nir. *Soldiers, Rebels, and Drifters: Gay Representation in Israeli Cinema*. Detroit: Wayne State University Press, 2012.

Dyer, Richard. "Don't Look Now", *Screen* 23.3-4 (1982), pp. 61-73.
Dyer, Richard. "Male Sexuality and the Media". In id. *The Matter of Images: Essays on Representation*. London / New York: Routledge, 1993, pp. 88-99.
Eisenstadt, Shmuel N. *The Transformation of Israeli Society*. London: Weidenfeld and Nicolson, 1985.
Elon, Amos. *The Israelis: Founders and Sons*. Tel Aviv: Schocken Publishing House, 1971. [Hebrew]
Epstein, Yoram. "The 'Eilat Metula Trek': The Research That Put an End to 'Water Discipline'", *HaRefua HaZvait* 8.1 (2011), pp. 65-69. [Hebrew]
Eshed, Eli. "Toothpicks in the Bonfire: Poochoo and the Palmach", *Eli Eshed's Multi Universe* (2009), https://no666.wordpress.com/2009/04/30/%D7%A7%D7%99%D7%A1%D7%9E%D7%99%D7%9D-%D7%91%D7%9E%D7%93%D7%95%D7%A8%D7%94-%D7%A4%D7%95%D7%A6%D7%95-%D7%95%D7%94%D7%A4%D7%9C%D7%9E%D7%97/ (last retrieved 12 October 2020). [Hebrew]
Fainaru, Edna. "The Stuttering Erotica of the Israeli Film", *Laisha* 1629 (1978), pp. 18-20, 96, 99. [Hebrew]
Feldmesser Yaron, Rivi and Boaz Cohen. "And Now Take Off Your Bra", *Monitin* (June 1992), pp. 54-56. [Hebrew]
Feldstein, Ariel L. *Pioneer, Toil, Camera: Cinema in Service of the Zionist Ideology 1917-1939*. Tel Aviv: Am Oved Publishers, 2009. [Hebrew]
Feuer, Dror. "To Undress or not to Undress", *Maariv - Sofshavua* (13 October 1995), pp. 40-45. [Hebrew]
Foucault, Michel. *The Archeology of Knowledge* [1969]. New York: Pantheon Books, 1972.
Foucault, Michel. "The Subject and Power". In Dreyfus, Hubert L. and Paul Rabinow (eds.) *Michel Foucault: Beyond Structuralism and Hermeneutics*. New York / London / Toronto / Sydney / Tokyo: Harvester Wheatsheaf, 1982, pp. 208-226.
Foucault, Michel. *The History of Sexuality: An Introduction* [1976], Vol. 1. New York: Vintage Books, 1990.
Freud, Sigmund. "Jokes and their Relation to the Unconscious" [1905]. In Strachey, James (ed.) *The Standard Edition of the Complete Psychological Works of Sigmund Freud*, Vol. 8. London: Hogarth Press, 1960.
Freud Sigmund. "Humour" [1927]. In Strachey, James (ed.) *The Standard Edition of the Complete Psychological Works of Sigmund Freud*, Vol. 21. London: Hogarth Press, 1960, pp. 161-166.
Friedman, Régine-Mihal. "Between Silence and Abjection: The Cinematic Medium and the War Widow". In Gertz, Nurith, Orly Lubin and Yehuda-Judd Ne'eman (eds.) *Fictive Looks: On Israeli Cinema*. Tel Aviv: Open University Publications, 1998, pp. 33-43. [Hebrew]
Galily, Yair and Michael Bar-Eli. "From Tal Brody to European Champions: Early Americanization and the 'Golden Age' of Israeli Basketball, 1965-1979", *Journal of Sport History* 32.3 (2005), pp. 401-422.
Gertz, Nurith. *Motion Fiction: Israeli Fiction in Film*. Tel Aviv: Open University Press, 1993. [Hebrew]
Gertz, Nurith. *Holocaust Survivors, Aliens and Others in Israeli Cinema and Literature*. Tel Aviv: Am Oved Publishers, 2004. [Hebrew]
Gertz, Nurith, Orly Lubin and Yehuda-Judd Ne'eman (eds.) *Fictive Looks: On Israeli Cinema*. Tel Aviv: Open University Publications, 1998, pp. 33-43. [Hebrew]

Gilman, Sander L. *Difference and Pathology: Stereotypes of Sexuality, Race, and Madness*. Ithaca / London: Cornell University Press, 1985.
Gilman, Sander L. *Jewish Self-Hatred: Anti-Semitism and the Hidden Language of the Jews*. Baltimore / London: The John Hopkins University Press, 1986.
Gilman, Sander L. *The Jew's Body*. New York / London: Routledge, 1991.
Gilman, Sander L. "'Jewish Humour' and the Terms by Which Jews and Muslims Join Western Civilization", *Leo Baeck Institute Year Book* 57 (2012), pp. 53–65.
Ginat, Gali. "Making Scenes", *Zman Tel Aviv* (27 April 2007), pp. 54–55. [Hebrew]
Ginat, Gali and Roni Arison. "My First (and Last) Time", *Zman Tel Aviv* (27 April 2007), pp. 50–53. [Hebrew]
Gledhill, Christine. "Rethinking Genre", in Gledhill, Christine and Linda Williams (eds.) *Reinventing Film Studies*. London: Arnold, 2000, pp. 221–243.
Gluzman, Michael. "'Suffer More, Be a Victim': On the Aesthetics of the Dismembered Body in Moshe Shamir's He Walked through the Fields". In id. *The Zionist Body: Nationalism, Gender and Sexuality in Modern Hebrew Literature*. Tel Aviv: Hakibbutz Hameuchad, 2007, pp. 182–208. [Hebrew]
Goldberg, Harvey E. and Chen Bram. "Sephardic / Mizrahi / Arab-Jews: Reflections on Critical Sociology and the Study of Middle Eastern Jewries within the Context of Israeli Society". In Medding, Peter Y. (ed.) *Studies in Contemporary Jewry: Sephardic Jewry and Mizrahi Jews*, Vol. 22. New York: Oxford University Press, 2007, pp. 227–256.
Golomb, Jacob. "Thus Spoke Herzl: Nietzsche's Presence in Herzl's Life and Work", *Leo Baeck Year Book* 44 (1999), pp. 97–124.
Grant, Barry K. "Introduction". In id. *Shadow of Doubt: Negotiations of Masculinity in American Genre Films*. Michigan: Wayne State University Press, 2011, pp. 1–12.
Greenspan, Ezra. *The Schlemiel Comes to America*. Metuchen, NJ / London: The Scarecrow Press, 1983.
Gross, Natan. "The Blowup and the Child", *Al HaMishmar* (1 December 1967). [Hebrew]
Gross, Natan and Yaakov Gross. *The Hebrew Film: Chapters in the History of Silent and Taking Movies in Israel*. Jerusalem: Self-Published, 1991. [Hebrew]
Gurevitz, Zeli. "The Mask of Mischief". In Broshi, Michal (ed.) *Dosh – Caricaturist, 1921–2000*. Tel Aviv / Jerusalem: Eretz Israel Museum / Ben Zvi Institute, 2007, pp. 1–23. [Hebrew]
Hadas, Eran. "Full Nude", *Yedioth Ahronoth – Yedioth Plus* (31 March 1993), pp. 11–12. [Hebrew]
Hagin, Boaz. "Margot Klausner and the pioneering of Israeli cinema", *Screen* 59.2 (2018), pp. 158–175.
Hakak, Lev. *Modern Hebrew Literature Made into Film*. Maryland: University Press of America, 2001.
Halachmi, Joseph. *No Matter What*. Jerusalem: Steven Spielberg Jewish Film Archive, 1995. [Hebrew]
Harell, Yehuda. "Thirty Years of Israeli Cinema". In id. *The Cinema from its Beginning to the Present Day*. Tel Aviv: Yavneh Publishing House, 1956, pp. 216–240. [Hebrew]
Harris, Rachel S. *Warriors, Witches, Whores: Women in Israeli Cinema*. Detroit: Wayne State University Press, 2017.
Hattis Rolef, Susan. "Mizrahim", "Egypt and Israel". In *Political Dictionary of the State of Israel*. Jerusalem: Keter Publishing House / Jerusalem Publishing House, 1998, pp. 209–210, 228–231. [Hebrew]

Hattis Rolef, Susan. "The Domestic Fallout of the Yom Kippur War". In Kumaraswamy, P. R. (ed.) *Revisiting the Yom Kippur War*. London / Portland: Frank Cass Publishers, 2000, pp. 177–194.

Heikaus, Ulrike. *Deutschsprachige Filme als Kulturinsel: Zur kulturellen Integration der deutschsprachigen Juden in Palästina von 1933–1945*. Potsdam: Universitätsverlag Potsdam, 2009.

Hernández, Josafat. "Dialectics in the epistemological anarchism of Paul Feyerabend" (2013), http://criticadenuestrotiempo.blogspot.de/2013_04_01_archive.html (last retrieved 12 October 2020).

Hetsroni, Amir and Shmulik Duvdevani. "On Tel-Avivian Hedonism in Avi Nesher's Cinema", *Resling A Multi-disciplinary Stage for Culture* 7 (2000), pp. 99–112. [Hebrew]

Hobbes, Thomas. *Leviathan* [1651]. London: J. M. Dent & Sons, 1914.

Hunt, Lynn. "Introduction: Obscenity and the Origins of Modernity, 1500–1800". In id. *The Invention of Pornography: Obscenity and the Origins of Modernity, 1500–1800*. New York: Zone Books, 1993, pp. 9–45.

Hutcheson, Francis. "Reflections upon Laughter". In id. *Reflections Upon Laughter and Remarks Upon the Fable of the Bees*. Glasgow: Printed by R. Urie for Daniel Baxter, 1750, pp. 5–38.

Inbar, Efraim. "Israel Strategic Thinking After 1973". In id. *Israel's National Security: Issues and Challenges Since the Yom Kippur War*. London / New York: Routledge, 2008, pp. 3–23.

Inda, Jonathan X. "Analytics of the Modern: An Introduction". In id. (ed.) *Anthropologies of Modernity: Foucault, Governmentality, and Life Politics*. Malden, MA / Oxford / Carlton Victoria: Blackwell Publishing, 2005, pp. 1–22.

Iskovitz, Gili. "The Establishment Finally Pays Respect to George Obadiah, the Most Disregarded Director of the Israeli Film Industry", *Haaretz – Gallery* (18 September 2015), http://www.haaretz.co.il/gallery/cinema/.premium-1.2731211 (last retrieved 12 October 2020). [Hebrew]

Israel, Yael. "A Small 'Quickie' on the Floor", *Al Hamishmar – Hotam* (2 September 1994), pp. 10–11. [Hebrew]

Jacob-Arzooni, Ora G. *The Israeli Film: Social and Cultural Influences 1912–1973*. New York / London: Garland Publishing, 1983.

Jankélévitch, Vladimir and Béatrice Berlowitz. "Die Falle des guten Gewissens". In id. *Irgendwo im Unvollendeten*. Wien: Turia & Kant, 2008, pp. 138–145.

Juni, Samuel, and Bernard Katz. "Creative Pseudo-Reality as a Defensive Factor in Jewish Wit: A Dialectical Perspective", *Journal of Psychology and Judaism* 22. 4 (1998), pp. 289–300.

Kappelhoff, Hermann. *Matrix der Gefühle: Das Kino, das Melodrama und das Theater der Empfindsamkeit*. Berlin: Vorwerk 8, 2004.

Kappelhoff, Hermann. *Realismus: Das Kino und die Politik des Ästhetischen*. Berlin: Vorwerk 8, 2008.

Kappelhoff, Hermann. "Schmutzige Bilder, glänzende Unterhaltung: die saubere Trennung des Postmodernen Kinos". In Malinar, Angelika and Martin Völker (eds.) *Un/Reinheit: Konzepte und Praktiken im Kulturvergleich*. München: Wilhelm Fink, 2009, pp. 279–292.

Karsh, Efraim. "Preface". In Kumaraswamy, P. R. (ed.) *Revisiting the Yom Kippur War*. London / Portland: Frank Cass Publishers, 2000, pp. ix–x.

Katsnelson, Anna Wexler. "Belated Zionism: The Cinematographic Exiles of Mikhail Kalik", *Jewish Social Studies: History, Culture, Society* 14.3 (2008), pp.126–149.

Katzir, Judith. "To David Greenberg, with Gratitude", *Time Out Israel* (21 November 2013), http://timeout.co.il/%D7%AA%D7%9C-%D7%90%D7%91%D7%99%D7%91-%D7%A9% D7%9C%D7%99/%D7%9C%D7%93%D7%95%D7%93-%D7%92%D7%A8%D7%99%D7% A0%D7%91%D7%A8%D7%92-%D7%91%D7%AA%D7%95%D7%93%D7%94 (last retrieved 12 October 2020). [Hebrew]

Kedem, Eldad Meshulam. *The Kibbutz and Israeli Cinema: Deterritorializing Representation and Ideology*. PhD Dissertation, Amsterdam University, 2007.

Kimchi, Rami. *The Israeli Shtetls: Bourekas Films and Yiddish Classical Literature*. Tel Aviv: Resling Publishing, 2012. [Hebrew]

Klausner, Margot. *The Dream Industry: Memories and Facts: 25 years of Israel Motion Picture Studios Herzliya Ltd, 1949–1974*. Tel Aviv: Israel Motion Picture Studios Herzliya, 1974.

Klein, Uri. "Glossy Product with no Relations to What Really Counts", *Kolnoa* 1 (1978), p. 6. [Hebrew]

Klein, Uri. "When did We Start to Talk about Cinema", *Haaretz – Gallery* (22 June 2012), http://www.haaretz.co.il/gallery/cinema/1.1737312 (last retrieved 12 October 2020). [Hebrew]

Konigsberg, Ira. "'The Only 'I' in the World': Religion, Psychoanalysis and the Dybbuk", *Cinema Journal* 36.4 (1997), pp. 22–42.

Kronish, Amy W. *World Cinema: Israel*. Trowbridge Wiltshire / Cranbury NJ: Flicks Books / Fairleigh Dickinson University Press, 1996.

Kronish, Amy W. and Costel Safirman. *Israeli Film: A Reference Guide*. Westport Connecticut / London: Praeger, 2003.

Kumaraswamy, P. R. "Revisiting the Yom Kippur War: Introduction". In Kumaraswamy, P. R. (ed.) *Revisiting the Yom Kippur War*. London / Portland: Frank Cass Publishers, 2000, pp. 1–10.

Landmann, Salcia. "'Der Dibbuk' von An-Ski. Zur Aufführungsgeschichte". In An-Ski, Salomon *Der Dibbuk: Dramatische Legende in vier Bildern*. Frankfurt a. M.: Insel Verlag, 1989, pp. 117–156.

Lehman, Peter. *Running Scared: Masculinity and the Representation of the Male Body*. Philadelphia: Temple University Press, 1993.

Lewis, Paul. "Joke and Anti-Joke: Three Jews and a Blindfold", *Journal of Popular Culture* 21.1 (1987), pp. 63–73.

Lima, Luiz C. "Are You Convinced that the Earth is Egg-Shaped?", *Crossroads: An Interdisciplinary Journal for the Study of History, Philosophy, Religion and Classics* 4.2 (2010), pp. 112–119.

Lord, Amnon. "Not on our screens", *Yedioth Ahronoth – Yedioth Tel Aviv* (9 September 1994), pp. 66–67. [Hebrew]

Loshitzky, Yosefa. *Identity Politics on the Israeli Screen*. Austin: University of Texas Press, 2001.

Lubin, Orly. "From the Margins to the Centre: The Subversion of Transit Camp Films", *Zmanim a Historical Quarterly* 39–49 (1991), pp. 141–149. [Hebrew]

Lubin, Orly. "Boundaries of Violence as Body Boundaries", *Theory and Criticism* 18 (2001), pp. 103–138. [Hebrew]

Lubin, Orly. "Woman as Other in Israeli Cinema". In Fuchs, Esther (ed.) *Israeli Women's Studies: A Reader*. New Brunswick / New Jersey / London: Rutgers University Press, 2005, pp. 301–316.

Maiberg, Ron. "Cinema Truth", *Monitin* (June 1982), pp. 98–102. [Hebrew]

Marks, Laura U. *Touch: Sensuous Theory and Multisensory Media*. Minneapolis / London: University of Minnesota Press, 2002.

Meiri, Sandra and Yael Munk. "The Return of the Repressed: Sexual Stereotypes of the Old Jew and the Case of *Gift from Heaven*". In Abrams, Nathan (ed.) *Jews & Sex*. Nottingham: Five Leaves Publications, 2008, pp. 66–76.

Mulvey, Laura. "Visual Pleasure and Narrative Cinema" [1975]. In Nichols, Bill (ed.) *Movies and Methods*. Berkeley: University of California Press, 1985, pp. 303–315.

Munk, Yael. *Borderline Cinema: Space and Identity in Israeli Cinema of the Nineties*. PhD Dissertation, Tel Aviv University, 2004. [Hebrew]

Munk, Yael. *Exiled in Their Borders: Israeli Cinema at the Turn of the Century*. Raanana: Open University Press, 2012. [Hebrew]

Munk, Yael and Nurith Gertz. *Revising Israeli Cinema: 1948–1990*. Tel Aviv: Open University Publications, 2015.

Neale, Steve. "Masculinity as Spectacle: Reflections on Men and Mainstream Cinema", *Screen* 24.6 (1983), pp. 2–16.

Ne'eman, Yehuda-Judd. "Zero Degrees in Film", *Kolnoa* 5 (1979), pp. 20–23. [Hebrew]

Ne'eman, Yehuda-Judd. "The Death Mask of the Moderns: A Genealogy of New Sensibility Cinema in Israel", *Israel Studies* 4.1 (1999), pp. 100–128.

Ne'eman, Yehuda-Judd. "Modernism, the Unpublished Manifesto" [1992], *South Cinema Notebooks* 1 (2006), pp. 133–141. [Hebrew]

Nevo, Ofra. "Appreciation and Production of Humor As an Expression of Aggression: A Study of Jews and Arabs In Israel", *Journal of Cross Cultural Psychology* 15.2 (1984), pp. 181–198.

Nevo, Ofra and Jacob Levine. "Jewish Humor Strikes Again: The Outburst of Humor in Israel during the Gulf War", *Western Folklore* 53.2 (1994), pp. 125–145.

Nuriel, Yehuda and Gon Ben Ari. "Dizengoffing", *Yedioth Ahronoth – 7 Leilot* (27 February 2009), pp. 31–33. [Hebrew]

Oren, Rachel. "He Walked Through the Fields", *Davar* (8 December 1967). [Hebrew]

Oring, Elliott. *Israeli Humor: The Content and Structure of the Chizbat of the Palmah*. Albany: State University of New York Press, 1981.

Padva, Gilad. "Cinema Sissy: The Image of the Effeminate Man in the Israeli Cinema", *Terminal: Journal of Art in the 21st Century* 34 (2008), pp. 8–11. [Hebrew]

Pattir, Dan. "Wisdom of the Eye, Creative Imagination, Straight Heart and Love of Humanity". In Broshi, Michal (ed.) *Dosh – Caricaturist, 1921–2000*. Tel Aviv / Jerusalem: Eretz Israel Museum / Ben Zvi Institute, 2007, pp. 100–131. [Hebrew]

Peri, Menachem. "Polyphonic Voices in Genesis", Lecture given at the Conference *The Female Voice in Biblical Poetics*, Tel Aviv University (20 March 2000). [Hebrew]

Peri, Menachem. "What kind of God", *Haaretz – Books* (11 October 2005), http://www.haaretz.co.il/literature/1.1050089 (last retrieved 12 October 2020). [Hebrew]

Pinsker, Sanford. *The Schlemiel as Metaphor: Studies in the Yiddish and American Jewish Novel*. Carbondale / Edwardsville: Southern Illinois University Press, 1971.

Raberger, Ursula. *Israelischer Queerer Film*. Wien: Zaglossus, 2015.

Rapaport, Azaria. "Murder of all Motives", *Maariv* (19 December 1966). [Hebrew]

Raveh, Yair. "Undressed Cinema", *Pnai Plus* (23 April 2008), pp. 130–131. [Hebrew]

Raveh, Yair. "The State's Eyes. How We Made the Documentary Series *Celebration for the Eyes*", *Cinemascope: Yair Rave's Cinema Blog* (19 June 2015), http://cinemascope.co.il/archives/21398 (last retrieved 12 October 2020). [Hebrew]

Ravid-Hameiri, Dalit, et al. "Tel Aviv Seaside", *Centre for Educational Technology* (2008), http://lib.cet.ac.il/pages/item.asp?item=18829 (last retrieved 12 October 2020). [Hebrew]
Rivlin, Yuval. *The Mouse that Roared: Jewish Identity in American and Israeli Cinema*. Jerusalem: Tobypress, 2009. [Hebrew]
Rolef, Naomi. "The Melodrama of War in *Judgement Day*", *mediaesthetics – Zeitschrift für Poetologien audiovisueller Bilder* 1 (2016), https://www.mediaesthetics.org/index.php/mae/article/view/44/100 (last retrieved 12 October 2020).
Roman, Zipporah. "Rape in Front of the Camera", *Laisha* 2545 (1996), pp. 34–37. [Hebrew]
Sartre, Jean-Paul. *Anti-Semite and Jew* [1946]. New York: Schocken Books, 1965.
Sasson, Yasmin (Max). "The Missing Woman: Another Attempt to Crack the Safe". In Niv, Kobi (ed.) *Big Shots: A Script by Chaim Merin*. Gedera: N. B. Books, 2008, pp. 171–178. [Hebrew]
Schnitzer, Meir. *Israeli Cinema*. Tel Aviv: Kineret, 1994a. [Hebrew]
Schnitzer, Meir. "Short, Filthy and with No Dignity", *Maariv – Sofshavua* (2 September 1994b), pp. 64–66, 68, 71. [Hebrew]
Schorr, Renan. "The Cinematic Experience – Sabra Reflection in the Films of Uri Zohar", *Kolnoa* 15–16 (1978), pp. 32–41. [Hebrew]
Schorr, Renan. "Israeli Cinema – Israeli History: Periodisation of Israeli Cinema", *Skira Hodshit* 31.5 (1984), pp. 37–45. [Hebrew]
Schweitzer, Ariel. *The New Sensibility: Israeli Modern Cinema of the Sixties and Seventies*. Tel Aviv: Babel Publishing House, 2003. [Hebrew]
Shalev, Meir. "Das erste Weinen". In id. *Aller Anfang: Die erste Liebe, das erste Lachen, der erste Traum und andere erste Male in der Bibel*. Zürich: Diogenes, 2010, pp. 123–144.
Shalit, David. *Projecting Power: The Cinema Houses, the Movies and the Israelis*. Tel Aviv: Resling Publishing, 2006. [Hebrew]
Shapira, Anita. "The Myth of the New Jew". In id. *New Jews Old Jews*. Tel Aviv: Am Oved Publishers, 1997, pp. 155–174. [Hebrew]
Shaul, Ilan. "Sex is not Bourekas", *Lehiton* (6 September 1983), pp. 8–9. [Hebrew]
Shehori, Idit. "'Circles' – Producers' Sex", *Monitin* (June 1982), p. 102. [Hebrew]
Shemer, Yaron. "Trajectories of Mizrahi Cinema". In Talmon, Miri and Yaron Peleg (eds.) *Israeli Cinema: Identities in Motion*. Austin: University of Texas Press, 2011, pp. 120–133.
Shiram, Matan and Itay Rom. "Go Naked", *Globes* (26–27 October 2003), pp. 20–21. [Hebrew]
Shohat, Ella. *Israeli Cinema: East/West and the Politics of Representation*. Austin: University of Texas Press, 1989.
Shohat, Ella. *Israeli Cinema: History and Ideology*. Tel Aviv: Brerot, 1991. [Hebrew]
Shohat, Ella. "Mizrahim in Israel: Zionism from the Standpoint of its Jewish Victims". In id. *Forbidden Reminiscences: A collection of Essays*. Tel Aviv: Kedem Publishing, 2001, pp. 140–206. [Hebrew]
Shuv, Yael. "The Female Figure and the Dynamics of Broken Narrative in the Modernist Israeli Cinema". In Gertz, Nurith, Orly Lubin and Yehuda-Judd Ne'eman (eds.) *Fictive Looks – On Israeli Cinema*. Tel Aviv: Open University Publications, 1998, pp. 215–223. [Hebrew]
Shuv, Yael. "They Concurred in the Beds", *Haaretz – Articles part 2* (02.11.2001), p. 11. [Hebrew]
Smith, Paul. "Eastwood Bound". In id. *Clint Eastwood: A Cultural Production*. Minneapolis / London: University of Minnesota Press, 1993, pp. 151–172.
Sobchak, Vivian. *Carnal Thoughts: Embodiment and Moving Image Culture*. Berkley / Los Angeles: University of California Press, 2004.

Steir-Livny, Liat. "The Image of the Mythological Sabra in *He Walked Through the Fields* – Revisited", *Kivunim Hadashim* 15 (2007), pp. 290–304. [Hebrew]
Steir-Livny, Liat. *Two Faces in the Mirror*. Jerusalem: Magnes Press, 2009. [Hebrew]
Studlar, Gaylyn. "Valentino, 'Optic Intoxication', and Dance Madness". In Cohan, Steven and Ina Rea Hark (eds.) *Screening the Male: Exploring Masculinities in Hollywood Cinema*. London / New York: Routledge, 1993, pp. 23–45.
Talmon, Miri. *Israeli Graffiti: Nostalgia, Groups, and Collective Identity in Israeli Cinema*. Tel Aviv: Haifa University Press / Open University Press, 2001. [Hebrew]
Talmon, Miri and Yaron Peleg (eds.). *Israeli Cinema: Identities in Motion*. Austin: University of Texas Press, 2001.
Tryster, Hillel. *Israel Before Israel: Silent Cinema in the Holy Land*. Jerusalem: Steven Spielberg Jewish Film Archive, 1995.
Utin, Pablo. *The New Israeli Cinema: Conversations with Filmmakers*. Tel Aviv: Resling Publishing, 2008. [Hebrew]
Weiss, Meira. "Sanctifying the Chosen Body: Bereavement and Commemoration". In id. *The Chosen Body: The Politics of the Body in Israeli Society*. Stanford, CA: Stanford University Press, 2002, pp. 65–93.
Wilden, Anthony. *The Rules Are No Game*. London / New York: Routledge & Kegan Paul, 1987.
Willemen, Paul. "Anthony Mann: Looking at the Male", *Framework* 15 (1981), p. 16.
Williams, Linda. "Film Bodies: Gender, Genre, and Excess", *Film Quarterly* 44.4 (1991), pp. 2–13.
Williams, Linda. "Corporealized Observers: Visual Pornographies and the 'Carnal Destiny of Vision'". In Petro, Patrice (ed.) *Fugitive Images: From Photography to Video*. Bloomington / Indianapolis: Indiana University Press, 1995, pp. 3–41.
Williams, Linda. "Melodrama Revised". In Browne, Nick (ed.) *Refiguring American Film Genre*. Berkeley / Los Angeles / London: University of California Press, 1998, pp. 42–88.
Williams, Linda. *Hard Core: Power, Pleasure and the "Frenzy of the Visible"* [1989]. Berkeley: University of California Press, 1999.
Williams, Linda. *Screening Sex*. Durham / London: Duke University Press, 2008.
Winkler, John J. "Introduction". In id. *The Constraints of Desire: The Anthropology of Sex and Gender in Ancient Greece*. New York / London: Routledge, 1989, pp. 1–13.
Wisse, Ruth R. *The Schlemiel as Modern Hero*. Chicago / London: University of Chicago Press, 1971.
Yosef, Raz. *Beyond Flesh: Queer Masculinities and Nationalism in Israeli Cinema*. New Brunswick / New Jersey / London: Rutgers University Press, 2004.
Yosef, Raz. *To Know a Man: Sexuality, Masculinity and Ethnicity in Israeli Cinema*. Tel Aviv: Hakibbutz Hameuchad Publishing House, 2010. [Hebrew]
Zanger, Anat. "Filming National Identity: War and Woman in Israeli Cinema". In Lomsky-Feder, Edna and Eyal Ben-Ari (eds.) *The Military and Militarism in Israeli Society*. Albany: State University of New York Press, 1999, pp. 261–279.
Zanger, Anat. "Hole in the Moon or Zionism and the Binding (Ha-Ak'eda) Myth in Israeli Cinema", *Shofar: An Interdisciplinary Journal of Jewish Studies* 22.1 (2003), pp. 95–109.
Zanger, Anat. *Place, Memory and Myth in Contemporary Israeli Cinema*. London / Portland, OR: Vallentine Mitchell, 2012.
Zerubavel, Yael. *Recovered Roots: Collective Memory and the Making of Israeli National Tradition*. Chicago / London: University of Chicago Press, 1995.

Zerubavel, Yael. "Female Images in a State of War: The Israeli War Widow in Fiction and Film". In Weiner, Amir (ed.) *Landscaping the Human Garden: Twentieth-Century Population Management in a Comparative Framework*. Stanford, CA: Stanford University Press, 2003, pp. 236–257.

Zimmerman, Moshe. *Sighs of Movies: History of Israeli Cinema In the Years 1896–1948*. Tel Aviv: Dionon / Tel Aviv University Press, 2001a. [Hebrew]

Zimmerman, Moshe. *Tel Aviv Was Never Small*. Tel Aviv: Ministry of Defence Publishing House, 2001b. [Hebrew]

Zimmerman, Moshe. "Jewish and Israeli Film Studies", in *The Oxford Handbook of Jewish Studies*. Oxford: Oxford University Press, 2002, pp. 911–942.

Zimmerman, Moshe. *Hole in the Camera: Gazes of Israeli Cinema*. Tel Aviv: Resling Publishing, 2003. [Hebrew]

In the course of my research I also made use of the following websites:
  http://www.amalnet.k12.il
  https://www.wikipedia.org/
  https://www.biblegateway.com/ (all last retrieved 12 October 2020).

Filmography

999 ALIZA THE POLICEMAN [999 ALIZA MIZRACHI]. Director: Menahem Golan. IL 1967.

ADAM. Director: Yona Day. IL 1973.
THE ADVENTURES OF GADI BEN SUSSI. Directors: Baruch & Yizhak Agadati. PS 1931.
AMERICAN GRAFFITI. Director: George Lucas. USA 1973.
ATALIA. Directors: Tzvika Kertzner & Akiva Tevet. IL 1984.
AVODAH. Director: Helmar Lerski. PS 1934.

BIG EYES [EYNAYIM G'DOLOT]. Director: Uri Zohar. IL 1974.
BIG SHOTS [MITACHAT LA'AF]. Director: Jacob Goldwasser. IL 1982.
BLAZE ON THE WATER [LAHAT BAMAYIM]. Director: Jacob Hameiri. IL 1969.
BLAZING SAND [HOLOT LOHATIM]. Director: Raphael Nussbaum. IL, FRG 1960.
THE BOY ACROSS THE STREET [HAYELED ME'EVER LERECHOV]. Director: Yosef Shalhin. IL 1965.
A BOY AND A CAMEL [HAGAMAL V'HAYELED]. Director: Osamu Takahashi. IL 1968.
BOYS WILL NEVER BELIEVE IT [HATARNEGOL]. Director: Uri Zohar. IL 1971.

CEASEFIRE [HAFUGA]. Director: Amram Amar. IL 1950.
CHARLIE AND A HALF [CHARLIE VACHETZI]. Director: Boaz Davidson. IL 1974.
CLOUDS OVER ISRAEL [SINAIA]. Director: Ilan Eldad. IL 1962.
THE CONTRACT [KATZ VECARASSO]. Director: Menahem Golan. IL 1971.
COVER STORY [PARASHAT WINCHELL]. Director: Avraham Heffner. IL 1979.

DALIA AND THE SAILORS [DALIA VEHAMALACHIM]. Director: Menahem Golan. IL 1964.
DAN QUIXOTE AND SA'AD PANCHA [DAN VESA'ADIA]. Director: Nathan Axelrod. IL 1956.
DAUGHTERS, DAUGHTERS! [ABU EL BANAT]. Director: Moshé Mizrahi. IL 1973.
DAY AFTER DAY [YOM YOM]. Director: Amos Gitai. IL 1998.
DEEP THROAT. Director: Gerard Damiano. USA 1972.
DIZENGOFF 99. Director: Avi Nesher. IL 1979.
THE DREAMER [HATIMHONI]. Director: Dan Wolman. IL 1970.
THE DYBBUK [DER DIBUK]. Director: Michal Waszynski. PL 1937.
THE DYBBUK [HADYBBUK]. Director: Ilan Eldad. IL, FRG 1968.

EAST OF EDEN. Director: Elia Kazan. USA 1955.
EIGHT AGAINST ONE [SHEMONA B'EKVOT ECHAD]. Director: Menahem Golan. IL 1964.
ELDORADO. Director: Menahem Golan. IL 1963.
ERVINKA. Director: Ephraim Kishon. IL 1967.
ESCAPE TO THE SUN [HABRICHA EL HASHEMESH]. Director: Menahem Golan. IL 1972.
EVERY BASTARD A KING [KOL MAMZER MELECH]. Director: Uri Zohar. IL 1968.

THE FAITHFUL CITY [KIRYA NE'EMANA]. Director: Józef Lejtes. IL 1952.
FISHKE GOES TO WAR [FISHKE BEMILUIM]. Director: George Obadiah. IL 1971.
FLOCH. Director: Dan Wolman. IL 1972.
THE FLYING MATCHMAKER [SHNEI KUNI LEMEL]. Director: Israel Becker. IL 1966.
FORCED TESTIMONY [EDUT ME'ONES]. Director: Raphael Rebibo. IL 1984.
FORTUNA. Director: Menahem Golan. IL 1966.
THE FOX IN THE CHICKEN COOP [HASHUAL B'LOOL HATARNEGOLOT]. Director: Ephraim Kishon. IL 1978.

https://doi.org/10.1515/9783110694741-020

GET ZORKIN [HASAMBA VENA'AREI HAHEFKER]. Director: Joel Silberg. IL 1971.
GIFT FROM ABOVE [MATANA MISHAMAIM]. Director: Dover Kosashvili. IL, FR 2003.
GIRLS' PARADISE EILAT [HAVU BANOT LE'EILAT]. Directors: Nathan Axelrod & Leo Filler. IL 1964.
GROWING PAINS [PIZEI BAGRUT 80]. Director: Ze'ev Revach. IL 1980.

HAGIGA: THE STORY OF ISRAELI CINEMA [CHAGIGA LAEINAYIM – SIPURO SHEL HAKOLNOA HAISRAELI]. Director: Noit Geva. IL 2015. [TV series]
HAMSIN. Director: Daniel Wachsmann. IL 1982.
HE WALKED THROUGH THE FIELDS [HU HALACH BASADOT]. Director: Yosef Millo. IL 1967.
THE HERO'S WIFE [ESHET HAGIBOR]. Director: Peter Frye. IL 1963.
HIGHWAY QUEEN [MALKAT HAKVISH]. Director: Menahem Golan. IL 1971.
HILL 24 DOESN'T ANSWER [GIVA ESTIM VE'ARBA EINA ONA]. Director: Thorold Dickinson. IL 1955.
A HISTORY OF ISRAELI CINEMA [HISTORIA SHEL HAKOLNOAH HAISRAELI]. Director: Raphaël Nadjari. IL, FR 2009.
HOLE IN THE MOON [CHOR BALEVANA]. Director: Uri Zohar. IL 1965.
THE HOUSE ON CHELOUCHE STREET [HABAYIT BERECHOV CHELOUCHE]. Director: Moshé Mizrahi. IL 1973.

I DON'T GIVE A DAMN [LO SAM ZAYIN]. Director: Shmuel Imberman. IL 1987.
I LOVE YOU ROSA [ANI OHEV OTACH ROSA]. Director: Moshé Mizrahi. IL 1972.
IRIS. Director: David Greenberg. IL 1968.
IS TEL AVIV BURNING? [SHISHIM SHAOT LESUEZ]. Director: Kobi Jaeger. IL 1967.

JACKO AND THE PROSTITUTES [JACKO VEHAYATZANIOT]. Director: Paul L. Smith. IL 1972.
JUDGEMENT DAY [YOM HADIN]. Director: George Obadiah. IL 1974.

KAZABLAN. Director: Menahem Golan. IL 1973.

LACKING A HOMELAND [BE'EIN MOLEDET]. Director: Nuri Habib. IL 1956.
THE LAST TANGO IN PARIS. Director: Bernardo Bertolucci. FR, IT 1972.
THE LAST WINTER [HACHOREF HA'ACHARON]. Director: Riki Shelach Nissimoff. IL, USA 1984.
LATE MARRIAGE [HATUNA MEUHERET]. Director: Dover Kosashvili. IL 2001.
LITTLE MAN [SHRAGA KATAN]. Director: Ze'ev Revach. IL 1978.
LEMON POPSICLE [ESKIMO LIMON]. Director: Boaz Davidson. IL 1978.
LEMON POPSICLE 2 – GOING STEADY [ESKIMO LIMON 2 – YOTZ'IM KAVUA]. Director: Boaz Davidson. IL, FRG 1979.
LIGHT OUT OF NOWHERE [OR MIN HAHEFKER]. Director: Nissim Dayan. IL 1973.
LOVESICK ON NANA STREET [CHOLEH AHAVA BESHIKUN GIMEL]. Director: Savi Gabizon. IL 1995.

MARRIAGE GAMES [CHACHAM GAMLIEL]. Director: Joel Silberg. IL 1973.
MOMENTS [REGA'IM]. Director: Michal Bat-Adam. IL, FR 1979.
MOTIVE TO MURDER [HAMENIA LARETZACH]. Director: Peter Freistadt. IL 1966.
A MOVIE AND BREAKFAST [SERET VEARUCHAT BOKER]. Director: Alfred Steinhardt. IL 1977.
MY FATHER'S HOUSE. Director: Herbert Kline. PS, USA 1947.
MY MICHAEL [MICHAEL SHELI]. Director: Dan Wolman. IL 1975.

NIGHT AND FOG [NUIT ET BROUILLARD]. Director: Alain Resnais. FR 1956.
A NIGHT IN TIBERIAS [PITZUZ BECHATZOT]. Director: Hervé Bromberger. IL 1966.
NIGHT SOLDIER [CHAYAL LAILA]. Director: Dan Wolman. IL 1984.

NOA AT 17 [NOA BAT 17]. Director: Isaac Zepel Yeshurun. IL 1982.
NOT MINE TO LOVE [SHLOSHA YAMIM VEYELED]. Director: Uri Zohar. IL 1967.

ODED THE WANDERER [ODED HANODED]. Director: Chaim Halachmi. PS 1932.
ON A NARROW BRIDGE [GESHER TZAR ME'OD]. Director: Nissim Dayan. IL 1985.
ONCE UPON A TIME [VAYEHI BI'YEMEI]. Director: Chaim Halachmi. PS 1932.
ONLY TODAY [RAK HAYOM]. Director: Ze'ev Revach. IL 1976.
OVER THE RUINS [ME'AL HACHURVOT]. Director: Nathan Axelrod. PS 1938.

PARATROOPERS [MASA ALUNKOT]. Director: Yehuda-Judd Ne'eman. IL 1977.
PEEPING TOMS [METZITZIM]. Director: Uri Zohar. IL 1972.
THE PIANO. Director: Jane Campion. AU, NZ, FR 1993.
THE PILL [HAGLULA]. Director: David Perlov. IL 1972.
A POUND A PIECE [RAK BELIRA]. Director: Yoram Gross. IL 1963.
THE POLICEMAN [HASHOTER AZOULAY]. Director: Ephraim Kishon. IL 1971.
THE PRODIGAL SON [HABEN HAOVED]. Director: Yosef Shalhin. IL 1968.

RACHEL. Director: Nuri Habib. IL 1960.
REBEL WITHOUT A CAUSE. Director: Nicholas Ray. USA 1955.
REPEAT DIVE [TZLILA CHOZERET]. Director: Shimon Dotan. IL 1982.
ROCKING HORSE [SUS ETZ]. Director: Yaky Yosha. IL 1978.

SABINA [SABINA V'HAGVARIM]. Director: Peter Freistadt. IL 1966.
SABRA [TZABAR]. Director: Aleksander Ford. PL, PS 1933.
SAINT COHEN [CHAGIGA LA'ENAYIM]. Director: Assi Dayan. IL 1975.
SALACH SHABATI. Director: Ephraim Kishon. IL 1964.
SALOMONICO. Director: Alfred Steinhardt. IL 1972.
SAVE THE LIFEGUARD [HATZILU ET HAMATZIL]. Director: Uri Zohar. IL 1977.
SIEGE [MATZOR]. Director: Gilberto Tofano. IL 1969.
SINGIN' IN THE RAIN. Directors: Gene Kelly & Stanley Donen. USA 1952.
SEX. Director: David Avidan. IL 1970.
SWEET AND SOUR [LO LA'ALOT YOTER]. Director: Ze'ev Revach. IL 1979.
SPLENDOR IN THE GRASS. Director: Elia Kazan. USA 1961.

TAKE OFF [HITROMEMUT]. Director: Uri Zohar. IL 1970.
A TALE OF A TAXI [MA'ASEH BEMONIT]. Director: Larry Frisch. IL 1956.
THEY WERE TEN. Director: Baruch Dienar. IL 1961.
THE THIN LINE [AL HEVEL DAK]. Director: Michal Bat-Adam. IL 1980.
THIS IS THE LAND [ZOT HI HA'ARETZ]. Director: Baruch Agadati. PS 1935.
A THOUSAND AND ONE WIVES [ELEF NESHOTAV SHEL NAPHTALI SIMAN-TOV]. Director: Michal Bat-Adam. IL 1989.
THREE AND ONE [SHLOSHA VEACHAT]. Director: Mikhail Kalik. IL 1974.
THE TROUPE [HALEHAKA]. Director: Avi Nesher. IL 1978.
TWO HEART BEATS [SHTEI DEFIKOT LEV]. Director: Shmuel Imberman. IL 1972.
TZANANI FAMILY [MISHPACHAT TZAN'ANI]. Director: Boaz Davidson. IL 1976.

THE VALLEY TRAIN [RAKEVET HAEMEK]. Director: Jonathan Paz. IL 1989.
VIVRE SA VIE. Director: Jean-Luc Godard. FR 1962.
THE VULTURE [HA'AYIT]. Director: Yaky Yosha. IL 1981.

THE WILD ONE. Director: Laslo Benedek. USA 1953.
A WOMAN'S CASE [MIKREH ISHA]. Director: Jacques Katmor. IL 1969.
THE WOODEN GUN [ROVEH HULIOT]. Director: Ilan Moshenson. IL 1979.
WRONG NUMBER [TA'UT BAMISPAR]. Director: Ze'ev Revach. IL 1979.

YERACHMIEL THE SCHLEMIEL [YERACHMIEL HASCHLEMIEL]. Director: Nathan Axelrod. PS 1928/29/30.

Name Index

Aftergood, Steven 150
Agadati, Baruch 82
Agadati, Yizhak 79
Ahad Ha'am (Asher Zvi Hirsch Ginsberg) 64
Almog, Oz 10, 11, 17–19, 22, 80, 81, 183–185, 229, 233, 234, 249
Alterman, Nathan 61
Amar, Amram 9
Anderman, Nirit 11
Arendt, Hannah 52–56, 66, 67, 76, 137
Arison, Roni 15
Aristotle 78
Ashkenazi, Ofer 24, 27, 28, 31, 33, 102, 104, 209, 211
Augé, Marc 61
Avidan, David 185
Avisar, Ilan 34, 42
Axelrod, Nathan 79, 112, 148
Ayin Hillel (Hillel Omer) 81

Bakhtin, Mikhail 71, 72, 79, 80, 137, 144
Bar-Eli, Michael 231
Bar-Haim, Gabi 15, 16
Bashan, Rafael 116
Bat-Adam, Michal 19, 20, 150
Bataille, Georges 120
Becker, Israel 112
Ben-Amos, Dan 73–76, 79
Ben-Amotz, Dahn 184, 233
Ben Ari, Gon 184, 232, 254
Ben-Ari, Nitsa 3, 4, 17, 18, 22, 110, 112, 141, 184
Ben David, Benny 34, 42
Benedek, Laslo 139
Ben-Shaul, Nitzan 32, 35, 61, 62, 190, 209, 210
Bergson, Henri 70–72, 77, 79
Berlin, Isaiah 46
Berlowitz, Béatrice 76, 78
Bernstein, Deborah 207
Bertolucci, Bernardo 184
Bialik, Hayim Nahman 249

Bordwell, David 136
Boshes, Heda 231
Boyarin, Daniel 3, 6
Bram, Chen 207–209
Brando, Marlon 138
Bregman, Ahron 120, 188
Bromberger, Hervé 149
Broshi, Michal 87, 89, 90
Bruno, Michael 188
Buber, Martin 49
Bursztyn, Igal 19, 22, 28, 29, 63, 82, 140, 164, 195, 229
Bush, George W. 52
Butler, Judith 3, 21, 44, 50–58, 67

Campion, Jane 7
Canetti, Jonathan 15
Carroll, Noël 6
Cavell, Stanley 68, 69
Certeau, Michel de 61
Cohan, Steve 178
Cohen, Ayelet 33
Cohen, Boaz 15
Cohen, Nir 31, 33

Damiano, Gerard 184
Danon, Rotem 15
Davidson, Boaz 14, 15, 185, 210, 232
Day, Yona 187
Dayan, Assi 187
Dayan, Nissim 19, 150
Descartes, René 5
Dickinson, Thorold 9
Dienar, Baruch 106
Donen, Stanley 238
Dosh 87, 90
Dotan, Shimon 11
Duvdevani, Shmulik 16, 35, 229–232
Dyer, Richard 123, 124

Eichmann, Adolf 55
Eisenstadt, Shmuel N. 230

Eldad, Ilan 100, 148
Elon, Amos 89, 90
Engels, Friedrich 38
Epstein, Yoram 133
Eshed, Eli 88

Fainaru, Edna 14, 15, 232, 233
Feldmesser Yaron, Rivi 15
Feldstein, Ariel L. 24
Feuer, Dror 14, 15, 241
Filler, Leo 112
Ford, Aleksander 11
Foucault, Michel 3–6, 12, 13, 37, 40–42, 50–52, 55, 59
Freistadt, Peter 101, 106
Freud, Sigmund 39, 48, 72–75, 77, 79, 124, 155
Friedman, Régine-Mihal 30, 31
Frisch, Larry 9
Frye, Peter 11

Galily, Yair 231
Gabizon, Savi 11, 15
Gertz, Nurith 10, 19, 25, 28, 29, 31–33, 36, 63, 101, 131, 133, 151, 153–155, 158, 160, 165, 229, 231–234, 237, 238, 244
Geva, Noit 42
Gilman, Sander L. 44–49, 51, 56, 58, 75
Ginat, Gali 15, 16
Gitai, Amos 80
Gledhill, Christine 190–192, 198
Gluzman, Michael 85
Godard, Jean-Luc 220
Golan, Menahem 11, 12, 100, 117, 148, 187, 210, 229
Goldberg, Harvey E. 207–209
Goldwasser, Jacob 20
Golomb, Jacob 65
Gorki, Maxim 189
Grant, Barry K. 178
Greenberg, David 12, 165
Greenspan, Ezra 74, 76, 79
Gross, Natan 24, 149, 165, 229
Gross, Yaakov 24, 165, 229
Gross, Yoram 112
Grotjahn, Martin 75
Gurevitz, Zeli 87, 89, 90

Habib, Nuri 9, 11
Hadas, Eran 15
Hagin, Boaz 24
Hakak, Lev 29, 153, 155, 156, 159
Halachmi, Chaim 60, 79
Halachmi, Joseph 24
Hameiri, Jacob 12
Harell, Yehuda 9, 24
Harris, Rachel S. 19, 21, 31
Haschemi Yekani, Elahe 178
Hattis Rolef, Susan 188, 189, 207, 208, 231
Heffner, Avraham 187
Hegel, Georg W. F. 37–39
Heikaus, Ulrike 24
Hernández, Josafat 38
Herzl, Theodor 64
Hetsroni, Amir 35, 229–232
Hobbes, Thomas 69, 70, 72, 77, 80
Hogarth, William 217
Hunt, Lynn 3, 8
Hutcheson, Francis 70–72

Imberman, Shmuel 187, 195
Inbar, Efraim 188
Inda, Jonathan X. 55
Ingres, Jean-Auguste-Dominique 170
Iskovitz, Gili 189, 190
Israel, Yael 15, 16
Ivgi, Moshe 80

Jacob-Arzooni, Ora G. 10, 24, 25
Jaeger, Kobi 119
Jankélévitch, Vladimir 76, 78
Juni, Samuel 74–76, 78, 79

Kalik, Mikhail 185, 189, 191
Kappelhoff, Hermann 11, 59, 68, 191
Karsh, Efraim 188
Katmor, Jacques 125
Katsnelson, Anna Wexler 188–191, 199, 205
Katz, Bernard 74–76, 78, 79
Katzir, Judith 165
Kazan, Elia 118, 132
Kedem, Eldad Meshulam 29, 31, 32
Kelly, Gene 238
Kertzner, Tzvika 140
Kiczales, Yishai 15

Name Index

Kimchi, Rami 28, 63, 64, 80, 207–209
Kishon, Ephraim 25, 112, 187, 210, 229
Klausner, Margot 24
Klein, Uri 25, 229, 232
Kline, Herbert 148
Kluge, Alexander 59
Konigsberg, Ira 116
Kosashvili, Dover 14, 20
Kristensen, Hans M. 150
Kronish, Amy W. 19, 29
Kumaraswamy, P. R. 188

Lacan, Jacques 124
Landmann, Salcia 117
Lapid, Haim 230, 231
Lehman, Peter 123, 124, 146
Lejtes, Józef 148
Lerski, Helmar 11
Levinas, Emmanuel 56, 57
Levine, Jacob 50, 74, 76
Lewis, Paul 78
Lima, Luiz C. 12
Lord, Amnon 11, 15, 16, 186
Loshitzky, Yosefa 19–21, 30, 31, 63, 80, 86, 209
Lubin, Orly 19–22, 31, 36, 164, 209, 238, 252
Lucas, George 233

Maiberg, Ron 15, 16, 186
Marks, Laura U. 7
Marx, Karl 38
Meiri, Sandra 20–22, 34, 80
Michaels, Yvonne 240
Millo, Yosef 12, 131
Mizrahi, Moshé 28, 31, 150, 187, 207, 211
Morag, Raya 178
Moshenson, Ilan 150
Mulvey, Laura 117, 123
Munk, Yael 20–22, 28, 32, 34, 80, 90

Nadjari, Raphaël 42
Neale, Steve 123, 124
Ne'eman, Yehuda-Judd 25, 26, 30–33, 209, 210
Nesher, Avi 19, 184, 229
Nevo, Ofra 50, 74, 76
Nietzsche, Friedrich 53, 64–65

Nordau, Max 48, 49
Nuriel, Yehuda 184, 232, 254
Nussbaum, Raphael 9

Obadiah, George 150, 187, 189, 191
Oren, Rachel 131
Oring, Elliott 75, 103, 104

Padva, Gilad 31, 209
Panofsky, Erwin 68
Pattir, Dan 89, 90
Paz, Jonathan 140
Peleg, Yaron 36
Penley, Constance 178
Peri, Menachem 84, 85
Perlov, David 150
Pinsker, Sanford 74–79

Raberger, Ursula 31
Rancière, Jacques 59
Rapaport, Azaria 101, 102
Raveh, Yair 15, 43
Ravid-Hameiri, Dalit 168
Ray, Nicholas 239
Rebibo, Raphael 150
Reik, Theodor 75
Resnais, Alain 135
Revach, Ze'ev 150, 185, 187, 210, 211
Rice-Davies, Mandy 171
Rivlin, Yuval 33
Rolef, Naomi 190, 192–194, 196, 198
Rolland, Romain 189
Rom, Itay 15
Roman, Zipporah 15

Sadat, Anwar 231
Safirman, Costel 29
Sartre, Jean-Paul 44–47
Sasson, Yasmin (Max) 20
Schnitzer, Meir 10, 15, 16, 34, 101, 131, 165, 167, 190
Schorr, Renan 25–28, 31–33
Schweitzer, Ariel 29, 33, 135, 142, 165–168, 170
Shalev, Meir 84, 85
Shalhin, Yosef 150
Shalit, David 10, 24, 184

Shapira, Anita 64–66
Shaul, Ilan 15
Shehori, Idit 15
Shelach Nissimoff, Riki 140
Shemer, Gideon 116, 147
Shemer, Yaron 209
Shiram, Matan 15
Shohat, Ella 12, 25–29, 31–33, 79, 118, 119, 151, 168, 207–209, 223
Shuv, Yael 14–16, 170
Silberg, Joel 150, 187
Sirk, Douglas 190
Smith, Paul L. 123, 124, 217
Sobchak, Vivian 7
Spivak, Gayatri Chakravorty 52–54, 56, 67
Steinhardt, Alfred 187
Steir-Livny, Liat 34, 133, 134
Studlar, Gaylyn 124

T. Carmi, (Carmi Charney) 81
Takahashi, Osamu 150
Talmon, Miri 19, 29, 30, 33, 36, 62, 63, 88, 90, 91, 106, 107, 131–133, 178, 215, 229, 230–234, 243, 249, 250, 254
Tevet, Akiva 140
Tofano, Gilberto 140
Tryster, Hillel 24

Utin, Pablo 35, 42

Wachsmann, Daniel 20
Waszynski, Michal 117
Weiss, Meira 80, 81, 85, 86
West, Russell 178
Wilden, Anthony 38–42, 44
Willemen, Paul 122
Williams, Linda 3, 8, 11, 13, 21, 120, 124, 175, 176, 184, 185, 190, 191, 251
Winkler, John J. 6
Wisse, Ruth R. 74–79, 239
Wolman, Dan 19, 150, 187

Yehoshua, Abraham B. 152
Yeshurun, Isaac Zepel 150
Yosef, Raz 3, 4, 22, 31, 134, 136, 138–143, 146, 192, 200, 208, 209, 211
Yosha, Yaki 140, 150

Zanger, Anat 30, 34, 35, 81, 86, 152
Zerubavel, Yael 80, 81, 134
Zimmerman, Moshe 24, 25, 31, 32, 34
Zohar, Uri 11, 12, 19, 25, 100, 150, 152, 164, 184

Film Index

999 ALIZA THE POLICEMAN 100, 112

ADAM 187
AMERICAN GRAFFITI 233, 234
ATALIA 140
AVODAH 11

BIG EYES 187
BIG SHOTS 20
BLAZE ON THE WATER 12, 150, 165
BLAZING SAND 9, 106, 140
THE BOY ACROSS THE STREET 150
A BOY AND A CAMEL 150
BOYS WILL NEVER BELIEVE IT 12, 19, 164, 169, 187, 233

CEASEFIRE 9
CHARLIE AND A HALF 210
CLOUDS OVER ISRAEL 148
THE CONTRACT 187, 210, 233
COVER STORY 187

DALIA AND THE SAILORS 11
DAN QUIXOTE AND SA'AD PANCHA 148
DAUGHTERS, DAUGHTERS! 187, 210
DAY AFTER DAY 80
DEEP THROAT 184
DIZENGOFF 99 19, 184, 231, 232, 243–245, 247, 249, 251–253, 255
THE DREAMER 150, 165, 187, 232
THE DYBBUK (1937) 117
THE DYBBUK (1968) 100, 116–117, 119, 124, 141

EAST OF EDEN 132
EIGHT AGAINST ONE 148
ELDORADO 11, 121, 122, 127, 129, 132, 134, 143, 144, 185, 203, 216, 221
ERVINKA 112
ESCAPE TO THE SUN 187
EVERY BASTARD A KING 100, 119, 120

THE FAITHFUL CITY 148
FESTIVAL AT THE POOLROOM
FISHKE GOES TO WAR 187
FLOCH 150, 232
THE FLYING MATCHMAKER 112, 114
FORCED TESTIMONY 150
FORTUNA 116–119, 124, 141, 211, 212
THE FOX IN THE CHICKEN COOP 187

GADI BEN SUSSI 79
GET ZORKIN 150, 165
GIFT FROM ABOVE 20, 22
GIRLS' PARADISE EILAT 112, 114
GROWING PAINS 150

HAGIGA: THE STORY OF ISRAELI CINEMA 42
HAMSIN 20
HE WALKED THROUGH THE FIELDS 12, 34, 131, 132, 134, 139, 144, 252
THE HERO'S WIFE 11, 132, 134–138, 141, 145, 147, 166, 174, 185, 198, 200, 252
HIGHWAY QUEEN 12, 185, 210, 211, 217, 218, 222, 225–228, 255
HILL 24 DOESN'T ANSWER 9
A HISTORY OF ISRAELI CINEMA 42
HOLE IN THE MOON 25
THE HOUSE ON CHELOUCHE STREET 150, 210

I LOVE YOU ROSA 150
IS TEL AVIV BURNING? 119, 120, 125

JACKO AND THE PROSTITUTES 217–219
JUDGEMENT DAY 150, 189–200, 202, 205, 206, 231, 255

KAZABLAN 210

LACKING A HOMELAND 9, 148
THE LAST TANGO IN PARIS 184
THE LAST WINTER 140
LATE MARRIAGE 14

LEMON POPSICLE 14, 150, 229, 230
LEMON POPSICLE 2 – GOING STEADY 232–243
LIGHT OUT OF NOWHERE 150, 183, 185, 233
LITTLE MAN 210, 211, 213, 215, 217, 222, 228, 255
LOVESICK ON NANA STREET 11, 14

MARRIAGE GAMES 187, 210–212
MOMENTS 19, 252
MOTIVE TO MURDER 101–107, 111, 114, 118, 163, 191, 249
A MOVIE AND BREAKFAST 187
MY FATHER'S HOUSE 148
MY MICHAEL 187

NIGHT AND FOG 135
A NIGHT IN TIBERIAS 148–151, 178, 179, 193, 198
NIGHT SOLDIER 19
NOA AT 17 150
NOT MINE TO LOVE 12, 19, 148, 150–152, 161, 164–166, 178, 179, 184, 185, 187, 193, 194, 198, 252, 253

ODED THE WANDERER 60–63, 76, 78, 79, 82, 84, 86, 87, 91–94, 101, 148, 190, 219
ON A NARROW BRIDGE 19
ONCE UPON A TIME 79, 137
ONLY TODAY 187, 210
OVER THE RUINS 148

PARATROOPERS 11
PEEPING TOMS 150, 164, 165, 187, 232, 238
THE PIANO 7
THE PILL 150, 165, 232
A POUND A PIECE 112–114
THE PRODIGAL SON 150

RACHEL 11
REBEL WITHOUT A CAUSE 239
REPEAT DIVE 11, 140
ROCKING HORSE 150, 187, 232

SABINA 106
SABRA 11
SAINT COHEN 187
SALACH SHABATI 25
SALOMONICO 187
SAVE THE LIFEGUARD 187
SINGIN' IN THE RAIN 238, 239
SWEET AND SOUR 185, 187
SPLENDOR IN THE GRASS 118

TAKE OFF 11, 187
A TALE OF A TAXI 9
THEY WERE TEN 106
THE THIN LINE 150
THIS IS THE LAND 82, 84, 137, 140
A THOUSAND AND ONE WIVES 20
THREE AND ONE 185, 189–201, 204–206, 252, 255
THE TROUPE 229, 232, 253
TWO HEART BEATS 187
TZANANI FAMILY 185, 187, 210, 233

THE VALLEY TRAIN 140
VIVRE SA VIE 220
THE VULTURE 140, 190

THE WILD ONE 138
A WOMAN'S CASE 125, 169
THE WOODEN GUN 150
WRONG NUMBER 187

YERACHMIEL THE SCHLEMIEL 79

Subject Index

abjection 31
abortion 134, 232
aesthetics 12, 24, 25, 28, 68, 74, 100, 130, 135, 168, 191, 221, 232
agency 6, 41, 51, 52, 73, 91, 251
aggression 16, 48, 50, 57, 72, 73, 75, 90, 101, 103, 108, 109, 130, 154, 155, 158, 172, 174, 199, 201, 205, 238, 242, 254
alterity see also Otherness 44, 46, 51, 52
American 46, 52, 53, 190, 208, 233
– American cinema / film 11, 131, 178, 184, 238
– American film character 120, 193, 194, 222
– Americanisation 229, 232, 234
anti-Semitism 44, 45, 47, 48, 90
– anti-Semitic 22, 33, 34, 46, 49, 80
– anti-Semite 44, 47, 48, 75
anxiety 22, 45, 47, 83, 120, 126, 188, 190, 209
army see also military 133, 188, 211
art cinema/film 26–30, 35, 136, 165, 185, 190, 209–210
Ashkenazi see also European Jews 27–28, 31, 209, 211
auteur film 25, 26, 151, 165

bathroom 237, 238, 245, 246
battle 81, 86, 89, 120, 181, 192, 194, 199, 206
beach 128, 165, 196, 197, 201–203, 215, 235, 240
Bedouin 60, 63, 77, 78, 91, 93, 148, 149
bereavement 81, 85–86, 135, 140, 143
Bible 85
– Biblical 78, 81, 84, 89, 110, 120, 205, 224
birth 84, 225
bite 109, 130, 132, 154, 162, 201, 251
Black Panthers 208, 210
bombardment 142, 144, 146
bourekas films see also ethnic fim 209–210
bourgeois see also middle class 19, 28, 40, 58, 71, 144, 151, 164
breach of privacy 102–103, 107, 113, 114, 115, 121–122, 138, 178, 201, 213, 215, 239, 246

breakdown 174, 189, 198
breasts 11, 128, 172, 200, 201, 203, 205, 224, 225, 244, 245, 247, 248
brutality 175, 205, 223, 225

caress 112, 117, 130, 132, 143, 144, 156, 157, 162, 175, 195, 201, 203, 239, 240, 245, 246, 251
carnival 71, 135, 137
castration 21, 22, 123
censorship 8, 10–11, 41, 71, 101, 150, 184, 185
child abuse 148, 150, 158
Chizbat 103–104
Christian 3, 4, 5, 45, 47, 135
– Judeo-Christian morality 65, 66, 78, 86
cityscape 122, 151, 152, 165, 167
clash 32, 75, 76, 77, 78, 79, 138, 150, 152, 193, 238, 255
class 4–5, 13, 27, 71, 207, 210, 228
– middle class see also bourgeois 5, 194, 223, 229, 234, 248
club 141, 193, 196, 198, 200, 201, 217, 224
collectivism 17, 28, 29, 32, 63, 65, 66, 82, 137, 217, 222, 229
colonialism 32
commercial cinema/film 15, 19, 25, 26, 27, 28, 29, 34, 35, 185, 189, 190, 209–210, 229, 232
communal identity 17, 37, 43, 59, 65, 69, 91, 179, 183, 186, 187, 206, 232, 249
crisis 28, 63, 90, 135, 138, 162, 167, 169, 174, 183, 188, 189, 191, 197, 230–231, 242
– masculinity crisis 178–179

death 30, 80–82, 85, 88, 116, 119, 120, 125, 126, 133, 134, 195
death sentence 55
desire 13, 21, 106, 112, 119, 140, 141, 158, 159, 171, 176, 177, 201
Diaspora 22, 26, 33, 37, 65, 76, 77, 79, 81
Dimona 117, 217

Subject Index

discord / disharmony 51, 62, 63, 106, 130, 136, 156, 160, 169, 185, 201, 237, 239, 240, 244, 252, 255
disempowerment 178
divorce 165, 167, 169, 192

ecstasy 112, 144, 158, 236, 250–251
education 17, 64, 65, 141, 183–184
Eilat 112, 192–193, 194, 197, 200, 234
elitist 14, 28, 29
empowerment 3, 21, 53, 62, 147, 223
eroticism *see also* Spectacle 7, 112–113, 116–117, 118, 122–125, 126, 138–139, 143, 147, 149, 153–154, 157, 159–160, 171, 183, 200, 203, 205–206, 212, 216–217, 223, 225, 237, 251, 255
– anti-erotic / loss of eroticism 15–16, 106, 110–112, 115, 119, 140–141, 163, 172–173, 186, 200, 238, 243, 248, 249
ethnicity *see also* Ashkenazi, Mizrahi, European Jews, *and* Oriental Jews 21, 78, 207, 209–210, 211, 212, 223
– ethnic film *see also* Bourekas film 26, 27, 35, 79
European cinema 12, 15, 18, 26, 167, 184
European Jews *see also* Ashkenazi 33, 47, 48–49, 74, 80, 217, 223
exhibitionism 123, 154
explicit (content) 3, 8, 9–10, 12, 184, 185
extravagant 105, 114, 137

fallen soldiers 80–81, 85–86
femininity 123, 155, 218
fire 142–143, 144, 172, 192
flirtation 133, 159, 171, 196, 203, 212, 244, 245, 246, 252
fragmentation 135, 136, 146, 160

gang 88, 223–224
grief *see also* berevement *and* mourning 56, 83, 85, 174, 191, 198, 246–247

Haganah 88, 103
Haifa 217

harmony 108, 137, 154, 156, 162, 163, 199, 218, 239, 240, 244, 250, 251–252
hedonism 35, 193–194, 229
hegemony 3, 5, 6, 20, 30–32, 42, 52–53, 57–58, 86, 211
heroism 25–26, 29, 33, 42, 43, 50, 74, 80, 81, 92, 93, 133, 143, 147
historiography 34–35, 37, 40–43, 223
Holocaust 44, 101, 114, 116, 142
– Holocaust survivor 30, 34, 134, 148
homosexuals / homosexuality 21, 31, 53, 56, 122, 249

identity politics 21, 22, 86
immigrant/s 22, 31, 76, 87, 88, 103–104, 117, 131, 207
impotence 203
implicit 8–10, 11, 108
individualism 17, 28, 29, 63, 65, 66, 141, 216–217, 229
innocence 77, 81, 88, 90, 149, 150, 177, 193–194, 199, 206, 217
intrusion/intrusiveness 14, 61, 62, 63–64, 65, 67, 102, 107, 114, 119, 122, 126–128, 132, 154, 157, 186, 193, 230, 237, 238, 239–240, 243, 246
Israeli-Arab conflict 27, 188
Israeli culture 2, 3, 5, 18, 60, 88, 89, 90, 103, 110, 233
Israel-Egypt peace agreement 37, 183, 231

Jaffa 121, 122, 128
Jerusalem 35, 151, 152, 156, 194, 197, 252
Jewish humour 47, 48, 50, 69, 73–76, 77–79
Jewish tradition 17, 18, 33, 43, 56, 64, 143
Jewishness 47, 49, 57

kibbutz 29, 88, 131, 133, 134, 136, 138, 141, 142, 144, 151, 152, 155, 217, 220, 221, 222
– kibbutznik 27
kiss 11, 108, 112, 113, 117, 118, 126, 128, 130, 132, 138, 144, 146, 154, 156, 158, 160, 162, 170, 171, 175, 195, 201, 203, 213, 214, 235, 239, 241, 244, 245, 246, 250, 251

Subject Index — 281

landscape 90, 91, 122, 131, 135, 140, 144, 168, 194, 216, 220
love 17, 31, 116, 130, 144, 151, 156, 173, 200, 216, 242, 243
– love affair 19
lovemaking (make love) 158, 196, 217, 222, 252
lover 105, 106, 108, 117, 130, 144, 149

marriage 116, 140, 149, 169, 198, 201
martyrdom 30, 80–81, 82, 86, 216, 233
masculinity 22, 31, 33, 92, 122, 123, 178–179
– emasculation 173, 239
masochism 6, 75, 123, 124
melodrama 26, 82–84, 116, 130, 131, 146, 189–191, 195, 198, 199, 205, 206, 210, 211, 224, 225, 228
military *see also* Army 16, 31, 35, 56, 119, 120, 133, 134, 142, 149, 189, 192, 212, 214, 216
Mizrahi *see also* Oriental Jews 27, 28, 30, 31, 207, 211
mobilisation 33, 34, 37, 50, 63, 79, 94, 150, 198, 199, 234
mourning *see also* berevement *and* grief 56, 80, 141, 206
morality 8, 10, 41, 43, 55, 57, 58, 60, 65, 66, 70, 72, 78, 85, 86, 93, 105, 148, 191, 194, 195, 205, 206, 209, 231, 232
muscle Jew 49, 93
music 122, 135, 139, 143, 144, 154, 155, 193, 196, 197, 198, 199, 200, 215, 216, 219, 220, 233, 235, 244, 246, 253
– bossa nova 152, 156, 160
– classical music 104
– jazz music 138, 139, 143, 217
– mediteranean music 119
– pop music 167, 174, 193, 239, 240, 242, 243, 253
– rock music 125, 166, 224, 233,
– song 85, 141, 198, 199, 200, 239, 253
myth 30, 34, 35, 42, 81, 86, 90, 148, 193, 199
mythical/mythological 27, 32, 33, 34, 43, 64, 80, 88, 92, 141, 142, 178

national cinema 28, 29, 31, 80
national identity 206, 256
National Water Carrier 110, 150
neo-phenomenology 7
New Jew 22, 30, 32, 34, 50, 64–65, 179
new sensibility 29, 151, 168
nostalgia 30, 88, 155, 168, 176, 198, 229, 234
Nouvelle Vague 135
nuclear family 192, 197, 198
nuclear weapons 150
nudity 10, 11, 14, 15, 120, 153, 160, 166, 170, 172, 193, 203, 214, 216, 221, 222, 235, 240–241, 242, 245, 248, 251, 252, 254, 255

objectification 19, 28, 106–107, 123–124, 125, 147, 164, 167, 169, 195, 225, 235, 254
orgasm *see also* ecstasy 221, 251
Oriental Jews/Jewish *see also* Mizrachi 22, 27, 74, 80, 186, 189, 208–210, 212, 217, 218, 222–224, 227, 228
Otherness *see also* alterity 22, 30–31, 33, 35, 42, 44–50, 51, 57–58, 62, 95

pain 81, 82, 114, 116, 132, 133, 134, 179, 236, 246
Palestine 9, 10, 24, 60, 79, 148
– Palestinian 16, 27, 30, 31, 34, 53, 56, 57
Palmach 88, 103, 133, 192
peripheral 5, 12, 26, 31, 49
personal cinema *see* New sensibility
phallus 6, 21
– phallic 7, 31, 123
– phallocentric 251
pioneers 24, 32, 33, 82, 84, 140
police 101, 105, 114, 125, 126, 128, 130, 149, 219
pornography 3, 8–9, 20, 109, 233, 249, 252
– pornographic films 176, 184, 185, 248, 249, 253
post-coital scenes 9, 11, 26, 108, 163, 209
post-colonialism 26, 209
post-ideology 230
Post-Zionism 33, 37

private sphere / space *see also* breach of privacy 54, 56, 57, 62, 63, 66–67, 103, 116, 146, 153, 186, 221, 256
promiscuity 17, 107, 173, 193, 195, 205, 254
prostitution 19, 217, 219–220
– prostitute 126, 195, 217, 221, 227, 232
psycho-semiotics 6–7, 21, 22, 123, 124
public sphere (space) 5, 52, 54, 56, 57, 62, 66–67, 102–103, 113–114, 121, 128, 137, 138, 146, 153, 167, 172–173, 178, 186, 241, 249, 256
Purim 135, 137–138

rape 16, 19, 165, 166, 173, 174–177, 179, 217, 225, 227
rescue 60, 83, 93, 120–121, 130, 134, 149, 162–163
ritual 22, 53, 56, 80, 90, 140

Sabra 26, 27, 32, 33, 80, 88, 103
sacrifice 57, 81, 86, 203
– self sacrifice 30, 64, 82, 126, 130, 131, 133, 143, 144, 198, 205, 210, 216
sadism 6, 122, 123, 124–125, 216, 237–238
schlemiel 47, 74–76, 77, 78, 80
Sea of Galilee 134, 139, 140
security forces 149
seduction 107, 108, 109, 113, 149, 219, 232, 233
– cinematic seduction 146, 149, 254, 255
Sephardi *see* Oriental jews *and* Mizrahi
sex
– fellatio 203
– group sex 211, 214
– intercourse / sexual act 8, 9, 11, 13, 15, 19, 108, 143–144, 154, 157, 164, 172, 184, 185, 218, 221, 235, 237
– manual 158
– partner swap 247–248
– penetration 11, 20, 132, 160, 175, 214, 219, 220, 225, 227, 228, 236, 251
– threesome /three-way 232, 233, 247, 250–252, 254
sexual assault 165, 179, 205, 254
sexual fantasy, fantasies 18, 123, 149, 237, 238, 252, 255

sexual harassment 138, 139
siege 35, 61
Sinai War 148
Six-Day War 27, 29, 32, 119–121, 134, 150, 188, 195
slapstick 244, 245, 250, 253
social ascendancy/mobility 210, 211–212
social injustice 210, 227, 228
socialism 65
– socialist 14, 64
socialist realism 32
sociology 17, 25, 208, 230
Spectacle 119, 122, 137, 191, 198, 234, 237, 249
– anti-spectacle 163–165
– erotic spectacle *see also* male spectacle and female spectacle 252, 255
– girl spectacle 170–171
– female spectacle 117, 122, 123, 146
– male spectacle 92, 122–124, 126, 130, 132, 133, 139, 143, 146, 179
Srulik 87, 89–90
subjectification 107, 225
subversion 3, 20, 22, 26, 31, 41, 51, 72, 209, 253

Tel-Aviv 112, 121, 125, 128, 166, 167, 168, 187, 192, 197, 211, 212, 217, 243
terrorist attack 149
Tiberias 139, 142
trauma 43, 135, 142–143, 144, 152, 160, 166, 178, 188

ulpan 134, 136, 141, 144
uniform 193, 218, 234
– military uniform 134, 192–193, 213
Utopia 32, 33, 43, 61, 64, 71–72, 80, 92, 93, 137, 176, 252
– film utopia 59

violence 11, 22, 53, 56, 57, 117, 125, 163, 166, 174–175, 177, 178, 185, 205, 216, 217, 225, 227, 237, 238
virginity –loss of 118, 241
voyeurism 6, 21, 123, 237

– Peeping Tom 105, 237, 252
vulnerability 90, 91, 102, 153, 175,
   220–221, 225

War of Independence 81, 84, 88, 121, 134,
   143, 148, 188, 192, 199
The West
– Western culture/ civilisation 5, 12, 17, 66,
   190, 233, 234
– Western ideology 18, 32, 74
– Western society 4, 33, 47
widow 134, 140
wilderness 32, 62, 82, 86, 92, 148
womanhood 21, 171

Yiddish 63, 64, 74, 80, 112, 116, 200
Yom Kippur War 32, 186, 188–189, 191, 192,
   194, 196, 206, 230, 253, 254, 255
youth 87–89, 152, 159, 173, 178, 201, 233,
   240, 253, 254, 255
– youth culture 88, 90, 234
– youth films 19, 186, 229–232
– youth movement 173, 234

Zionism 17–18, 22–23, 26, 27, 30, 31, 32,
   33–34, 35, 37, 42, 43, 49, 57, 63–64,
   65, 79, 80, 81, 86, 94, 164, 205, 238

www.ingramcontent.com/pod-product-compliance
Lightning Source LLC
Chambersburg PA
CBHW020223170426
43201CB00007B/296